A CITY IN CIVIL WAR
Dublin, 1921–4

A CITY IN CIVIL WAR

Dublin, 1921–4

PÁDRAIG YEATES

Gill & Macmillan

Gill & Macmillan
Hume Avenue, Park West, Dublin 12
www.gillmacmillanbooks.ie

© Pádraig Yeates 2015
978 0 7171 6726 5

Index compiled by Grainne Farren
Typography design by Make Communication
Print origination by Síofra Murphy
Printed by ScandBook AB, Sweden

This book is typeset in Minion 10.5/13.5 pt.

The paper used in this book comes from the wood pulp
of managed forests. For every tree felled, at least one
tree is planted, thereby renewing natural resources.

A CIP catalogue record for this book is available from
the British Library.

5 4 3 2 1

To Karl Kautsky and renegades by hindsight everywhere.

> The deciding battles for Ireland's independence in recent years were won mainly by the energy and devotion of her proletariat. In spite of this, that proletariat is threatened by the independent state which it won, not with an improvement, but with a further decline of its position.

(From *Irland*, published January 1922 in Vienna, after Dáil Éireann had approved the terms of the Treaty with the British government. Translated by Angela Clifford and published by the British and Irish Communist Organisation, January 1974)

To Charlie Gilmore, who kept the faith.

> They come again through forty years
> When tired feet stumble by my door;
> The leggings and the bandoliers
> Of boys who cross the glen no more.
>
> Their passing stirred a little breeze
> Among the dead leaves crisply curled;
> But sap still rises in the trees
> And tempests roar around the world.

(*The Leggings and the Bandoliers*, a poem by Charlie Gilmore, published by Repsol Publications, Dublin, 1976)

To Katherine O'Donnell, Justice for Magdalenes campaigner, who wants to live in a republic that cherishes all its people equally.

> The first National Gay Conference took place in 1981 in Connolly Hall, the ITGWU headquarters in Cork, at a time when male homosexuality was still criminalised in Ireland. Since then, lesbian, feminist and gay activists have ensured unions not only led the struggle for economic justice but have helped empower everyone, irrespective of sex, marital status or sexual preference, to participate fully in the social, cultural and political life of our country with freedom, dignity and equality.

(SIPTU-LGBTQ conference, Liberty Hall, Dublin, 24 February 2014)

And to Geraldine Regan, a Liberties girl who has travelled far.

CONTENTS

PREFACE AND ACKNOWLEDGEMENTS

Like its predecessors, *A City in Wartime: Dublin, 1914–18*, and *A City in Turmoil: Dublin, 1919–21*, this book grew out of one written fifteen years ago called *Lockout: Dublin, 1913*. It picks up the story from the Truce that marked the end of the War of Independence in July 1921, extends through the Civil War and concludes with the abolition of three of Dublin's great institutions: the City Council, the South Dublin Union and the Dublin Metropolitan Police. From being the cockpit of revolution, Dublin became the seat of reaction.

As with the previous books, I have tried to show how major public events affected ordinary citizens in their everyday lives. The revolutionary elite that set much of the agenda in previous years was deeply divided by the Treaty. As a result other forces, within the business community, among farmers and the labour movement, began to challenge the hegemony of militant nationalism. A new conservative consensus manifested itself in this desperately poor city, with the Catholic Church not alone filling many of the gaps in social services left by a government that was too busy fighting for survival to pay much attention to the wider needs of society but, in the process, determining the ethos for the city's denizens.

Among the anti-Treaty ranks various public figures struck revolutionary poses, but few proposed practical policies that would either defend the Republic or advance the radical policies outlined in the Proclamation of the Irish Republic (1916) and the Democratic Programme of Dáil Éireann (1919). At the national level, the outbreak of civil war would see the dissipation of the 'national struggle' into a series of localised conflicts that would simultaneously centralise administrative power in the Free State and prepare the way for the return of parish-pump politics.

Many people assisted me during my research. I wish to make particular mention again of the Dublin Civic Archives, a wonderful resource for everyone interested in Dublin and its past. Mary Clarke, Máire Kennedy and their colleagues facilitated my requests with unfailing courtesy. I also wish to thank the staff of the National Archives and especially Catriona Crowe, who has helped revolutionise access to public records in Ireland and has been unstinting in her support, Diarmaid Ferriter for his encouragement and Katherine O'Donnell for bringing articles on women and militarism to my attention and above all for her unfailing kindness and patience when she had many other calls on her time.

Miriam Moffitt gave me great assistance and advice regarding Dublin loyalist claims for compensation, and her briefing ensured that I made the best use of my visit to the British National Archives at Kew. Jim Herlihy pointed me in the right direction on the DMP, Oriel House and much else.

Commandant Padraic Kennedy and his colleagues at the Bureau of Military History have always facilitated my requests for access to material at short notice.

Kieran Murphy and Tom MacSweeney facilitated access to the archives of the Society of St Vincent de Paul, which still battles poverty and deprivation in the city.

Brendan Byrne, Ed Penrose, Jack McGinley, Francis Devine, Theresa Moriarty and their colleagues in the Irish Labour History Society have helped with their comments and discussion of aspects of the history of the period.

My thanks also to Gerry Kavanagh, Keith Murphy and their colleagues at the National Library of Ireland and the National Photographic Archive, Noelle Dowling at the Dublin Diocesan Archives, Seamus Helferty and his colleagues at the UCD Archives. Eamon Devoy of the Technical, Engineering and Electrical Union provided access to early records of the Irish Engineering, Shipbuilding and Foundry Trade Union.

I wish to thank Eamon O'Reilly, Pat Ward and Charlie Murphy at Dublin Port for facilitating access to its records, Brian Kirby for access to the Irish Capuchin Provincial Archives, Noel Gregory and Terry Fagan for information on the north inner city, Joe Mooney, John Dorney, Eve Morrison, Ann Matthews, Margaret Ó hÓgartaigh and Tom Morrissey SJ for their insights into the era, and Peter Rigney for access to the files of the Irish Railway Record Society and his unique knowledge of industrial relations in this area. A special word of mention for Shane Mac Thomáis, who gave to me so freely of his vast knowledge of life and death in Dublin, as he did to everyone. The city and its history are infinitely the poorer for his passing.

At Gill & Macmillan I wish to thank Deirdre Rennison Kunz for managing the manuscript through the production process, Jen Patton for picture research, Teresa Daly for spreading the word, Fergal Tobin (now retired) for inadvertently initiating the project, and his successor, Conor Nagle, for staying with it. Thanks also to Don O'Connor for another magnificent jacket, Séamas Ó Brógáin for the depth of knowledge he brings to the editing process, and Síofra Murphy for her meticulous typesetting.

Finally, my son Simon for his support and Geraldine Regan for her encouragement over many years. As in the past, I have tried to recruit my prejudices and predilections constructively to the task of writing this book.

ABBREVIATIONS

ASU	Active Service Unit
CID	Criminal Investigation Department
DATI	Department of Agriculture and Technical Instruction
DMP	Dublin Metropolitan Police
DUTC	Dublin United Tramways Company
DWC	Dublin Workers' Council
GSWR	Great Southern and Western Railway
IAOS	Irish Agricultural Organisation Society
IEIU	Irish Engineering and Industrial Union
IES&FTU	Irish Engineering, Shipwrights' and Foundry Trade Union
IFU	Irish Farmers' Union
ILP&TUC	Irish Labour Party and Trade Union Congress
INTO	Irish National Teachers' Organisation
ITGWU	Irish Transport and General Workers' Union
ITUC	Irish Trades Union Congress
ITUC&LP	Irish Trades Union Congress and Labour Party
IWWU	Irish Women Workers' Union
LNWR	London and North-Western Railway
MRA	Municipal Reform Association
NPGCA	Non-Permanent Government Clerks' Association
NSPCC	National Society for the Prevention of Cruelty to Children
OC	officer commanding
RIC	Royal Irish Constabulary
RMRPC	Railway Maintenance, Repair and Protection Corps
YMCA	Young Men's Christian Association

Terminology

Terminology in this area is always contentious. 'The IRA' is used to describe republican armed forces until the split in its ranks began to emerge immediately after the acceptance of the Treaty by Dáil Éireann. Subsequently the terms 'anti-Treaty IRA' and 'National Army' are used to describe the rival forces. 'Sinn Féin' generally refers to political opponents of the Treaty and 'pro-Treaty Sinn Féin' to its supporters.

A note on money

The pound (£) was divided into twenty shillings (s) and the shilling into twelve pence (d). Intermediate amounts were written in a combination of denominations, e.g. £2 10s; 3s 6d. Some relatively small amounts in pounds might be written entirely in shillings, e.g. 42s (£2 2s).

'IT WOULD BE ONLY ... RUSSIA WHERE A WOMAN WHO SERVED HER KING WOULD BE ALLOWED TO DROP TO SUCH AN EXISTENCE'

D ublin suffered from a severe shortage of good-quality hotels in the summer of 1921. Hardly had the Truce between the Irish and British forces been declared on 11 July than public attention was directed to the demands of peace. 'One of the effects of the war and the rebellion of 1916 has been to put out of action eleven city hotels ...' the *Irish Times* commented. 'All of these were catering for the public in 1913, the year of the last pre-war Horse Show.' The Horse Show was to be resurrected in all its former glory at the Royal Dublin Society grounds in three weeks' time, and crowds of visitors were expected not alone from all parts of Ireland but from Britain and the Continent.

The newspaper called for the 'living-in' quarters of workers in shops, warehouses and pubs to be converted into temporary hotel rooms. It urged the owners of 'large, well furnished, houses to let them advantageously in view of the pleasant prospect that presents itself.' The city's leading draper, Edward Lee, was commended for his enterprise in establishing the Avenue Hotel in Kingstown (Dún Laoghaire) to meet expected demand, for 'a little enterprise and foresight now would mean much in attracting people to the city.'

The sudden concern of the *Irish Times* that the city should look its best was born of the 'optimism prevalent everywhere ... since the political truce began and hopes are high that Dublin will regain some of its former glory as the Irish capital.' Only the previous day the President of the Irish Republic, Éamon de Valera, had arrived in London for talks with the British Prime Minister, David Lloyd George, to be met by rapturous crowds of London-Irish. For the vast majority of Irish people at home, relief at an end to the fighting had transformed itself into a belief that peace was imminent.

Still fixated on the Horse Show, the *Irish Times* leader mused that 'three weeks hence the Royal Dublin Society will open its gates at Ballsbridge to all and sundry. The London Conference may not have come to an end by that time, but in all probability the issue will have ceased to be in doubt.' It looked forward to the 'large amount of money' that would be spent in Dublin 'to compensate our traders for some of the losses of the dismal period of Civil War.'[1] That the *Irish Times* could characterise the conflict as a civil war while many of the combatants saw it as a war of independence suggested that the gap was wider than the newspaper's leader-writer realised.

Meanwhile, authorisation of a return to normal train schedules by the military on the day before the editorial was published, and the lifting of restrictions on the use of motor transport on the day of publication, reinforced the impression that the years of conflict were over. Work was nearing completion on the restoration of the southern half of O'Connell Street, destroyed during the 1916 Rising, and new wage rates were struck for the building trade to usher in an era of industrial peace. Craftsmen could expect to earn between 1s 10d and 2s 2d an hour, while labourers were entitled to at least three-quarters of the relevant craft rate. These were vast increases on the old pre-lockout rates of 1913, when a craft worker might earn 6s a day and a labourer 3s 4d.

The physical regeneration of the city extended to 'some talk in Municipal circles regarding the erection of a new City Hall which would afford accommodation for all Corporation departments and staff, and also a large public hall for the use of citizens.' This was a pipe dream, given the parlous state of the finances of Dublin Corporation (as Dublin City Council was called at the time). In fact a political settlement offered 'the only hope of escape from the crushing burden of compensation for malicious injuries' imposed as a collective punishment on the community for rebel activities.[2] It is unlikely that there would have been any discussion at all about building a new City Hall if the British army had not remained in occupation of the old one, along with adjoining Corporation offices in Castle Street.

Nor did the early release of a handful of leading Republicans, such as Alderman Michael Staines, a member of the Dáil for St Michan's constituency, herald an end to the troubles.[3] Staines was despatched immediately to Galway to act as an IRA liaison officer with British forces in the west. Another Dublin deputy, Éamonn Duggan, acted as chief liaison officer for Ireland and for the capital.[4] Meanwhile almost 4,500 IRA suspects remained in internment camps, including more than a thousand Dubliners, among them the Corporation's secretary, the veteran Fenian

Fred Allan. There were another 1,600 convicted Republican prisoners. All were hostages to fortune and the peace process.

———

An ominous sign that peace was far from imminent was the fact that prisoners arrested immediately before the Truce were still being processed through the courts-martial system. The terms of the Truce had specifically left this issue for resolution at a later date.[5] In Dublin eight men tried by military courts in the days after the Truce came into effect faced the death penalty for being arrested in possession of weapons or being in the company of armed men, while two more were charged with the attempted murder of a military police sergeant. Most of those arrested refused to recognise the jurisdiction of the court. These included James Doyle of 263 Clonliffe Road, arrested on 2 July with a revolver and fourteen rounds of ammunition, as well as three men arrested on 21 June in South Richmond Street by a patrol of Auxiliaries. John Aloysius Haslam was charged with carrying a loaded Smith and Wesson revolver, James Cluskey had a grenade, and Martin Haugh carried nothing and at first denied to the patrol that he knew his companions; but when he appeared with them before the military court he sealed his fate by refusing to recognise the proceedings.

On 2 July, John O'Connor was arrested in Great Britain Street (Parnell Street) with an unloaded revolver. While he declined to recognise the court or to defend himself, he did offer evidence in support of Michael Kerrigan, who had the misfortune to bump into him when a military patrol arrived on the scene. Kerrigan recognised the court, was carrying neither a weapon nor ammunition and had no known political affiliations. Nevertheless he too now faced the prospect of the gallows.

Two men, Robert Butler and John Richmond Church, were charged with the attempted murder of a sergeant in the Royal Garrison Artillery on the night of 18/19 April. The sergeant was not identified in court, because he was working under cover for the intelligence service. He had shot one of his attackers, whose fate was unknown. Butler and Church strenuously denied involvement in the attack or any interest in politics. They also produced witnesses stating that they were at home at the time of the attack; but because the sergeant was on active service they had no prospect of trial in a civilian court. The fact that both men recognised the court and the nature of their testimony suggests that the incident may not have been politically motivated.

Not that political crime was always of an elevated nature. Patrick Keogh and James Doyle of Malahide were charged with 'depriving two private soldiers of their boots' at Cloghran, Co. Dublin, on 29 May. The soldiers said they were enjoying a drink in a public house when a group of armed men held them up. They had no weapons—and, after the brief encounter, no boots either. Keogh refused to recognise the court but Doyle pleaded not guilty, perhaps feeling that a pair of boots was not worth dying for.

The jurisdiction of the court-martial system, which sentenced most of those appearing before it to internment or terms of imprisonment rather than death, was already under appeal to the House of Lords. A case had been taken on behalf of two Cork prisoners, Patrick Clifford and Michael O'Sullivan, sentenced to death in April for unlawful possession of arms, and the proceedings were keenly watched as they dragged on through July and into August 1921. The appeal proved unsuccessful. As Lord Shaw put it, 'the King's law is for the King's lieges and other people cannot claim protection if they forswear allegiance.' The Law Lords found that the field courts-martial were not courts at all but 'committees' established by the local officer commanding British forces to make sure martial law was enforced in areas under his control. As they were not courts, they did not fall under the jurisdiction of the law.

Like the IRA, the Law Lords were refusing to recognise the courts-martial, with the same potentially lethal results.

The balance of terror was not entirely one-sided. Hostages of war were held by Republicans, albeit far fewer in number. The release of loyalist prisoners, such as Lord Bandon, a leading Southern unionist, and P. S. Brady, a resident magistrate in Cork, was welcomed as part of the peace dividend but posed questions about the fate of others still missing, such as seventy-year-old Mary Lindsay. It later emerged that she had been executed for aiding the enemy, along with her chauffeur, James Clarke. Rebels cited lack of facilities for holding and trying prisoners as mitigation for summary justice.

Another sign that much unfinished business remained a hostage to fortune was the decision of the government to suspend the Irish Land Bill then wending its way through the House of Lords. Despite protests from some Irish peers, it was decided that there was little point in trying to resolve the land question until it was clear which regime would be responsible for administering any new scheme for redistributing farms and compensating landlords.[6]

————

Dáil Éireann's *Irish Bulletin* was still in war mode in July, with its latest issue publishing 'stirring stories' of the heroism of Volunteers in the concluding hours of the conflict, and there were continuing reports of death and injury from Ulster. Unfortunately, what Ulster loyalists denounced as 'the farcical Truce' had come on the eve of the Twelfth, and there were twelve funerals in Belfast alone on 14 July for the latest casualties of sectarian violence in the Northern capital.[7] Anyone who doubted the true state of affairs received a sharp reminder in a public appeal from the Irish Republican Dependants' Fund for help in supporting the families of political prisoners, who included thirty-eight women. It pointed out that a 'Truce is not Peace': it 'is only a suspension of hostilities, rights no single one of our wrongs, and provides no cure for the suffering of our country.'[8] Even the optimistic *Irish Times* conceded that, should the talks fail, the loss of the Horse Show would prove 'a minor calamity' in the general scheme of things.[9]

Fortunately, some progress was made on the vexed issue of hostages well before then, when the British government decided at the beginning of August to release thirty-six of the thirty-seven Dáil deputies in custody. The exception was Commandant Seán Mac Eoin, deputy for Longford and Westmeath, who had been condemned to death by field court-martial on 14 June for the murder of an RIC district inspector who was killed in a skirmish at Ballinalee, Co. Longford, the previous February. The Republic's leaders responded with a warning that a meeting of Dáil Éireann convened for 16 August would not take place if Mac Eoin could not attend, and the Truce itself would be put in jeopardy.

Within three days the British side climbed down and the field court-martial system was suspended. As Austen Chamberlain told the House of Commons, the decision to release a prisoner condemned to death 'was based solely upon the existing situation in Ireland and the importance at the present time of avoiding conflict.'[10]

––––

It was against this happier backdrop that the Dublin Horse Show finally went ahead. More than 55,000 people attended, far more than in the troubled years of 1919 and 1920 but still not as many as flocked to the pre-war events. Still, a new national assertiveness was in the air. The IRA threatened to stop proceedings if the Union Jack was flown or other manifestations of Empire allowed. Dublin's ubiquitous Lord Mayor, Laurence O'Neill, appealed to de Valera, only to be advised 'to be very careful not to give any offence to the Army.' O'Neill, a dedicated peace-maker, negotiated an agreement whereby only the RDS's own flag would be flown, no anthems would be played, and the traditional reception for the Lord Lieutenant would be cancelled.[11]

Widespread dissatisfaction was also expressed at the majority of judges being English. The society defended itself by stating that outsiders were needed to ensure that there would be 'no suggestion of favouritism' in the decisions made, though the *Irish Independent* commented that 'Irishmen are surely as good judges of horseflesh as any Englishman.'

The show at least provided an opportunity to display Irish manufactures, which included presentation boxes of Gallaher's cigarettes provided by Clondalkin Paper Mills and matches made of cardboard. Other domestic products included

Longford wool and dolls from Co. Mayo. No heavy industry or light engineering products were in evidence, but then the boycott of Belfast goods in retaliation for the pogroms remained part of the political landscape of the South.

The ubiquity of organised religion further tainted hopes for the future. Cardinal Michael Logue expressed the hope of many when he told a novitiate of the Fathers of Charity in Omeath, Co. Louth, that 'the people, thank God, amidst their present sufferings, are good and fervent Catholics.'

————

The same month another gathering took place in the Mansion House in Dublin whose participants shared the cardinal's confidence in the future. The Irish Labour Party and Trade Union Congress could look back on a period of enormous growth since the employers' pyrrhic victory in the Dublin Lockout of 1913. In 1913 its affiliated unions had 100,000 members; now the figure stood at 300,000.[12] In fact the strength of the movement was in decline, as *de facto* union recognition, introduced during the Great War, was ending in many industries, and rising unemployment took its toll.

Whether the still formidable organisational strength of the movement could be converted into political power was the question that concerned delegates. Thousands of workers expelled from the shipyards and other work-places in Belfast remained unemployed, and the annual report of the ILP&TUC admitted that 'we can see no light ahead' on that front.

There had been other, more welcome manifestations of work-place militancy. A large number of 'soviets' had been established, with workers in pursuit of better pay and conditions occupying and operating concerns rather than mounting pickets in the traditional way. Knocklong Creamery in Co. Limerick and the Arigna Mines in Co. Roscommon were the best known. These creamery workers and miners seized the means of production and paid themselves from the proceeds. In both cases the men secured pay increases. Joe McGrath, formerly an accountant with Craig Gardner and finance officer of the ITGWU, said: 'They had one complaint in Knocklong, and that was that the workers in the rest of Ireland were more or less asleep in regard to their efforts'; but Louie Bennett of the Irish Women Workers' Union cautioned the ILP&TUC Executive that 'if we want to secure control of our industries … we need an Advisory Committee.' Efforts in Dublin to assert workers' control over enterprises had foundered from a lack of expert advice.

An even bigger problem was securing employment for men who had lost their jobs because of union activity or, as a Dundalk delegate put it, 'because of the fight they made for the Irish nation.' For the moment, the leadership of the ILP&TUC was happy to welcome the manifestation of 'soviets'; however, in acknowledging the successes the secretary, Thomas Johnson, echoed Bennett, saying, 'It cannot be done immediately, and not in every strike or on every occasion that the employers or owners refuse to continue their functions as organisers of production.'[13]

It was the political rather than the economic crisis that dominated the debate, and this was led, in turn, by those with advanced nationalist views within the ILP&TUC leadership, men who had been closest to the Dáil Éireann government before the Truce. Rather than challenge the supremacy of Sinn Féin and the IRA, the Congress nominated members to the Irish White Cross, a body established by the President of the Irish Republic, Éamon de Valera, as an alternative source of relief to the British Red Cross Society. It gave priority to victims of British and loyalist outrages.

Earlier in the year, when elections were held under the Government of Ireland Act, which partitioned the country and established separate parliaments in Belfast and Dublin, the ILP&TUC declared that 'the Labour Party should take no part ... beyond calling upon all workers, North and South, to demonstrate their loyalty to Ireland and freedom by voting only for those candidates that stand for the ownership and government of Ireland by the people of Ireland.' The movement even baulked at establishing a fund to help the families of trade unionists interned by the British, in case it would be interpreted as a split in the national ranks; instead the Executive referred members to the White Cross and Republican welfare bodies.

Trade unionists had paid a high price for their close association with the Republican movement in the South, especially in Dublin city and county. Besides the hundreds interned, the secretary of the Skerries Branch of the ITGWU, Tom Hand, had been killed by Auxiliaries, and four of the six Dublin IRA members hanged in Mountjoy Prison on 14 March 1921 were trade unionists, including Captain Paddy Moran, president of the Irish National Union of Grocers' and Vintners' Assistants.[14]

At least the Truce meant an end to the Dublin curfew, which had seen unions and other organisations meeting as early as 3 p.m. to make sure they could conclude their business and their members get home before the military deadline.[15] Workers in many occupations refused to work late in case they were arrested for breaking the curfew. Shipping was particularly affected, and the turnaround times on vessels could double, depending on the state of the tide. The retail trade, railways, banks, entertainment and even street dealers selling fruit and vegetables had been crippled by the curfew.

Unfortunately, the return to normality brought a new threat, that of a sustained assault by employers on earnings and living standards. The post-war boom was over, and workers in Britain had already suffered savage pay cuts, with miners' wages reduced from 80s a week to 44s. Even the traditionally militant and well-organised engineering trades had agreed wage cuts of 6s a week in the weeks before the ILP&TUC conference. Some unions promised 'to consider a further reduction equalling ... 10s or 12s in September.' The question was how Irish workers would respond to the employers. Ironically, the disturbed state of the country had masked the seriousness of the threat. Economic activity may have been disrupted in many places, but the lack of law and order had made employers hesitate to impose cuts. Some labour leaders misread the signs badly. The president of Congress, Tom Foran, told delegates in August that 'if the miners in England ... had acted as the miners in Arigna had acted [i.e. with a soviet] we would be a long way towards the social revolution.'

The ever-moderate secretary of the ILP&TUC, Thomas Johnson, questioned the cost-of-living index used by the British government's *Labour Gazette*. He said it failed to take account of Irish conditions. Retail prices had risen by 240 per cent during the First World War and had fallen back to 128 per cent by May 1921, according to the *Gazette*, but Congress had conducted its own survey, which showed that the price of basic household items in Ireland was still 175 per cent of what it was before 1914. Because Irish workers generally had lower wages, worked longer hours and spent a higher proportion of their income on necessities, the ILP&TUC proposed 'the guiding policy of the [Irish] unions to be ... to claim advances in the lower paid occupations,' and to oppose any reduction in 'real wages; that is to say, a reduction greater than the decline in the cost of living.' To work more effectively in support of this strategy, Congress urged the formation of workers' industrial councils or joint committees—at the local and the national level—in businesses and industries where they did not already exist.[16]

———

The battle was joined by the Irish Engineering, Shipwrights' and Foundry Trade Union, which formed an alliance with branches of the British unions from which it had recently broken away. The ITGWU, which represented labourers in the sector, also joined the fray. The omens were not propitious. The boilermakers, who sought a pay increase of 23s 6d a week in August 1920, had been forced to settle at the end of January 1921 for a British Industrial Tribunal award of 1s 9d.[17] Already, on 27 July, the eve of the ILP&TUC conference, the Engineering Employers' Federation in Britain told the engineering unions in Ireland that it wanted a cut of 6s in pay, together with the elimination of a 12½ per cent bonus scheme agreed the previous year. Nor was the federation prepared to accept negotiation on the cuts at the company level, because of 'the unsettled political situation' in Ireland.

The main engineering firms in Dublin aligned themselves with the federation and made it clear that they regarded themselves as 'an integral part of the United Kingdom.' Employers in Cork and other centres followed suit. Reporting back on negotiations to the IES&FTU, the president of the union, Jack Redmond, said that even employers previously prepared to consider localised negotiations had committed themselves to the hard-line British strategy.

If the men expected support from Dáil Éireann's Ministry of Labour, they were disappointed. It suggested that they accept the cuts in the hope that employers would engage in localised bargaining on future changes when the political crisis was resolved. The IES&FTU ordered an immediate strike. The British craft unions were in a dilemma, as their parent organisations had already accepted pay cuts in the rest of the United Kingdom; but some of their shop stewards pledged to support the strike, even if they had to do so unofficially.[18] It was a defining moment for the new Irish craft union, which said it was rejecting the pay cuts because it did not accept that Ireland was 'an integral part of the United Kingdom,' nor was it bound by agreements reached there. Jack Redmond became secretary of the strike committee, and Thomas Foran, president of the ITGWU and of the ILP&TUC, endorsed the craft workers' contention that 'the negotiations for a settlement in England, without the workers of Dublin being consulted, were not going to be accepted in this country.' He warned that employers in the Irish shipping, flour-milling and chemical industries were planning similar wage cuts in August, and said that Congress would help all its affiliates 'to stand together in the coming attack.'[19]

Despite public displays of solidarity, tensions ran high behind the scenes between the IES&FTU and some of the British craft unions, which remained reluctant to support a dispute over pay cuts already conceded in Britain. The dockyards, where British unions remained strong, had to be excluded from the strike. Funds were tight, and many workers were hard pressed to stay out. The IES&FTU (which changed its name to the Irish Engineering and Industrial Union on 1 August) had to establish a £60 emergency float after complaints about its failure to anticipate the widespread hardship caused by the strike. In one highly embarrassing incident a deceased member could not be buried until his family could obtain access to the union's death benefit.[20]

Meanwhile the railway companies demanded that their unions accept a reduction in pay of 6s a week once military controls ended. The shipping companies sought a pay cut of 2s a week, having first mooted a cut of 4s. The main British engineering union, the Amalgamated Engineering Union, threatened to break ranks in the railways and accept the proposed reduction. Somehow, unity was maintained.[21] Tensions eased only when control over pickets was ceded to a Joint Strike Committee, which gave the IEIU increased representation to reflect its growing strength.[22]

In September 1921 the IEIU further consolidated its position by affiliating to the relatively new Dublin Workers' Council rather than the traditional Dublin Trades Council. This was probably due in part to its need to keep in with the founders of the DWC, Thomas Foran and William O'Brien, leaders of the dominant faction within the ITGWU, but the DWC was also recognised by Dublin Corporation as the nominating body to the Arbitration Board that dealt with disputes involving skilled employees in the city.

The success of the DWC in overshadowing the old Trades Council reflected the closeness of many trade unionists to Sinn Féin, the largest party in the City Council. William O'Brien and the 'Republican Labour' councillors were in effect junior partners in the Sinn Féin-Labour coalition that controlled the Corporation. Several IEIU members had run as Sinn Féin candidates in the 1920 municipal election, although only one, the general secretary of the IEIU, P. J. (Patrick) McIntyre, had been elected.[23] A further indication of republican leanings came in early September when the union referred a demand for £2 3s 5d in respect of income tax from the British Collector of Taxes 'to the responsible official of Dáil Éireann for advice.'[24]

None of this did anything to resolve the engineering dispute, which now involved about a thousand craft workers.[25] McIntyre used his position as a city councillor to raise the engineering strike at a meeting of the Corporation on 3 October, and the Lord Mayor, Alderman Laurence O'Neill, called a conciliation conference with the employers but failed to break the deadlock.[26]

——

There was more progress on the railways, where another conference under the auspices of the Lord Mayor reached a settlement.[27] Unfortunately, the terms caused serious damage to the internal cohesion of the IEIU. Many members, particularly in the Great Southern and Western Railway works at Inchicore, vowed to continue the struggle.[28] A mass meeting in the Banba Hall in Parnell Square on 18 September proved so acrimonious that the following night two founder-members of the union, Christy Farrelly, representing the iron-moulders, and John Rooney, representing the coach-builders, proposed the expulsion of the GSWR men, and one of the leading dissidents, Joe Quinn, was suspended from his position as treasurer of the union.[29] Eventually the executive instructed all dissidents to return to work on 26 September and withdrew strike pay from those still on the picket line, as well as unemployment benefit from those laid off as a result of the dispute.[30]

Several of these men had worked closely together in a special intelligence unit Michael Collins established to 'smash up' British unions and establish the IEIU in order to control important branches of the economy, such as the power stations and railways, as well as liaising with other nationally minded unions, such as the ITGWU, in such areas as Dublin Port. However, the lack of any clear industrial strategy or long-term political outlook made it inevitable that they would fall foul of demarcation disputes, the curse of the craft unions, and unity in the IRA was splintered on the factory floor.[31] As it happened, the IRA itself was soon to divide.

The sense of betrayal among the Inchicore men ran deep over acceptance of the wage cut. It took a provincial delegate to tell the Dubliners bluntly that 'reductions at the present time were inevitable.' If 'the shop men go on strike they will be attempting the impossible, and in the process ... ruin the future of the union.'[32] Of course the same analysis could be applied in the engineering industry, but these firms were far more numerous and their economic circumstances more varied than those of the railway companies. Some were profitable enough to continue paying existing rates, or to implement less drastic cuts than the 6s a week demanded by the Employers' Federation. That was why the basic demand of the engineering unions remained local bargaining.[33]

Their strike finally ended on 22 October when agreement was reached at yet another conference in the Mansion House under the auspices of the Lord Mayor. The unions were forced to accept the cut of 6s a week and had to settle for guarantees that there would be no victimisation.[34] The failure to secure work-place bargaining was a serious setback, and the fact that they had fought much harder than their British counterparts only underlined the inevitability of the outcome. Pay cuts in other sectors followed.[35]

On 16 September, the day after the railway settlement, the IEIU stopped paying benefits to members interned by the British authorities. Following the ILP&TUC precedent, it said it did not wish to be seen to discriminate in favour of its own members; but in truth the union could no longer afford to.[36] The general president, Jack Redmond, described the financial situation as 'extremely critical.'[37] The following week he resigned, deciding to become self-employed rather than unemployed. He told the Executive that, as 'he was about to enter into business on his own account ... it would not be at all fitting for an employer to occupy that position.'[38] He was a significant loss, having held the line with the Inchicore men, maintained good relations with Dáil Éireann and the ITGWU, found suitable head office premises for the union and overseen its finances. He was typical of a generation of dedicated trade unionists whose instincts were separatist rather than socialist.

The union's finances were now so bad that it could not afford to give him a testimonial. It even began holding bingo sessions in the head office and enquired about acquiring a bar licence from the Dáil Éireann Ministry of Home Affairs, as well as pursuing tenants who were in arrears with the rent. Although the latter included the Dublin Brigade of the IRA[39] and the James Connolly Labour College, it was a commercial tenant, Hampton Leedon Ltd, that was the worst offender. Meanwhile the bingo sessions were dropped at the end of the year. They raised £18 8s 9d but cost £24 4s 4d to run.[40]

────

By far the greatest setback for the trade union movement was the abolition of the Agricultural Wages Board on 1 October 1921 by the British government. While the spread of socialist ideas and trade union organisation had fuelled the campaign for improved pay rates and conditions in Co. Dublin and further afield, it was the establishment of the board in 1917 that provided structures that facilitated the growth and increased militancy of the rural workers who flocked to the ITGWU. Pay for agricultural labourers reached a peak of 34s a week for a 55-hour week in May 1921 and some 37s 6d for ploughmen.[41] In some places, such as north Co. Dublin, men won 40s a week (the maximum rate for women was 19s 6d). The driving force behind *de facto* union recognition for rural workers was the same as for their urban cousins: the British government's need to ensure industrial peace in wartime. But now the Hun was beaten, and ploughman and fitter alike would be left to their own devices just as the economic recession bit.

––––

If Dublin's trade unionists were in reactive mode in the Truce period, some former supporters of the late John Redmond were beginning to exert a significant influence on the course of events. Joseph Brennan came from a wealthy Co. Cork family that was able to send him to Clongowes Wood College and University College, Dublin, and then to the University of Cambridge after he complained of poor teaching and study facilities in Dublin. At Cambridge he studied mathematics and then classics, winning a first in Latin and Greek as well as various prizes before securing a place in 1911 in the first division of the British Civil Service.

Although he was now securely ensconced in London, Brennan continued to show an intense interest in Irish affairs. He spoke on a platform supporting the Redmondite candidate in his native Bandon in 1910, in defiance of the All for Ireland League, which was the dominant force in local nationalist politics.

When the opportunity came in 1912 of a posting to Dublin Castle, Brennan took it. He epitomised the younger generation of educated, public-spirited nationalists ready to put the Home Rule project into operation. At Cambridge, writing in the Christ's College magazine under the pseudonym 'Corcaigh', he had advocated a federal structure for the British Empire. He holidayed in the west of Ireland, where he took strong objection to the activities of local proselytisers as a manifestation of 'aggressive Protestantism' and wrote to the Archbishop of Tuam suggesting that Connemara hotels be supplied with notices showing details of Masses in the locality.[42]

Brennan's outlook may have been conservative (he met his wife at a Clongowes Social Services Conference), but he enjoyed the theatre and had a wide circle of friends, who stood him in good stead in the coming decade of revolution. Meanwhile, when war came, two of his brothers served in the British army and a sister in the Women's Army Auxiliary Corps. The 1916 Rising did not dent his faith in the Home Rule project or in Redmond, and he stuck by the stricken leader until his death marked the political demise of the Irish Party in 1918. When Brennan's brother Jerry died in France during the closing stages of the war, he could still take comfort in the thought that 'he died for Ireland and doing his duty.'[43] Now a deputy clerk in Dublin Castle, Brennan did his best to maintain a moderate nationalist position in discussions with his superiors, who were increasingly intolerant of any dissent.

Whatever about his own views, Brennan's social circle outside work was becoming radicalised by default. When Edward Shortt was appointed Chief Secretary for Ireland he considered making Brennan his private secretary, until he was shown a captured document reporting that 'so long as Joe is in the Castle everything will be all right.'[44] Brennan was indeed becoming increasingly sceptical of the efficacy of British policy. When he returned to Co. Cork to visit his father in late 1920 he saw at first hand the state of the country: family members had been threatened and assaulted for employing 'Sinn Féiners', the family's hosiery factory had been burnt down and the family home at Kilbrogan House attacked. 'You are no doubt aware that for some days past the town of Bandon, Co. Cork, has been subjected to outrage, arson and general terrorism by forces of the Crown,' he told his friend Cornelius Gregg, the Chief Secretary's private secretary in London. After itemising attacks on his family and their property in a telegram to Gregg, he demanded 'proper redress' and asked, 'Is it not possible to have some steps taken to establish discipline among the troops or otherwise allay the apprehensions of good citizens?' He was reproved by his superior in Dublin Castle, Sir John Taylor, for using the telegraph service to transmit the message, but Gregg told Brennan: 'I am getting daily sicker and sicker of the news from Ireland.'

An inquiry into events at Bandon was promised by Sir Nevil Macready, the officer commanding British forces in Ireland, but it proved a whitewash. When Brennan resorted to having a question asked in the House of Commons to publicise what was happening in his home county it only added fuel to the flames of his indignation because of the combative response of the Chief Secretary, Sir Hamar Greenwood. MPs were told that the trade of James Brennan and Sons was built on the boycott and murder of a local loyalist businessman.[45]

A few months later, when negotiations opened between the Irish and British delegations in London on the shape of the Treaty, Brennan's moment had come. By October 1921 he had been put in charge of the Finance Division of the Chief Secretary's Office. The link between Dáil Éireann's Minister for Finance, Michael Collins, and the disaffected Brennan was made through another former Clongowes boy, Patrick McGilligan, then private secretary to Dáil Éireann's Assistant Minister for Local Government, Kevin O'Higgins. O'Higgins was not part of the negotiating team but he was secretary of the Economic Relations Committee reviewing taxation issues. Like Collins, O'Higgins was deeply aware of the shortcomings of the Irish team on financial matters.

The first meeting between Collins and Brennan took place in McGilligan's flat in Leeson Street. Brennan was extremely nervous, not so much at the prospect of meeting Collins as at being followed and having his job put in jeopardy. He agreed to help the enemy, salving his conscience by recalling that the facts and figures he was producing for Collins were available in official publications, provided one knew where to look.

The Irish team certainly needed all the help it could obtain, as the British negotiators on financial matters included senior Treasury officials as well as members of the British premier's formidable Irish support team, such as Sir John Anderson, Andy Cope and Lionel Curtis, all of whom were Brennan's superiors at Dublin Castle. Brennan therefore had the unenviable task of working all day on British government briefs, only to spend his nights producing rival papers for the other side. He produced eight papers in all, some of them highly technical, covering such issues as making reliable estimates of Irish revenue, determining Irish liability for Britain's war debts and contributions to pensions for Irish ex-servicemen, as well as RIC and DMP members, not to mention the judiciary, and of course calculating compensation for landlords under the various Land Acts. Brennan did not sign any of these documents, as the results of his duplicity would have been fatal to his career, and possibly in other ways if the Treaty talks had broken down and hostilities resumed.

As it happened, the specialist subcommittee never reconvened, and financial issues were dealt with in direct talks between Lloyd George and Collins and the other principals. This made Brennan's advice all the more vital. While partition and the oath of allegiance would feature far more prominently in negotiations and the subsequent debate on the Treaty, the economic gains would have a far greater bearing on the daily lives of citizens in the new Irish dominion. It was partly as a result of Brennan's surreptitious contribution to the negotiations that the British conceded the right of the new Irish government to full fiscal autonomy, including the power to impose duties 'for the encouragement of infant industries and for economic development,' while the measures for fisheries protection and revenue collection contained the seeds of an Irish naval service.

From 16 January 1922 Brennan would find himself embarked, like thousands of other public servants, on a new career, serving the nascent Irish Free State. Collins appointed him Comptroller and Auditor-General on 1 April. Although he was not formally appointed Secretary of the Ministry of Finance until 1923, he was the directing force behind it, even before his nominal superior, William O'Brien, was moved sideways to chair the Revenue Commissioners. By the summer of 1922 Brennan was in London meeting Sir John Anderson and other former colleagues to continue negotiations on unfinished business.

If Brennan was one of the most significant members of the existing administrative hierarchy who facilitated the transfer of power, he was by no means the only one. The fact that colleagues unhappy with the change of regime could transfer to Northern Ireland or Britain eased the change process. The leading historian of the Irish public service, Martin Maguire, concludes that 'the Provisional Government, by seizing control of the civil service, seized control of the entire existing machinery of the State. Thus, a revolutionary act was cloaked in a constitutional and parliamentary form.' The only outward manifestation of the change was the decision to abandon Dublin Castle and make City Hall the temporary administrative headquarters of the Free State. There was even talk of using explosives to demolish the Castle and eradicate this hated symbol of British rule.[46] A similar debate was taking place simultaneously in Russia, where some members of the new communist regime wanted to demolish the Kremlin.

———

The Truce that prevailed from July 1921 was something of a misnomer. As Emmet Dalton, who took over the role of chief liaison officer for the IRA with the British forces on 1 December, put it,

> a most unprecedented outburst of brigandism swept the whole country. Armed hold-ups and motor thefts were a daily occurrence. Towards the latter end of December six motor thefts were reported to my office all upon the same day. The C.I. [Criminal Investigation] Department not then functioning, the police work was directed from my headquarters in the Gresham Hotel.[47]

Alice Howard, Countess of Wicklow, was one of many members of the Anglo-Irish ascendancy in the greater Dublin area who feared the consequences of a general breakdown in law and order. Shortly after Dalton took over his new post she travelled into the city centre 'to Mitchell's to see about my fur jacket [which needed altering]. Then we went to the "Distressed Ladies" Sales at Shelbourne [Hotel] to meet V. [Viscount] Holmpatrick—met a good many friends—All in despair at the state of the country.' She was further depressed by the weather, which was 'Dark and Gloomy,' and complained that she was frequently confined to the house, because 'we cannot take the car out as they are being stopped and stolen every day.'[48]

She might have taken some comfort from knowing that the South Dublin Brigade of the IRA, within whose operational area she now lived, was also concerned about unauthorised expropriations of transport. In a 'special memorandum' it told Volunteers that 'seizures shall only be carried out when sanctioned by the Brigade O/C. RECEIPTS should be given for all goods commandeered for Army purposes.' Concern had been prompted when a car had been commandeered from a local loyalist by a Southern Division officer en route to the Four Courts garrison.[49]

Generally speaking, intimidation of Southern loyalists was far more prevalent outside Dublin, where they were more physically and socially isolated. Besides, the continued presence of large numbers of British troops in the capital inevitably curbed the worst excesses of lawless elements among Republicans and their opportunist fellow-travellers. Nevertheless, some Dublin unionists did find themselves very exposed, such as Annie Hole, who ran a boarding-house at 22 Lower Mount Street. This had been the scene of an IRA attack on suspected British intelligence officers on Bloody Sunday, 21 November 1920. One of her lodgers, a 'Mr McMahon' (otherwise Temporary Captain Henry Angliss), had been shot dead, and another, Temporary Captain Carl Peel, narrowly escaped assassination. 'From that time onwards … her house was continually watched by rebels,' her solicitor subsequently told the Irish Grants Committee, established to compensate loyalists who suffered losses because of their support for the British government. She had run her business as a landlady in Dublin for thirty years but now found it impossible to make ends meet, where previously she claimed to have enjoyed an income of £600 a year from her lodgers and was able to employ two servants. In June 1922 she finally sold the house, with all its contents, for £300 and moved to Britain, where she earned £35 a year as a part-time housekeeper. Her solicitor told the committee that

> she has lost everything that she had in the World and all due to her loyalty to the British connection. When other people in Dublin would not take in British Officers she welcomed them and was a mother to them, and when the murders took place in her home it became a marked house into which no loyalist dare enter … Owing to the state of her health, which is very bad since the terrible shock she received at the time of the murders, she is not now able to accept any employment that might offer …
>
> Whilst she was living in Lower Mount Street, she frequently supplied the military with useful information and detectives came regularly in motor cars to her house to take her to the Castle, all of which was, of course, observed by her neighbours, and the wonder is that she herself was not murdered for having done so.

In spite of her ordeal, she told the committee 'she would gladly go through it all again' to serve her country. The committee gave her £350, although she had to wait until 1927 for the final instalment, together with £20 7s 6d for damage caused to her property by gunfire. The British government would prove consistent in its parsimony when rewarding loyalty.

———

Charles Thompson was another loyalist casualty of the changing times. He had been in the printing and stationery business, 'in quite a large way previous to the Rebellion of 1916,' according to the Southern Irish Loyalists Relief Association.

> In addition to very considerable business with the British Army and Police, he had a good general connection. After Easter 1916 he was rigidly boycotted and lost all his general business. He was just able to carry on by reason of the business he did with the Army and Police, but when the Treaty came into force he found it impossible to keep going.

He was given £50 compensation. In 'most gratefully' acknowledging the amount, Thompson confessed that he was 'much disappointed that you could not see your way to grant me £100.' It was not, he believed, an extravagant claim,

> after supplying the Military for 36 years with printing and stationery. 32 of these years in Ireland and years supplying troops with goods of many kinds, when it was most dangerous to be seen entering or leaving barracks or having troops coming to your place of business. I have been a marked man ever since and [my] business gone to the dogs.
> I have turned 76 years and growing very feeble and past active service. You will see by the enclosure that I am on the point of being turned out of my house and home for non-payment of rent. Now with another £50 my wife would be able to start a new apartment house where we could make a decent living by letting apartments. I pray you once more to do me this good turn and see justice done me, for which for the rest of my wife's and mine own [life] we shall feel most grateful.[50]

One of the oddest, and most poignant, cases of loyalists left stranded by the ebb tide of Empire was Emily Katherine Harris, founder and former matron of the Red Cross Hospital in Kingstown, though it is hard to avoid the conclusion that she drew some of her misfortunes on herself; even some of those trying to assist her confessed that she 'is not easy to deal with.' From about September 1920 she was met with open hostility in the area and was 'spat upon,' according to her subsequent claim for compensation to the Irish Grants Committee. Confrontations with local republican activists and their supporters appear to have increased significantly after she hired ex-servicemen to carry out work on a cottage she had acquired adjoining her home, The Hall, at Crosthwaite Park, Glenageary. Her furniture was damaged or stolen, lead guttering taken, 'trees cut down, crops in garden destroyed, rose trees, including other choice plants and bulbs were ruthlessly torn up and left lying after breaking in pieces.' Two arson attacks took place on her house, one in late 1920 and another in 1921.

The situation worsened in 1922, when she reported three incidents of shots being fired into the house, telephone wires cut, and being assaulted in Nassau Street and later in her own home. Jewellery, silver and books were stolen. She believed the cause of such animosity was her role in founding and promoting the Red Cross Hospital during the First World War. Neighbours appear to have been reluctant to come to her assistance. They may perhaps have felt that there was an element of paranoia in some of her claims, such as her description of being 'tripped in the streets by women carrying golf sticks, especially on turning corners,' or they may simply have declined to run the risk of becoming involved in her lonely combat with the rebels in case they brought retribution down on themselves.

However, Major Reid Jameson of the Irish Grants Committee in London believed her and told the commission that she was singled out 'as a direct consequence of her loyalist sympathies.' There was a sad inevitability about the next phase in her story.

> Although my powers of endurance were very great, and my nerves of iron, fear not entering into my composition, the long strain of keeping myself taut to show what kind of mettle English People are made of, coupled with the injuries inflicted eventually ended up in a severe attack of General Neuritis and double Sciatica, with dilations of the heart.

She spent much of 1922 and 1923 undergoing medical treatment, and Major Jameson believed her health had been 'permanently impaired.' In February 1926 she sold her interest in the Hall and the adjoining cottage and moved to Cuxton in Kent, where she kept a poultry farm. The 150 fowl appeared well fed and well looked after when a representative of the British Red Cross Society called in 1928, but Miss Harris was living 'in a kind of hut which has been condemned by the District Council.'

She claimed compensation of £6,000 from the Exchequer, and Major Jameson estimated her losses at £4,000. The problem was that she could provide no supporting evidence for her losses. The transfer of her claim, with an estimated 19,000 others, from the Irish to the British Exchequer further delayed matters, while the reorganisation of policing in the Free State meant that the new Garda Síochána had no proper records of the incidents on which her claim was based. The investigating officer for the Irish Grants Committee, Major Charles Coleman, expressed considerable scepticism about the size of the claim, questioning why the insurance policy had been increased from £750 in 1919 to £1,500 in 1923.

Eventually Emily Harris was awarded £500, but as £350 had been paid in advance this left her only £150 on which to survive in straitened circumstances. On receiving the news of her final award she asked rhetorically whether 'it would be only one other country, perhaps Russia, where a woman who served her King would be allowed to drop to such an existence.'[51]

Nor were casualties restricted to the middle classes. Albert Pennycook was a fitter and turner with the Great Southern and Western Railway at its Inchicore works. His steady progression through the ranks from apprentice to charge hand in the carriage and wagon shop when only twenty-two was put down to favouritism by many workmates because he was a Protestant. When he was appointed piecework checker over 140 other employees his situation became increasingly fraught. He found himself in the unenviable position of having

> to go around the shop checking what the men were doing, and on a number of occasions some of the men who would be absent from their work [were] carrying out murderous acts against the British Crown; at the end of the week when it was time to return a report of their work, they would not have enough ... done to pay them their wages. It was then that they threatened me and told me I would get a bullet and if I did not send in their wages they would get rid of me and put one of their own in my place.

In August 1921 his home was ransacked after IRA Volunteers found his name in a membership list during a raid on the Orange Order's head office in Rutland Square (Parnell Square). His family was held at gunpoint and his Orange sash thrown on the kitchen fire, while he was warned that 'if he were ever seen ... near the Lodge, or wearing the sash, they would destroy him.' The following month his brother was told by a 'friendly' IRA Volunteer that Pennycook was 'on a list to be shot.' Ostracised by his neighbours, he became too ill to work. Though he did not want 'to lose the benefit of his twenty-two years in his employment and his membership of the Engineers Society,' he decided to take his young family, including 'a son in a very delicate state of health,' to Canada in 1924. He found work with a local subsidiary of a Northern Ireland firm, but his health broke down again and he went to London, where he threw himself on the mercy of the Irish Grants Committee. Unlike many other claimants, he could at least produce figures based on his former wages to calculate his losses. Nevertheless he was awarded only £700 of the £1,500 sought, and that was not paid until January 1930.[52]

———

Most Dubliners were as indifferent to the travails of Albert Pennycook, Emily Harris and their fellow-loyalists as the British Exchequer. Those who were ratepayers were far more interested in proposals to reform the Corporation. In May 1921 a Reorganisation Committee, first proposed a year earlier, had finally been established, and it produced its report in July. All political parties were represented, and it concentrated on improving basic organisation and procedures. Among the main proposals were:

- Holding two regular meetings each month instead of one
- Having proposals costed before being debated
- Sharpening guillotine procedures on debates
- Reducing and rationalising the number of committees
- Synchronising committee meetings to avoid clashes
- Bringing all employee posts under a unified appointments system
- Making the Town Clerk responsible for overseeing the records of all committees.

Centralising the secretariat under the Town Clerk made sound organisational and financial sense. The decision stemmed from a bitter pay dispute in 1920 with white-collar employees and a belief that some senior staff members, including the former Town Clerk, Sir Henry Campbell, had colluded with Dublin Castle to undermine the city's administration after it transferred its allegiance to Dáil Éireann. But some senior personnel who supported the new regime, such as the IRB veteran Fred Allan, the Town Secretary, also faced the axe because of the high salaries and other perks they had accumulated through the years.

Sinn Féin councillors had been particularly alienated by Campbell and a number of other senior officials because of their hostility to the Irish language and the separatist agenda generally. Most senior officials had been supporters of the old constitutional nationalist regime. Labour councillors also disliked these City Hall mandarins. Every councillor in the group was a trade union official representing manual workers, and they had little sympathy for the Corporation's white-collar employees, whom they regarded as snobs and lacking in sympathy for any socialist agenda. Even the Municipal Reform Association, formed from an alliance of former unionists and constitutional nationalists, regarded City Hall as full of expensive bureaucratic time-servers whose main preoccupation was featherbedding.

By the summer of 1921 there was a growing demand from ratepayers for economies, faced, as they were, with a mounting bill for compensation from companies and individuals who had been subjected to attacks by the IRA. The war may have ended, but the British Government was adamant that reparations should be paid.

By subsuming the secretariats of the various committees in the Town Clerk's office the Corporation could suppress eight senior posts. Further savings could be made by reducing the pension of retired employees to reflect general wage trends in the deepening economic crisis. Naturally, the proposals provoked a furious reaction from the Local Government Officials (Ireland) Trade Union, which argued that pensions were already too low and that the abolition of long-standing promotional opportunities would lead to staff members seeking better positions elsewhere. These protests evoked little sympathy. The argument about promotional outlets held little water, as some senior officials already held more than one position, and staff members were welcome to depart for a labour market in which unemployment was soaring.

The official person with most positions was Fred Allan. As well as being Secretary to the Corporation he had alternated as City Treasurer, Commercial Manager and secretary of the Electricity Supply Committee, and secretary of both the Public Lighting Committee and the Cleansing Committee. As an active member of the IRB and former member of its Supreme Council he had powerful allies in the government of the Irish Republic, including Harry Boland and Michael Collins. Above all, he enjoyed a halo of martyrdom from his present status as an internee at Ballykinler. Nevertheless the reform current was strong enough to see him divested of his duties in absentia, although he was consoled with a pension of £603 a year when he was only entitled to one of £362.[53]

However, progress was being made on other fronts. In June 1920 Councillor Hanna Sheehy Skeffington (Sinn Féin) had secured the passing of a resolution that

this Council declares (and that committees be instructed accordingly) that in future no woman should be disqualified by reason of her sex from holding any appointment under the council, and, that women be eligible to compete at all future examinations on the same terms and conditions as men.

In December 1921 the Corporation built on that initiative, passing a motion that 'no woman employee should, by reason of her sex, receive less remuneration than a male employee performing work of equal value.' The increasing acceptability of the equality principle was reflected in the fact that it was the Corporation's most populist member, Alderman Alfie Byrne, who had seconded the Sheehy Skeffington motion. The surprisingly modern-sounding equal-pay proposal came from Alderman Tom Lawlor of Labour (a member of the Trades Council faction) and was seconded by Alderman Bernard Shields (Municipal Reform Association).[54] If the move towards greater equality proved illusory in the decades ahead it was in part due to the extraordinary events of the next few months, culminating in civil war. Ironically, many women republicans played a leading role in the armed struggle while losing the battle for equality by default.

————

The Corporation made one of its least contentious decisions in September when the members voted unanimously to congratulate the new Catholic Archbishop of Dublin, Dr Edward Byrne, on his appointment. Byrne had been auxiliary bishop to the late Dr William Walsh from the previous year, and Walsh had groomed him for the position. While intelligent and energetic, he lacked the political skill that had made his predecessor such a formidable participant in the events of the previous thirty-five years. Byrne was essentially a pastor with good administrative skills, whose instincts were cautious. He had worked for many years in the Pro-Cathedral parish in the inner city, where proselytism and prostitution were seen as greater threats to the faith than poverty. However, he realised that many poor families were giving children to Protestant orphanages only in return for material aid to help make ends meet. He was involved in various social initiatives to counter the proselytisers and also attempted to reach out to prostitutes. However, he was hampered by public attitudes that had been largely fashioned by the Church itself. For instance, his decision to offer the last sacraments to seriously ill women in brothels was considered very radical, though there was a provision that, however ill they were, they had to be carried to the front door, 'as the priest could not be seen to enter such a house.'

Byrne's elevation coincided with a significant new initiative by Catholic lay activists, the foundation of the Legion of Mary, which would have a significant impact in this area. Pillars of the new charitable dispensation, such as Margaret Pearse (sister of Patrick Pearse) and Lillie Connolly (widow of James Connolly), belonged to St Joseph's Guild of Rescue, which concerned itself with the children of poor unmarried Catholic mothers who might be tempted to give them for adoption to Protestant societies. Lillie Connolly, who was herself a convert from the Church of Ireland, gave a young Frank Duff, future founder of the Legion of Mary, a copy of her husband's book *Labour in Irish History*. For her and for many followers of the dead revolutionary there was no clash between class and creed.

The Legion itself was established in the autumn of 1921, and from the outset it was a lay auxiliary body intended to extend the ideological reach of the Catholic diocesan clergy through visitations.[55] As many early members were also in the Society of St Vincent de Paul and the Pioneer Total Abstinence Association, they were apostolic social engineers in the city, seeking to refashion existing lay activist structures to meet new conditions. Whether such an initiative would have been welcomed, or even tolerated, by Archbishop Walsh is doubtful. He had squashed similar lay initiatives in the past and was acutely aware of the need to accommodate as well as contain the Protestant community in the city.

Inevitably, hopes were high that Byrne would not only display the same dazzling political acumen as Walsh but would exceed him. The congratulations proffered to the new archbishop by Lorcan Sherlock, a former Lord Mayor and former political confidant of Walsh, were typical.

May I in common with the man in the street express the hope that your reign will coincide with the settlement of political affairs in Ireland … And may I further predict that during your reign the most pressing of all our local problems housing the working class will be tackled and dealt with in a thorough manner.[56]

As Tom Morrissey, biographer of both Walsh and Byrne, has pointed out, the problems facing the national movement in the Truce period would have taxed even Walsh's machiavellian skill at the height of his powers. Byrne would prove an adaptor to political developments rather than their architect. Walsh's own radical nationalist stance, combined with Dublin's role as cockpit of the Irish Revolution, also meant that the clergy in Byrne's archdiocese were divided on the Treaty. While thirty-eight members of the regular clergy who took public positions on the issue would support the Treaty, twenty-one would oppose it. Among the religious congregations the pattern was reversed, with thirteen supporting the Treaty and twenty-eight opposed. The anti-Treatyites were strongest among the Capuchins, while the only order in which the pro-Treatyites constituted a majority was the Jesuits.[57]

Chapter 2 ∾

'WE WOULD NOT RECOGNISE THE COURT, BECAUSE THE GOVERNMENT THAT DOES NOT REDRESS OUR GRIEVANCES IS NOT WORTH RECOGNISING'

In the early hours of 6 December 1921 Laurence O'Neill received a call from Sir James MacMahon to tell him that a treaty had been signed, 'but no particulars were to hand.' MacMahon was an under-secretary at Dublin Castle and the senior member of the administration closest to O'Neill. Both were survivors, O'Neill from the old nationalist elite swept away by Sinn Féin; MacMahon was the first Catholic 'Whig' to rise through the senior ranks of the civil service. Both were involved in a wide range of religious charities and were attentive to the concerns of the hierarchy while seeking to reconcile unionists to the prospect of change.

O'Neill had been a member of the first Irish delegation to London, in recognition of his role in helping to initiate peace talks as well as allowing Éamon de Valera and his cabinet colleagues to more or less take over the Mansion House, where Dáil Éireann normally sat. However, O'Neill was a power facilitator rather than a power broker, and his role in London was largely confined to 'a mixture of public relations and catering for the welfare of … members of the party.'

Unlike the euphoria with which crowds around the Mansion House had welcomed the Truce in the glorious summer of the previous July, O'Neill found the reception of the latest news distinctly chilly. 'There was no enthusiasm in the city,' he recalled, 'no flags, no bells, everyone looked solemn instead of gay, a cloud appeared to have spread over the spirits of the people.' The conclusion of talks took everyone by surprise. De Valera had been reviewing Volunteers down the country but fortuitously had arranged to be back in Dublin that evening to preside at a lecture in the Mansion House by Count Plunkett on Dante. He asked O'Neill, astounded, 'Surely they have not signed a treaty without taking it back to be dealt with by the Cabinet; that was the solemn undertaking given by Griffith on behalf of the plenipotentiaries.'

Already people were taking sides. O'Neill recorded that 'one man during the lecture ... created a scene by loudly shouting "Collins is a traitor." I was sitting beside de Valera [on the platform] and he seemed like a man in a dream.'[1]

The crucial meeting of an already fractured Dáil cabinet took place in the Mansion House on 8 December. O'Neill wrote:

The memory of that night is as fresh before me, now as I write ... over nine years ago, as if it were yesterday ... The fierceness of the language could be heard outside. The pent up animosity of Brugha [Minister for Defence] towards Collins was let loose. De Valera pleading, and Cosgrave made many visits to the study, where the Lord Mayor of Cork, Donal O'Callaghan and I were. Cosgrave was battling with his conscience, and speaking to himself [said], 'I cannot leave Dev. He stood by me when others wanted me turned down. My oath to the Republic haunts me.'

According to O'Neill, Cosgrave asked his advice.

I said, 'Willie I am in a different position to you by being for the Treaty, and because I have never taken an oath to be true to the Republic.' And putting my hand on his shoulder, and knowing the deeply religious man he was, I said to him—'If I were you I would be guided entirely by prayer.' Cosgrave came back in a few minutes looking very much relieved. He returned to the drawing room and declared for the Treaty.[2]

While O'Neill may have had a gilded recollection of his discussion with Cosgrave, they knew each other well from over a decade of mutual acquaintance and friendship serving on Dublin Corporation. All this was soon to change; but for a moment more the intimacy of Dublin politics, which was such an essential element in the national drive for self-determination, would continue to prevail.

Cosgrave's vote was crucial in securing a majority of four to three in favour of the agreement and ensuring that it survived the first hurdle so that it could be referred to a full meeting of the Dáil. This would convene on 13 December 1921 at a new location, University College in Earlsfort Terrace. Meanwhile on 10 December, Liam Lynch, commander of the 1st Southern Division, the largest in the country, had written to the chief of staff, Richard Mulcahy, notifying him that all the commanding officers in his division rejected the Treaty.

Fundamental shifts in the balance of power within the independence movement were under way. As far back as 11 March 1921, when pressure from the British was beginning to tell and attendance at sessions of the Dáil was reduced to twenty-five, de Valera had proposed that if arrests prevented it from functioning effectively then governmental power should pass to the IRA. Mulcahy, the chief of staff, favoured a less militarist option, whereby Sinn Féin should nominate substitutes for deputies arrested to take their seats in the Dáil. It had been decided instead that if the number of deputies fell to five they could reconstitute themselves as a 'Provisional Government'. No attempt was made to decentralise the political administration, although there was no opposition to the idea in principle.

Decentralisation began instead with the IRA. The creation of divisions was intended not simply to replicate the structures of a regular army or to strive for greater coherence among very diverse units but, as Mulcahy put it, to ensure that 'if headquarters was wiped out there would be sufficient authority and prestige attached to local groups … to get on if they were driven to get on without us.'[3]

The Republic had been a unitary state, driven from Dublin at the centre, but the creation of IRA divisions can be seen as the first move towards localising Irish politics once more, albeit in a military context. This coincided with the growing involvement of local IRA units in political decisions, ranging from the nomination of candidates for the second Dáil to public appointments, such as dispensary doctors and rate-collectors. Regional IRA structures gave the organisation power centres outside Dublin that would, inadvertently, facilitate civil war when the time came.

It would be difficult to overestimate the importance of the IRA in the political and social as well as military life of the rebel administration. The second Dáil had 125 deputies, by courtesy of the Government of Ireland Act, as opposed to the 73 who constituted the first Dáil after the 1918 election. Almost half the deputies (42 per cent) were members of the IRA and nearly a third were IRA officers, compared with 20 per cent in the first Dáil. Like their fellow-deputies, these men would no longer be answerable to either the civil government in Dublin or GHQ but to their local units and constituents.[4]

Even before the Dáil adjourned on 22 December to enable members to consult their constituents, various interest groups around the country, from trades councils to chambers of commerce and farmers' associations, were taking positions on the Treaty and, in the process, hoping to influence the outcome of the vote. At a meeting of Co. Dublin farmers Paddy Belton, a leading Sinn Féin activist who had taken up farming after being sacked from the civil service but whose main claim to fame was having recruited Michael Collins to the IRB, proposed that Dáil deputies vote for 'the very good bargain, considering the circumstances,' brought back by the negotiators. Arthur Griffith and Michael Collins 'knew the country better than any other two men.'

The annual meeting of the Irish Commercial Travellers' Association in Dublin on 31 December was fairly typical of growing public sentiment. The president, P. F. Holland, said that members had been sorely tried over the previous year in trying to carry out their duties. 'Nobody knew the feelings of the public better than commercial travellers and 95 per cent of the population favoured peace.' In what was another straw in the wind, Cathal Brugha, a prominent member of the association and one of the most vociferous opponents of the Treaty, failed to be elected to its committee.[5]

———

If all politics are local, a comforting reminder came at the Corporation's first meeting of the new year on 2 January 1922 when M. J. Moran, a survivor of the Home Rule old guard now ensconced in the Municipal Reform Association, raised the hardy annual of 'objectionable cinematograph films.' He warned that 'something more than ordinary vigilance was necessary.' His fellow-councillors agreed, and it was decided to ask Dublin's new Catholic archbishop, Dr Byrne, 'to nominate a few censors to act in conjunction with six who have been appointed by the Priests' Guild.' The *Irish Times* welcomed 'this new effort to purify the atmosphere of Dublin's cinematograph establishments.' A film was 'not necessarily immoral because it comes from England, or even from America'; nevertheless unsuitable offerings were eluding the censor's vigilance. 'Erotic "dramas" with predominant sex motifs are capable of infinite harm.'[6]

It was a reassuringly habitual preoccupation and inadvertently showed how much better off Dubliners were during the Truce than Belfast's citizens. In Belfast four people, including a soldier, were killed by loyalist snipers that day and four more civilians wounded, including a 21-month-old boy. Since the start of the pogroms in July 1920, 202 people had been killed and 1,288 wounded. Dublin had been largely spared the obscenity of sectarian violence, whatever about erotic films, for more than six months.[7]

A far more serious problem that confronted councillors that day was related to the political conflict. A letter from the Dáil Minister for Local Government, Alderman W. T. Cosgrave, dated 6 September 1921, was presented, outlining the Dáil's attitude to claims for malicious damages made by some solicitors on behalf of their clients since the Truce. These sought garnishee orders (whereby a debt can be collected by attaching a debtor's property when it is in the hands of a third party) for debts that 'arose out of the conditions of war which the British Government had forced on this country by its refusal to acknowledge the right of the Irish people to determine for themselves the form of government under which they would live,' Cosgrave wrote. 'Decrees for huge amounts were light heartedly issued by English Judges against the ratepayers of Ireland.' Solicitors 'and holders of these decrees have been warned against taking any steps to seize, in satisfaction of their claims, rates which have been struck and issued to maintain vital public services. To do so is to make war upon the sick, helpless poor, or the mother, the aged and the infant.'

By far the largest claim in the greater Dublin area was from Balbriggan, which, as Cosgrave pointed out, had been sacked by the British government's 'guardians of law and order' in September 1920 after an RIC inspector had been killed in a row in a local pub. Claims amounted to £83,727, of which the biggest component was £62,000 from the English hosiery firm of Deedes, Templer and Company.

> That sum has not been paid. It will not be paid. Its payment would involve the closing of the Dublin Union and the Richmond Asylum.[8]
>
> The Crown forces burn and loot, and the ratepayers are invited by decree of an English Judge to foot the bill. The people of Ireland are not merely to have their throats cut, they are to be charged for the knife.
>
> The solicitor or barrister who attempts to obtain payment on foot of a 'Criminal and Malicious Injury' decree out of the public rates is waging war on the community and can have no grievance if the country, or those entitled to act in its name and for its protection make war on him.
>
> The people must jealously watch and safeguard the principle that public rates must not be held liable for war damage ... While the Truce lasts there is naturally some difficulty in meting out to such people the punishment, the full punishment they deserve, but even under Truce conditions the public has it in its power to make the professional man who is guilty in this respect feel the weight of its resentment.

The draconian nature of the malicious damages legislation united ratepayers of all political persuasions. But there was little the council could do beyond referring the matter to the Estates and Finance Committee on the motion of the former Unionist, now leader of the MRA group, Alderman James Hubbard Clark.

Meanwhile the British authorities simply dipped into the dog-licence money they were holding for the city to begin paying off claimants. If nothing else, such arbitrary acts reduced the interest facing the ratepayers on outstanding claims; but they also fuelled resentment against British rule during the Truce.[9]

––––

On 3 January 1922 Dáil Éireann resumed the debate on the Treaty. As the *Irish Times* leader-writer put it, the issues were clear.

> The Dáil must choose between peace and war. If it prefers war, it will doom Ireland to misery and unrest—perhaps, a return of bloodshed, and certainly

widespread poverty, to economic disaster and to permanent partition ... The Irish people are knocking impatiently on the door of freedom. Will their own janitor refuse to open it?

While the paper believed that Dáil deputies were of a higher moral calibre than their Home Rule predecessors, it cautioned against the 'autocracy in the blood of youth' that would be 'disposed to ignore the wishes of their constituents.' Thirty-eight per cent of deputies were under the age of thirty-five, and 75 per cent were under forty-five. Local celebrity as war heroes meant that some may have had 'a somewhat elevated view of the importance of their opinions,' but the chants of the crowd outside the Dáil venue of 'Ratify, ratify!' no doubt reinforced the pressure coming from the increasing peace sentiment in the constituencies.[10]

Any doubts that the focal point of power was finally moving out of the city's realm, if not its premises, came quickly once the vote accepting the Treaty was passed on 7 January. Arthur Griffith replaced de Valera as President of Dáil Éireann on 9 January, and on the 14th the pro-Treaty members of the Dáil met, along with the four Unionist members representing the University of Dublin (Trinity College), as the 'House of Commons of Southern Ireland' to approve the Treaty and elect a Provisional Government for the Irish Free State.

Michael Collins was elected chairman of the interim administration, the Provisional Government. On 16 January he arrived at Dublin Castle, untypically late because of a railway strike on the line from Longford, where he had been visiting his fiancée, and accepted the transfer of the building from the Viceroy, Lord Fitzalan.

Sir Henry Robinson, who was the longest-serving senior civil servant in the British administration during the War of Independence, has left a graphic account. According to Robinson, he waited with his colleagues outside while Lord Fitzalan, having gone through the formalities with Collins,

left by the door to the State Apartments, and so avoided meeting his trusty and well-beloved civil servants with a *sauve qui peut* [every man for himself], which was the only advice he would have had to offer them. After his departure the Irish Ministers designate were marched into the Council Chamber to join Mr. Collins, and took their seats around the council table. James MacMahon then proceeded to call in all the heads of departments to make them known to their new chiefs, and I, being senior in the service, was called in first and then was marched around and introduced to each one in turn, just as a newly sworn privy councillor is presented to other members of the Council. What struck me most was the extreme youth of most of the new Ministers; they seemed scarcely out of their teens and all looked pale and anxious. No doubt they had been through a period of terrible anxiety, and they certainly looked gloomy and over powered with the consciousness of the responsibility for the future government of the country. Michael Collins, their spokesman, however, was cordiality itself, and there was none of the 'top dog' attitude about him at all events. I was rather amused to hear people asking each other whether the civil servants would be expected to shake hands with these men whose hands were stained with outrage and crime, but, if the civil servants had any doubt on the subject themselves, they were speedily dispelled by Michael Collins, who grasped their hands with his iron grip and shook them warmly with the greatest bonhomie.[11]

The act was largely symbolic. Like its Dáil predecessor, the new government met briefly to conduct its business in the Mansion House and then on 21 January moved to City Hall, which had finally been evacuated by its British garrison. It was the first military post to be evacuated in the capital.

Freed of their guests, O'Neill and his fellow-councillors could once more concentrate on running the city. On 30 January they re-elected him Lord Mayor, although not without a contest that reflected the changing allegiances within the city and the country. Seán Mac Coillte (Seán Woods), a Sinn Féin councillor, was proposed by Alderman Seán McGarry TD, a former president of the IRB, and seconded by Councillor Jennie Wyse Power, a leading figure in Cumann na mBan. McGarry would serve in the National Army during the Civil War, while Wyse Power would be a founder-member of Cumann na Saoirse, established as a pro-Treaty breakaway from Cumann na mBan. Both would also serve in the new Free State legislature, McGarry as a Cumann na nGaedheal TD and Wyse Power as a senator. Eight other Corporation members who supported Mac Coillte's nomination would become strong supporters of the new regime. They were drawn from the old Unionist and Home Rule pools as well as Sinn Féin. Nevertheless O'Neill won the election comfortably, by 41 votes to 27. Characteristically, he voted for his opponent.

The primary repository of militant nationalism, the IRA, was polarising more rapidly. On 6 January, the day before the Treaty was ratified, Séamus Robinson, a TD for Tipperary and deputy OC of the 2nd Southern Division, demanded that an army convention be called. On 11 January several senior IRA commanders, including Liam Lynch and the commander of the Dublin Brigade, Oscar Traynor, wrote to Richard Mulcahy requesting a general army convention, at which they would be proposing that the IRA reaffirm its allegiance to the Irish Republic, rather than Dáil Éireann, where deputies had voted by a narrow majority for the Treaty. They would also be proposing that the IRA assert its autonomy, resurrecting the self-governing structures it had enjoyed as the Irish Volunteers up until 1920.

Mulcahy, who had replaced Brugha as Minister for Defence, rejected the proposal. He refused to call a convention, whereupon the dissident commanders formed an Acting Military Council. A showdown was averted only when Mulcahy relented and agreed to hold a convention within two months.[12]

Despite its paper strength, the anti-Treaty majority in the IRA faced a formidable diarchy in Mulcahy and Collins at the centre. Both were IRB men and skilled military managers and had political outlooks that complemented each other. Mulcahy saw the IRA as the apolitical arm of the government, while Collins regarded it for all practical purposes as an extension of his own political power base. He would offer all sorts of inducements to bring anti-Treaty elements in the IRA over to his side. His approach was devastatingly pragmatic: he would dismiss any past differences with Volunteer officers by saying, 'If you are prepared to do the right thing now, you are the man I want.'[13]

Later, many on the anti-Treaty side would see Mulcahy and Collins as deliberately playing for time. One Civil War pamphleteer complained that 'the Army of the Republic lost opportunity after opportunity since December last and wasted its strength in unavailing efforts to secure unity and peace,' while alleging that 'our efforts and anxiety were utilised by our opponents to gain time ... and finally to strike us unexpectedly in the back.'[14]

Ironically, the avowedly apolitical nature of an IRA devoted to the defence of the Republic, combined with an internal democratic power structure and a belief 'in the power of the gun alone to cure all our ills,'[15] proved a fatal combination. It gave the anti-Treaty IRA all the trappings of militarism and fuelled popular fears, which its opponents exploited to the full, but denied it the capacity to seize state power. When the new Provisional Government denied funds even to meet previously authorised bills, the anti-Treaty forces imposed levies, including the collection of the much-abused dog licence, and resorted to a wave of armed robberies that culminated in a series of co-ordinated raids on 1 May 1922, netting more than £50,000.[16]

But such measures could not match the steady flow of funds and weapons available to the nascent Free State, supported, as it was, by the British government and a functioning civil service apparatus that ensured that Volunteers joining the National Army received £1 a week, all found, without arbitrary and haphazard sequestrations, and that their pay would increase as the prospect of civil war loomed. (See chapter 10 for the myriad terms and conditions on offer to recruits.)

Not surprisingly, policing was one of the crucial issues on which talks between the anti-Treaty IRA and the Provisional Government broke down, with the latter insisting that the newly constituted Civic Guard, later to be redesignated An Garda Síochána, would be responsible for all civilian policing.

One incident that particularly illustrated the need for a unified policing force in Dublin was the death of Max Green, chairman of the Irish Prisons Board. He was on his way to his office in St Stephen's Green on 3 March 1922, after leaving his twin sons at the Loreto Convent School nearby, when he was killed. A few minutes earlier armed men had robbed part of a Ministry of Labour payroll as it was being delivered by taxi cab in Molesworth Street. They made off with an attaché case containing £50 of the £600 consignment. Members of the DMP and Republican Police gave chase. It was as he was emerging from the Green that a pursuing DMP constable called on Green to stop one of the raiders. As he attempted to do so the man shot him at point-blank range.

Although the gunman and one of his two accomplices were taken prisoner minutes afterwards, it proved impossible to secure a conviction for murder, though many people saw the shooting. Essential witnesses failed to turn up in court, evidence went missing from the Bridewell after it was occupied by National Army personnel in the attack on the Four Courts, and one of the accused claimed to have been a member of the Republican Police in pursuit of the robbers at the time of his arrest. Laurence Dowling, a nineteen-year-old draper's assistant from Harold's Cross, was eventually convicted at his third trial of robbery under arms and sentenced to ten years' imprisonment. The man who claimed to be in the Republican Police, James O'Neill of Francis Street, was tried four times, but each time the jury disagreed; eventually he was discharged in April 1924 with a *nolle prosequi* after spending more than two years in custody.[17]

Max Green was no ordinary civilian. His wife, Johanna, was a daughter of the former Irish Party leader John Redmond. While Green had become a controversial figure in the War of Independence after presiding over the regime that saw the death of Thomas Ashe from forcible feeding in 1917, he appears to have rehabilitated himself politically, and his death was widely condemned across the political spectrum, increasing the pressure on the Provisional Government to restore order in the capital.

Public outrage did nothing to loosen the public purse strings. Green was never replaced as chairman of the Prisons Board; the state thus saved the taxpayer the £1,700 a year in salary. His widow received a pension of £100 a year but died a few months later, before it was approved. It subsequently went to their children.

Although armed robbery was common enough, and Dublin had been spared the large-scale revolutionary sequestrations that occurred elsewhere, the Max Green incident underlined the fact that, while the Republican Police enjoyed a better reputation in the capital than elsewhere, their status was at best ambiguous and their reputation was becoming increasingly besmirched, like the Black and Tans before them.

Meanwhile Collins and Mulcahy worked desperately to convert their small core of committed activists within the GHQ staff and 'Dublin Guard' into a National Army in substance as well as name. The IRA had begun using the Dublin Mountains extensively for training in the months after the Truce. Cobbs Lodge in Glenasmole, which belonged to Howard Hely, a leading member of the Dublin Citizens' Association, was used as the main training base by the Dublin Brigade for the south city battalions and Kilmore House for those on the north side. Among the weapons the Volunteers used were newly imported Thompson sub-machine guns. In the autumn, GHQ took over these premises from the Dublin Brigade.

While the camps continued for all Volunteers, special training was provided for the Dublin Guard, a combination of Collins's old 'Squad' and the Dublin Active Service Unit, who were reassembled at Celbridge as the core unit of the National Army. On 31 January 1922, fitted out with new uniforms and arms, this unit, under Captain Paddy O'Daly and Lieutenants Joe Leonard and Pádraig O'Connor, marched through the city and past City Hall, where the salute was taken by Collins, to Beggarsbush Barracks in Haddington Road, one of the smallest barracks in the country but the first to be occupied by the new force. O'Daly, the former head of Collins's Squad, was promoted to brigadier-general and his two lieutenants to the rank of colonel as the force rapidly grew from less than 50 to 3,500 by April.[18]

Inevitably, some Volunteers subsequently defected to the anti-Treaty side, but the essential point was that the Provisional Government had secured the first vacated barracks in the capital. As it grew in size, the National Army would systematically occupy the rest, recognising that Dublin was the military key to the country, something to which their opponents were seemingly blind.

———

As early defections showed, allegiances within the Dublin Brigade were severely tested by the Treaty split. Like those in most parts of the country, Dublin battalions experienced a large influx of Volunteers during the Truce. De Valera's old unit, the 2nd Battalion, grew from 250 members to between 1,200 and 1,400.

Preference in recruiting members to the nascent National Army went to men who had seen service in the War of Independence. One of these was John Pinkman, a Liverpool-Irishman who served time in Dartmoor Prison for arson attacks in England and now wanted to do some 'real soldiering' for Ireland. When he arrived at Beggarsbush Barracks, 'almost everything about it appeared lackadaisical ... Only a mere handful of soldiers in the barracks were fully uniformed.' A fellow-Volunteer who was refused a commission went off to join the impromptu anti-Treaty garrison at the Four Courts; another Volunteer who had served in the British army was made an NCO because he was the only member of the section capable of drilling the rest. Pinkman became a member of A Company, which, along with B Company, would form the 1st Battalion of the Dublin Guards Brigade. 'Morale in our two companies was very high because almost all of us had seen active service in the IRA prior to the Truce,' he wrote later. His unit was soon despatched to

Kilkenny to confront anti-Treaty forces, seen off at the railway station by a band playing 'The Red Flag'.[19]

Laurence Nugent, who owned a shop in nearby Baggot Street and was assistant quartermaster of the 3rd Battalion, had a very different experience.

> All Volunteers at this time were supposed to be members of the new regular army and any man wishing to join the uniformed army could do so by applying to his Commandant or Brigadier and he got his transfer. While the Brigadier was signing transfers for the uniformed forces he gave me a cheque for £100 for the possible purchase of arms from the Auxiliaries in Beggar's Bush Barracks. While engaged in this pursuit I was ordered out of Beggar's Bush one day by Major Swan, the Auxiliary Commander. The Free State Army took over next day and I was ordered out [again] under guard by Shaun McMahon [sic], Q.M.G.

'I had the key of a room where arms were hidden by an Auxiliary and in the hope of getting in, I kept close to the area,' Nugent said. J. J. 'Ginger' O'Connell, former IRA director of training and now a colonel in the National Army, offered him the job of quartermaster at Beggarsbush, but Nugent refused to take it, as he did offers from Michael Collins. The triumph of principle over expediency was to be a besetting problem for IRA members opposed to the Treaty.

Nugent had been a late convert to militant republicanism. He remained with the Redmondite National Volunteers until 1916, when he was one of several shopkeepers who tried to arrange a truce in the Rising. However, he subsequently became heavily involved in the War of Independence and, the decision being made, there was no turning back: 'I was not at any time prepared to accept the Treaty and I continued to train men during the Truce for the purpose of preventing it coming into operation.' His objections were widely held among the anti-Treaty members of the IRA and included 'liability for Public Debts and Payment of War Pensions and the Oath of Allegiance ... There was the question of the ports and posts to remain in occupation of the British Army and the question of the Governor General.' He felt that the latter appointment 'was very obnoxious to any republican,' because

> in all our propaganda for a great number of years ... objection of the general population to this individual as a symbol of oppression for over seven hundred years was well recognised.
>
> While he might be an Irishman, he could not be appointed without the sanction of the British Government ... had the right to summon or dissolve the Dáil and he sanctioned the commission of all military or police officers: in fact, he was a dictator in the interest of England any time he wished to use his powers in that direction. Was it any wonder we fought?

Nugent added that 'this attitude personally was no easy one ... with a wife and nine children ... at home.'[20]

Liam Archer, a veteran of the Howth gun-running and the 1916 Rising, was undecided about what to do after the Treaty's terms were disclosed. During the War of Independence he had come to know several GHQ figures well, including Collins, for whom he conducted intelligence work through his job in the Post Office, and Rory O'Connor, the director of engineering. It was through conversations with the latter that he finally came to a conclusion, although not the one O'Connor wanted.

O'Connor told Archer he would oppose the Treaty 'if I could get enough to support me.' When it became clear that O'Connor's aim in having the Treaty rejected was to ensure that the British would 'return in force for the purpose of establishing "Law and Order" and we would be plunged into complete submission or complete anarchy,' Archer opted for the National Army. Besides, he wanted to marry, which probably made anarchy less appealing than it may once have been.[21]

Many Volunteers appear to have made their decision on what were basically bread-and-butter issues. The economic recession meant that jobs were scarce, and full-time soldiers of the Republic in particular found they had a choice of continuing to be paid by entering the ranks of the National Army or reverting to the status of unpaid, and unemployed, Volunteers.[22]

Nugent reported that in his own company only fourteen men joined the Free State Army and about seventy remained with the Irish Republican Army. In the neighbouring 6th Battalion, defections seem to have been much greater. The battalion intelligence officer reported that large numbers of Volunteers 'were defecting to an army that is a disgrace.' There was inevitably a strong judgemental aspect to his assessments of the defectors. He reported that an apartment in the old Sinn Féin head office in Harcourt Street 'is being used by some women as a Free House and it is mostly frequented by FREE STATE OFFICERS who generally stay 'til early in the morning.' The conduct of the Free State garrison sent to man the RIC Barracks in Dundrum was

> disgraceful, falling about drunk in the village when they went off in Taxis and went into a public house in Merrion and caused a row in it. They said they were insulted by an Orange Man there, which is not true. Then they came back to Dundrum in the Taxis singing and started to fight in the village.

He listed 22 members of the Milltown Company as defecting by May, 22 more from the Windy Arbour Company, 69 from the two Blackrock companies, 16 from the Dean's Grange and Cornelscourt Company, and 15 from the Ticknock and Barnacullia Company. The Glencullen and Glencree companies went over *en bloc* to the new army, while IRA units showed a 'very poor turnout at parades.'[23] The majority of the 2nd Battalion in the city—which had been the workhorse of the

IRA in the War of Independence and was particularly strong on the docks and in the industrial area around the port—supported the Treaty.

C. S. 'Todd' Andrews found that of more than a hundred men in his own unit, E Company of the 4th Battalion, only four, including himself, were anti-Treaty. Personal friendships were often sundered in the spring of 1922, and in his own case the hardest break was with F. X. Coghlan, his company commander in the War of Independence. Originally from Co. Cork, Coghlan took command of the pro-Treaty 4th Battalion in March 1922 when the anti-Treaty IRA reasserted its independence from Dáil Éireann. In his thirties and considered 'oldish' by the younger activists who made up the bulk of the battalion, Coghlan was nevertheless respected 'as a man we could trust,' Andrews recalled years later. Besides, he had been out in 1916. He had been sacked from his civil service job with the Land Commission after the Rising and now sold insurance from door to door. If this meant a severe drop in income and social status, it proved handy for keeping out of reach of the law. His 'mildly socialist' views appealed to the young student, who considered himself a 'Jacobin'; and, most importantly, they had fought together in the War of Independence, including the Bloody Sunday operation.

They fell out not so much over the Treaty as over the company's hard-won arms. Andrews lifted the weapons from the dump in the grounds of St Enda's School in Rathfarnham, where Patrick Pearse's former gardener helped him, and gave them to the anti-Treaty IRA Executive.

> I dreaded the thought of meeting Coghlan, knowing how deeply offended he would be by the seizure of the dump ... I decided to get the unpleasantness over quickly. I was on my way to seek him out when I encountered him on the street in Rathfarnham. Coghlan never raised his voice, never displayed anger nor was he by nature a resentful man. He did not now raise his voice but he left me in no doubt that he was resentful, angry, even bitter with me. He felt he had been betrayed, that the men in the Company had been robbed, that the Army Executive were a collection of disgruntled men aiming at military dictatorship and I should be ashamed of myself and my behaviour. He did not want anything more to do with me or my companions in what he insistently called the robbery of the arms.
>
> I made no apologies for what I had done but I felt sick at heart that so close a friendship should come to such a miserable end.[24]

Of course Coghlan also had a wife and two children to support, and after a decade of upheaval he probably felt, as Liam Archer did, that the Treaty was as much as could be won in 1922 and far more than either had envisaged when they went to the Rotunda in November 1913 to enrol in the Irish Volunteers in support of Home Rule. Men such as Laurence Nugent, who had personal resources to fall back upon, or young single men like Andrews without responsibilities, were probably inclined to give more weight to matters of principle than those who yearned for a return to normality. And, while there is often a tendency to regard those who voted against the Treaty as the most socially radical element in the second Dáil, it is worth remembering that business people comprised the only occupational group of TDs in which anti-Treatyites constituted a majority. By contrast, professionals such as teachers and journalists voted by 32 to 19 for the Treaty, white-collar workers by 8 to 3 in favour, farmers by 9 to 7, and all three artisans supported it. The average age of Dublin deputies who rejected the Treaty was forty-eight, compared with thirty-five for its supporters.[25]

At the same time there were many leading figures in the pro-Treaty ranks, such as Kevin O'Higgins and Eoin O'Duffy, who had no time for the 'Red Flaggers'. It was to be Labour's misfortune that it was seen by the new government as clinging to the coat-tails of the anti-Treaty forces in the hope of social revolution and by the anti-Treaty side as propping up the Free State regime by contesting the election with the intention of taking seats in the new Dáil. The future anti-Treaty IRA chief of staff Liam Lynch would describe the Labour manifesto when it was published as 'gas'.[26]

How Dáil deputies for Dublin City and County voted on the Treaty

Against the Treaty	Occupation and age	For the Treaty	Occupation and age
Kathleen Clarke	Businesswoman (41)	Philip Cosgrave[IV]	Businessman (37)
Constance Markievicz	Gentlewoman (53)	Michael Derham[IV]	Businessman (25)
Seán T. O'Kelly	Manager (39)	George Gavan Duffy	Lawyer (39)
Margaret Pearse	Widow (65)	Desmond Fitzgerald	Journalist (34)
Phil Shanahan	Businessman (44)	Thomas Kelly*	Businessman (50)
		Frank Lawless[IV]	Farmer
		Daniel McCarthy[IV]	Clerk (38)
		Seán McGarry[IV]	Businessman (35)
		Joseph McGrath[IV]	Businessman (33)
		Richard Mulcahy[IV]	Soldier (35)
		Charles Murphy[IV]	Manager
		Séamus Dwyer	Businessman (25)
		Michael Staines[IV]	Clerk (36)

[IV]Member of Irish Volunteers.
*Kelly was too ill to attend the Dáil but wrote a letter to the Ceann Comhairle expressing support for the Treaty.

As the IRA fragmented and fears of renewed conflict grew, other issues slid down the political agenda, including the city's most abiding social evil, its tenement slums, home to poverty and pestilence. The continuing high mortality rate in the city was directly attributable to the appalling housing conditions. Yet the situation had worsened during the War of Independence. The city councillors had been unwilling to increase the rates (the local property tax), and various attempts to raise funds from private investors or central government failed.

The housing crisis was actually worse by the time of the Truce than in 1914, when a government report on conditions, held in the wake of the Church Street tenement collapse that killed seven people, had shocked the nation. While nearly a thousand dwellings were closed as unsafe by 1918, only 327 new houses had been built. Between 1918 and 1921 the Corporation built no houses at all, weighed down, as it was, by industrial strife and the exigencies of the War of Independence. These included the crippling burden of malicious damages claims and the withdrawal of substantial subsidies from the British Local Government Board, which accounted for a fifth of its revenue, after it transferred its allegiance to Dáil Éireann.

An aggravating factor was the high cost of construction. The power of the construction unions, particularly the bricklayers, was considerable, and in 1921 they were conducting a more effective defence of pay rates than their counterparts in Britain. The comparatively high rates for bricklayers of 2s 2d an hour, as opposed to 2s 0½d in London, was a result of strong organisation, militancy and strike action. Unfortunately the strike had led, among other things, to the abandonment of the Corporation housing programme for 1921. Compensation for landlords whose properties were condemned was also prohibitively expensive. Some landlords deliberately ran down premises to secure compensation, and the landlords' lobby remained powerful in the City Council despite the changes wrought by the municipal election of 1920, which saw Sinn Féin replace the nationalists as the dominant party.

One of the greatest offenders was Alderman Patrick Corrigan, a friend of the Lord Mayor, Laurence O'Neill. Another friend of Corrigan was the leader of the Sinn Féin group on the Corporation for many years, Tom Kelly. Corrigan had disposed of explosives for Kelly after the latter's arrest in 1916. But Corrigan had also pocketed £10,000 for the sale to the Corporation of 22 acres at Fairbrother's Fields, between Donore Avenue and Blackpitts, hiding his identity behind the ground landlord, the Earl of Meath.

Some members of the new regime were no better. The Republican Labour councillor Thomas P. O'Reilly emerged as the largest slum-owner in the city in the early 1920s, and the Lord Mayor himself was a slum landlord; so there was little appetite for exposing corruption in the council chamber. Far from considering a large-scale building programme at the beginning of 1922, the Corporation sought to sell off 1,172 self-contained cottages and artisans' dwellings to generate income and reduce expenditure on housing maintenance, under the slogan 'Every man his own landlord.' Nevertheless, it was decided to lay the foundations for 198 houses in Fairbrother's Fields, for which Corrigan had received such generous compensation. On the motion of Trades Council Labour councillors it was also agreed to call for an immediate report on plans for housing at East Wall and Marino, where developments had been put on the long finger during the War of Independence.

The underlying problem of providing housing for those most in need simmered into the summer and surfaced again in June 1922, when Councillor Tom Lawlor of the Trades Council wing of Labour demanded that the sale of Corporation houses be postponed until there was a full investigation of claims that they were being 'given by members of the [housing] committee to their own personal friends over the heads of people who were entitled to get them.' The houses, which had cost the city between £1,016 and £1,025 to build, were being sold at between £500 and £600 on a tenant-purchase scheme. When Dillon, the superintendent of Corporation dwellings, was examined by Lawlor at a council meeting on 6 June 1922 he admitted that 'it would be safe to say that there were 2,000 applicants for houses who were better entitled to get them than the persons to whom they were given.' He had prepared a list of a hundred suitable applicants, but, as far as he knew, 'not one from the list had received a house,' nor had two transfer tenants whom he had recommended.

The Housing Committee took the precaution of hiring a leading barrister, J. C. R. Lardner KC, to represent them against Lawlor's charges. Lardner sought to justify the decision to allocate the houses on the grounds of ability to pay rather than need because of the state of the Corporation's finances but then admitted that the houses had been undervalued by up to a third and that the annuities schedule of sixty years was too long. (This was later reduced to forty years.) Lardner even conceded that some were going to people who did not live in the city, but he challenged Lawlor to prove they had been allocated to friends of the committee. Lawlor had to backtrack on this claim, which undermined his more fundamental point about the departure from the principle of housing those most in need.

Officials also defended the system. John Sherwin, clerk of the Housing Committee, said the sales scheme was 'a novel departure ... on the right lines. It was a good commercial bargain which would not be a burden on the rate payers for it would relieve them of the enormous cost of maintenance. The scheme created new ratepayers.'

Fairbrother's Fields houses[27]

House type	Initial price	Adjusted price	Annuity
A	£246	£327	Reduced from 60 years to 40
B	£303	£361	Reduced from 60 years to 40
C	£379	£429	Reduced from 60 years to 40

The deputy chairman of the Housing Committee, J. J. Murphy, said the allocation had been made by ballot. The chairman, Alderman James Hubbard Clark, who headed the Municipal Reform Association on the council and was a leading figure in the Citizens' Association, a commercial ratepayers' lobby, was equally unapologetic.

> During the last few years the city was appalled by the loss on the existing houses. The sale scheme was discussed in all details and approved by the Council. The first idea was a reduction in the rates and to give people a greater interest in their homes by the fact of possession or the feeling of ultimate full possession. The trouble was that they could not get an economic rent for the houses at the price that they cost.

The scheme was also defended by Thomas Farren, a senior ITGWU official and a member of the Republican Labour bloc on the council, which was aligned with Sinn Féin. He said he knew a man

> who had been an applicant for a house for many years, and who only lived yards outside the city boundary, but who worked all his life in the city ... [He] had got a house and he ... was perfectly entitled to it. There was no partiality in the allocation of the houses. He and other members of the Committee had exercised their just and fair discretion.

Lawlor had no choice but to retreat. Alderman Hubbard Clark said he knew that 'Mr. Lawlor was not imbued by a personal animosity, but had great courage in bringing the charges.'

The controversy would simmer on into 1923, but the lasting animosity was between the two Labour groups on the council rather than with conservatives, such as Hubbard Clark, who wanted value for money on behalf of the ratepayers rather than helping the needy. The Fairbrother's Fields case was an example of how to achieve neither.[28]

By comparison, the British War Office was building 465 houses for ex-servicemen and their families in a garden city development at Killester, three miles from the city centre. Another forty houses were being built by Pembroke Urban District Council on the former grounds of Shelbourne Football Club at Sandymount Road. Killester was the largest scheme in Ireland, where the War Office would ultimately build 2,626 houses.

Far from welcoming such urgently needed initiatives, many city councillors, particularly in the ruling Sinn Féin bloc, objected to them.[29] One reason was that, unlike similar schemes in Britain, the Killester houses were exclusively for ex-servicemen, who also supplied most of the labour. But then the unemployment rate for ex-servicemen was exceptionally high, at 46 per cent, and Killester would house only a small fraction of the 5,200 British veterans living in the Dublin slums.

Nor was discrimination a one-way process. Dublin Corporation agreed in January 1922 to give preference to unemployed members of the Dublin Brigade in filling job vacancies. Oscar Traynor, the officer commanding the brigade, said that five hundred of his members had no means of livelihood, an unemployment rate almost as high as that of ex-servicemen, given that, on his own estimates, the brigade had no more than 1,250 members during the War of Independence.[30]

The dwellings for ex-servicemen set a new standard for social housing. A description of the Sandymount houses in the *Irish Times* noted that they comprised semi-detached and detached dwellings with a 'super' kitchen of 164 square feet and a parlour of 108 square feet as well as a 'well lighted staircase' leading to two large bedrooms and a bathroom upstairs, 'facilities of which tenement-dwellers could only dream.'[31] At Killester many of the houses were even bigger; 247 of them were bungalows with large gardens. Ranging in size from 675 to 1,007 square feet, they were allocated in accordance with rank.

An Irish Sailors' and Soldiers' Land Trust was established to manage the housing programme for ex-servicemen in the Free State. It would be beset by difficulties, as budgetary pressures from the British Treasury and lack of adequate support from the new Irish government meant constantly increasing rents. Nor was there any entitlement for the families of war veterans to remain in occupation when they died. This caused constant tension, and by the mid-1920s rent strikes and evictions had become a feature of life in these estates. The schemes were supposed to pay for themselves, but by 1925, when two-thirds of the schemes had been built throughout the country and the £29,650 in rent should have yielded a surplus of £3,400 a year to repay the capital expenditure, there was a deficit of £4,200, 'owing to organised rent strikes and to a demoralisation largely due to outside pressure.' Weekly rents ranging from 8s to 21s 6d, and sometimes higher, were hard to meet when the average earnings of many breadwinners were between £2 10s and £3 10s, and when many ex-servicemen had difficulty finding work.[32]

Rising pay rates would eventually ease the problem, but it was only when the British government passed legislation in 1952 allowing the trust to sell houses to occupants that a bitter legacy of strife ended. Despite the harsh realities of living in houses 'fit for heroes,' tenants treasured family memories of military service. Armistice Day and other commemorative events would remain central features of life in the community into the 1930s, and photographs of local parades featured regularly in press coverage of Armistice Day commemorations. The rent strikes may have weakened affection for the British connection but it added to the sense of solidarity in communities such as Killester.[33]

———

Increasing tension over the Treaty did nothing to help the economy, which was already in recession, with workers facing pay cuts and lay-offs. On 18 January 1922 the Dublin Council of the Unemployed took over the Rotunda Concert Hall, raised the Red Flag and put up posters denouncing capitalism. A front for the infant Communist Party of Ireland, the group was calling for a ban on overtime and a levy on property-owners to finance relief work at trade union rates. It had demanded accommodation from the Lord Mayor in the Mansion House, but O'Neill, having only recently secured the full use of the premises from Dáil Éireann and Free State politicians, refused to accommodate them.

The leaders of the group that seized the Rotunda were Liam O'Flaherty, a founder-member of the Communist Party, and Jim Phelan, a left-wing member of the IRA. Both were colourful characters, O'Flaherty a veteran of the First World War who had joined the Industrial Workers of the World (the 'Wobblies') in America before returning to Ireland and Phelan a member of the 2nd Battalion of the Dublin Brigade. Both would take the anti-Treaty side in the Civil War and both would subsequently become successful authors.[34] O'Flaherty told the press it was a peaceful protest 'against the apathy of the authorities' in the face of rising unemployment. 'If we are taken to court, we would not recognise the court, because the Government that does not redress our grievances is not worth recognising.'

From the outset the occupation met with hostility. At least one collector of funds for the Council was beaten up in Parnell Square on 19 January. By Saturday the 21st tension had reached boiling point. Hostile crowds, aroused apparently by the sight of the Red Flag, attacked the building. At about 8:30 p.m. a youth attempted to tear down the flag, only to fall and be taken to Jervis Street Hospital, but a second youth succeeded in tearing it down, to loud cheers. At 10:30 p.m. the building was stormed, and 'hand to hand fighting' took place before order was restored by the combined forces of the DMP and Republican Police. Three or four shots were fired from the building over the heads of the crowd after the two police forces had cordoned off the hall, and it was obvious that the position of the hundred occupiers was becoming untenable. Negotiations were opened by the Communist Party with Eoin O'Duffy, deputy chief of staff of the IRA, to evacuate the building peacefully shortly after midnight.[35]

The occupation lasted only four days but attracted much attention, not alone because unemployment was such a serious problem, affecting more than 130,000 of the 440,000 insured workers in the new state,[36] but because it provided a disturbing example of how political and economic crises were converging to create open conflict on the streets.

While crowds surged around the Rotunda 'soviet' a taxi cab was robbed at gunpoint under the noses of the police on duty outside. On the same day an RIC touring car was seized at gunpoint in Dawson Street, an RAF car in St Stephen's Green, a military car in Gardiner Row and another military vehicle in Middle Abbey Street, not to mention two military motorbikes and a private vehicle. The thieves were well armed and organised but it was not clear whether they were criminals or were acting on behalf of IRA units in the city. The once-feared Auxiliaries, who had toured the streets maintaining order before the Truce, were themselves now locked in dispute with the British government over redundancy payments, having just rejected an offer of £10,000.[37] The power vacuum was attracting predators.

The unemployed were not the only workers feeling the sharp edge of the recession. At the beginning of January more than 250 Dublin tailors went on strike after the Merchant Tailors' Association cut wages by 12s a week, double the 6s cut inflicted on engineering workers in the city and three times what the railwaymen conceded. The association declared that members could no longer afford to pay 'boom time' wages.[38] So many members of the recently formed Engineering Union, itself a creation of the IRB, were claiming assistance that the Executive decided in March 1922 that benefit would be paid only to members who could prove they were unemployed as a result of victimisation by their employer for trade union activities. Not only did it reject the application of a member claiming assistance because he had been 'on the run' in Clonmel but the Executive decided that being on the run did not in itself constitute victimisation, or prevent a member from looking for work.

In some of the more protected sectors of the labour market small victories were still possible. For instance, the Hospitals of Industry in Dublin (the Richmond, Hardwicke and Whitworth Hospitals) agreed to give boilermen an increase of 15s a week and their assistants 10s.[39] Nevertheless, unions were generally in retreat, with membership falling steadily, from 229,000 in 1920 to 189,000 by 1922. The decline would continue, to 186,000 in 1923 and 175,000 in 1924 and would finally bottom out at 92,000 in 1929.[40]

The Dublin Trades Council cut its quarterly fee for affiliated unions from 2d per member to 1d at its annual general meeting on 25 March 1922. Straitened finances meant that a decision by the Engineering Union to form a branch in

Belfast was deferred.[41] Instead, events in the North were affecting Dublin, where many workers resisted efforts to find jobs for the 7,500 refugees from the pogroms. The IEIU refused to give union cards to Northerners, or to allow its members to work alongside any craftsmen not already in the IEIU. It was a policy fraught with pitfalls and sparked a lockout when a man from Belfast was given a job in late 1921 at the Ross and Walpole foundry. The firm agreed to take him after representations from the Belfast Victims' Committee, which the IEIU helped finance. Unfortunately, he was a member of the Amalgamated Iron Dressers' Society, a British union, and local people refused to work with him, although he was willing to transfer to the IEIU; instead they wanted the job to go to a local man who, as it happened, was in the same union as the Northerner but was not prepared to join the IEIU.

The IEIU preferred sacrificing the prospect of recruiting Northern refugees to ensuring that local men had priority in obtaining the few jobs available.[42] It even appealed to Dáil Éireann to intervene, on the grounds that the Dáil 'was out to stop emigration.'[43] This showed poor judgement, as Dáil Éireann was the main sponsor of the Belfast Victims' Committee. In reality the Dáil could not tell the employer what to do, only offer mediation. Eventually it helped negotiate a return to work for the strikers.

In a post-mortem on the dispute the general secretary of the IEIU, P. J. McIntyre, who was a Sinn Féin councillor and IRB member, said he thought 'a rather narrow view had been taken by members of the Iron Dressers Section and their decision [to reject the Belfast man] would not be likely to assist us when we set out to organise further north than Dundalk or Greenore.'[44]

That was a decision for another day, as the union struggled to stay solvent. The Resident Executive Committee called a general meeting for New Year's Day, 1922, in the Abbey Theatre to discuss the situation. Jack Redmond, the former president, agreed to chair the meeting in the absence of an elected successor. Members agreed to increase subscriptions to 2s 6d a week to keep the IEIU afloat. They further agreed to voluntary levies of between 10s and £10, to be recorded on special cards.[45] Their response was generous and showed faith in the officers, especially as the latter could not supply a proper set of accounts, as Joe Quinn, the former general treasurer and leader of the dissident Inchicore members, refused to hand over the books.[46] However, craft workers in other railway workshops strongly opposed the Inchicore stance, and the meeting ended on a high note with a motion passed to be forwarded to the next ILP&TUC conference calling for the nationalisation of the railways.[47] By the end of January it had a balance of £578 13s 4d, against outstanding debts of £433 13s 7d. In its first burst of largesse for some time the Executive agreed to allow the general secretary to put down linoleum in his office.[48]

In February 1922 the union felt financially confident enough to organise a collection for the Dublin Destitute Children's Committee and to appoint a full-time organiser for Munster—on a trial basis.[49]

Finally, the IEIU achieved a breakthrough by negotiating an agreement with the Dublin Building Trade Employers' Association. This became the precursor of collective bargaining agreements that set minimum rates of pay and working conditions for construction, electrical contracting and many other industrial sectors for almost a century. The first rate, negotiated on 31 March 1922, was 1s 10d an hour, or £4 0s 8d for a basic 44-hour week.[50]

Meanwhile the IEIU sought a meeting with the Minister for Trade and Commerce in the new Provisional Government, Ernest Blythe, over the loss of jobs and transfer of work to cheaper British plants.[51] He agreed to conduct an investigation into the state of the engineering industry, where unemployment was now running at over 20 per cent.[52] But the reality was that if employers could meet orders more profitably by subcontracting the work to British firms where workers had accepted bigger pay cuts, they would do so. Independence was quickly found to have its limitations, especially in a state that had yet to establish its sovereignty either internally or with regard to London.

———

If the trade union movement continued to fight a fairly coherent rearguard action on the industrial front, it was deeply divided on political strategy. The core leadership, most of them veterans of the Dublin Lockout a decade earlier and supporters of James Connolly's motion at the 1912 ITUC Congress to form a political party, wanted to contest the forthcoming general election.[53] There had been a massive growth in trade union membership during the First World War, when it more than doubled to 270,000. Even with the recession it still stood at 189,000 in 1922 and had extended its reach to almost every corner of rural Ireland through the recruitment of tens of thousands of agricultural labourers to the ITGWU. The introduction of proportional representation also greatly increased the possibility of securing seats, because of transfers from Sinn Féin. In the 1920 municipal elections in Dublin a first-preference vote of 12 per cent had translated into 16 per cent of the seats, thanks to transfers from Sinn Féin. Above all, the Government of Ireland Act had partitioned the country, thus eliminating the danger of the movement itself dividing on the issue of self-determination.

However, there was now an almost equally divisive issue in the South, namely the Treaty. For an organisation such as the IEIU, itself a creation of the IRB, this posed a serious problem, as its own activist membership was deeply divided on the Treaty. Thomas Leahy, a boilermaker and founder-member and trustee of the union, said years later:

> I will never forget the day at 6, Gardiner's Row, when the news came through on the [Treaty] vote. Our EC had arranged a meeting that evening on other

matters and advantage was taken after business to test members' feelings on it. When introduced one could feel the cold and fear of a lost soul departing when the result was declared by John Redmond. Most of them supported the decision of Collins and Griffith on the vote: those of us who thought of ourselves as a Labour Union within the Republic came away with sad hearts, but determined to carry on as Connolly, Pearse, Tom Clarke and company would like us to have done—carry on to the complete separation of our country from England.[54]

When its Resident Executive Committee met again on 20 February 1922 to discuss the special delegate conference called by the ILP&TUC for the next day in the Abbey Theatre, it decided to mandate delegates against participation by Labour in the election. A number of other Dublin craft unions, such as the Vehicle Builders and the Typographical Society, did likewise. This reflected the heavy involvement of their leaderships in the IRB and republican movement generally. Many of these union activists had no interest in class politics and saw the Labour Party as the voice of the unskilled and urban poor. Both OCs of the Dublin Brigade in the War of Independence, Dick McKee and his successor, Oscar Traynor, were printers by trade, and many other members were skilled workers.[55]

Nor were unions with a distinctly left-wing viewpoint, including the ITGWU, by any means united in their approach to the elections. The ILP&TUC was still torn between the aspiration towards a workers' republic and the need to deal with the harsh realities of defending workers' rights in a strife-torn, recession-ridden society where the last recourse to order remained the commander of British forces, Sir Nevil Macready, in the Royal Hospital, Kilmainham. The ILP&TUC leadership reflected bitterly on the changes in its own political status since the Truce. Previously, Tom Johnson, secretary of the ILP&TUC, reported to delegates,

> Dáil ministers had frequently conferred with them … on matters of public concern. But on this matter of the relations between England and Ireland, though it now appears that the Southern Unionist Party and the Ulster Unionist Party, and probably other parties also were consulted and secured promises, the Labour Party was not approached nor informed of anything that was proposed or suggested.

Nevertheless, when members of the ILP&TUC Executive had the opportunity of meeting Arthur Griffith, the new President of Dáil Éireann, on 10 January to outline their concerns, their demands were important in trying to defend workers' living standards but hardly revolutionary. They asked for a compulsory Tillage Order to protect the jobs of 20,000 agricultural labourers being laid off to make way for cattle, relief work projects to ease unemployment, 'done as far as possible by local Trade Union labour,' new housing schemes that would use Irish materials and designs, and restrictions on cheap foreign-milled flour to protect jobs in Irish mills.

The most innovative proposal was for a trade agreement with Soviet Russia, exchanging Irish agricultural surplus for Russian raw materials and agricultural machinery. This proposal reflected revolutionary wishful thinking, rather like the 'Address to the Workers of Ireland' that the National Executive issued as its public response to the Treaty. Even this document was only released after the Treaty vote, 'so it did not influence debate.'[56] It reminded workers that

> during the period of crisis in the Nation's life you have subordinated your claims and demands to the need for National solidarity. Individually and collectively the workers have borne their full share of the pain and sacrifices of recent years ... have freely given of their lives and substance.

It reminded the leaders of Dáil Éireann that

> the Republic conceived of and demanded by the workers is a Republic in which those who give labour and service to the commonwealth—and none but they—are the citizens, the rulers, and the owners; a Republic in which wealth is the servant, not the master, of mankind.

It concluded with a stirring summons for workers to 'unite and stand fast! Do not allow yourselves to be drawn into opposing camps. As you have shown solidarity in the Nation's cause, let you now show the same solidarity in your struggle for bread.' But the Executive itself was divided when it came to drafting a course of action for the conference. Instead of taking a position on the Treaty the Labour leaders wanted a plebiscite, but when this was ruled out by Griffith they decided to drop the demand from the final motion put to the delegates at the special conference on 21 February. So was the most radical proposal of all, that in the event of a hung Dáil, with Labour holding the balance of power, its deputies should

> vote for the re-election of the Republican Government. Such a contingency will have proved the existence of a deep and widespread revolutionary purpose amongst the mass of the people, sufficient to carry the country forward a long way towards transforming the Republic into our ideal Workers' Republic.[57]

The decision to drop this paragraph can be seen as either a failure of faith in the 'revolutionary purpose' of the masses or a cold realisation that such a platform was merely offering Labour as a second-best alternative to de Valera's anti-Treaty group, not to mention alienating the Provisional Government and potential Labour voters who belonged to the great majority of the populace demanding peace. The central question confronting delegates when they assembled in the Abbey Theatre, therefore, was not the Treaty but the more modest one of whether to contest the election at all.

Cathal O'Shannon, who chaired the conference in place of the ailing president, Tom McPartlin,[58] asked delegates 'not to think of the contending parties outside, Free Staters or Republicans, but to … reach a decision that … would be the best for the Labour Party and the Labour movement.' Tom Johnson, who, along with William O'Brien, was the movement's leading strategist, put the best gloss he could on the situation by saying that the presence of Labour representatives in the new parliament, whatever its composition, would be welcomed 'as a breath of fresh air' and would serve as a rallying-point for 'all those elements that were democratically inclined and had social ideals, but who had hitherto been bound up with one or other of the political movements in the past.' He also argued—and it was his most potent point—that the new assembly, whatever its composition, would 'have to build a constitution for the future Government of Ireland.'

Opposition came from several sources. As we have seen, many Republican activists wanted Labour to wait, as it did in 1918. On whichever side of the Treaty debate they stood, these delegates were united in discouraging anyone from contesting the election and thus challenging the political hegemony of Sinn Féin and the IRA. There were also militants on the left of the republican and labour movements, such as the IES&FTU founder and Citizen Army member Thomas Leahy and the veteran female suffrage campaigner Cissy Cahalan, president of the Irish Drapers' Assistants' Association, who were opposed to both the Treaty and partition. Cahalan, who was a delegate at the ILP&TUC conference, argued that participation in the election would split the labour movement and weaken the republican cause. As a member of the Congress executive she knew how far it had retreated from its original position. By dropping proposals that Labour TDs should vote for the restoration of the Republic in a hung Dáil and demanding a plebiscite on the Treaty she believed Labour had become a *de facto* pro-Treaty party.

The Irish Women Workers' Union opposed Labour participation in the election on the grounds of outright opposition to 'parliamentarism,' as Helena Molony characterised it. She proposed an amendment that Labour not contest the election. Her colleague Helen Chenevix said that Labour MPs in the British Parliament 'had sold the interests of the workers.' The IWWU 'stood for the overthrow of capitalism and the establishment of a Workers' Commonwealth, and these could only be achieved by direct action.' The general secretary of the IWWU, Louie Bennett, put the union's objections to Labour participating in the election in more moderate terms, arguing that an election campaign would divert resources from the industrial field.

At this important crisis in the trade union movement was that a wise thing to do? Could they spare men and women? The probability was that only a handful of labour men would be returned. Would they have the power to control legislation? Would they be strong enough to resist temptation to compromise?

James Hughes of the Clerical Workers' Union was more dismissive, saying that 'the strength of trade unions and labour lay outside and not inside Parliament,' which 'would be dominated by the farmers. The only way to get at the farmers was by organising farm labourers.'

The sharpest criticism of the ILP&TUC leadership came from Walter Carpenter, a founder-member of the Communist Party, who accused them of hypocrisy in talking about a workers' republic.

> Those who worked for a Workers' Republic were the men who seized the mills, the creameries, and the railways. Russia did not bring the Workers' Republic into operation by going into Parliament. [A voice: 'It did.'] No, but through direct action by Lenin and Trotsky.

Like most of the outright opponents of Labour participation in the election, Carpenter represented a relatively small union. Nor could membership numbers be taken as an indicator of real sentiment. Thomas Boyle of the Vehicle Builders said he had been instructed by two Dublin branches, with 800 members, to vote against the Executive's proposal. Only 130 members turned up to vote, 'with 80 against the proposal and 50 supporting it.' He disagreed with the outcome, as did his fellow-delegates. They would have to vote as directed, but they all hoped Labour would fight the election.

P. J. Rooney of the 1,500-strong Clerical Workers' Union acted diametrically against his mandate. He said he was going to defy his members' instructions to support the Executive proposal, which 'practically endorsed the Treaty.' The ILP&TUC leaders 'had not the courage or manliness to come out and pledge themselves Free State candidates.'

But the real threat came from within the mainstream of the ILP&TUC, from among those who still felt the time was not ripe for Labour to enter the electoral arena. E. P. Hart of the Transport and General Workers' Union, a British union, believed the 'few candidates they would get elected would be so small as to be useless,' except to 'get the political parties up against labour.' A Limerick Trades Council delegate called Keyes said they would be able to 'count the number of successful candidates on the fingers of one hand, or at most two hands. It would only mean subverting labour.' When 'the present issue was decided between Free Staters versus Republicans, then the time would come to launch their policy.'

James Mitchell of the Automobile and Mechanics' Trade Union said there was 'never ... a worse time than now. The question of the Treaty versus Republic at the elections would defeat the whole labour movement.'

Even some ITGWU delegates questioned the wisdom of entering the fray. Thomas Kennedy, a veteran of the 1913 Lockout and Citizen Army and long-time associate of William O'Brien, said:

> It was all right talking about the Workers' Republic, but when they went before the working-class electors the question they would have to decide was 'whether you are for peace or war, and whether you are prepared to support the element prepared to carry the Treaty into effect, or oppose it and put up with the consequences.' Could the National Executive inform them why they had not given an opinion on it?

Some of the strongest support for participation came from delegates in Northern Ireland. H. T. Whitley of the Typographical Association explained why.

> At the time of the election in the North they were told not to interfere between the Unionists and Sinn Féin, because if they put up labour candidates Sinn Féin would not go in. In the present Ulster House of Commons they had not a single direct labour representative.

Now they were in a situation where 'if they went up for election they would be asked were they Free Staters or Republicans, and labour men in the North would be asked if they were Unionists or Sinn Féin.' Whitley said he was

> a labour man pure and simple, and on political questions he reserved the right to exercise his own discretion. He did not care what a man was if he were going to improve his class. They should try and get even half-a-dozen into the assembly, and not have to resort to delegations to members of Parliament. Though politicians might divide the country, they were not strong enough to divide the labour world. The Labour Party should enter the contest and fight their corner.

David Campbell, representing the Belfast Trades Council, reminded delegates that he was the only member of the Executive, apart from the chairman, Cathal O'Shannon, to oppose the decision not to contest the 1918 general election. 'Whatever excuse there might have been for standing down then, there was not a shred of an excuse for standing down now.' The new parliament would not be elected on one issue, and it would be entrusted with 'building up the Constitution,' something they should endeavour to participate in, 'however small a measure' they could contribute. It was suggested that they go along organising on industrial lines. Were they to go back to the days of passing resolutions and sending deputations to the Irish Party or London? He saw no alternative if they decided not to go forward at the elections but to scrap their whole constitution and start a fife-and-drum band.

One of the strongest defences of the Executive's proposal came from J. T. O'Farrell of the Railway Clerks' Association. He said that unity was 'essential to attain complete success, but unity at the expense of doing nothing was absolutely useless and worthless.' There would always be divisive issues, but, 'unemployment, housing, profiteering were the great questions at present convulsing the economic and social world.' These were things they should be able to discuss as of right, not by permission.

It was absolutely unthinkable that in a country so highly organised as Ireland, labour should not have a single representative in the first assembly elected under Irish auspices after the forces of the British Crown have been withdrawn. Was it because they had individual opinions as to the merits of the dispute between the contending parties they were going to allow to design and build the house in which they were going to live? Take care instead of building a house, they might not build a Bastille. They should not overlook the danger of the whole country being brought under the heel of militarism. It was interesting sometimes to hear each party claiming to have a majority of the IRA. Did not that mean that the party who controlled the most bayonets were going to control the lives of the people? ... What was the use in talking of industrial action if the party in power had the authority to stop strike pickets? They should aspire to capture the political machine.

He believed that even half a dozen Labour members would command influence out of proportion to their numbers.

It was left to William O'Brien, general treasurer of the ITGWU, to sum up for the ILP&TUC leadership. He said he

had attended every Congress since 1909 and he was never more disappointed than today. In the old days they were told Labour could achieve its objectives by remaining strictly neutral and Home Rule would be the proper time for labour to enter the political arena.

At the Trades Congress in Clonmel in 1910 [sic] on a motion of James Connolly, they got a resolution passed that the Congress should be a political party. For twelve years that motion had been in operation and when a member moved to put it into effect, some reason was put forward why it should be postponed to some distant date ... If the majority of the workers did not want labour representation let them say so.

Some of those opposed to Labour entering the political arena were 'steeped up to their lips in politics and put forward this argument because they wanted to range themselves under the banner of either side of the contending political parties.' If delegates felt that they only wanted industrial activity they could propose the deletion of political representation as an objective.

When O'Shannon put the amendment that the ILP&TUC not contest the election he appealed to 'adherents of one or other of the political parties' not to vote 'but leave the question to those who would only exercise their vote on labour grounds.' The amendment was defeated by 115 votes to 82, suggesting that few of the delegates took notice of the chairman's injunction.[59]

An ITGWU delegate and Citizen Army member, Frank Robbins, then tried to mend fences by seeking to reinsert in the Executive's motion the call for a plebiscite on the Treaty, to be held separately from the general election. Although a strong ILP&TUC loyalist, Robbins had friends in the anti-Treaty camp and was particularly close to Liam Mellows. He probably saw the call for a plebiscite as a way of maintaining the labour movement's neutrality between the warring republican factions. His proposal was seconded by William Whelan of the Dublin Typographical Society and by the IEIU delegates.[60]

Any hopes of this being seen as a conciliatory move were demolished by Thomas Farren, a senior ITGWU figure and secretary of the Dublin Workers' Council. First of all, he pointed out that there was no machinery that would enable the Executive to take a plebiscite of workers in their various unions. Then he went on the offensive.

> They heard a lot of talk about unity, but it struck him that the people who were against the recommendations of the National Executive were the people who did not want to bring about unity. The only way to bring about unity was to elect 20 or 30 trade unionists. There were Republicans and Free Staters in that hall, but he was neither, but of the working class. He knew the Republicans, through their Home Department, to have insulted the working classes up to their teeth by issuing a panel of referees of arbitrators to decide between workers and employers. That panel contained none but names of farmers, shopkeepers, civil servants, or the middle classes, but not a working man or woman. A greater insult was never hurled in the face of the working classes of Ireland by ignoring them, and suggesting that they had not sufficient sense of justice or responsibility to act as referee or arbitrator. If they could not have an honest working man or woman to do the job they could not have an honest employer either. The election would be held no matter what demand they made for a plebiscite.

It was a powerful outburst from a man who had even stronger links to militant nationalism than Robbins. He had been one of the leaders of the Dublin Lockout, a founder of the Irish Citizen Army and a member of the committee that organised the funeral of the veteran Fenian Jeremiah O'Donovan Rossa in 1915. He had taken part in the 1916 Rising, been interned, served on the Executive of the National Aid Association, set up to help Republican prisoners and their dependants, and then worked for Sinn Féin in the by-elections of 1917. He believed Labour should have contested the 1918 election in alliance with Sinn Féin and was disillusioned with his former allies.

His dismissal of the Dáil Éireann arbitration system was unfair but showed how deep his disenchantment with Republicans of all hues went. Yet, perversely, he was so taken aback at the size of the vote against participating in the election that he told delegates angrily that 'in the face of the vote that day he did not think the National Executive would be justified in putting forward candidates.' He went on to warn them that the new Free State assembly

> would set up a Constitution that would govern the lives of future generations of men and women, and they, by their action at the Congress, wanted to see there would be no one there but the farmer, the shop keeper and the middle classes, the same as on the panel of arbitrators ...
>
> There were men who claimed to be leaders of the labour movement in this country speaking about direct action, and who were so blinded with political prejudice that they were going to betray the working classes of Ireland, and lose the greatest opportunity that ever presented itself to any generation of Irishmen or women. Constitutions were not made for a day, but to last for years. If they decided the working classes should not be represented they shouldered a terrible responsibility.

However, he now felt that 'with the minority so strong there was no hope whatever of the Labour Party entering the elections, and, personally, he was glad it was so. He was in favour of holding back until the big question was settled.'

There was no doubt that the ILP&TUC leadership was badly rattled by the strength of the opposition to participating in the election. When C. P. Kelly of the Postal Workers' Union proposed that the question be referred back for further consideration, Tom Johnson said the argument in favour 'was very strong in view of the new situation.' He assured delegates that

> there was nothing in the recommendations of the National Executive which limited in the slightest degree their faith in industrial action. The Executive as a whole, and every member of it, placed much more faith in industrial action in the country than it did in political action, but it put forward political action

as a splendid protection for industrial work. They would find later that the National Executive was wise in their advice, and that the big minority had been very far astray in their vote today.

This did not prevent him from announcing that he would support Kelly's amendment, even though he was the mover of the proposition.

It was the delegates who led on this occasion: they ignored Johnson and defeated the amendment to refer back the question of participating in the election, by 72 votes to 55.

Having survived the challenge, Johnson's motion was then passed, by 104 votes to 49. Robbins's motion calling for a plebiscite on the Treaty to be taken separately from the general election was passed even more overwhelmingly, by 128 to 12. However, some unions refused to give practical effect to the decision, and others, including the IEIU, continued to oppose the plan to put forward Labour candidates. When James Carr, a member of the IEIU executive, proposed that the union donate £50 to the Dublin Labour Party's election fund and £50 to any union member who ran for the Dáil and signed the Labour Party's election pledge, he could find no seconder.[61]

The *Irish Times* next day dismissed the idea of a plebiscite on the Treaty as 'preposterous' and took the same attitude as so many of the opposition delegates at the ILP&TUC conference by counselling that 'the Irish Free State must be established before Labour can grind its axe.'[62]

———

By contrast, the *Irish Times* gave a warm welcome to the decision by the Irish Farmers' Union to contest the election, although the latter also had divided counsels about the wisdom of doing so. Like the trade union movement, farmers faced serious problems in the spring of 1922. Prices had toppled since the wartime boom ended, reaching a peak at 192 per cent of pre-war prices in 1920 and then falling to 119 per cent in 1921, resulting in a drop of £40 million in cattle prices alone. Calls for increased tillage to offset unemployment met with little sympathy, as farmers claimed the Agricultural Wages Board had failed to take account of the downturn, making the use of more labourers for intensive cultivation methods too expensive.

This did nothing to curb militancy throughout the countryside, where pay rates had stagnated after the abolition of the Wages Board. In March 1922 there were widespread strikes by the ITGWU, with the largest dispute in Co. Dublin. The Irish Farmers' Union offered to increase basic pay from 34s to 37s a week but eventually had to settle at 43s for a 54-hour week, maintaining the half day off on Saturdays and the £3 harvest bonus. Similar increases were secured elsewhere, although rates of 34s to 36s were the most conceded outside Co. Dublin. Labourers in north Co. Dublin around Balbriggan and Skerries were offered only 40s.

These figures were predicated on agricultural prices rallying, but by the end of 1922 they had fallen to 169 per cent of their pre-war level and would drop to 157 per cent in 1923. In other words, the increases were conceded on the strength of union militancy and the disturbed state of the country rather than on economic realities. One result was that, while agricultural wages went up, the number of labourers employed continued to fall.[63]

Not surprisingly, the IFU wanted more law and order. At first its National Executive decided not to put forward Farmer candidates in the election but to support the pro-Treaty section of Sinn Féin. It was the threat from the 'soviets' phenomenon that forced the IFU to consider the possibility of political action. When Sir Thomas Cleeves, a prominent unionist businessman in Munster, had his milk factories in Co. Tipperary taken over by the workers and declared 'soviets', the IFU demanded that 'the Government ... take immediate steps to re-establish law and order.' The IFU 'pledge them full moral and physical support in any steps they deem necessary to this end.' Its National Executive 'did not want Russian Methods in this country and ... had no intention of allowing them.' Public utilities such as the gasworks in Tipperary and Waterford were also seized, the latter by its predominantly female work force.[64]

At a meeting of the IFU Executive on 18 May in Dublin the consensus was that if the 'government did not govern they should be told to get out and let people who would govern take over the government of the country.' A Wexford delegate said that 'revolvers and guns were being used, and they were stronger than treasury notes.' While there was apparent agreement with the ILP&TUC on the issue of militarism, a Co. Carlow delegate warned that the one-day general strike against paramilitarism 'was to throw dust in the eyes of the Irish people. Their intention ... was to seize property, and it was time for the farmers to be up and doing.'

Ironically, it was the pre-election pact between de Valera and Collins that finally decided the IFU on participating in the election. Its secretary, Michael O'Hanlon, said that

> up to the present it was believed by the vast majority of Irish farmers that any attempt on their part to enter the political arena would merely result in clouding the national issue. That they would not do. However, the agreement signed on Saturday last clears the way.

He added that in some instances he expected that accommodation could be reached with business or ratepayer interests over the selection of suitable candidates. That certainly seems to have been the case in north Co. Dublin, where John Rooney was the candidate. Rooney had previously been a member of the Irish Volunteers, Sinn Féin and the Gaelic League, not to mention the Black Raven Pipe Band, founded by the Republican martyr Thomas Ashe.[65] Now he ran on a farmers' ticket.

The Ratepayers' Association also decided to take the electoral plunge, although none of its candidates would be elected. At least equally exercised was the Dublin Chamber of Commerce, which condemned 'the Provisional Government's attempt to function.' Its president, William Hewat, encapsulated the fears of his members when he said that Ireland was pervaded with fear—'fear to purchase anything, fear to have anything for sale, fear of violence, fear your life's work may be destroyed before your eyes, fear of being driven from your home.' Like the farmers, the chamber was much exercised by the fact that the Minister for Labour in the new government, Joe McGrath, had until shortly before been a trade union official, albeit a rather unconventional one. Hewat ventured to suggest that, having failed, the government had, 'perhaps wisely, thrown up the sponge and decided to coalesce' with the anti-Treaty forces.[66]

Chapter 3 ～

| 'GOODNIGHT, MR O'MALLEY'

It was the breakdown in law and order that united farmers, trade unionists and business interests in *de facto* support for the Provisional Government. The labour movement may have had the most ambiguous stance, but on 24 April 1922 it held a formidable demonstration against militarism when the Irish Labour Party and Trade Union Congress called a general strike. It was the last general strike of the revolutionary period; it was also the largest and, if it was the least effective, at least it reflected the very real popular opposition to further disorder and the underlying threat of war. More than 75,000 workers took to the streets in Dublin alone and, for the first time in a general strike, there were no trains to Belfast and all the country's post offices closed. The Free State came to a standstill. In the words of the *Irish Independent,*

> no games or pastimes were indulged in. Football and hurling grounds and golf courses were deserted as if it was a day of national mourning. Labour pickets were on duty in all parts of the city … There was little or no necessity for their presence; for there was not an establishment in the city, outside of a few dairy shops, that had not its doors locked and barred. Banks, offices, business houses, factories, restaurants, theatres, picture houses and newspaper offices were one and all shut down.[1]

Even the courts and the schools, both Catholic and Protestant, closed for the day, and not a ship entered or left Dublin port. It even had the backing of the business community and of Southern unionists, which did not prevent the labour leadership from warning the 'ascendancy' and all those 'who have always been found on the side of the enemies of liberty' that workers would not be diverted from their objective of a workers' republic. The ILP&TUC Executive told its class enemies to

> be under no delusion regarding our intentions. We take our stand against militarism, because we know that the military spirit will surely be exploited by the reactionary elements in defending the tyrannies of capitalism and the entrenchment of the old order.[2]

However, militarism had developed such a hold on the popular consciousness that the ILP&TUC drew its stewards for the demonstration in Dublin from the ranks of the Irish Citizen Army. Any fears, or hopes, that the Citizen Army would play a leading role in events, as it had in 1916, proved groundless. Talks had indeed taken place between the ITGWU and the Citizen Army in the preceding months, with the aim of building a much larger workers' army throughout the country, based on the union's branch network. The concept was appealing, as the Citizen Army could provide the cadre for training a much larger militia, capable not alone of fighting the British forces but of providing protection for strike pickets and 'soviets', which were also falling foul of the IRA.

Unfortunately, relations between the Citizen Army and the union had been fraught, even in James Connolly's time, and some Citizen Army officers were suspicious that the ITGWU leadership was more interested in ending the organisation's autonomy than in advancing the cause of the workers' republic. The Labour Party's decision to contest the general election and enter the 'Free State' Dáil if the Treaty secured an electoral mandate reinforced a fear among some Citizen Army members that their organisation might end up being used to defend the Provisional Government at a time when the majority of its members were veering towards the anti-Treaty side.

Connolly's successors at the top of the ITGWU were fond of citing him, none more so than his old friend William O'Brien, but none had the temperament or the appetite for his blood-red brand of revolutionary socialism. Not that the revolutionary instincts of the Citizen Army should be over-emphasised. Members looked askance at approaches from the newly founded Communist Party, despite the presence of Connolly's son, Roddy, among the leadership of this minuscule revolutionary body. Ironically, the Citizen Army invoked the authority of its first leader, James Larkin, to assert its independence from the ITGWU and to reject approaches from the Communist Party, either ignorant of Larkin's own affinity to the Communist International in the United States or wilfully ignoring it.

There were many reasons for the Citizen Army's marginalisation after 1916, including lack of numbers and resources, but the most crippling of all was its lack of a revolutionary ideology or long-term strategy.[3] In this it had much in common with the anti-Treaty IRA. Faith in the power of the gun rendered both politically impotent.

The last flourish of left militarism was on 27 June 1922 when a Citizen Army member, Walter Carpenter, who had sung the praises of Lenin and Trotsky at the ILP&TUC conference in February, was involved in organising a mass meeting of the unemployed in the Mansion House. The moving spirit behind it was probably the Communist Party, and the main demand was for minimum payments of 30s a week to unemployed men, 25s for women, and £1 for boys and girls aged sixteen to eighteen. Michael McCabe, a Communist Party member, said that workers had 'fought everyone's battle but their own'; now it was time to fight their own war. A Council of Action would be formed, and once 'certain instructions' were given 'there should be no questioning or turning back.'

Carpenter also called for the unemployed 'to steer clear of capitalist armies … If they wanted an army let them get one of their own—a workers' army.' The means and the day were 'near at hand.'[4]

War was nearer than he thought. In the early hours of the following morning the National Army began bombarding the anti-Treaty forces in the Four Courts.

Meanwhile the mainstream trade union movement remained committed to reclaiming the streets of Dublin, Cork and other towns by peaceful means, although the violence continued unabated. On the day before the general strike the platform from which the Chairman of the Provisional Government, Michael Collins, was to address a crowd in Killarney was burnt down, and the day after the strike Brigadier-General George Adamson was fatally wounded in Athlone by anti-Treaty forces, becoming the first senior officer in the National Army to be killed. By 6 May 1922 forty-nine members of the anti-Treaty IRA and National Army had been wounded and eight killed in various clashes.

Lieutenant-Colonel F. F. McCabe, a veteran of the First World War, tried to bring home the impact of these clashes in a letter to the *Irish Times* written on the day of the general strike.

I should like very much to occupy a few minutes in an endeavour to make some of the young gentlemen who are nightly parading our streets letting off revolvers and rifles know something of the seriousness of what is often lightly spoken of as 'only wounded.'

It is an unfortunate fact that, while nature reserves her very worst and long drawn out agonies for those who have received a severe gunshot wound, these agonies are hidden away behind hospital walls, so that nobody except the patients themselves, the doctors, and the nurses know anything at all about the horrible state to which the previously healthy human body is quickly reduced … Few learn by other people's experience, but I venture to say that no man could ... walk through the surgical wards of a war hospital, seeing there the agonised faces of the wrecks of humanity, without resolving to do what he could to get quarrels settled in some way other than shooting at healthy men and women.

I myself have seen many hundreds of men suffering such agonies for month after month, as the result of severe gunshot mutilations that they have repeatedly asked surgeons to put an end to their lives. I have seen men grasp the anaesthetic from the doctor's hand and press it closer to their nose and mouth, begging for quicker insensibility, while they shook with the agony of the daily dressing. I have seen men die of pain that no art could cure. I have read of crucifixions and other tortures, which lasted some three hours, but I have seen, as a result of gunshot wounds, months of unspeakable agony, ending in death caused by the exhaustion of pain. And now Irishmen are trying to shoot one another, because one party prefers the word 'Republic' to 'Free State'!

Many of them, I feel sure, would cease fighting if they saw a bleeding nose or a black eye directly in front of them, but they let off their revolvers freely because they have no idea what the result means to their comrades who are hit ... I am speaking of severe wounds, where bones are shattered into little bits, where nerves and other sensitive structures are lacerated and torn. I am speaking too of wounds received when the skin is dirty or when particles of dirty clothing have been carried into the wound in front of the bullet in its passage. Indeed, if this terror is to go on the citizens of the Free State would be well advised if it were impressed upon them that they must never neglect to have a daily bath and must ever have clean clothes upon them ...

To fight over a word is only resulting in killing our businesses and giving for the time being an unanswerable argument to those who have said that 'Irishmen were unfit to govern themselves' ... Truly, indeed, must the angels weep, if they have tears to shed, when they see Irishmen killing and crippling one and another because England insisted upon giving the name 'Free State' to what is indeed and in fact a Republic, because, once it is established, no one can say nay to the will of the people as expressed through their elected representatives. Why, then, not wait and vote?[5]

Cork, which had witnessed some of the worst excesses of militarism, had also experienced the largest demonstration outside Dublin of trade union strength against it. A delegate to the ILP&TUC conference in August said the demonstration had such a 'moral effect ... that for two or three weeks afterwards there was a very marked change in the attitude of the military people towards the civilian population.' But all he could suggest in the midst of civil war was 'that we in the Labour movement can demonstrate again.' It was Labour's dilemma that it lacked the capacity to convert the latent power of 189,000 members into effective political action. Instead events would turn on the small Free State executive, ensconced behind barricades and sandbags, defended by one army against the other.

———

As we have seen, the electoral pact agreed by Michael Collins and Éamon de Valera on 20 May 1922 was welcomed by the Irish Farmers' Union, the ILP&TUC and the Dublin Chamber of Commerce. It was in many ways a master stroke by Collins, although some of his colleagues did not think so at the time. Arthur Griffith never called him 'Mick' again. He did not realise, nor perhaps did Collins, that the pact would give other interest groups the confidence to participate in the democratic process at a time when continuing lawlessness was a forbidding deterrent to joining the contest.

In Dublin, the intimidation of advocates of the Treaty does not appear to have been as serious as in other parts of the country. One of the worst incidents occurred on 12 June when a group of anti-Treaty Volunteers led by Robert Briscoe, a former intelligence operative for Michael Collins, raided the home of Darrell Figgis, a Sinn Féin member standing as an independent pro-Treaty candidate, and shaved off half his flaming red beard, of which he was enormously proud. He subsequently topped the poll in south Co. Dublin. However, the raid had a traumatic effect on his wife and may have been a contributory factor in her suicide two years later. (See chapter 6.)

The violence in Dublin paled in comparison with rural Ireland. Perhaps the worst individual incident occurred in Co. Tipperary, one of the most disturbed counties. At 1 a.m. on 16 June a dozen armed members of the anti-Treaty IRA raided the home of E. M. Biggs, a gentleman farmer, at Hazel Point, near Dromineer. He ran a small market gardening business with his wife, Harriet. The raiders seized Biggs and a lodger, Thomas Webb, tied them back to back, beat them and then locked them in a room. Five of the raiders, including the officer in charge, raped Harriet Biggs and 'kept her husband fully informed of what they were doing.' Her ordeal concluded with a severe kicking. When her husband and the lodger managed to free themselves they found her 'insensible' and her injuries so severe that it was feared they might necessitate the amputation of her leg. She would spend the next few years in hospital, first in Dublin and then in London. Her husband suffered a complete nervous breakdown, and the couple had to abandon their market gardening business.[6]

This is the only recorded case of rape during the War of Independence or Civil War, and it caused widespread anger within the British ruling class. Edward Carson told the House of Lords that 'of all the horrible outrages that we have had … this to my mind is one of the worst.'[7] But it did not merit much consideration in the Irish league of atrocities, although the claim for compensation from the Irish Free

State Compensation (Personal Injuries) Committee was the largest of its kind. The new government proved no less parsimonious than its British predecessor, first offering £1,200, which would not even cover medical expenses. Eventually Harriet Biggs received £6,000; but the most shocking aspect of the case in some respects is what happened to the perpetrators.

Three of them were captured by the National Army in the opening weeks of the Civil War and were charged with the rape. Neither of the Biggs couple was fit to give evidence when the men came to trial, and their lodger, Webb, proved a reluctant and not very convincing witness. Nevertheless all the men were found guilty. One was fined £3, another was bound over to keep the peace, and the third was given a caution. The anti-Treaty officer concerned, who was one of the rapists, was never charged. One of the convicted men belonged to a family that had been involved in disputes with the Biggs couple previously over unpaid wages. The breakdown in law and order was now allowing such feuds to develop from threats and harassment to something far worse. Given the outcome of the trial, it is hardly surprising that other women opted not to report rape during these years.

––––––

The new-found swagger of IRA units in some parts of the country was part of a general erosion of social deference that led groups such as farmers and businessmen to mobilise more actively and to throw their weight behind the Provisional Government. The Farmers' Union provided the former with a national structure that could be converted into an electoral machine in suitable places, including north Co. Dublin. Not so the various chambers of commerce. The Dublin chamber could not even find unity on important economic issues, such as protective tariffs and the proposed nationalisation of the railways. William Hewat, the chamber's president, believed nationalisation would turn every station-master into a 'local High Priest' and result in 'the taking on of armies of unnecessary employees.' But William Field, a former Fenian and radical Home Rule MP who had important business interests in the live cattle trade, said he had been in favour of nationalisation for forty years, while James Brady, a solicitor and another survivor from the Home Rule era, took Hewat to task for his attacks on the Provisional Government, which 'had a most difficult task'; ministers 'had done their best.'

Hewat was on firmer ground in criticising the Provisional Government for not providing any indication of its fiscal policy. 'If a clear pronouncement ... could be made it would clear the air greatly,' he said. He also held that partition was 'unnatural and not in the best interests of the country' but did so from the standpoint of a Southern unionist. 'Whatever ... extremists might think and feel about past history, self-interest lay in the direction of [a] close business relationship' with the United Kingdom, 'as well as with all countries within the British Empire, the most glorious creation of time, founded on liberty and progress.'

The Chamber of Commerce, like the old Irish Party, was a victim of its own longevity. The city's oligarchs had hardly changed since the 1913 Lockout. Its current president, Hewat, and vice-president, Sir William Goulding, had been leading figures in the chamber and in Southern unionist ranks from before the First World War, as was Sir Maurice Dockrell, the sole remaining Dublin MP in the House of Commons. The old constitutional tradition was represented not alone by such figures as Brady and Field but by the Lord Mayor, Laurence O'Neill, his deputy, Alfie Byrne, and Sir Horace Plunkett, a former Liberal Unionist MP.

Plunkett said he 'would support by voice and vote' the Provisional Government, 'because it was doing its best to get people freedom, and was showing high courage in the effort.' But he also warned of the danger of the 'transfer of authority from the orb and the sceptre to the bayonet and the bomb. [Hear, hear.] They did not see that that involved the maintenance of an army Ireland could not possibly afford.' Speaking as a unionist, he added that

> they must be allowed to live their lives without hindrance, so long as they obeyed the laws of the properly constituted authority. If they must, in their complete exclusion from all public affairs, organise their forces for the defence of their elementary rights, let it be known that they did so with good will to all men, with faith in their country, and with hope for the future. [Hear, hear.]

This was strong language from a man who had pioneered reconciliation with his nationalist fellow-countrymen as a founder of the co-operative movement and of the United Irishwomen (precursor of the Irish Countrywomen's Association) and as chairman of the failed Irish Convention, which sought to resolve the constitutional impasse in 1917 and 1918.

Dockrell was also very conscious that Southern unionists must now rely on themselves. As a member of the House of Commons he could tell the Chamber of Commerce that British ministers were 'washing their hands of us. They said that they had handed everything over to Irishmen, and if they fought between themselves it was their own affair, and if they burned property it was their own property.'

Field, who had served for over thirty years as a member of Parliament for the city, said he was 'a supporter of the Free State because he believed it was the legalised government ... and it ought to be the duty of every man in the community to give his active support to the government.' The chamber unanimously called on the government to provide 'such conditions of security and tranquillity as will permit of Irishmen living their lives in peace and quietness, and developing to the utmost the resources of their native land.'[8]

The Chamber of Commerce could at least take comfort from the fact that the conflict in the South had yet to yield casualty lists approaching those of Belfast, where seven people had died and twelve had been wounded in an attack on St Matthew's Church in Ballymacarret the previous weekend, or to be presented with bills such as the 6d on the rates that Mayo County Council imposed to reimburse local businesses for goods seized by IRA units.

———

It is an ill wind that provides no business opportunities, and the mass mobilisation against militarism inspired one Dublin firm, Stephens and Bourke of St Stephen's Green, to advertise its new foot scanner. It advised mothers to protect their children's feet by using the shop's 'Ped-o-Scope'. This 'wonderful X-Ray instrument enables her … to see how the feet rest in the shoes. Chance fitting is absolutely eliminated.'[9]

———

Throughout the new Free State the march towards renewed conflict continued, aided and abetted by the British army, which evacuated barracks with no regard to whether the IRA units replacing them supported the Treaty or not. This led to several tense situations, of which the most serious was in Limerick at the end of February. The anti-Treaty forces won the tactical stalemate but suffered strategically when the Provisional Government retaliated by banning the proposed IRA convention the following month.

Despite this, on 26 March 1922 the anti-Treaty IRA units held a convention in Dublin. They reasserted their allegiance to the Republic and saw no contradiction in repudiating the authority of Dáil Éireann as well as the Provisional Government. The delegates confirmed the appointment of a new GHQ Staff, headed by Liam Lynch, commander of the 1st Southern Division, and they reintroduced the Belfast boycott, abandoned by the Provisional Government.

In a low-key but practical response the military leadership of the Provisional Government set up new headquarters for the Dublin Brigade and its constituent battalions around the city. The brigade headquarters was in City Hall, where the Provisional Government was ensconced. The 1st Battalion was allocated 22 Manor Street, the 2nd Battalion was based at 100 Seville Place, the 3rd Battalion at 24 Great Brunswick Street (Pearse Street) and the 4th Battalion at the RIC Barracks in Rathfarnham.[10] These provided a means for recruiting reliable pre-Truce activists into the new army, which was being built incrementally as British army posts were taken over.

The propensity of the anti-Treaty forces to hold conventions was due largely to their inability to agree a strategy for meeting the growing threat to the Republic. At times the leadership appeared to be trying to catch up with the most radical or militant elements in the rank and file. The day before the March convention about forty armed men had taken possession of the Orange Hall and adjoining Fowler Memorial Hall in Rutland Square (Parnell Square). A spokesman for the group declared that it was taking over the premises 'in the name of the expelled workers of Belfast' and 'on the instructions of the IRA.' In the past the IRA had enforced a boycott of Belfast goods on the instructions of Dáil Éireann as part of a policy aimed at dissuading loyalists in the North from attacks on the minority nationalist community. It had proved largely counter-productive, as the companies with the strongest links to the South tended to be owned by members of the nationalist business community that employed Catholics. The large engineering and shipbuilding enterprises that employed many of the militant working-class unionists involved in the pogroms had little or no business south of the border. Probably the only important unionist enterprises affected by the boycott were the banks, whose customers opened accounts at that bastion of Southern unionism the Bank of Ireland to conduct business in the Free State. The main effect of the boycott was to reinforce the partition mentality, north and south, and destroy any possibility of a rapprochement, however unlikely, with the new Stormont regime.

The occupation of the national offices of the Orange Order to house victims of the pogroms marked not only a resumption but a significant stepping up of the boycott. This was followed by raids on shops suspected of selling Northern goods and on freight trains from the North. Suspect cargoes were removed, and on at least one occasion a whole wagon was set on fire. Consequently the Great Northern Railway suspended night services between Belfast and Dublin and between Derry and Dublin.

The boycott was a relatively easy means by which the anti-Treaty IRA could keep Volunteers occupied and simultaneously served to reassert its hegemony on the streets when other social actors, such as trade unions, farmers' organisations and chambers of commerce, were attempting to re-enter the public arena. The chairman of the committee that occupied the Orange premises in Rutland Square said the Belfast refugees 'were absolutely starving' since they came to Dublin and had 'nowhere to go.' The intention was to use the premises as a temporary shelter until the families could 'find employment and other accommodation.'

There was little apparent planning involved. The organisers had between 26s and 27s with which to buy food, augmented by a donation of £1 from Maud Gonne. These funds provided breakfast on the first morning of the occupation, but there was nothing else to eat until provisions arrived in the evening, consisting of seventy loaves donated by a local bakery, some tinned meat and condensed milk.[11] The operation was reminiscent of the 'Rotunda Unemployed Soviet' set up by Liam O'Flaherty and Jim Phelan, but instead of attracting public hostility there was considerable sympathy for the Belfast pogrom victims.

Within a few weeks the Kildare Street Club and the Freemasons' Hall in Molesworth Street had been seized to accommodate the refugees. The seizure of buildings so strongly associated with unionism cannot have reassured Southern unionists, such as Plunkett, Dockrell or Andrew Jameson, the banker. It also alarmed the Provisional Government. When the veteran suffrage campaigner and icon of militant nationalism Maud Gonne approached Arthur Griffith and asked him to provide twenty beds from one of the barracks being occupied by the National Army he warned her that the occupation of the Fowler Hall could 'cause trouble.'[12] Nor were the premises concerned particularly suited to the task in hand. Nora O'Sullivan, a national teacher who visited the hall, found that there were twelve families living there, comprising seventy-one individuals. She added that

neither the White Cross, Provisional Government or IRA have come to the assistance of these people. I found in the men's dormitory a complete absence of beds. 17 men sleep on boards on the floor and on a few forms [benches]. Their covering consisted of a few blankets contributed by a Christian merchant of the city. The women and children were provided with a few beds on which were a few bags of straw ... The women and girls, also the men, apologised for not having the place spotless, but could not have it so as they had neither a supply of soap, brushes, buckets, towels, or disinfectants, and what was worse they could not buy them as the voluntary contributions they got only provided them with the bare necessities of life. I was amazed to learn from them that the White Cross refused them, and gave as their reason that once residence was taken up in the hall they could not do so.[13]

Another visitor, Seán O'Casey, was more favourably impressed when he brought a young Oxford student and aspiring journalist, R. M. Fox, to the hall. Fox would later move to Dublin and write extensively about radical movements and figures from the era, including the authorised history of the Irish Citizen Army.

The refugee centres at the Kildare Street Club and Freemasons' Hall appear to have operated directly under the auspices of the anti-Treaty forces and were better run.[14] In June families in all three centres were moved to Marlborough Hall in Glasnevin after it was evacuated by Provisional Government troops, who were transferred to the Curragh. The Freemasons were relieved to find that their premises had been well looked after, although Rory O'Connor had broken into the safe, hoping to find incriminating papers, much to the anger of Joseph O'Connor, the local officer in charge. As O'Connor predicted, the Freemasons had taken the precaution of removing all their important records early in 1922, anticipating that it might be occupied. The Freemasons operated out of the Hibernian Hotel around the corner during the occupation, by courtesy of the manager, G. Murray Ross, who was one of the brethren.[15]

The refugees, on the other hand, were disappointed to find that their plight evoked little sympathy or assistance from the Provisional Government. Too busy struggling to create the sinews of a new state, the government left the problem to be solved by private charity. Nor were unions generally sympathetic. Dublin workers were willing to subscribe to the relief of distress in Northern Ireland but generally resisted efforts to find jobs for refugees. As we have seen, even staunchly militant nationalist unions, such as the IRB-inspired IEIU, refused to give union cards to Northerners and called on Dáil Éireann to stop the flood of refugees.

————

On 13 April, Liam Mellows, a friend of Frank Robbins and a leading leftist in republican ranks, called on Dáil Éireann to finance the anti-Treaty IRA. He had just been appointed quartermaster-general, a position not dissimilar to that of director of purchases that he had occupied on the old GHQ Staff. He also called for the disbanding of the newly formed Civic Guard so that the IRA could continue policing the country. This would be one of the crucial stumbling-blocks in negotiations to stop the drift to war. Incidents such as the killing of Max Green in the centre of Dublin, regular requisitions of food from shops, hotels and delivery carts to feed garrisons and continuing attacks on British military personnel only confirmed Griffith and other hard-line members of the Provisional Government, such as Kevin O'Higgins, that war was preferable to chaos.

There was a particularly senseless shooting of a British soldier in Kingstown (Dún Laoghaire) when Private A. T. Taylor of the Service Corps was killed when he was loading furniture.

On the same day the anti-Treaty forces occupied the Four Courts as a more suitable headquarters than their previous residence, the Gaelic League Hall in Parnell Square. The hall had been the scene of a stalemate with the National Army a few weeks earlier, which underlined its vulnerability as a defensible position. Rory O'Connor used the opportunity of the occupation of the Four Courts to remind the press that the anti-Treaty forces were not now associated with any political organisation and that, in accepting the Treaty, the deputies of Dáil Éireann had 'done a thing they had no right to do.' Asked if the seizure of the Four Courts and other buildings heralded a military dictatorship, O'Connor reportedly replied, 'You can take it that way if you like.'[16] It was a phrase that would come back to haunt the anti-Treaty camp.

To add to the confusion, Liam Lynch's forces took over Barry's Hotel in Gardiner Place. Frank Robbins, a Citizen Army 1916 veteran who was now active in the ITGWU and Labour Party, sought out his old friend Liam Mellows at Barry's to discuss the situation. 'A tallish man with rimless glasses appeared and, in a voice of some arrogance,' demanded to know his business. It was Liam Lynch, who told Robbins that Mellows was not there but omitted to mention that he had gone off to occupy the Four Courts. When a frustrated Robbins finally tracked Mellows down the next day and demanded to know if the occupation was intended to provoke the British into a resumption of war, 'he looked at me and smiled, but it was a very sad sort of smile and he made no reply to my outburst.'[17]

Mellows tried to justify the occupation on the grounds that it was the most suitable premises in the city to serve as a military headquarters, but practically all the other premises that had been looked at, such as the Fowler Hall and Kildare Street Club, were similar symbols of British power. In fact few premises taken over by the anti-Treaty forces in the city had any military value.

An exception was the Ballast Office, on the corner of Westmorland Street and Aston Quay, which was garrisoned on the same day as the Kildare Street Club. The building commanded the O'Connell Bridge crossing of the Liffey; it was also the nerve centre of operations in Dublin Port, and within twenty-four hours business there was paralysed. Four days later 1,500 unemployed dockers marched on the building. Following a tense confrontation it was evacuated after negotiations between the National Army headquarters in Portobello Barracks (Cathal Brugha Barracks) and the Four Courts garrison. It was one of the few occasions in the period when workers confronted with a threat to their livelihood were able to face down military diktat. By Monday 8 May the sandbags and barbed wire were gone from the Ballast Office, with just a few shattered windows to testify to the brief military occupation.[18]

The occupation of the Ballast Office may have been part of a wider attempt by the anti-Treaty forces to impose their authority in the port. The managing director of the Great Southern and Western Railway at Kingsbridge Station (Heuston Station) received a letter headed *Óglaigh na hÉireann, North East Boycott Department, Four Courts Barracks,* from Leo MacHenry (Henderson) dated 1 May.

A Chara, I am informed that your Co is assisting the Belfast Shipping Co which delivers Coal twice weekly at Waterford. I have to inform you that this is contrary to the Boycott Order and must cease.

I have also to inform you that the minimum fine for any infringement of the Boycott Order is £100, and before deciding upon the amount of fine to be imposed in this case I am giving you an opportunity of putting forward any points or case you may care to put forward.

The GSWR decided to make its case instead to Michael Collins, Minister for Finance in the Provisional Government. The company secretary, Richard Crawford, explained that a six-month contract had been entered into with John Kelly Ltd of

Belfast 'for the Sea Freight of our Steam Coal from South Wales to Waterford, and the Contract expires at the end of this month.' Collins's department responded promptly with a request 'for definite particulars of the protection which you will require, when the matter will have the earnest attention of the Provisional Government.' Crawford suggested

> that a Military Guard at Kingsbridge might be effective, but this is a matter my Board desire to leave to the judgement of the Provisional Government. They do think, however, that the Company should be indemnified from loss, as large taxpayers to the State, against the threat we have submitted.[19]

The indemnification does not appear to have been granted, but the military protection was.

———

Meanwhile various peace initiatives continued, with the Catholic Archbishop of Dublin, Dr Byrne, and the Lord Mayor, Laurence O'Neill, organising a conference even as the Four Courts were being occupied. Negotiations took place under their auspices between 19 and 29 April involving Collins, Griffith, de Valera and Brugha.

Byrne and O'Neill saw themselves as peace brokers, and O'Neill endorsed the ILP&TUC manifesto against militarism that was issued during the talks in the same spirit. In the period before the general strike he proposed a motion in the City Council, seconded by Councillor Thomas Loughlin of Sinn Féin, endorsing the manifesto. It not alone supported the strike but directed all Corporation offices and works, except essential services, to close for the day.

Unfortunately, by the time Labour delegates were invited to participate in talks, on 28 April, it was clear that they were going to fail. Undeterred, O'Neill visited the Four Courts with the treasurer of the ILP&TUC, William O'Brien, who was also a city Alderman, to meet Rory O'Connor, Liam Mellows and Joe McKelvey. O'Brien, who, like several Labour leaders, had friends in both Republican camps, went on to meet Liam Lynch, Seán Moylan, Peadar O'Donnell and Séamus Robinson as well. It is not clear if O'Neill accompanied him, but nothing came of these discussions either. Ominously, de Valera issued a public warning that 'Republicans maintain that there are rights which a minority may justly uphold, even by arms, against a majority.'

O'Neill tried desperately to keep the city council neutral. When Alderman Cosgrave, who was now Minister for Local Government in the new dispensation, proposed on 9 May that the Corporation transfer its allegiance from Dáil Éireann to 'the Provisional Government of Ireland ... set up and clothed with authority by virtue of the Treaty,' O'Neill tried to rule him out of order. O'Neill had already blocked a proposal on 7 March that the Corporation submit three nominations to the new administration for City Sheriff on the grounds that the Corporation had given its allegiance to Dáil Éireann on 3 May 1920. He had succeeded on that occasion in deferring the inevitable debate on where the city's allegiance lay by pointing out that the majority of the council had not questioned Dublin's allegiance to the Republic up till then. Now Cosgrave was putting a proposal to test the issue, and it was clear that he had canvassed support among fellow-councillors. The motion was seconded by George Lyons, a Sinn Féin councillor, who said they 'wanted no more camouflage' or 'sniping at the Provisional Government ... In adopting this resolution they were carrying out due allegiance to Dáil Éireann. The Provisional Government was native and the national authority.'

Alderman Seán T. O'Kelly, whose long service on the Corporation matched Cosgrave's, had taken the anti-Treaty side in the Dáil, and he called for the postponement of any vote that 'would take away from the sovereign authority of Dáil Éireann'; instead he proposed an amendment that the council 'reaffirms its allegiance to Dáil Éireann' rather than 'a so-called Government set up by England.' Councillor Joe Clarke, a veteran of the Battle of Mount Street Bridge in 1916, seconded O'Kelly's amendment.

An early straw in the wind came from James Gately, one of the few nationalist survivors from the Home Rule era, who said he would support Cosgrave's motion because

it was a step in the right direction for peace in the country. The people of Ireland wanted some controlling agency to protect life and property, and the Provisional Government, acting under Dáil Éireann, was in a position to give that security ... The Irish people wanted peace, they were crying out for peace, and were sick of bloodshed and pillage ... Other parts of Ireland looked to the Corporation for a lead, and they had the opportunity of giving that lead now.

The leader of the Municipal Reform Association, Alderman James Hubbard Clark, pointed out that the Provisional Government was actually recognised by both Dáil Éireann and the British government. Like Gately, he believed people 'wanted peace and good will.' Alderman Andrew Beattie, another former Unionist in the MRA, urged that the motion be passed, while Seán O'Callaghan, a pro-Treaty Sinn Féin councillor, accused 'the minority beaten in Dáil Éireann' of 'endeavouring to use the machinery of local government to defeat the will of Dáil Éireann.'

In reply, Hanna Sheehy Skeffington said the fact that the Provisional Government was 'recognised by the stranger ... was sufficient argument for turning down the motion.' Councillor Michael Lynch, an anti-Treaty IRA officer, attacked Cosgrave, the council and Dáil Éireann for not doing enough to promote the use of Irish before challenging the assertion that the Provisional Government was acting in conformity with Dáil Éireann.

Two senior Dáil deputies who were also councillors contributed to the debate: Joe McGrath, who argued for the motion, and Joseph MacDonagh, who argued against. The final word went to Thomas Cassidy, one of the Sinn Féin councillors who had proposed that Dublin Corporation give its allegiance to Dáil Éireann in May 1920. A veteran of the 1916 Rising, Cassidy said the opposition 'don't want anything but disruption and disorder. The people were asking when in heaven's name were things going to settle down.' In exasperation at the anti-Treaty councillors, he declared: 'The whole lock, stock and barrel want to be swept aside completely, and let someone with some common sense and some love of country get into the saddle and carry on the government of the country.'

Certainly opponents of the motion showed little tactical sense in handling the debate. Not only was there little coherence in their contributions but they rejected an offer from Cosgrave to accept O'Kelly's amendment as an addendum to his own motion. If they had agreed it would have neutralised much of the political value of the vote to the Treaty's supporters in the period before the general election. In the event, the amendment was defeated by 44 votes to 13.

Significantly, no councillor voted for the amendment outside the ranks of the anti-Treaty Sinn Féin councillors, whereas supporters of Cosgrave's motion included MRA members and Labour councillors from both factions. The only councillor to abstain was the leader of the Trades Council Labour faction, P. T. Daly, who, unusually, did not contribute to the debate. O'Neill, with his customary courtesy, congratulated Cosgrave on his victory, even though it had ended the period of neutrality by placing the Corporation firmly in the Provisional Government camp. He concluded by saying that 'the time was rapidly coming … when common people, of whom he claimed to be one, could decide the destinies of this country and take it from those little demi-gods who thought, God help them, that they could not be done without.'[20]

It is hard to believe that O'Neill's departure from his usual studied neutrality was not deliberate. He was an experienced politician and, having failed to avert the vote, he would have wanted to assure the electorate that this did not mean he was on the side of the 'little demi-gods', as he would be running for a seat in the third Dáil himself. What was perhaps the most significant aspect of the debate was the vehemence with which the Sinn Féin councillors from the pro and anti-Treaty camps attacked each other.

———

One of the Sinn Féin councillors who voted for Cosgrave's motion was Jennie Wyse Power. She had been a leading member of the feminist and militant nationalist movements since the days of the Ladies' Land League in 1881. A successful businesswoman who ran the Irish Farm and Produce Company in Dublin, she typified the generation of advanced nationalists who had led the independence struggle. As the Treaty election loomed on 16 June she simultaneously sought to mobilise support for her own pro-Treaty faction and to keep open links with friends on the other side. A former president of Cumann na mBan, she had founded Cumann na Saoirse to provide an alternative organisation for members unhappy at the takeover of the former by Mary MacSwiney and others opposed to the Treaty.

In a letter of 6 June 1922 to one of MacSwiney's young lieutenants, Sighle Humphreys, Wyse Power said that 'things have calmed down since the [Collins-de Valera] "pact" and Larry [O'Neill] appears as a treaty card, and of course will head the poll.' But hopes of maintaining some thread of unity, or even civility, proved vain, and relations with many of her former comrades sundered when, as joint treasurer of Sinn Féin with the Dublin solicitor Éamonn Duggan, Wyse Power froze the party's funds, causing severe difficulties for de Valera and other leading political opponents of the Treaty.

On the eve of the poll Michael Collins advised the electorate 'to vote for the candidates you think best of.' While the anti-Treaty camp accused him of treachery, the pact still allowed anti-Treaty TDs to be returned for seventeen uncontested seats. This was almost half the thirty-six they had secured in the third Dáil, which they refused to recognise or attend.

The general result confirmed that there was overwhelming support for the Treaty. Forty-one pro-Treaty candidates were elected from the Collins-de Valera 'panel', along with seventeen Labour candidates, seven farmers and six independents. Six of the independents elected were for Dublin constituencies, as were two of the seventeen Labour TDs and one Farmers' candidate. Richard Mulcahy, the former IRA chief of staff and now Minister for Defence in the Provisional Government, headed the poll in Dublin North-West. He was elected on the first count, as was W. T. Cosgrave's brother Philip, as pro-Treaty candidates. Another leading figure in the War of Independence in the city, Michael Staines, was elected on the second count. Joe McGrath secured the last seat by thirteen votes from J. T. Farrell, the Labour candidate, amid allegations of widespread personation.

As Jennie Wyse Power had predicted, Laurence O'Neill topped the poll in Dublin Mid-West, with 9,465 votes, followed by another independent nationalist, Alfie Byrne, with 7,899. Both were elected on the first count, while the pro-Treaty Sinn Féin candidate Seán McGarry had to wait for the third count to secure his seat. Seán T. O'Kelly was the only anti-Treaty Sinn Féin candidate in the constituency to win a seat, on the sixth and last count. The other two outgoing Sinn Féin TDs, Phil Shanahan and Kathleen Clarke, widow of the 1916 leader Tom Clarke, lost their seats.

In Dublin South one of the anti-Treaty camp's best-known campaigners, Constance Markievicz, lost her seat, while a relatively unknown Daniel McCarthy, a senior apparatchik within Sinn Féin whose power base lay in the GAA, topped the poll as a pro-Treaty candidate. Another long-standing Sinn Féin campaigner, Tom Kelly, was elected on the pro-Treaty ticket, although he was too ill to campaign. Alderman William O'Brien took a seat for Labour, and Myles Keogh, a popular local doctor and veteran of the old Home Rule political establishment in the city, took the last seat.

In Dublin County the prospects of the anti-Treaty candidates had never looked good. The southern townships in particular, with their long-standing unionist traditions and high turn-out, could be expected to deliver for the pro-Treaty candidates. Monkstown had the distinction of having the highest turn-out in the country, with 97 per cent of those eligible to vote doing so. Darrell Figgis, the man who had been subjected to the indignity of having half his beard shaved off by anti-Treaty Volunteers a week before the election, topped the poll with 15,076 votes as an independent. It was very much a sympathy vote: Briscoe and his fellow-barbers had done the impossible and made the arrogant, irascible Figgis popular. Although he had helped organise the Howth gun-running and had been a leading figure in the Dáil Éireann government during the War of Independence, Figgis owed his failure to secure a nomination from the pro-Treaty bloc within Sinn Féin to his innate ability to antagonise colleagues. Only Arthur Griffith's patronage ensured him a role in the new regime.

One other candidate was elected on the first count: Tom Johnson of Labour, with 8,220 votes. George Gavan Duffy, the sitting pro-Treaty Sinn Féin candidate who had represented the constituency since the Sinn Féin landslide of 1918, was elected on the second count. John Rooney, a former Sinn Féin activist and Volunteer officer, was elected as the sole farmers' candidate in Co. Dublin on the sixth count.

Desmond Fitzgerald, 1916 veteran and Dáil Éireann's director of publicity for most of the War of Independence, was elected on the eighth count, along with John Derham, whose family's chief claim to fame was having their business burnt down by the Black and Tans in the 'Sack of Balbriggan'. Derham defeated the outgoing anti-Treaty TD Margaret Pearse, mother of Patrick Pearse, by fifty votes.

As in Dublin North-West, the Labour Party complained of widespread personation, although on this occasion it did not deprive it of a seat.[21]

Dublin, once the stronghold of the radical nationalist and labour movements, now had only one anti-Treaty deputy, Seán T. O'Kelly, and two Labour deputies, Tom Johnson and William O'Brien. It would be hard to decide which of the three could be considered the most conservative within their respective constituencies. All of them were more comfortable in the debating chamber than on the barricades; perversely, all three were also authors of the most radical social document to emerge from the Irish Revolution, apart from the 1916 Proclamation. This was the Democratic Programme of Dáil Éireann, adopted by the first Dáil in January 1919. Johnson and O'Brien wrote the first draft, and O'Kelly had been nominated by his IRB colleagues to remove their worst socialist excesses.

———

While the election campaign was in full swing Dublin witnessed the last great display of British power in the Phoenix Park, where nine thousand soldiers took part in a pageant to celebrate the King's birthday. The officer commanding British forces, the Right Honourable Sir Nevil Macready, Bart, GCMG KCB, recalled in his memoirs that

> among the spectators, the old pensioners from the Royal Hospital wearing many medal ribbons of bygone wars, and the boys of the Royal Hibernian Military School, who marched past in [the] rear of [the] infantry, made up a picture that could not fail to appeal to those who realised that never again would British troops salute the flag on that ground …

It was a colourful reminder for the electorate and the anti-Treaty forces that Britain retained the capacity to unleash the 'immediate and terrible war' threatened by Lloyd George during the peace negotiations.

By contrast, the anti-Treaty IRA remained unable to agree a viable policy for defending the Republic. A second convention was held on 9 April 1922 in the Mansion House, by courtesy of the Lord Mayor. It was essentially about electing a new leadership completely independent of Dáil Éireann and the Provisional Government. The only political issue debated was whether to ban the forthcoming election. The proposal was defeated.

The third convention was held on 18 June, two days after the election. Tom Barry, commander of the 1st Southern Division, proposed that if British troops (including the nine thousand who had paraded in the Phoenix Park a fortnight earlier) did not evacuate Dublin within seventy-two hours the war should resume. Far from uniting the delegates by reigniting the War of Independence, as Barry had hoped, it divided them. When the proposal was defeated, by 118 votes to 103, the militant minority, including Barry, withdrew to the Four Courts and set up new command structures, with Joe McKelvey of Belfast, commander of the 3rd Ulster Division, as their chief of staff. Liam Lynch, still chief of staff as far as the majority of delegates were concerned, moved into the Clarence Hotel, his third Dublin headquarters within three months, just downriver from the Four Courts. Lynch went to the Four Courts the next day, only to be turned away at the gates.

The timing of this split was unfortunate. On 22 June, Field-Marshal Sir Henry Wilson was shot by IRA members outside his home in London after unveiling a war memorial at Liverpool Street Station. Wilson, a Southern unionist, had recently retired as chief of the imperial general staff in order to act as security adviser to the Northern Ireland government. Ironically, he advocated giving the military primary control of security in the North, rather than the newly formed Royal Ulster Constabulary and its 'B Special' auxiliaries. This might have spared the Catholic population some of the worst excesses of the pogroms.

The suspicion for Wlson's killing immediately fell on the anti-Treaty forces in the Four Courts, although such evidence as there is suggests that the attack originated in an order issued by Collins in 1920 and never rescinded. Wilson's assassins, Reginald Dunne and Joseph O'Sullivan, had served in the British army in the Great War and owed their capture to the fact that O'Sullivan had lost a leg and Dunne would not abandon him in the police pursuit. The London Brigade had split over the Treaty, with Dunne voting in favour. Dunne subsequently said the pair went to confront the field-marshal, not shoot him, which suggests that it was events in Northern Ireland and the perception of Wilson as a unionist diehard that sealed his fate. If anyone else, including Collins, was implicated, then Dunne and O'Sullivan took the secret with them to the scaffold. By the time of their execution, on 10 August, they had already been forgotten in the storm of civil war.

Wilson's assassination appalled the British political establishment. Macready was summoned to London, where he was asked by Lloyd George if he had sufficient troops to attack the Four Courts. He said it was a comparatively easy military operation but feared it would see a large proportion of National Army personnel defect and lead to renewed hostilities and serious civilian casualties, for all of which the British government would bear the responsibility. Thinking he had dissuaded his political masters from hasty action, Macready returned to Dublin, only to receive a telegram ordering him to attack the Four Courts regardless. He bought more time by pleading the necessity of bringing military personnel and dependants scattered around the city into the British-controlled sector before the attack took place. He then sent a memorandum reiterating the serious political risks of an attack on the Four Courts, endorsed by all his senior military subordinates. London concurred.

The whole episode increased Macready's contempt for the cabinet and especially the Colonial Secretary, Winston Churchill, although he did not underestimate how perilous the situation had become following Wilson's assassination. In his memoirs he would write:

Had there been a shadow of proof to connect those responsible for the occupation of the Four Courts with the murderers of Henry Wilson it would have been a justification for the risk of reopening the whole Irish question, although such a move would have been wholly inconsistent with the instructions of the Government two months before … It can only be supposed that panic and a desire to do something, no matter what, by those whose ignorance of the Irish situation blinded them to possible results, was at the root of this scheme.[22]

As it happened, the Four Courts Executive would solve all its opponents' problems for them. On the morning of 26 June a convoy of fifteen armed men with an armoured car and tender drove from the Four Courts to the garage of Harry Ferguson and Company in Lower Baggot Street, seized several vehicles, and smashed equipment at the site. They were under the command of Leo Henderson, the director of the Belfast boycott, who had warned the GSWR that it faced fines of £100 if it continued importing coal in ships from Northern Ireland. Ferguson's was a Protestant-owned firm and, it was alleged, had ignored the boycott.

In fact none of the vehicles on the premises appear to have originated in Belfast, but the boycott had been extended to manufactured imports from Britain, making any mechanically propelled vehicle fair game. According to some anti-Treaty sources, the seized vehicles were required for military purposes; according to others they were needed to help Belfast refugees. Whatever the reason, that afternoon a force of National Army troops arrived with two armoured cars under the command of Frank Thornton and blockaded the Four Courts group. Thornton had worked for Collins during the War of Independence; Henderson, by contrast, had been attached to the Dáil Éireann civil service and had incurred Collins's ire by drawing his full salary while in prison, when he was only entitled to half, as he had no dependants. Henderson was now arrested after refusing to return the seized vehicles.

On 27 June a small group of Four Courts Volunteers under Ernie O'Malley arrested Lieutenant-General Ginger O'Connell, assistant chief of staff, on his way back to Beggarsbush Barracks from Gilligan's public house. O'Malley phoned Eoin O'Duffy, the National Army's new chief of staff, and said O'Connell would be released in return for Henderson.

'Is that all?' O'Duffy replied.
'Yes, Mr O'Duffy. Good night.'
'Good night, Mr O'Malley.'[23]

————

Instead of negotiating, the Provisional Government responded to O'Malley's ultimatum with one of its own: it demanded the evacuation of the Four Courts and the surrender of the garrison by midnight. National Army troops began occupying positions in the city centre and took over the Four Courts Hotel alongside the anti-

Treatyites' stronghold and the Bridewell Police Station at the rear of the complex. Snipers were placed in the tower of St Michan's in Church Street and Jameson's Distillery in Bow Street.

Meanwhile Emmet Dalton, the National Army's director of operations, called to see Macready at Kilmainham to ask for 18-pounder field guns and ammunition. The British government, which had been urging Macready to do the job himself four days earlier, agreed with alacrity.[24] At seven minutes past four on the morning of 28 June 1922 many Dubliners awakened by artillery and machine-gun fire thought it was the British army 'bombarding the city, perhaps from a gunboat in the Liffey, as in 1916.' It was indeed British artillery but it was being operated by National Army gun crews.

Nothing had happened at midnight, because when O'Duffy ordered Frank Carney, the supplies officer at Portobello Barracks, to provide munitions for the attack he resigned, as did several other members of the garrison. They were all placed under arrest. Macready's earlier assessment of the slender hold Collins and Mulcahy had on their troops had not been far off the mark.

At this point the pro-Treatyites attempted to reopen communications with the Four Courts, first through O'Daly and then through another old Squad member, Tom Ennis, who was in command of the National Army's new 2nd Eastern Division, responsible for the greater Dublin area. Ennis's note arrived at 3:40 a.m., but the Executive, which was meeting under the Dome in the great central chamber of the Four Courts, told Volunteer Tommy 'Skinner' O'Reilly, who took the note from the National Army despatch rider, that there was no reply. O'Daly made one last attempt to phone his former comrades at 4 a.m. There was still no answer. By now Dalton had his guns in place, and the bombardment began.

Hubris is the only word to describe the behaviour of the IRA leadership in the Four Courts. They had an unconcealed contempt for their opponents. A few months earlier, when Richard Mulcahy had shown Oscar Traynor a meticulously prepared document by his deputy, Eoin O'Duffy, and asked, 'Isn't that a magnificent report?' Traynor replied, 'What strikes me about the man is that he must have a lot of time on [his] hands.' O'Duffy did indeed lack the operational experience and political nous of Traynor, but, as his biographer Fearghal McGarry has pointed out, he owed his rapid rise through the ranks to his organisational abilities rather than his active service record, and his career thrived in these months on creating order out of chaos. The military bureaucrats would quickly demonstrate that in fighting on a large scale, logistics and organisation were more important than being able to set up an ambush. The pen was indeed mightier than the sword.

Meanwhile Dalton was having a hard time maintaining a bombardment with untrained crews and had to operate one of the 18-pounders himself for three hours. Besides, the shrapnel ammunition had barely any effect. It was with undisguised relish that Macready later wrote:

The noise went on all day with very little impression on the Four Courts, but with much amusement and interest to the inhabitants of Dublin, who lined up on either bank of the Liffey about a hundred yards east and west of the battle, being kept in their places by policemen in the same way as at a festival or a Lord Mayor's Show.[25]

Liam Lynch's reaction was less sanguine. Once the attack began he called a meeting of all available officers in the Clarence Hotel. It was decided that the priority must be to return to their areas and mobilise local units in support of the Four Courts garrison. On his way to Kingsbridge he was detained by a National Army unit under the command of Liam Tobin, Collins's deputy director of intelligence in the War of Independence. In an uncharacteristic lapse, the pro-Treaty side was unaware that a rapprochement had been reached between Lynch and the Four Courts garrison shortly before the assault began. According to Liam Deasy, one of the men detained with Lynch, they were individually interviewed by Eoin O'Duffy. Deasy described it as 'one of the shortest interviews I have ever experienced.'

'This war is too bad, Liam,' said O'Duffy.
'Yes indeed it is,' I replied.
'Where were you going when Liam Tobin met you?' he asked.
'To get a train at Kingsbridge for Mallow,' I replied.
He stood up saying, 'Ah, you better be on your way,' offering me his hand, which I gladly accepted and with this act of mutual friendship we parted.[26]

If Lynch had a similar interview he must have put on an uncharacteristic display of duplicity. The group was allowed to catch the Cork train.

Looking back, awaiting the prospect of execution as a prisoner six months later, Deasy would reflect on their release that 'there was no enthusiasm for this war. At most we could only say that we were protesting in arms. The tragedy was that our protest did not end with the fall of the Four Courts.'[27] But, as Liz Gillis has pointed out, 'any hope the Provisional Government had of restricting the fighting to Dublin, or indeed ending the Civil War swiftly, ended with the release of Liam Lynch.'[28]

Meanwhile in Dublin, Oscar Traynor summoned a meeting of local anti-Treaty officers. He established his headquarters at Barry's Hotel in Gardiner Row and sent garrisons to occupy strongpoints in the north-east quadrant of the city and to await the onslaught. No attempt was made to link up with the Four Courts garrison, which itself had no viable plan for either holding or retreating from their stronghold. As far back as early April, when the Four Courts complex was seized, it was obvious that it required a much larger garrison than the hundred or so Volunteers who drifted in and out. Without the financial resources of the

Provisional Government and the staff training needed to make use of what resources there were, the headquarters of the most militant element within the anti-Treaty forces constituted an open prison rather than a threat to the British or to the 'Free Staters' and 'Irish recreants,' as it now characterised former comrades.

The only plan was to provoke the British or pro-Treaty forces into an attack; but Macready had been too wily to take the bait. Yet, despite their belligerent stance, the Four Courts Executive's determination not to start a shooting war was such that it ordered men to stop mining the quays in front of the building as a defensive measure when National Army troops arrived to prevent the work going ahead.

Once the attack began, anti-Treaty IRA units tried to stop reinforcements reaching the besiegers. 'Our plan ... was to establish posts to intercept supplies reaching the forces attacking the courts,' Joseph O'Connor, commander of the anti-Treaty forces south of the Liffey, explained. 'This was the reason for the occupation of many houses on the various routes from Portobello and Beggars Bush.' He based himself at 41 York Street, the offices of the Dublin Total Abstinence League and Workmen's Club, which had long served as a meeting-place for south city Volunteers. 'De Valera reported to me for duty and he was accompanied by a goodly number of prominent people. Few however, had military training.' Cathal Brugha also called to York Street after attending early morning Mass but only to tell O'Connor that he was taking the 4th Battalion across the river to support Traynor. 'I agreed, although certainly I could have used them.'

There were hopes that Lynch would mobilise Volunteers in the provinces and return rapidly to turn the tide of the fight for Dublin. On paper the balance of forces was still in favour of those opposed to the Treaty, and the strength of the National Army at this time was no more than four thousand. But no-one took the obvious step of seizing the railway stations and rushing reinforcements to the capital, as the British had done in 1916 to crush the Rising.

The reality was that credible military resistance to the new state was not feasible while a large British garrison remained in Dublin and the last British troops would not depart until December, by which time the military outcome of the Civil War was irreversible. The only remotely realistic strategy was Tom Barry's proposal to attack the British forces in the hope that Collins and Mulcahy would return to the militant nationalist fold, but that had been rejected, albeit narrowly, in April. Again, most hardliners would not accept the Treaty but showed little appetite for fighting for the Republic. What followed could be described as passive militarism, while everyone waited for the 'recreants' to impose a solution.

———

Traynor remained stubbornly on the defensive, although forces attacking the National Army units besieging the Four Courts hardly constituted a ring of steel. Máire Comerford, one of the Cumann na mBan members of the Four Courts garrison, was able to carry despatches to Traynor on her bicycle. On one occasion she returned with ammunition supplied by a Free State soldier. O'Malley would later write acerbically about the failure of the 3rd and 4th Battalions to intervene, yet the Four Courts garrison had not shown much initiative either. There was an armoured car in the complex, a Rolls-Royce, the best model of the era. It is lovingly described in his Civil War memoir by Ernie O'Malley, who hijacked it from Templemore during the Truce. The garrison christened it *The Mutineer* but never seem to have thought it might more usefully have been employed by anti-Treaty forces in the city than kept as a trophy. When the fighting began, the pro-Treaty forces made sure it remained barricaded inside the complex, where it served as a mobile firing platform until the tyres were shot out.

Even less understandable was the failure to use the three months of occupation to adequately defend the building. When the fighting broke out, many of the windows were unprotected or blocked with unsuitable material, such as sandbags. Few communications tunnels or trenches had been dug, making safe contact between different sections of the complex impossible. There had not even been an attempt to rig up an internal telephone system, so that when the Post Office cut the external lines it automatically reduced communication within the Four Courts to men, and Fianna Éireann boys, running a deadly gauntlet between the buildings.

Ironically, Ernie O'Malley, who listed many of these shortcomings afterwards, had brought a large library of military books with him. He even offered them to their prisoner, Ginger O'Connell, and recommended Tolstoy's *War and Peace*. 'I'd like to read it,' O'Connell said, 'but I think it will be browsing because I won't have time to finish it.'

The weakest point in the defences was the north-west section, which came under direct fire from the Four Courts Hotel, National Army positions in Church Street and the Bridewell as well as artillery fire from Haymarket. It was defended by members of Fianna Éireann, who also provided the garrison's orderlies. Worst of all, it was where the munitions store was placed, sharing the site with the Public Record Office of Ireland, including one of the most complete sets of mediaeval records in the world. Some of the archives had been used, along with law books and legal files, for barricading windows. Surveying the complex from a rather exposed position on the Four Courts Dome, Seán Lemass, the garrison adjutant, told O'Malley and the garrison commander, Paddy O'Brien: 'The garrison are kids. We should have put older men with them.'

And yet the 'kids' showed no sign of breaking, although their position was increasingly untenable.[29] O'Brien decided that the only thing to do was to burn the dump, but enemy pressure was now driving events, as National Army soldiers finally began to penetrate the defences. Heavy rifle and machine gun fire from the Four Courts, supplemented by desultory sniping from behind the lines, were only some of the problems facing Dalton, O'Daly and Ennis. On the evening of 28 June, Macready had received frantic phone calls from Eoin O'Duffy and from Andy Cope, the senior British civil servant remaining in Ireland, demanding more field guns and ammunition. Macready said they would have to wait until the next day, when he expected a destroyer with fresh supplies. Characteristically, O'Duffy told him the shortage of shells was his fault, and he intended telling the Colonial Secretary, Winston Churchill, so. Equally characteristically, Macready dismissed it as 'an Irishism for which I was quite prepared. I then asked if Dalton could be sent to me. The poor man arrived about 9.30 p.m. thoroughly worn out but full of fight. After he got outside a drink or two he told me his story.'

It was a tale of training unwilling gunners from scratch and having to replace casualties resulting from enemy action, desertion and hunger, as no arrangements had been made to feed the attacking party. However, the kernel of the problem, they both agreed, was that 'he could never get his men to risk their lives in an assault' without artillery support.

Macready, who liked Dalton, agreed to supply him with shrapnel shells, 'simply to make a noise through the night, as he was afraid that if the guns stopped firing his men would get disheartened and clear off.'[30] In fact the fighting, which had now spread to other parts of the city, was giving the 'Staters' a new cohesion, and by Thursday they were coming to close quarters with the Four Courts garrison.

By Friday 30 June it was only a matter of time before the Four Courts fell. Ironically, Traynor had finally succeeded in sending a small force of anti-Treaty members of the Citizen Army along Abbey Street to within four hundred yards of the complex that morning to try to break through. But it was no more than a relief unit—a case of too little too late. Fortunately for the Citizen Army force, it never reached its destination.

By 11 a.m. a large fire had broken out in the headquarters section of the Four Courts. At 11:45 a.m. Paddy O'Daly called the fire brigade, but the chief fire officer, John Myers, refused to send his men, some of whom were anti-Treaty Volunteers, unless there was a ceasefire. O'Daly refused to allow one, saying, 'Ireland is more important than the fire at the Four Courts.' Fifteen minutes later the munitions exploded, bringing the siege to a spectacular end and providing one of the iconic photographs that encapsulate the foundation of the Irish Free State and the fall of the Irish Republic. It was also a vivid way of capturing the end of a priceless mediaeval manuscript archive.

In Dobson's public house on the corner of Abbey Street and Capel Street, where Commandant John Hanratty of the Citizen Army had gathered his relief force for the final push to the Four Courts, there was a stunned silence after the explosion, followed by 'a rushing sound—a pounding on the road and the pavement as if a whole army were advancing at the double.' The men cocked their weapons and peeped out, expecting waves of Free Staters, only to see law books bounding along the road outside as a cloudburst of paper fell on the city and spread across the suburbs as far as the heather on the Hill of Howth.[31]

The explosion made the position of the Four Courts garrison untenable, but the Volunteers and Fianna Éireann boys continued to fight on through two further explosions at 3:15 p.m. that spewed more ancient documents over the city. The chief fire officer had finally allowed his men to enter the complex to put out the growing conflagration, despite O'Daly's refusal to grant a ceasefire. Three of them became casualties, one of whom, Bernard King, who had sixteen years' service, would be forced to retire as a result of his injuries.

Meanwhile a message came through from Oscar Traynor informing the garrison that he would be unable to fight his way through to them, 'even at terrific sacrifice. I am expecting reinforcements at any moment. If the Republic is to be saved your surrender is a necessity.' This led to further debate within the Four Courts as men tried to reason how their surrender could save the Republic, especially if reinforcements were imminent.

Characteristically, O'Malley was for fighting on; but the majority saw the hopelessness of their situation, and Father Albert Bibby, one of the Capuchin friars who risked death daily on the streets to bring succour to the injured and dying, acted as go-between with O'Daly.

The former Squad commander had not mellowed with promotion; he insisted that the surrender had to be unconditional. Liam Mellows, Joe McKelvey and Ernie O'Malley told the men 'with tears in their eyes' that there was no dishonour in surrender. They might be compelled to give up their guns, but they would never surrender their principles. In fact they did not surrender their weapons but stripped them, broke the working parts, doused them with kerosene and set them alight.

Despite the length of the struggle, only three members of the 140-strong garrison were killed and eight wounded. The National Army lost seven killed and seventy wounded, mainly in the storming of the building. The three injured firemen should also be added to the casualty list.

———

While the Four Courts provided the initial focal point of the battle for Dublin, the Provisional Government was determined to keep the initiative elsewhere in the city as well. Even before the assault on the Four Courts began it was decided to evict the anti-Treaty forces from the Orange Order premises and Fowler Hall in Rutland Square, which had been occupied since March. With the Belfast refugees recently departed for Marlborough Hall there was nothing to inhibit the National

Army attack, which was led by Frank Bolster, a former member of the 'Squad' who would become notorious for his treatment of anti-Treaty prisoners. His men were supported by an armoured car and machine-gun fire. The garrison held out for eight hours before setting the buildings alight and departing at about 12:30 p.m. on 28 June. One National Army soldier was killed, along with three civilians in cross-fire. One civilian fatality may have been caused by British troops who had called to the Rotunda Rink to collect mail and opened fire, under the impression that they were being attacked.

By now sporadic shooting had begun around the city as word spread of the fighting at the Four Courts and rival detachments encountered each other. Two National Army officers were killed and two soldiers wounded in an ambush at Leeson Street Bridge, and an anti-Treaty Volunteer was killed in an exchange on the quays. The anti-Treaty forces had the advantage in that the great majority were not in uniform. Most tram services operated normally, but there was considerable disruption of train services entering the city.

The fire in the Orange Hall and Fowler Hall added £17,000 to the rapidly mounting list of compensation claims that would soon assail the Dublin ratepayers. The claim from Ferguson's Garage, where the Civil War might be said to have begun, would be £8,356. By the end of the conventional fighting in July claims against the city would total over £3¼ million, more than 60 per cent higher than the figure for 1916. They even included some of the same claimants, such as the veteran Home Ruler and confectioner Sir Joseph Downes, known colloquially as 'Lord Barmbrack'.

There would seem to have been a disproportionate number of premises damaged as a result of occupation by the anti-Treaty forces that were associated with the old unionist order, such as the Hibernian Bible Society, which claimed £40,000, the Young Men's Christian Association, which claimed £20,000, and the Church Representative Body, which claimed another £20,000. The Freemasons claimed only £1,108, showing that the anti-Treaty forces could behave reasonably well under a responsible commander such as Joseph O'Connor. The Royal Hibernian United Services Club in St Stephen's Green came off more lightly still, with a claim for £345. But then, the anti-Treaty occupants neither systematically wrecked nor set fire to these buildings.

Of course Protestant and unionist institutions and businesses formed a disproportionate number of those premises in the centre city, where the worst fighting took place. Some, such as the railway companies, were attacked for strategic reasons. Between 27 June and 28 July there were 123 attacks on the permanent way of the Great Southern and Western Railway, sixty attacks on bridges, eighteen attacks on signal boxes and other premises and three trains derailed, leading to claims of £100,000. The GSWR traversed the most strongly held Republican areas in the country. By contrast, the Dublin and South-Eastern Railway claimed a mere

£3,425 for the same period. Significantly, the anti-Treaty forces already saw railways as a strategic threat rather than a potential asset, a means by which the war could be brought to them rather than a way of bringing it to the enemy.

The fact remains that premises belonging to bodies associated with loyalism were often regarded as legitimate targets and their occupation or destruction seen as a natural stepping up of the Belfast boycott. The focus on symbols of unionism and the urge to help the nationalist minority in the North was a potent factor in distorting anti-Treaty IRA policy in the period leading up to the Civil War. There had been a consensus among senior military commanders and IRB members on both sides that something had to be done to protect the minority, and in April it had been agreed to transfer weapons from anti-Treaty units, along with experienced personnel from Cos. Cork and Kerry, 'to stiffen the Northern IRA' before an offensive across the border. The transfer of weapons was needed for fear that if they came from the munitions that the British were supplying to the Provisional Government and were captured it would expose the duplicity of Collins, Mulcahy, O'Duffy, Mac Eoin and other National Army commanders.

The northern offensive, which took place in May and early June, proved 'a dismal failure,' degenerating into hostage-taking, clashes with the A Specials and a temporary return of British troops, who established a demilitarised zone on both sides of the border. Michael Hopkinson has assessed the strategy as 'nothing more than an attempt to embarrass and destabilise the Northern government while having the useful additional role of aiding the search for army unity.' It certainly left many IRA units, particularly in Northern Ireland and the border areas, off balance, besides feeding the illusion that a joint offensive against the British was still possible.

Once Collins and his military cabal realised that this gambit would fail they withdrew. Needless to say, the weapons handed over were never replaced, adding to the bitterness some senior anti-Treaty commanders felt against their former comrades. On the other hand, quite a few Northern Volunteers headed south to join the National Army.

Meanwhile in Dublin the material cost of the attack on the Four Courts was mounting. The largest claim against Dublin Corporation was from the Honourable Incorporated Law Society, which sought £300,000 for damage to its premises. There would be multiple claims on top of these as lawyers and their clients demanded compensation for lost documents, especially deeds, and consequential losses for beneficiaries. Not perhaps surprisingly, the largest claims for the loss of personal belongings came from the judiciary, totalling £1,837. Other significant claims for collateral damage included the trustees of the Franciscans' church (popularly known as Adam and Eve's) at Merchants' Quay, opposite the Four Courts. They were looking for £1,000. The British War Office put in a bill of £7,284 17s 6d for the destruction of military vehicles in the Four Courts complex (including, presumably, the *Mutineer*). The Four Courts Hotel, which played such an important role as the base for the National Army attack on the west side of the complex, put in a claim for £30,000 and was soon functioning as a National Army post to protect the complex from further attacks.[32]

In 1916 the British government had paid compensation to property-owners on the grounds that most of the damage was done by its own artillery, and it wanted to assuage nationalist sentiment. The Provisional Government would prove far more tight-fisted, and the Corporation was left to pay most of the claims itself, which meant that ratepayers outside the city centre had to compensate their wealthier neighbours. Inevitably, cuts in services meant that the poor were indirectly subsidising the conflict as well.

———

Oscar Traynor's decision to order the surrender of the Four Courts cleared the way for the National Army to turn its attention on him. Although he had been advocating a return to guerrilla war, he ordered his men to take up fixed defensive positions in the city, based on strongpoints in the string of hotels along the east side of Upper O'Connell Street and Barry's Hotel in Gardiner Place, which once more served as a headquarters for the anti-Treaty forces. Tom Ennis took command of the Provisional Government forces in the area and brought one of the field guns with him from the Four Courts to bombard enemy positions from cover in Henry Street.

Seán Prendergast, OC of C Company of the 1st Battalion of the anti-Treaty IRA and a veteran of the 1916 Rising, was leaving a show at the Plaza Picture House in Granby Row with other members of the company when they were 'waylaid' and 'served with the mobilising order, which we were inclined to treat as a huge joke.' Nevertheless the mobilisation of the company proceeded quickly, and the men gathered at the appointed rendezvous, the Tara Hall in Gloucester Street (Seán MacDermott Street). The turn-out was surprisingly high, given that the venue was in the 2nd Battalion area. However, the company quartermaster was not contactable, so there were not enough arms to go round—far fewer than in 1916, Prendergast recalled. His unit was ordered to take up a post on the junction of Strand Street and Capel Street, but by now heavily armed patrols of the National Army were blocking their way in O'Connell Street. They were then ordered to take over Hughes's Hotel in Gardiner Street instead.

> Everything requisite for our welfare was seen to, such as the commandeering of supplies, arranging guards, sniping posts, cooking, first-aid posts, sleeping quarters, securing of an ample supply of water, and everything considered to be of use in case of a prolonged fight or a siege. Our weakness, however, was in arms.

Over the next few hours the forty Volunteers mobilised in Prendergast's unit were joined by thirty members of other companies of the 1st Battalion and 'a Belfast refugee whose name I disremember.' Men were sent out to collect weapons held by Volunteers who had not turned out.

> Had we rifles for all our men, proper serviceable rifles, more than half of our troubles would have been solved. After repeated appeals to the Battalion for a supply of rifles, we secured the modest number of five which, we were informed, were all that could be spared, when fifty would not have been in excess of our requirements.

They discovered that another unit had occupied the houses on the far side of Gardiner Street, including Moran's Hotel, which had been one of Collins's haunts during the War of Independence. This garrison was made up mainly of members of the 5th (Engineers) Battalion, who laid a mine in Talbot Street. There was no command structure linking these adjoining strongpoints.

> We were not aware of any hard and fast rules on the matter but it did seem a bit contradictory to have independent authorities exercised by both a Commandant controlling one garrison and a Captain [Prendergast] a neighbouring one. Some form of co-operation was necessary. Hence I contacted Commandant O'Doherty, explained our situation and that we were acting under orders of our Battalion Commandant, P. Holohan. It was obvious that Commandant O'Doherty was equally perplexed, thought the situation peculiar but it must be said to his credit that he did not seek to impose any undue influence in regard to our operations or our status.[33]

Similarly, when an order arrived instructing Prendergast to take over a distillery in 'Brunswick Street' it did not state whether it was North Brunswick Street or Great Brunswick Street (Pearse Street). It might have been obvious that Jameson's in North Brunswick Street was the intended objective—a move south of the river made little operational sense—but neither was it a 'very rosy prospect in moving our men and materials ... to North Brunswick Street, to cover a distance of about two miles and get away with it.' Prendergast's unit refused to obey, reasoning that they did not have 'the remotest chance of being successful'; instead they remained in place until they received another order on Thursday from Holohan to move to a position in Upper O'Connell Street, which 'would bring us nearer our Battalion Headquarters.'

When Prendergast informed O'Doherty in Moran's Hotel that they were leaving the area 'he was none too pleased' and declared he would withdraw as well, as he lacked the men and material with which to defend the whole area, which was now coming under attack from National Army forces based in Amiens Street Station and on the railway line overlooking the Talbot Street and Lower Gardiner Street area. Eventually 'two of the girls who were assisting in cooking, Marcella Crimmins and Nan Tobin,' were sent 'with a report to Brigadier Traynor in the Hammam Hotel Headquarters [Upper O'Connell Street] explaining the dilemma in which we were placed as a result of the exercise of dual authority.'

Prendergast obviously felt guilty about sending the women through heavy sniper fire on 'that dangerous mission' but argued that 'we could not have employed any of our men ... because they were generally too well known, and, besides, we could ill afford to spare them from their other duties.' Traynor told Prendergast to place his unit under O'Doherty, and they remained in position.

Besides the impression of chaos this account gives of the situation in Dublin in the week in which the Four Courts were attacked, the striking feature of the dispositions of the anti-Treaty forces is that, of the eighteen strongpoints occupied, eleven were hotels and two, the Catholic Young Men's Society in O'Connell Street and the St Stephen's Green Club, had accommodation and catering facilities. Todd Andrews, who was part of the garrison in the O'Connell Street hotels, recalled being 'supplied with the necessities—even luxuries—of life in abundance. We had deep mattresses, thick blankets ... joints of lamb, boxes of chocolates, Turkish or Egyptian cigarettes ... or any other brand we wanted.' While this solved urgent logistical problems it made little military sense. In contrast, the National Army, able to make use of all the barracks in the city and having ample transport and supplies of weaponry, could concentrate on seizing strategically important buildings and engaging in a level of aggressive patrolling that made it impossible for their opponents to liaise effectively, let alone undertake offensive operations.

John Pinkman, the Liverpool-Irish Volunteer who had come straight from prison to join the National Army in Beggarsbush Barracks, found himself deployed in Amiens Street Station, where he slept with his comrades in empty railway carriages. While they were engaged in a duel with enemy snipers outside the station 'a stout, elderly lady' among the onlookers gave him an envelope for Paddy O'Daly, who had moved his command post to the railway station. It contained a map of the area with all the enemy positions marked.[34]

In a separate incident, National Army troops took over my grandmother's flat overlooking Rutland Place, because it gave a clear view of Barry's Hotel, and used it to snipe at the anti-Treaty garrison. The Volunteers on the receiving end returned fire at the ruins of the Orange Hall, assuming that was where the shots were coming from. Every time they did so they exposed themselves to counter-fire.

It was Constance Markievicz, who had joined the Barry's Hotel garrison with a contingent of anti-Treaty Citizen Army members, who realised what was happening. One Citizen Army veteran said: 'She told us not to bother trying to hit the sniper, just fire together on her command at the corner of the window. She said the splinters of glass and brickwork would blind him.' As it happened, the National Army snipers were uninjured, but they knew the game was up and moved on.

During this time my grandmother and her sons sheltered under the bed. The soldiers shared their rations with them to save her hunting for food in the surrounding streets. Civilian support for the Provisional Government, implicit in my grandmother's story and explicit in Pinkman's, seems to bear out John Dorney's contention that co-operation with the National Army was not regarded in the same light as co-operation with the British in the War of Independence.[35]

The soldiers who commandeered my grandmother's flat were by then engaged in mopping-up operations after the anti-Treaty forces had been cleared from the O'Connell Street strongpoints. By a strange symmetry, the lower half of O'Connell Street had been destroyed by British artillery in 1916. They had stopped short of extending their fire beyond Cathedral Street, thanks to the heroism of D. Brophy, traffic manager of Dublin United Tramways Company, who stayed in the company's head office at 9 Upper O'Connell Street throughout the fighting and stopped British gunners from flattening the offices by proving to their commanding officer that there were no snipers inside.

In June 1922 the anti-Treaty forces occupied the DUTC offices and the adjoining buildings, which were mainly hotels, including the Hammam and the Gresham. Together these constituted 'the Block'. The anti-Treaty forces, with limited firepower, could not counter the National Army's armoured cars and artillery deployed in the O'Connell Street area.

Todd Andrews recalls seeing Éamon de Valera (former President of the Republic), Austin Stack (former Minister for Home Affairs), Cathal Brugha (former Minister for Defence) and Oscar Traynor (commander of the Dublin Brigade) 'standing around, apparently without purpose,' in a large room in the Gresham 'otherwise bustling with armed men coming and going. They had been great names to me; now they seemed like wraiths.' There were a number of priests with the garrison of the Block, 'who stayed with us inspired no less, it must be said, by patriotic than by religious motives.' These would say the Rosary at intervals, to which the whole garrison responded, 'crouching under the window sills' to avoid incoming fire. The priest who organised the Rosary was Father Albert Bibby, the Capuchin friar who had been with the Four Courts garrison and somehow managed to bring 'a beautiful statue to Our Lady' into the large room where de Valera was and that served as the general headquarters of the anti-Treaty forces. A lamp was kept 'burning continually' in front of the statue, and Art O'Connor, the former Minister for Agriculture in the second Dáil, designed a scroll bearing the words *A Mhuire Mháthair, guidh orainn* (Mary, Mother of God, pray for us), which was placed overhead. The redoubtable Father Albert pinned a Sacred Heart badge on the coat of Commandant Robert Barton, 'a non-Catholic,' and had him and Oscar Traynor organise a special recitation of the Rosary on Sunday 2 July. 'The response was magnificent,' the friar would recall later.

That day the heavy fighting in the city centre saw local churches closed, and Father Albert organised recitations of the Rosary at various places in the embattled inner city. He stopped the evacuation of Marlborough Hall by Belfast refugees and persuaded families in local tenements to stay in their homes rather than flee the fighting.[36]

In the event it proved a wise decision, because of the short duration of the conflict. The main reason was, of course, the disparity in equipment and organisation between the increasingly confident National Army and its opponents. Todd Andrews was given a personal demonstration of the imbalance in forces the following afternoon when

> a single armoured car approached, opening up this time exclusively on the Tramway Office. I was returning fire rather futilely with my rifle when a hail of bullets caught my firing slit blasting sand from the barricades with great force into my forehead, right eye and cheek. A large bullet splinter penetrated my clothing, lodging in my forearm. I was stunned for a while. My face looked as if a pepper canister had been shaken over it. I could not use my right eye which felt as if it was irreparably damaged. My arm was bleeding a good deal although there was no bone broken nor much pain. I was helped … to a first aid station in the Gresham where an elderly lady doctor bandaged my arm and almost certainly saved my eye, extracting dozens of fragments of sand which had lodged in my eyeball by the unaesthetic method of licking them out.

After that, Andrews found himself in the Mater Hospital, a casualty of war.[37]

While the battle raged in O'Connell Street the men in Hughes's and Moran's Hotels in Lower Gardiner Street awaited their fate. 'We did not possess any fulsome information on the general plan of campaign,' Prendergast said—'little beyond the fact that we were placed there to occupy and defend the allotted premises. Our role, if we were to take our orders literally, was purely defensive. We were not so foolish as to imagine that our defence, or the extent of the resistance that we could put up, would be of a prolonged or even satisfactory nature.'

On Saturday, increasing sniper fire heralded the approaching assault, and the armoured cars that were causing havoc in O'Connell Street turned their attention on the rebel positions here as well. To the frustration of the defenders, these vehicles 'played fun-tricks when [in] the vicinity of the mine' in Talbot Street. Eventually the mine was detonated but it failed to catch its target, an armour-plated lorry full of soldiers. However, the force of the explosion caused considerable damage to the buildings held by anti-Treaty forces and to their barricades. Prendergast declared:

Confound the mine anyway! What a mess it left our position in. With our defences broken down and strewn about the rooms and in the hallways, our positions presented anything but a fortress then. It took time, patience and ingenuity in getting these places into some kind of protective shape.

On Sunday morning the main assault came, and 'in quite an unexpected way.' The National Army used the railway bridge between Amiens Street and Tara Street Stations not just for sniper fire but to bombard the rebel positions below with a trench mortar brought up on an armoured railway engine. Prendergast's garrison could only respond with ineffective rifle fire from loopholes before being forced to fall back. Contact with Moran's Hotel was possible only during lulls in the attack. Unlike the Four Courts, there was to be no costly assault on the rebel positions. As in O'Connell Street, bombardment and heavy fire would be used to break down resistance. Prendergast explained:

We had the uncanny consciousness of being isolated. As things stood ... we were at a decided disadvantage in practically every way, the only thing in our favour being that while we held on the Treaty forces might be delayed in making a grand assault on the garrison occupying portion of O'Connell Street.[38]

He quickly realised that 'we had no means of checking the pace which the Treaty forces imposed.' It was decided that a small rearguard of twelve would hold the position while the rest of the garrison slipped away with as many arms as possible. The rearguard quickly surrendered, as did the Moran's Hotel garrison, although the latter mined the building before evacuation. Members of a Cumann na mBan first-aid post in Moran's headed by Annie M. P. Smithson, the novelist and founder-member of the Irish Nurses' Organisation, remained in the building in case 'there might be someone hurt and perhaps left behind.' When the mine went off 'the walls shook, we were almost covered with dust and whitewash, but we were alive.'

On surrendering, both garrisons found themselves in the custody of former comrades of the 2nd Battalion who now formed the backbone of the National Army's Dublin Guard. They were paraded in front of Paddy O'Daly before being sent to Mountjoy Prison and, as that was already full to capacity, on to Portobello Barracks.

———

By the early hours of Monday the National Army was clearing the outlying enemy outposts that protected the Block in O'Connell Street. It was mainly a search-and-detain operation, as many of the anti-Treaty Volunteers appeared willing to surrender when confronted. In some cases the women seem to have been more determined than the men. After one furious exchange of fire in the Findlater building, on the corner of O'Connell Street and Findlater Place (Cathal Brugha Street), Pinkman's unit heard a woman's voice shouting from the other side of a hole in the wall: 'Stop firing! Stop firing! Don't shoot ... I'm a Red Cross nurse. I'm coming through.' The soldiers ceased firing and

> watched with great curiosity as a woman came crawling through the hole in the wall. When she emerged we could see she was wearing an improvised nurse's uniform with a red cross stitched on the front of her white apron, and as she straightened up we saw she was an attractive, fine looking woman.
> 'Don't touch me,' she said as she came forward. 'I'm a Red Cross nurse.'
> Despite her protest ... one of our lads shrewdly tapped the deep pocket on the right hand side of her apron.

'How dare you!' she shouted at him. 'I'm a woman!' But a soldier 'thrust his hand into her pocket regardless and pulled out a revolver—and we all stood still as we watched a thin wisp of smoke curl out of its barrel.' Pinkman also alleged that members of the main garrison in the Block escaped by using Red Cross armbands. This may well be true, for Traynor used Red Cross vehicles to send weapons out of the city in search of the hoped-for relief column. Ernie O'Malley, one of the recipients, said acerbically: 'The Red Cross, it seemed, could be pressed into IRA service when needed. Rifles were rifles; all thought it legitimate for us to abuse the Red Cross, but for no one else.'[39]

By the evening of Monday 2 July, Traynor had given up hope of reinforcements arriving from the provinces to swing the battle in his favour. The only response had been a column of a little over a hundred men from South Tipperary who made it as far as Blessington, Co. Wicklow, where they met elements of the anti-Treaty IRA from south Dublin, including Ernie O'Malley and Seán Lemass, who had escaped custody after the Four Courts surrender and arrived in a commandeered car. Some Co. Kildare Volunteers also arrived, bringing the total to about three hundred.

The National Army had created a cordon around Dublin by seizing all the canal and river crossings. O'Malley proposed that they retake bridges across the Grand Canal and then attack the College of Science in Upper Merrion Street, where the Provisional Government had moved, rather than try to link up with Traynor. 'That seemed to me more important than holding a street on the north side of the city,' he said dismissively of the Dublin OC's strategy. Then word arrived from the latter that he had abandoned O'Connell Street, leaving a rearguard under Cathal Brugha while the rest of the garrison made good its escape. This made any advance on Dublin difficult, with the National Army forces free to deal with such a small force.

Any doubts about what to do next were quickly resolved when the Blessington column heard that National Army units were converging on it from Dublin and the Curragh. The only attempt to relieve Dublin came to a hasty end as the column elements headed for their various home areas.

————

Traynor had had little option but to evacuate O'Connell Street, although a rearguard under Cathal Brugha managed to drag the defence of the Block into Tuesday evening, and from 9 p.m. onwards an 18-pounder joined the attack in support of the armoured cars and machine-gun crews. In spite of the danger, hundreds of onlookers came to watch the final hours of the siege, and several were injured by sniper fire. In the side streets, schoolboys played war games between 'Republicans and Staters'. Traynor sent word back to Brugha to surrender, but he refused. It was only at 6 p.m. on Wednesday 5 July, when the last intact building, the Granville Hotel, which had been used as a hospital, caught fire, that Brugha agreed to surrender.

As the garrison marched out, several members saw him make his last confession to a Capuchin friar. Only one member of the garrison remained behind with him, one of the Cumann na mBan nurses, Linda Kearns. She knew he had no intention of surrendering and asked him why he was determined to go to his death. According to Kearns, he said that if his death 'put a stop to the Civil War it would be a death worth while.' When they emerged from the rear of the building into Thomas's Lane, where the rest of the garrison had surrendered earlier, he drew two pistols and advanced on the National Army positions, firing and shouting 'No surrender!' The irony of his war cry would have been lost on Brugha.

Kearns thinks that the soldiers returning his fire deliberately aimed low. He was hit just once in the leg, and a bullet severed the femoral artery. Kearns, who staunched the wound with her hands, believed his death was primarily due to the delays in his treatment at the Mater Hospital.[40] He was quickly transformed into a republican martyr, and the inquest into his death had to be delayed until a sculptor had made a death mask. Mourners at the funeral included the Lord Mayor, Laurence O'Neill, as well as many anti-Treaty TDS. The ITGWU pipe band and a Cumann na mBan contingent swelled the funeral procession to Glasnevin, but the public attendance was relatively small compared with the thousands who would turn out for the funerals of Arthur Griffith and Michael Collins a month later.

Resistance elsewhere in the city faded away, with posts such as York Street, the centre of the anti-Treaty forces on the south side, being evacuated before they came under a sustained siege. The appetite for holding fixed positions had evaporated.

————

The practice of departing garrisons leaving mines or booby traps in evacuated buildings not only added to the claims on the ratepayers—in the case of Moran's Hotel £20,000—but was potentially ruinous to the owners. The owner of Barry's Hotel, Annie Farrington, a republican who had housed men on the run during the War of Independence at the Crown Hotel in O'Connell Street, was told to leave the war-ravaged building with the remnants of her staff because of the mines under the front door and under the roof. The Volunteers also left 'guns sticking out the window' to disguise the retreat.

> However, the three of us stayed and I asked the man who was preparing the mines to cut the wires if that was humanly possible, but that if he had to do his duty, he could do it, but that we were staying. We knelt down to pray and I believe I said prayers that were never heard before or since. The man at the mines touched me on the shoulder and said, 'It is all right, Miss, I have detached them.' Before they left, they went very hard on us to throw in our lot with them and take our chance with the other women of Cumann na mBan who were with them. I said 'If the house is going up I will go up with it. We have nowhere else to go.'

By contrast with the Moran's Hotel claim of £20,000, her claim for damage, caused mainly by the garrison boring holes between rooms and using furniture for barricades, was only £800. Nor were her troubles over.

> The night after the garrison left a couple of fellows, probably thinking there was nobody in the house broke in to loot. Miss Keogh, myself and the cook who had returned, had brought our beds downstairs to the dining room where there was a lift to the kitchen. We heard a noise and I went to the lift where we distinctly heard voices. We were afraid to go down so we called William [the porter] and Miss Keogh opened the front door and asked a passerby for help … Four or five Free State soldiers came with a machine gun. Some of them went down the kitchen stairs and called upon the intruders to come out. Instead they retreated to the scullery under the area steps. The soldier with the machine gun took up his position on the steps of the other house and fired. We heard a most awful scream and the soldiers went into the scullery and brought out the three looters. One of them was wounded by a bullet which entered through the mouth into the brain.

He was brought to the Mater Hospital, where he died almost immediately. There was relatively little looting by civilians during the fighting in Dublin compared with 1916, but anti-Treaty garrisons seem to have routinely 'requisitioned' goods from premises being occupied. So many clothes were removed from Hickey's and Boyer's drapery shops in North Earl Street that the Volunteers who removed them had to follow the vehicles they had used on foot, as there was no room left inside.

Any motor transport was at risk of seizure, the bigger the vehicle the better. A couple of days after their departure former members of the Republican garrison at Barry's Hotel returned with a van to retrieve some of the 'large quantity of food' they had left behind. If the anti-Treaty forces treated their supporters in this way it was hardly surprising that support was waning fast among the public at large.

As a result of her experiences Annie Farrington contracted 'neurotic rheumatism' (fibromyalgia) and had to go to England twice for treatment. She said later that her compensation 'barely covered what the contractor charged me. There was so much work of this kind to be done that the contractors were able to charge whatever they liked.' To make ends meet she began taking guests before the glass was put in the windows. 'I kept the shutters shut.'[41]

———

A Republican businessman who had to make hard decisions that week was Joseph Stanley. On 28 June 1922, the day the National Army attacked the Four Courts, Stanley resigned from H Company, 1st Battalion, the same battalion to which Seán Prendergast belonged. Stanley was a long-standing IRB member and a printer who had produced many mosquito publications during the First World War. He would probably have been commissioned to print the Proclamation of the Irish Republic in 1916, but his presses had been seized by the military authorities in the week before the Rising. Instead he sent what type he had left to James Connolly in Liberty Hall to help the ITGWU printers set the text of the Proclamation.

During the fighting Stanley regularly braved the risks inherent in passing through the British lines to meet Patrick Pearse in the GPO and printed the two war bulletins from hastily scribbled notes given to him by Pearse to keep the public abreast of events. After being interned in Fron Goch in Wales, Stanley became a close friend of Michael Collins. He was typical of the Sinn Féin activists who would develop the alternative state. He was a judge in the Dáil courts and a member of Drogheda Corporation and during the War of Independence branched out from publishing into cinemas. His picture houses showed the film promoting the Dáil Éireann loan. But by the time the Four Courts were attacked Stanley was thirty-two, was married and had four young children, and 'the necessities of life had become his priority. Besides, like many Volunteers, he had no appetite for fighting his fellow countrymen whose opinions may have happened to differ from his.'

He had also incurred significant business losses as a result of activities on behalf of the Irish Republic, which he estimated at £15,000. While the Criminal and Malicious Injuries (Amendment) Act would be introduced by the new Free State to provide reparation, compensation was backdated only to 21 January 1919, the day Dáil Éireann assembled for the first time. Unfortunately, Stanley's losses arose primarily from the period between the Proclamation in 1916 and the assembly of the first Dáil, including the loss of valuable printing equipment used for printing early editions of the Irish Volunteer bulletin, *An tÓglach*. Now any hope of recouping losses lay in personal friendships with members of the new government, such as W. T. Cosgrave and Éamonn Duggan, Minister for Home Affairs. But they were of little help. Stanley moved to London and worked as a sub-editor on the *Daily Mail*, a newspaper vilified by Republican propagandists such as himself for its coverage of Ireland during the War of Independence. He was one of the first of many Republicans to seek their fortunes abroad from 1922 onwards. In time he would save enough to return to Ireland and rebuild his fortune, but it would be in cinemas and film distribution rather than in publishing.[42]

———

There were many post-mortems on the IRA strategy in Dublin. Ernie O'Malley believed it had been a mistake to concentrate their strength in a few positions when the main purpose had been to provoke an attack by the Provisional Government or, better still, the British. This meant there were not enough Volunteers outside to undertake the other half of the strategy of containing the National Army. He maintained that

> we had enough men to isolate certain barracks and to attack others. Positions held by skeleton forces could have induced Staters to attack them. By pinning them to the ground, by carrying out the original plan, which would have meant much hard fighting, we could have restricted enemy movement, held Dublin until relieved, and have stimulated the fighting spirit in our men throughout the country. At any rate we should have been able to hold all approaches to the Four Courts until help arrived.

The aim of Collins and Mulcahy was to encourage the British to evacuate the 26 Counties as quickly as possible while maintaining IRA unity. The Northern offensive was part of this strategy, although it was also driven by genuine concern about the plight of Northern nationalists. Apart from being a dismal military failure, the offensive had the effect of drawing British forces back into the border area in strength. Meanwhile the Colonial Secretary, Churchill, reduced the rate of evacuation of British forces from the Free State to one battalion every three weeks and opposed supplying any further arms to the pro-Treaty forces until they showed a willingness to confront the Four Courts militants.

The Collins-de Valera election pact further fuelled the fears of Churchill and Chamberlain, the most hawkish members of the British cabinet, that a rapprochement between the Sinn Féin and IRA factions could see them seek to renegotiate the Treaty. Their hand was strengthened by growing support for drastic action among Conservative backbenchers. As we have seen, the assassination of Sir Henry Wilson brought the prospect of British military intervention perilously close. The nether stones of militancy turned by men such as O'Malley in the Four Courts and Churchill in London left the National Army commanders with no room to manoeuvre. Even after the attack on the Four Courts began on 28 June, Churchill was still pressing cabinet colleagues for the use of British troops and the Royal Air Force to force a quick decision. It took Lloyd George and Nevil Macready to contain the risk of a new Anglo-Irish war displacing an Irish civil war.[43]

Ernie O'Malley's proposed lunge for the College of Science to capture the Provisional Government and decapitate the Free State would have been an audacious riposte to the fall of Dublin and certainly less fatalistic than the alternative strategy of allowing the pace to be set by the enemy. However, like other IRA commanders, O'Malley chose to ignore the fact that, however successful his gambit might have been, it would not immobilise the Free State war machine, for the National Army leadership was now ensconced in Portobello Barracks in Rathmines, not in the College of Science.

Chapter 4 ∽

'THE GIRLS COME FROM IRELAND TO ENGLAND TO HIDE THEIR SHAME'

On 29 June 1922 Maud Gonne MacBride arrived in Dublin from Paris. Her son, Seán, was a member of the Four Courts garrison, and by 2 July she had gathered together a group of old comrades in the Mansion House in a renewed effort to bring about a peace agreement. Their names read like a roll of honour from the women's movement: they included Meg Connery, who had bearded Edward Carson and the future Tory leader Andrew Bonar Law on the steps of Lord Iveagh's house in 1913 to demand votes for women; the veteran suffragist and Sinn Féin councillor Hanna Sheehy Skeffington; Charlotte Despard, the most committed socialist in the group, whose activities reporting on British outrages in Ireland had acutely embarrassed her brother, the former Lord Lieutenant, Field-Marshal Sir John French; Agnes O'Farrelly, a founder-member of the Gaelic League and Cumann na mBan; Rosamund Jacob, who had helped secure a commitment at the Sinn Féin ard-fheis in 1917 that the party would support votes for women; and Louie Bennett, general secretary of the Irish Women Workers' Union. They were given the use of the Mansion House by the Lord Mayor, Laurence O'Neill, who also provided a Fire Brigade ambulance to allow them to traverse the city in relative safety and talk to the leading combatants.

Bennett would later recall how they met the leaders of the Free State in what was now Government Buildings. 'Collins was excited, obviously excited. Griffith was utterly depressed, an old, broken man. Cosgrave was outwardly unmoved, frigidly cold.' Despite their unprepossessing demeanour, the three agreed to meet representatives of the other side. The women then proceeded in the Fire Brigade ambulance to the parcels office of the Dublin United Tramways Company in O'Connell Street to make contact with the Anti-Treaty forces. Bennett described how

> we went into some sort of dark room, with sacks all around it. I sat on a sack of flour or something. We couldn't see any of the Republicans, but eventually someone—a General-somebody-or-other … had a long talk with Mrs. Sheehy Skeffington. But they would not negotiate any terms. They said they were into it now, and there was no way out but to fight it out.

Several of these women were opposed to the Treaty and would be attacked in the national press as unreasonable and unreasoning neurotics by their opponents, but at this stage in the conflict they were certainly seeking an end to the fighting.[1] By contrast, some of the most virulent opponents of the Treaty in the city were to be found among the Catholic clergy. On 21 July, Archbishop Byrne received a letter from W. T. Cosgrave complaining about a number of priests who had 'used their sacred position as a shelter for treasonable acts.' Cosgrave cited Father Albert Bibby and Father Dominic O'Connor of the Capuchins, who had both been involved in the Gaelic revival before administering to the spiritual needs of Republican prisoners from 1916 onwards. Father Albert had heard the confessions of many prisoners after the 1916 Rising, and Father O'Connor had been Terence MacSwiney's chaplain when he died on hunger strike in Brixton Prison in London. Cosgrave also singled out a member of the secular clergy, Father John Costello, for special mention. On 8 July, Cosgrave said the priest had visited a National Army post at the Lever Brothers premises in Parliament Street and called on them to lay down their arms. When they failed to respond he denounced them as murderers and 'Green Black and Tans'.[2]

Such denunciations did nothing to dampen the general rush to the colours when the Provisional Government issued a 'call to arms' on 12 July. The following day a public notice appeared in the national newspapers under the heading *Óglaigh na hÉireann*.

> Men of Dublin City and North County, Rathmines & Pembroke, who have handed in their names for Service in the National Reserve and who have not yet been called up, will present themselves at the City Hall, on Friday, 14th inst., between 10 a.m. and 2 p.m. or 4 p.m. and 8 p.m.
>
> C. Saurin, Captain, Adjutant, 1st Dublin Brigade.[3]

Crowds of men turned up, and by the end of the day many were ensconced in Wellington Barracks (Griffith Barracks) on the South Circular Road, where IRA prisoners were being held. Members of the 2nd Battalion were prominent among the National Army intake, and some had been inducted before the public notices had been issued. It was the battalion with which Collins and his old Squad cronies had the strongest personal links.

The call for new recruits probably went out through the IRB network as well as the pro-Treaty IRA recruiting offices. Men were signing up even as a new War Council was established by Collins, consisting of Richard Mulcahy, Eoin O'Duffy and himself, all members of the pro-Treaty core of the IRB. In February 1922 the IRB's Supreme Council had declared itself to be 'the sole government of the Irish Republic, until Ireland's complete independence is achieved, and a permanent Republican Government is established.' The decision to expand the National Army was probably known among many pro-Treaty Volunteers and IRB members on the streets of Dublin before the cabinet, which was presented with a *fait accompli*.[4]

Meanwhile, as captured anti-Treaty Republicans were discovering, their former comrades in arms showed even less concern for prisoners than their British predecessors. And, as the convening of the new Dáil had been deferred because of the disturbed state of the country, there were few forums where public concerns about the treatment of prisoners could be raised. One of them was Dublin Corporation. Hanna Sheehy Skeffington proposed that 'prisoners taken recently in action be treated while in captivity as prisoners of war.' She recruited the memory of past republican martyrs to her cause, pointing out that this was 'the principle to uphold which Thomas Ashe, Terence MacSwiney and many brave Irishmen have sacrificed their lives.' Her motion was seconded by the Lord Mayor, Laurence O'Neill, and passed by 23 votes to 15.

O'Neill's support was significant. He had been elected as an independent deputy to the new Dáil and was a canny political survivor, with friends on both sides of the Republican divide, as he had shown when seeing off the challenge for the mayoralty from Seán Woods and some of the pro-Treaty Sinn Féin elements on the city council. (See chapter 2.) On this occasion it was a combination of some pro-Government Sinn Féin councillors, such as Margaret McGarry, along with members of the Municipal Reform Association, who opposed treating the captured Republicans as prisoners of war. However, the majority of Sinn Féin councillors, including some prominent supporters of the Treaty, such as Jennie Wyse Power, supported the demand, as did councillors from both wings of the labour movement.[5]

Over the coming months, as the number of prisoners grew, so did the controversy over how they should be treated, providing one of the few issues on which Republicans opposed to the Treaty were able to mobilise public support. As early as 24 July, Count George Plunkett, father of the executed Easter Week leader Joseph Plunkett, was writing to the Catholic Archbishop, Dr Byrne, to complain about conditions in which prisoners, who would soon include two of his sons, were being kept. Like Cosgrave, he singled out priests who adopted partisan positions, except in this instance it was for being supporters of the Free State. He was particularly exercised about prison chaplains who were giving absolution and the sacraments only to prisoners who undertook never to take up arms again against the Provisional Government. This was a significant grievance in a country where people took religious observances seriously. Art O'Connor, a Republican prisoner, also wrote to Archbishop Byrne on the issue.

> We are soldiers of the Irish Republic [and] in common with hundreds of thousands of Irish people and many of the people's elected representatives, we deny the authority of the Provisional Government, and we respectfully submit that if a priest holds an opposite view in this matter he is not entitled to force his view as an article of the church's teaching.[6]

———

Now that the battles for the Four Courts and O'Connell Street were over, Dubliners, who had gathered in great numbers to watch the fighting, and not always from a safe distance, had to seek more conventional forms of entertainment. The Baldoyle races reported record crowds, and shoppers were treated to a blitz of summer sales by Switzer's and Roberts' in Grafton Street, McBirney's on Aston Quay and Edward Lee's chain of shops, from Mary Street to Bray. Lee's offered a discount of 20 per cent on all purchases over 5d. But some of the biggest discounts were in Clery's, where old stock was being cleared from the temporary shop in Abbey Street where it had been operating since 1916 before moving back into its old premises in O'Connell Street, which had been completely rebuilt.

Hotels that had been spared the destruction visited on Moran's, Hughes's, Barry's, the Hammam, Edinburgh, Granville, Holyhead and Gresham also took advantage of the restoration of order to exploit the misfortunes of their competitors with advertising campaigns aimed at visitors to the city. The Shelbourne even received an unsolicited endorsement from an unidentified IRA officer. Right Rev. P. J. O'Reilly, a native of Kells, Coadjutor Bishop of Peoria, Illinois, and Titular Bishop of Lebedos in Syria, had decided to resign and return to Ireland because of 'indifferent health and increasing years' and so that he could 'enjoy the long sought for fruits of peace and prosperity,' only to arrive at the Hammam Hotel as it became the epicentre of the Civil War. His efforts at mediation having failed, he told an *Irish Independent* reporter that 'the leader of the Irregulars' had advised him he would be better off in the Shelbourne. Dr O'Reilly, who was over seventy, bewailed the fact that his 'fondly cherished belief and earnest hopes' for Ireland had been shattered 'in such a cruel and unexpected manner as to leave upon his memory and his already enfeebled health ... a melancholy mark that can never be effaced.'

Some 280 workers employed in O'Connell Street hotels were even more upset as they found themselves out of work as a result of the fighting. The Society of St Vincent de Paul launched a distress fund to meet the crisis. The first donation of £250 came from Archbishop Byrne, followed by the nationalist historian Alice Stopford Green with £50 and Lady Fitzgerald Arnott with another £50.

Nor did charity end at home. Theatre life in the city resumed rapidly once the fighting subsided, and on 30 July an 'operatic concert' was held at the Theatre Royal in aid of the Belfast refugees, 'with selections from best operas in English and Italian.' Extracts were performed from *Carmen, Aïda, Cavalleria Rusticana, La Sonnambula* and *Pagliacci.* The reviews were kind rather than enthusiastic.[7]

——

The anti-Treaty IRA was so disorganised in Dublin after its defeat by the National Army in the conventional fighting that on 8 July a situation report recommended that men dump their arms, and quite a number of Volunteers left the city to link up with units in areas still under Republican control. It took several weeks for the IRA to reorganise in the city. Meanwhile Emmet Dalton, who had directed the attack on the Four Courts, discussed with the Irish Federation of Discharged and Demobilised Sailors and Soldiers the possibility of recruiting former British soldiers to the National Army. This was one of a number of ex-servicemen's groups that eschewed politics but lobbied the Irish and British governments on behalf of its members. With unemployment rising, they saw renewed job opportunities for members in their old line of work. While no formal agreements were made, Dalton appears to have made it clear that ex-servicemen were now welcome in the ranks of the National Army, which would no longer restrict itself to recruiting pre-Truce IRA Volunteers.[8] Ex-servicemen would come to constitute half the National Army's Civil War strength. By early August the Anti-Treaty IRA in the city was ready to assume offensive operations. The first major operation, the attempted destruction of the city's bridges on Saturday 5 August, backfired badly. Some senior officers in the city questioned the wisdom of the attack, whose strategic aim was unclear, but were overruled by GHQ. Liam Clarke, one of the headquarters officers involved, was taken prisoner in Rathfarnham on the night before the operation was due to take place with a map showing all the bridges to be destroyed. The officers in charge of the operation were alerted, 'but they insisted on carrying on and, when the various companies arrived at the scenes of action the Free State soldiers were waiting for them.'

Fatalism was becoming the dominant mood. Men such as Laurence Nugent felt that 'we were defending a principle ... We were at the time fighting physically a losing battle, but we were satisfied we were doing the right thing for Ireland.'[9]

In the south county, however, the IRA remained militarily more active. On 18 August 1922 it turned its attention to an old adversary, Sir Henry Robinson, former

Vice-President of the Local Government Board. His home at Kerrymount, near Ballybrack, was raided for arms. Robinson certainly confirmed that he possessed them by attempting to fight off the raiders, leading to a three-hour gun battle. 'One should give the devil his due,' Robinson said afterwards,

> and I am bound to say that, after my son and I ceased firing and surrendered to the Irregulars to save the house being burned over our heads, upon the undertaking given us by them that they would do no violence to person or property, they honourably kept their word, and so far from smashing things they seemed anxious in making their search for arms, binoculars, and other things they wanted to avoid doing damage.
>
> My grievance is that the two men who broke into the house first to reconnoitre opened fire upon us without a word of warning or explanation, and this, I think, gives me reasonable ground for complaint.[10]

He would certainly have grounds for complaint about his subsequent treatment by both the British and Irish governments. On the very day of the attack his former political master Lloyd George was telling a meeting in Leeds that he had brought peace to Ireland. As we have seen (chapter 2), Robinson had agreed to stay on beyond his retirement date in March 1922 to facilitate a smooth transition of the Local Government Board apparatus to his Free State successor, W. T. Cosgrave. He now appealed to Cosgrave for protection. On the day after the attack Cosgrave

> told me he was terribly pressed for men and the very utmost he could do for me was to give me protection for three days to enable me to get my furniture removed and stored in Dublin. This I did and I managed to get safely across to England with my wife and family.

It would be May 1923 before he was advised that it was safe to return, and he sold the house at considerable loss. A native Dubliner, he had to cash in a quarter of the £4,000 lump sum on his pension to help meet the costs of transferring his family to England. It was only in February 1927 that he received £250 as an advance on his claim for £1,000. He died in October that year, and it was not until 1928 that a further £150 was paid in final settlement to his estate.[11]

Robinson was widely respected for his work as head of the Local Government Board, for his wry humour and the courage he showed in continuing his duties through the years after 1916. His recollection of an incident he had witnessed a few days before his home was attacked was typically humorous and insightful. There was

> a very hot engagement with a large number of men on both sides near where I lived, and when it was over there was a small crowd of local sympathisers

standing around a furiously indignant Free State soldier who declared that one of the Irregulars, whom he knew well, during the engagement had deliberately taken aim and fired at him. Boiling with rage, he declared that two could play at that game and the next time he found himself face to face with Mr. Murphy in a battle that gentleman had better look out for himself as he would put daylight into him as sure as eggs were eggs. This feeling of sparing the foe died out much more rapidly with the Irregulars than with the Free State troops, and ambushes were later marked by real enmity and a genuine desire to kill.[12]

If Joseph Brennan demonstrated the flexibility of the younger generation of senior civil servant who could identify with the new state (see chapter 1), Robinson represented the old guard. He would fulminate in exile that

> I had never at any time thought or known that the Government contemplated a different sort of peace, namely the surrender to the forces of disorder and the announcement, coming as it did, just when the Rebels were believed to be on the point of collapse owing to lack of ammunition, money and supplies, came to me like a Bolt from the Blue, for I knew how my service to the British in Ireland was regarded by the rebels.[13]

Because Brennan had more access to British thinking in Dublin Castle than his senior contemporary had, ensconced in the Custom House, it was much easier for him to anticipate and accommodate to the changed circumstances.

Other members of the old Unionist rearguard to suffer under the new dispensation included near neighbours of Robinson, James Dudley Croftwell Murray and Sir Horace Plunkett. It would be hard to imagine two men more different in their outlook or circumstances. Murray was a former secretary of the Dublin Unionist Association who had been an outspoken critic of militant nationalism and would have regarded Plunkett's politics as dangerously liberal. With the break-up of the association, Murray decided to breed cattle and rented a farm at Shankill, Co. Dublin. Unfortunately it was strategically positioned, overlooking National Army posts in Bray and Enniskerry. Despite his political experience, or perhaps because of it, Murray lacked the diplomatic skill needed for dealing with local IRA or National Army units. During the Truce period he complained of 'constant trouble, threats and attempted robbery' by 'Sinn Féiners.' The outbreak of fighting in Dublin bought him some respite. 'I kept things fairly right until October 9th, 1922,' he said, 'when about 30 riflemen in full Free State uniform attacked.' It appeared that they wanted to burn the house down so that it could not be used by the enemy, but Murray's response was the same as Robinson's, and he opened fire on the would-be intruders until they beat a retreat.

The following day the house was 'completely robbed' while Murray was out and, assuming it was the work of the National Army, he went to Portobello Barracks to demand action. He was told that no protection was available, while he found that local people were 'afraid to have anything to do with me.' In a letter to the Irish Grants Committee in London he wrote that

> I gave up the land as it was useless trying to do business under such conditions. I have had to watch cattle all night with a loaded gun ... Some fowl were battered to pieces with sticks and left there. My two dogs were killed, one by a bullet meant for me. The owner of the house had asked me as a favour to leave it before it was levelled, which I did.

When he asked why he was being driven out, Murray was told it was because 'I was and always had been a British spy.' He sought £1,000 in compensation for loss of livelihood, accommodation and capital. His case was supported by the Southern Irish Loyalists' Relief Association and Sir David Harrel KCB, a former Commissioner of the DMP and Under-Secretary for Ireland. He was given £100 as a down payment. He spent the next six years living in hotels and rented rooms in Dublin awaiting the final resolution of his claim. His case was still being processed in April 1929 when the Relief Association notified the Irish Grants Committee that Murray had died on 20 December 1927, 'of pneumonia and starvation.' A further £200 was awarded to his estate.[14]

Compared with Murray, or even Robinson, Sir Horace Plunkett escaped relatively lightly. It helped that he was popular locally. During the War of Independence, IRA Volunteers had obligingly dug up the road on the Bray side of his house, Kilteragh, so that he would not be inconvenienced on his daily journey to the offices of the Irish Agricultural Organisation Society in the city. On the night of 29 January 1923, however, Kilteragh was burnt down, along with nine other large houses belonging to supporters of the Free State government in the area.

Plunkett, the founder of the Irish co-operative movement, was by then a Free State senator and, in the words of Poblacht na hÉireann, an 'Imperialist and Freemason. Denounced frequently by the late Mr. Arthur Griffith as a British spy.' It reminded readers that Plunkett had made such a 'bitter attack on Catholicism' in his book Ireland in the New Century twenty years earlier that it had required a rebuttal from Monsignor Michael O'Riordan, the late rector of the Irish College in Rome. The denunciation probably made little impact on Plunkett, who was on a visit to the United States at the time, researching the latest advances in agricultural science, or for that matter on the local IRA commander charged with destroying his house, George Gilmore. Gilmore was a Protestant socialist republican who respected Plunkett's pioneering work for the co-operative movement; however, he had little choice as a member of the IRA but to obey the order, however wrong-headed he might have thought it. Ironically, the reason for the destruction of Plunkett's house was that it had been a safe IRA refuge in the fight against the British, and there were fears that Free State forces might occupy it as a strongpoint while he was in America.[15]

Now quite elderly and, like Robinson and Murray, in failing health, Plunkett decided to move to England. He continued to campaign for the future of his beloved co-operative movement, which was now threatened not alone by the disruption of civil war but by partition. The annual subsidies to the IAOS by the British exchequer ceased in 1922 and were not resumed by the Free State government until 1926. An Ulster Agricultural Organisation Society was established to apply for grants from the new Northern Ireland government, but these proved short-lived and were withdrawn in 1924, on the grounds that the organisational work could be done directly by the Ministry of Agriculture, inevitably leading to rumours that the Unionist government wanted to use grants to reward supporters rather than distribute them through an autonomous non-sectarian organisation.

Meanwhile Plunkett continued his other abiding passion of establishing a centrist reform party in Irish politics. This was as doomed a project as his attempt to promote his own brand of liberal unionism in south Co. Dublin in the early 1900s. He was well aware of the quixotic nature of his politics and compared himself to a dog on a tennis court chasing balls and barking at the players who dominated the tribal politics of the day.

Even in death his opponents could not resist denigrating him. The *Catholic Bulletin* described him as 'this wealthy person Plunkett,' who stood condemned by his own 'gratuitous folly and garrulity.' In the event, many of his ideas stood the test of time better than those of his critics.[16]

——

The fate of Robinson, Murray and Plunkett and the futility of Republican radicals such as George Gilmore and Liam O'Flaherty were testimony to the resilience of conservative Catholic Ireland, now coming into its own. The Catholic Church was not only the largest religious denomination in the city but the greatest provider of social services, filling a gap left by the retreat of the British state on the one hand and the inadequate resources of the new Irish state on the other. Archbishop Byrne has been described as Dublin's 'forgotten Archbishop', wedged between his predecessor, William Walsh, and his successor, John Charles McQuaid, who were major architects of modern Ireland, but his very mediocrity serves to underline the momentum of the new dispensation.

A good indicator of the Church's role is provided by the reports of the Society of St Vincent de Paul for the Back Lane Shelter for Homeless Catholic Men. Founded by Archbishop Walsh in 1912, it had admitted 17,297 men in its first year, which surged to 33,462 in 1913, the year of the Lockout. There was a similar rise in the number of free meals provided, from 18,768 in 1912 to 37,271 in 1913. The Great War brought a significant degree of economic and social stability to the city's economy, demonstrated by average admissions of 14,459 between 1915 and 1919, with the number of free meals averaging 20,719. However, in 1920 the number of admissions rose to 16,768 and in 1921 to 30,361. There were 26,801 free meals in 1920 and 47,607 in 1921, far more than during the Lockout.

The end of the Civil War brought no end to the misery of this growing community of homeless, workless men. In 1923, 32,196 were admitted to accommodation and 60,150 meals were provided. By 1925 there were 35,022 admissions and 70,094 meals were provided.[17]

Every applicant was examined about the cause of his unemployment and particularly to establish if it was due to 'intemperance'. As in the Lockout, Rosary beads, medals, scapulars and prayer books were distributed along with clothing and boots. For instance, in 1923 there were 649 scapulars, 1,305 Rosary beads and 2,210 religious medals distributed with 815 items of clothing. In fairness to the committee it must be acknowledged that it would have distributed more clothing if it had been available, and it appealed for 'cast-off clothing, boots and shirts,' because the lack of them often prevented men from obtaining employment. The shelter also provided fares to Britain or to their native town or village for men who wished to leave the city.

Nevertheless, the primary emphasis of St Vincent de Paul activity was on implanting social discipline through religious instruction. 'A suitable meditation is read each evening ... followed by the Rosary and Evening Prayers, which are offered up for the benefactors to the Shelter and the men.' The annual reports, which are injunctions to action rather than mere commentaries, reminded members that

> the poor man who finds himself as an outcast without friends or a home, on whom the adversity of a merciless world has heavily fallen, and who in his dire circumstances has neglected the practice of his religious duties ... is reminded of the consolations Holy Church brings to the afflicted. It is within the knowledge of the Committee that many men received into the Shelter have left it with high hope and better fortified to face the trials of the world.[18]

It was in this context that the cult of Matt Talbot would become important after his death in 1925. Talbot was the archetypal unskilled worker. Born in the north inner city, in 1856 he left school at the age of twelve to become a messenger for a wine merchant and then a labourer with the Port and Docks Board. This was one of the best employments for unskilled workers in the city, and he secured it—as so many jobs were secured in Dublin—by virtue of his father already being employed in the bonded stores. His mother had been a domestic servant before marrying and worked thereafter as a charwoman. The bonded stores work, with its easy access to alcohol, proved the downfall of every male member of the family except Talbot's eldest brother, who was a clerk with the board and a teetotaller. Matt, who was a regular 'mitcher' from school, lacked the education to become a clerk; instead he 'swiftly became a heavy and obsessive drinker,' whose

> alcoholism consumed all his leisure and nearly all his wages; uninterested in any pursuit but drink, when money ran out he thieved, pawned clothing, or held horses for hours for a few pence; he shared a family propensity towards obstreperous pugnacity when intoxicated. Leaving his regular employment on his father's retirement in 1882, he worked some twenty years at casual labour, usually as a hod carrier with building contractors, or as a docker.[19]

His desperate need for drink famously led him on one occasion to rob a blind street musician of his violin, and yet, as his most recent biographer, Lawrence William White, recounts, Talbot's reformation was

> sudden, lasting, and absolute. On a Saturday evening in 1884, penniless and with credit exhausted, after loitering for hours outside a pub in vain expectation of being treated to drink, he walked to Holy Cross College, Clonliffe Road, where he consulted a priest, and took a three-month pledge of total abstinence.[20]

Religious devotion was central to Talbot's battle with alcoholism. One form of addiction was displaced by another, with a regime of prayer and physical mortification leading to physical renewal and spiritual ecstasy. When Talbot died, attendants at Jervis Street Hospital found a metal chain wound about his torso and knotted cords on his arms and below the knees, 'likely to cause pain when kneeling.' Regarded as a religious crank when alive, he was rapidly adopted by the Church as a role model that every Catholic working man should aspire to. A pamphlet on his life written by Joseph Glynn, president of the Society of St Vincent de Paul, and financed by a wine merchant sold 120,000 copies in three months.

The campaign for his beatification was a natural extension of the enthusiastic way in which the clergy promoted Talbot's devotion to education and self-improvement through his reading of devotional literature, his seeking after spiritual direction from priests, including Dr Michael Hickey, professor of philosophy at Holy Cross College, and his membership of the Pioneer Total Abstinence Association, the Third Order of St Francis and various sodalities and confraternities.

'A hard and tenacious worker, even in his drinking days, he was usually put first by the foreman to set the pace.' He joined Jim Larkin's new Irish Transport and General Workers' Union in 1911, and during the 1913 Lockout he would not pass pickets, though he did not join them either. He handed a portion of his strike pay to fellow-strikers with families. Even his diet, consisting largely of 'dry bread and tea, or a cold mixture of tea and cocoa,' with 'meat, fish, or eggs limited to small portions once or twice a week,' could be extolled as appropriate for the low-paid.[21]

An even more important constituency for the Catholic Church than the working man was the family, and especially children. Independence came just as the British state was about to engage in major reforms dealing with children at risk. The debate in Britain on the suitability of large institutions caring for children would lead to the abolition of industrial schools by 1933. The debate was largely ignored in Ireland, even though as early as 1913 an interdepartmental committee on reformatories and industrial schools had expressed concern at the lack of state supervision for these state-funded institutions. Far from seeking to deinstitutionalise care and make it more child-centred, the Catholic hierarchy succeeded in ending the system of fostering out, preferring to see youngsters consigned to industrial schools so as to protect them from exposure to Protestant proselytisers or other undesirable elements.

The economic imperatives of a new state desperate to balance its books after the massive damage and debts incurred in the Civil War, and religious orders anxious to generate funds to finance the Church's social control model, found the capitation system for industrial schools an attractive model. The capitation system was abolished in Britain in 1919 in favour of annual budgets to stop those running industrial schools from cramming them beyond their capacity to care properly for their charges, but this did not happen in Ireland until 1984.[22]

All the industrial schools in the Free State were run by Catholic religious orders, the last Protestant-controlled school having closed in 1917. They were excluded from supervision by the state's industrial inspectorate, as were the Magdalene laundries. The vast majority of children referred to such schools were victims of poverty. Only 11 per cent of boys and 1 per cent of girls had committed criminal offences, of which the most serious was housebreaking. The rest were invariably of a petty nature, such as stealing food or clothes, begging, or mitching from school. This last behaviour accounted for 10 per cent of all juvenile offences.[23]

Police magistrates preferred to use bail and the Probation Act to committing youngsters to incarceration; nevertheless the very fact of children being processed through the courts reinforced the image of child criminality. The possibility of being liable for the loss of £5 or £10 in forfeited bail was a powerful incentive for even the least responsible parent to keep children out of trouble; yet the great majority of children committed to custody (80 per cent of girls and 90 per cent of boys) were incarcerated in these institutions for 'lack of guardianship'.

In Dublin a fortunate few were sent to St Vincent's Orphanage, run by the Society of St Vincent de Paul, or the O'Brien Institute in Marino. But these were 'for the education of the sons of gentlemen in reduced circumstances,' and candidates were personally vetted by the Archbishop of Dublin. Children sent to St Joseph's Orphanage in Tivoli Road in Dún Laoghaire, run by the Daughters of the Heart of Mary, 'had happy memories,' but the order ran no industrial schools.

The savage reality of many of these institutions is now well known, but at the time many ratepayers believed the inmates of institutions such as 'St Kevin's Paradise' in Glencree had 'prime feeding three times a week,' were entertained by bands and had football games and 'excursion parties' regularly. One provincial newspaper opined that

> poor starving urchins must be either incorrigibly virtuous, [or] too inhumanly careless of life and its enjoyments, if they can resist the temptation of the very moderate amount of crime that is necessary to qualify them for admission.[24]

By 1924 there were more children in industrial schools in the Irish Free State than in England, Scotland, Wales and Northern Ireland combined; yet Joseph Glynn, president of the Society of St Vincent de Paul and of the Catholic Protection and Rescue Society, was proposing a hostel capable of looking after up to five hundred girls in Dublin. He suggested in the *Irish Ecclesiastical Record* that it be run by a lay committee under the direction of the hierarchy, 'owing to the difficulties of getting girls to enter a home controlled by nuns.' No-one seemed to question why girls were so reluctant to enter institutions run by religious orders.

On the other hand, Rev. M. H. MacInerny, who ran 'a small but active Rescue Committee', advocated a large number of rescue homes run by 'enterprising Congregations' of nuns as the best antidote to the 'huge Octopus' of Protestant proselytism. 'The absence of proper Catholic Institutions' for girls 'in trouble,' he wrote, 'simply drives them into the arms of the Soupers.' Other priests, such as 'Sagart', an anonymous contributor to the *Irish Ecclesiastical Record*, went so far as to warn against publicising the existence of 'Rescue Homes ... suggesting a certain indulgent attitude to moral lapses.' This 'would be calculated to lower the high ideals of our people.' He urged a continuation of the existing system, with 'its avoidance of scandal,' which 'seems to be the right method of dealing with this complicated and delicate problem.' This system, 'developed prudently ... would be able to catch in its net practically all the girls who now flee to proselytising homes, to unsafe maternity homes, to far-off Unions [workhouses] or to England.'[25]

Nor were agencies in England slow to take their Irish counterparts to task. Florence Russell, honorary secretary of the Liverpool and County Catholic Aid Society, wrote to Archbishop Byrne in June 1924 asking for your help in the great problem of reducing the number of unmarried expectant mothers coming to Liverpool ... The girls come from Ireland to England to hide their shame. This is not a Rescue Society and yet twenty-six girls from different parts of Ireland have been dealt with within the last nine months—all unmarried expectant mothers.

They come from Ireland in this condition. Some go into the Poor Law Institutions, others of the more fortunate type, as far as money is concerned ... get private attention.

It is rather hard on the ratepayers of this city to keep these girls and their babies, which they do for some considerable time, unless this Society, or some charitable person, sends them back. Their fate, if they are claimed out of Institutions by undesirable women, is often a very sad one. They drift into common lodging houses of the City and become the companions of prostitutes.

There is unfortunately, quite a large number of girls who have come from Ireland on the streets of Liverpool and we are obliged often to hear people say that the boast of the purity of Irish women is not a true one, and that the fallen Irish girls are turned out of their country to be supported by English charity. The numbers are certainly on the increase. The Irish women workers are ashamed of these girls. They bring disgrace on our religion and our country. Would it be possible to have the boats watched on the Dublin side and to prevent young women and girls from coming over here with only their fare and an address to go to?[26]

Archbishop Byrne told his secretary, Father Patrick Dunne, to assure Mrs Russell that he would give the problem his full attention but confided that he could not see 'how to stop this evil.' However, he did eventually liaise with her organisation and with the Liverpool Society for the Prevention of International Traffic in Women and Children, commonly known as the Port and Station Work Society, a non-sectarian body, which dealt with 2,292 out of the 3,240 Irish women who arrived in need of help between 1922 and 1927. The next-largest groups by nationality were English (982), Scottish (125) and Welsh (125).

Nor was Liverpool the only city that complained of Irish women throwing themselves on 'English charity'. Between 1923 and 1928 the Crusade of Rescue in London dealt with 1,278 similar cases, of which 450 were from Dublin, including a number of married women who did not want to keep their child.[27]

One initiative to help Archbishop Byrne 'stop this evil' was the Catholic Protection and Rescue Society, which had been conceived during the 1913 Lockout in Dublin as a response to the initiative of Dora Montefiore and a perceived increase in proselytising activities by the Irish Church Missions. Both were seen as exploiting hunger in the tenements to seduce Catholics from their religion. Montefiore, a socialist, had proposed bringing the children of Dublin's locked-out trade unionists to foster homes in Britain until the dispute ended. The scheme was denounced by Archbishop Walsh, and only a handful of children eventually travelled to England. Once the apparent threat subsided with the end of the Lockout, the efforts of the Catholic Protection and Rescue Society languished. The outbreak of war in 1914 saw British exchequer funds flow into the tenements through separation payments for soldiers' families as well as wages from increased employment for women in textiles, munitions and other war-related industries.

The proselytising threat that fed on hardship seemed to diminish, and relatively few cases were dealt with before a major reorganisation of the society took place and the constitution was redrafted in 1920. The society now committed itself

> to protect the Catholic poor against the evils of proselytism, as practised by a section of the Protestant community in Ireland, who offer money, food or material considerations to the needy, weak and depraved Catholics for a surrender of their faith and that of their children.

It aspired to become an all-Ireland body, co-ordinating Catholic efforts against proselytisers, to collect funds

> and, when necessary undertake legal proceedings to deal with cases of unmarried mothers and their children; to undertake such other works as may be needed to give effect to their programme; and to give to the Catholic Body a sense of strength and security in combating proselytism.

The society, which placed itself 'under the protection and patronage of the Holy Ghost and of the Holy Family of Jesus, Mary and Joseph,' extended its branch network throughout Ireland 'with the requisite ecclesiastical approval' of the local bishops. While priests could join the society, it was predominantly a lay body, operating under a General Committee and a 21-member Executive Committee that contained only four clerics. The new committee included Joseph Glynn, chairman of the Irish Insurance Commissioners and president of the Society of St Vincent de Paul; William Lombard Murphy, son and heir of the legendary William Martin Murphy; T. M. Healy, the former Irish Party MP and future Governor-General of the Irish Free State; and some luminaries of Southern unionism, such as Captain Stephen Gaisford-St. Lawrence of Howth Castle and Lady Corbally. These ecumenical Protestants were presumably concerned primarily with the material rather than the spiritual welfare of the women and their babies. It suggests that, even in 1921, they were coming to terms with the idea that social policy initiatives would have to be along lines determined by the dominant Catholic moral dispensation.

The reorganisation soon manifested itself in a dramatic increase in the number of cases. In 1920 the society dealt with 393 cases, compared with 125 in the years since 1913; in 1921 the number rose to 532. This put intense pressure on resources, and 124 of the children were boarded out. Twelve children were sent for adoption and four were transferred to industrial schools. No reasons are given for the transfers, but it may be that the mothers stopped making contributions towards their maintenance. Altogether, £658 12s 6d was contributed by mothers to the upkeep of the children, out of a total income of £3,203 13s 11d; in fact this was the largest source of income after the grant of £1,059 16s 11d from the Local Government Board.

The committee acknowledged the importance of the mothers' financial contributions 'towards the upkeep of their children from whom ... they never lose hope of being one day united in a little home of their own.'[28] This was a crucial difference between the Catholic Protection and Rescue Society and most institutions run by religious congregations. Not only was it less judgemental of its clients but its lay members seem to have shown more Christian charity than their co-religionists in holy orders. Above all, they held out the hope of keeping mothers and babies together. As the economic crisis deepened, this aim would come under increasing pressure as both parents and the society found it difficult to make ends meet.

Of course their clients were not 'fallen women', as were those of the Rotunda Girls' Aid Society and most of the St Patrick's Guild admissions. Although it was the younger of the two organisations, St Patrick's Guild handled the largest number of cases. The lists of admissions supplied to Archbishop Walsh's successor, Dr Byrne, showed that Dublin contributed between a quarter and a third of cases each year.

	Dublin	Nationally
1923	46	154
1924	34	135
1925	39	114
1926	57	173
1927	34	109
1928	51	156

Given the prior existence of the Rotunda Girls' Aid Society, one must ask why it was felt necessary to establish St Patrick's Guild. As it stated in its annual report for 1922, the society 'has grown old among the charitable Societies of Dublin. This year completes 41 years of wise and prudent work successfully accomplished.' Unlike St Patrick's Guild, and many 'mother and baby homes' that sprang up during this period, the Rotunda society was run by the Catholic laity. The Rotunda was a Protestant foundation, and the purpose of the society was to help Catholic girls who,

> still on the threshold of life ... have, alas, blundered very badly.
>
> Their sad lapse from virtue makes them, as it were, outcasts from society ... It is to those poor girls a helping hand is outstretched to lift them from their fall. A spark of hope for a brighter and happier future is kindled within their saddened hearts. A knowledge is given them that by a quick restoring to the ranks of self-supporting, self-respecting women, their serious lapse may in a great measure be retrieved by their future blameless lives. They are not freed from, but helped to bear the burden which motherhood has placed upon them.

While the language is judgemental, the approach of the society appears to have been more child-centred than many 'mother and baby homes' run by religious congregations. If a mother was required to contribute to the upkeep of the baby there was a policy of keeping her informed of the child's progress, and reuniting them where possible later. The rest of the children were usually boarded out and adopted by families nursing them. And, unlike other agencies dealing with the issue of 'illegitimacy', the society was not slow to remind its audience that

> in the vast majority of cases the burden and consequences of parenthood fall on the woman alone, and that for every unmarried mother that is condemned a father escapes a just share in her shame and punishment. This fact alone should obtain for these poor girls a sympathetic help and deep consideration.

Unfortunately it did neither, and Archbishop Byrne had to help tide the society over 1922 with an overdraft. The number of mothers and children cared for reached a peak in the aftermath of the Civil War and then fell rapidly. By 1931 it had sixty-nine cases, of whom forty-one were in permanent care. The much lower mortality rate experienced by these infants would suggest that fostering increased life expectancy compared with keeping them in institutions where, apart from spartan conditions, they were far more prone to infectious diseases.

What is important about the Rotunda Girls' Aid Society is that it showed that even within the prevailing Catholic consensus there were alternative approaches being practised in Dublin to dealing with single mothers and their children. The problem was that neither the religious congregations nor the laity seemed generally willing to engage with them. The Rotunda Girls' Aid Society was a survivor from an earlier, Victorian era, when the Catholic ethos was less dominant in Dublin society. Post-independence Dubliners appear to have preferred to keep the problem out of sight and out of mind in 'mother and baby homes'. Archbishop Byrne helped the society financially, but at no time does he appear to have promoted its objectives.

Cases dealt with by Rotunda Girls' Aid Society, 1922–6

	Children dealt with	Adopted (usually by foster-parents)	Taken by mothers	Placed in schools	Permanent care	Died
1922	124	26	6	21	59	12
1923 (missing)						
1924	133	54	3	8	54	14
1925	125	24	4	1	84	12
1926	130	30	5	0	78	17

The Rotunda Girls' Aid Society was as dependent on mothers' remittances as the Catholic Protection and Rescue Society. While only six mothers were in comfortable enough circumstances to take back their child in 1922, mothers' payments to the society amounted to £479 15s 6d out of a total income of £1,135 8s 8d. This pattern continued, with mothers contributing £495 5s in 1924 out of a total income of £1,394 8s 8d. By comparison, members' subscriptions brought in only £203 in 1924, compared with £218 4s 6d in 1922, which in turn was a drop of £123 18s 6d on the previous year. There was also a dramatic drop in bequests, from £330 in 1922 to £100 in 1924.

One factor that probably helped ensure that many mothers contributed was fear that their child might otherwise be placed in 'permanent care'. However, even this sanction appeared to fail as economic conditions worsened. As early as October 1921 the society wrote to Archbishop Byrne to inform him that its account at the National Irish Bank was overdrawn to the extent of £249 6s 6d. The reasons given were that (a) 'no cases of late have come for adoption, that would pay a sufficiently large fee', (b) in some cases the maintenance fees agreed with the mothers had been 'long since expended' because of inflation—clothing for the children had become particularly expensive—and (c) in other cases 'mothers have ceased to pay the monthly payments promised by them and are not to be found in the addresses given by them.'

The society had hoped for a grant from the Provisional Government but this was refused, 'on the plea of economy.' The situation was becoming so difficult that, rather than obtaining fees from prospective parents, the society was reduced to giving some women who nursed the older ones payments of £5 to £10 to adopt them. Gradually the society ceased to function as anything more than an adoption society.[29]

Some help would be forthcoming in the struggle against proselytism from the Order of the Knights of St Columbanus, established by wealthy lay Catholics before the First World War. Archbishop Byrne had been one of the first priest-members before being elevated to the archbishopric. However, the Knights faced competition from the Columbians, a Belfast variant that was organisationally and politically close to the Ancient Order of Hibernians. Byrne, as archbishop, insisted that the two bodies should resolve their differences and merge rather than continue 'walking on one another's heels.' In 1922 they finally did so, and Peter Maunsell, a senior knight, wrote to Archbishop Byrne on 22 June 1922 to assure him that this

> difficulty has now been overcome. The important Society of 'Columbians' has now united with our Order on terms which are mutually satisfactory. I may safely claim that the united body now represents the best elements and most energising influence in the Catholic laity of Dublin.

The Knights acquired Ely House in Ely Place early the following year from Lady Aberdeen, wife of the former Lord Lieutenant. She had used it to accommodate the Women's National Health Association, but from now on 'lady relations' of the Knights would be admitted to the premises only for designated annual events. The Knights combated the proselytisers by supporting such bodies as the Catholic Protection and Rescue Society, the Society of St Vincent de Paul, the Central Catholic Library and the Lourdes pilgrimage. Its approach to the latter was indicative of the way it would cultivate influence throughout Irish society. Not only did it pay 'for several poor pilgrims' on the trip but all the doctors and pharmacists attending the pilgrims were members of the Knights. In its first year Archbishop Byrne was informed that 'membership is now about 3,000 and ... councils are established in 30 cities and towns, each Council including several priests.'

Dr Byrne would attend the 'Complimentary Banquet to the Hierarchy of Ireland and the Clergy and Laymen associated with the work of the Catholic Truth Society of Ireland' on Thursday 23 October 1924. Sir Peter Reilly O'Connell, the supreme knight, was in the chair, and the toasts were 'the Pope, the Bishops and Clergy of the Irish Church, and the Catholic Truth Society of Ireland.'

———

The Catholic Girls' Club and Hostel served as a preventive agency, providing 'respectable lodgings' for young women coming to work in Dublin. It had been established towards the end of the Dublin Lockout by leading society ladies, including Viscountess Gormanston, Countess Fingall and Lady Howth. The hostel provided short-term accommodation for up to twenty-eight women a night, as its aim was to supply domestic servants for the upper middle class from respectable rural families. It had a jobs register for prospective employers, and throughput must have been high, as it catered for 990 women in 1920 and found situations for 550 of them. Like other lay Catholic social agencies, it provided religious instruction for residents and visitors, but it also provided recreational activities. Such was the demand for its services that it launched an appeal for the building of a recreational hall at the rear, and a temporary wooden structure was completed during the Truce.[30]

Viscountess Gormanston was still honorary president in 1921, and Lady Howth was vice-president. Women accounted for 17 of the 36-member Executive Committee, with a mere eight priests and no nuns. Like their female counterparts, the men were leading figures in the business community, including the ubiquitous William Lombard Murphy.

———

Nor did Catholic social services stop at the gates of institutions such as St Patrick's Guild, the Rotunda Girls' Aid Society and the Catholic Girls' Club and Hostel. A plethora of bodies acting largely under the auspices of the Society of St Vincent de Paul filled gaps left by an impoverished government still struggling to secure its grip on state power. One of the most significant was the Catholic Working Boys' Technical Aid Association, which was presided over by Sir Henry Bellingham and his fellow-commissioner of National Education Major Gerald Dease. It included representatives of St Patrick's Teacher Training College in Drumcondra and William O'Neill, headmaster of St Andrew's National School, Westland Row. The association was established in November 1914 to address the shortage of skilled workers in the city. It estimated that 6,000 boys a year left school early and more than 11,000 failed to achieve the minimum 150 days a year required by the School Attendance Act.

Not all the funds available for night schools and continuation classes were drawn, so that the amount available in grants from the British Exchequer for elementary evening classes had been gradually reduced from £23,000 a year to £8,000 in 1922. By then the association still appears to have been at the planning stage in developing links with 'recreation centres' and libraries to provide 'Religious Instruction, Physical Drill, and Medical Treatment' as well as indoor and outdoor games for these boys. Without such interventions, the association's report pointed out, they could be employed only 'as messengers, basket boys and the like.' Lacking any recognised skill, 'they have no prospect of an economically useful and self-supporting career, and become casual unskilled workers.' It urged reform of the school attendance legislation and the introduction of 'manual work' courses in schools catering for these youngsters.

But most of the practical work of the Society of St Vincent de Paul was done through its conferences (branches) and special works projects, such as the Prisoners' Aid Committee, the Penny Banks (which had twelve thousand members in 1922), the Seamen's Institute (which looked after sailors visiting Dublin port) and the

Labour Yard. The latter engaged 'in testing the bona fides of men who come to our Conferences seeking relief.' They were divided into those 'worthy of consideration' and 'non-triers,' who would be treated 'accordingly.' Conferences provided hospital visitors for the sick, including inmates of the South Dublin Union workhouse in James's Street,[31] provided coal for the elderly, helped families that had lost breadwinners through illness or accident, helped fishing families struggling with the collapse of prices, and organised boys' clubs and night schools. The motivation, as the annual report reminded members, was 'to show us how far we have discharged our obligations of personal service to God's poor[,] obligations which, as a matter of spiritual honour, are none the less blinding because voluntarily assumed.'[32]

It was an approach personified in Frank Duff, the founder of the Legion of Mary in 1921. If Matt Talbot encapsulated the devotional model for the edification of the working man, Frank Duff would become his young middle-class counterpart. Duff was as academically gifted as Joseph Brennan. Although he won a first-class exhibition (scholarship) as a pupil at Blackrock College, he had to forgo university and join the civil service to support his family because of his father's failing health and early death.

Like Brennan, Duff was a moderate nationalist. His ability was recognised when he developed a new method for calculating land annuities and was invited to the Treasury to discuss it. When the Free State was established he opted to transfer to the new Irish civil service. He worked briefly as personal secretary to Michael Collins until the latter's death and then with the Minister for Agriculture, Patrick Hogan, before transferring to the Ministry of Finance. He would almost certainly have become a senior civil servant if he had not chosen early retirement to devote himself to the Legion.[33]

Duff became the leading figure among a dedicated mass of Catholic lay activists who were moulding the city's dominant social ethos, even while the radical elements of the revolutionary elite were posturing in the Four Courts, having defined the issue of the moment as the re-igniting of the war with British imperialism, helpfully personified in the belligerent Colonial Secretary, Winston Churchill. Ironically, it was more competent military strategists such as Richard Mulcahy and Nevil Macready who were seeking to navigate a less bloodthirsty resolution to the conflict.

Not that the crisis in 1922 did not affect the Society of St Vincent de Paul, as it did so many organisations. Membership fell from a pre-independence maximum of 4,403 in 1921 to 3,852 in 1922, a drop of 12 per cent, and was still only 4,368 by 1924. Income also fell, though not as drastically, from £64,012 to £61,935, but the number of people helped remained almost constant, at well over seventy thousand. Fewer members worked harder.

If the motivation was primarily religious, it had an implicit class aspect that had received a spur from the Dublin Lockout, as Frank Duff's own career makes clear. His friend and first biographer Leon Ó Broin dates the origins of the Legion of Mary, appropriately enough, to a stable in Cheater's Lane, off Redmond's Hill. A young civil servant still only mildly interested in religion, Duff was recruited by Joe Gabbett, a shoemaker, former sergeant-major in the British army and convert to Catholicism. Duff had been instructed by the Society of St Vincent de Paul to mount a picket on a Protestant soup kitchen nearby that fed local homeless people, and Gabbett convinced him that it would be much more useful and effective to divert these 'poor dishevelled creatures' to an alternative source of nourishment.

It was Duff who provided the network of middle-class friends and supporters to finance and operate the premises so as to end what he described as 'an enormity against Heaven': stealing the souls of Catholics by preying on their hunger. The group not alone collected money to provide Sunday breakfasts for the homeless but 'washed their faces and combed their hair.' A statue of the Blessed Virgin was erected in the stable, and Duff began what would become a lifetime study of 'the entrancing but true eminence of the Woman on whom God had built His scheme from all eternity.'

Meanwhile his group set up classes to teach sewing, knitting and singing to local youngsters. These intensely active Vincent de Paul members went on to organise visits to cancer patients in the hospitals, including the workhouses. A second group identified places frequented by prostitutes, such as Biddy Slicker's at 25 Chancery Lane. One of Duff's helpers, Emma Colgan, found thirty-seven young women there 'sitting around in shawls.' They paid a shilling a time to borrow a coat from Slicker to go out and entertain clients. Another house identified was 48 New Market, which was 'packed with street girls.' One was

> a refined girl who passed as Honour Bright and 'had served her time in Switzers, never used bad language and was, Emmy said, 'a lovely person to talk to.' She had not been going to mass but promised to go 'next Sunday.' 'Maybe' said her companion Bridie Foran, 'you mightn't be alive next Sunday.' Nor was she. She was found dead on the Dublin Mountains. Murdered.

All this lay ahead, on 7 September 1921, when Duff formed his growing group of activists into the Legion of Mary. Although he was well aware of prostitution in the city, he was as ignorant of its causes and its culture as many other respectable citizens. He accidentally called to a brothel on a Vincent de Paul visitation during these years, Ó Broin recalled. 'For a moment he did not realise where he was. Then he saw, and was so intimidated that he backed out without saying a word.'[34]

————

The Irish Labour Party and Trade Union Congress, like its British counterpart, the Trade Union Congress, sought to involve the state more heavily in tackling the causes of poverty, as opposed to ameliorating its effects. At its conference in August 1922 the ILP&TUC called for compulsory education to be extended from fourteen to sixteen years of age for boys and girls, 'and that a co-ordinated system be devised whereby children of ability may be enabled to proceed from the Primary Schools to secondary and Intermediate Schools, and thence to Universities.' It also called for technical education to be free for the children of workers. 'The continuation schools for apprentices should be free, and they should be continued during working hours. Apprentices should get off during working hours to attend continuation schools.' The proposal had come from James Carr, a Limerick Trades Council delegate, who declared that

> the workers of Ireland will not send their children to school; if they do not there will have to be some form of compulsion. If the children of the workers are brought up in ignorance the Labour movement goes back. Now the average daily attendance for the whole of Ireland is only about 66 per cent. In England and Scotland it is over 90 per cent. The number of children absent from school every day in Ireland, practically all without any cause, is 220,000. The number of children not on the roll of any school is 200,000. That is nearly half a million away from school every day. Many of the cleverest children, some of poor parents, are forced to leave school at 10 or 11 years of age. In Limerick 90 per cent of the boys leave the primary schools about the age of 13; only 35 per cent of the people are in the fourth or higher standards [classes]. In some rural districts the figures are lower than these. There should be some system by which a clever child could be enabled to proceed from the primary to the higher schools, as in Scotland.[35]

But the Irish Free State was no longer part of the United Kingdom, although a British institution continued to be a major provider of children's services in the absence of alternatives. This was the National Society for the Prevention of Cruelty to Children. Its first Irish branch had been founded in 1889 in Dublin, and the city continued to be the main area of its activities within the new Free State. Unlike most providers of services for children, its membership was drawn overwhelmingly from suburban Protestant middle-class women. Realising that it was widely regarded—like most Protestant social agencies—as a proselytising threat, it quickly reached an accommodation with its Catholic counterparts.

As we have seen, distracted by civil war and largely bereft of social vision, the founders of the Free State had little time to consider, let alone implement, the commitments in the Proclamation of the Irish Republic or the Democratic Programme of Dáil Éireann to social justice, especially the latter's explicit commitment that 'it shall be the first duty of the Republic to make provision for the physical, mental and spiritual well-being of the children.' But then the Executive Council of the Free State could legitimately argue that it was not the government of the Republic but a much more modest project, morally as well as politically.

The key to the NSPCC's accommodation with the new dispensation was its capacity to meet the requirements of the growing network of industrial schools. At first the society had denounced the use of these schools as being at odds with its policy of working to maintain the family and encouraging parents' responsibility for children. Now it found that it could continue to ferret out cases of cruelty and neglect but could not adequately care for the children at risk, whereas the Catholic religious congregations claimed they could. With adoption illegal within the Free State until 1952 (which did not prevent 'mother and baby homes' from developing a profitable export trade for the adoption of children abroad), and boarding out increasingly discredited as cases of abuse and neglect came to light, a new welfare conveyor-belt was created that supplied children to religious congregations that were looking for capitation grants while facilitating the continuing retreat of the Free State government from providing for the well-being of the child. If the family could not care for the child, the religious would. No serious effort was made by the government to consider alternatives to the strategy of institutionalisation that had been developed in the nineteenth century.

Ironically, the British state had done a great deal to combat the poverty that posed the greatest threat to the children of Dublin's tenements through the separation allowances paid to the mothers, married and unmarried, of the children of soldiers during the First World War. This fact was freely acknowledged in NSPCC reports for the war years. With the end of the war most of those payments ceased,[36] and many of the returning soldiers were no longer very competent breadwinners or parents, because of physical or psychological disabilities.

The NSPCC continued to grow in the war years, from nine branches in 1913 (all but one of them in Dublin city or county) to twenty-nine in 1922 (including eight in the metropolitan hinterland of Cos. Wicklow and Kildare). However, it remained an almost exclusively Protestant body, wedded unapologetically to its British parent organisation. When collectors said it was hard to raise funds because members of the public complained that 'the money goes to England,' the organisation responded firmly that, 'as the Society has one policy in its works, one method with its cases, so it has one purse for its methods.' Nationalist perceptions were probably not helped by the fact that its head office in Molesworth Street adjoined that of the Freemasons, and that the building was called Victory House.

The NSPCC reports starkly delineate the fall and rise in the numbers of children at risk.

NSPCC, all complaints, 1911–24

	1911	1912	1913	1914	1915	1916	1917	1918	1919	1920	1921	1922	1923	1924
Neglect and starvation	1,353	1,466	1,372	1,438	1,311	1,203	1,051	698	797	772	785	706	676	699
Abandonment	24	0	0	0	0	0	0	0	1	1	1	1	3	2
Ill-treatment and assault	34	60	52	50	21	27	23	32	41	39	59	63	83	90
Baby-farming	0	0	0	0	0	0	0	0	0	0	1	0	1	1
Exposure	0	1	1	1	2	0	0	0	0	0	0	0	0	0
Exposure for the purpose of begging	6	3		5	1	0	1	0	3	0	3	4	0	13
Failure to notify receipt of nurse child	0	0	0	0	0	0	0	0	0	0	0	0	0	1
Criminal assault	0	0	1	1	3	3	0	0	1	0	0	0	0	0
Immoral surroundings	3	0	3	3	2	1	3	6	1	1	4	1	6	4
Other wrongs	1	6	7	7	12	4	5	4	23	28	10	7	23	7
Advice sought	0	0	0	0	0	0	0	38	0	0	0	17	37	38

Reports run from 1 April each year to 31 March of the following year. The reports from 1914 to 1919 are abbreviated because of wartime printing restrictions.

Breakdown of substantiated cases[37]

	Substantiated cases	Children	Illegitimate	Step-children	Unrelated to victim	At nurse	Boys	Girls	Offenders		Children who died
									Men	Women	
1911	1,397	4,046	37	0	1	27	-	-	934	698	36
1912	1,538	4,111	36	30	34	29	2,274	2,137	1,097	766	26
1913	1,441	3,993	50	23	64	55	2,028	1,965	970	719	30
1914	1,459	4,308	31	22	35	32	2,215	2,093	931	833	34
1915	1,308	3,981	29	24	55	45	2,010	1,971	695	847	16
1916	1,189	3,669	28	14	38	36	1,902	1,767	590	774	15
1917	1,049	3,023	44	12	52	44	1,591	1,432	509	679	8
1918	714	1,913	47	18	43	37	1,007	906	401	435	17
1919	832	2,162	36	26	41	?	1,098	1,064	970	719	18
1920	812	1,987	20	40	57	?	1,012	975	588	402	16
1921	831	2,043	67	32	58	?	1,078	965	970	719	30
1922	788	1,866	47	48		78	953	913	539	354	11
1923	811	1,966	63	37		50	1,025	941	539	354	6
1924											

The 1913 report attributes the reduction in the number of cases that year to the Lockout, because of the aid sent to Dublin's workers by the Trade Union Congress in Britain and other elements within the labour movement. The increase in the number of cases in 1914 reflected the underlying inadequacy of Irish services as well as the initial disruption caused by the outbreak of war. Again the gradual fall in demand for its services during the war years was attributed by the NSPCC to extra income flowing into the tenements in the form of separation allowances, which from 1916 included unmarried mothers if a serviceman accepted paternity of the children. By 1917 such allowances were the second-largest source of income in the tenements, after the wages of labourers.

Another characteristic of the war years was the fact that the majority of cruelty cases involved women, although the norm of men comprising the majority of offenders soon resumed after the war ended. The total number of cases of cruelty also rose after 1918 but never returned to pre-war levels.

The great majority of cases dealt with by the NSPCC involved 'neglect and starvation', with parents the main offenders. The one exception was children 'at nurse', where more than 90 per cent of cases investigated by the NSPCC found that some form of cruelty had been perpetrated. 'Baby farming and its attendant evils' were sharply denounced. 'Children are given out to nurse with false names and addresses, small sums are deposited, and the recipient hears no more of the real or pretended mother of the child. The natural result follows: the child is generally neglected.'[38] Whether this criticism extended to such bodies as the Rotunda Girls' Aid Society is not clear, but, as we have seen, such reports were used by religious congregations to promote the institutionalisation of mothers and babies, thereby discouraging the fostering out of children or anything smacking of 'baby farming'.

Despite its intentions, the NSPCC's image within the community was increasingly associated with the 'cruelty man'. This perception was not widespread in the early days. In 1925 there were five inspectors acting as front-line troops for the local committees, but within a few years elements within the Catholic Church, ranging from Archbishop Byrne's successor, John Charles McQuaid, to Frank Duff, became highly critical of the society and remained suspicious of its motives. In a famous exchange of correspondence in which Archbishop McQuaid asked for Duff's opinion on the numbers of children being referred through the courts to industrial schools, Duff accused the NSPCC, and one female inspector in particular, of 'simply shovelling children into Industrial Schools.'

The annual reports of the NSPCC always emphasised that its aim was to keep the child at home where possible, and its historian, Sarah-Anne Buckley, found that only 12 per cent of the cases she examined were placed in industrial schools. On the other hand, the Report on Child Abuse by Mr Justice Seán Ryan found that the society's inspectors facilitated 37 per cent of all committals to industrial schools.[39] Of course the NSPCC had no care facilities of its own, and the Irish section was out of sync with the mother ship in Britain, which operated in a very different social environment. The greatest irony was the assumption that once children were sent to industrial schools they would be protected from abuse. Ultimately, the fear of the 'cruelty man' in Dublin working-class communities proved more perceptive of the consequences of his (or her) activities than many expert professionals, lay or clerical.

———

There were also Protestant social agencies, such as the Nurse Rescue Society, that looked after foster-children from the Church of Ireland Magdalen in Leeson Street, while the Freemasons ran benevolent schools for the orphan sons and daughters of members as well as providing an annuitants fund to help the families of members who had fallen on hard times. The regime at the Masons' schools appears to have been more benevolent than that of its religious counterparts, and better funded.

Catholic institutions bore the great weight of caring for the vulnerable in the city. While the churches can certainly be criticised for their failings and the way many individual religious abused their power, no-one can be surprised that they created a system in their own image, by turns caring and authoritarian, charitable and brutal. Any alternative secular or pluralist vision to that of men such as Frank Duff was never a practical possibility. General Maxwell had decapitated the radical leadership of militant nationalism in 1916 when he executed the signatories of the Proclamation. Now their successors were too busy slaughtering each other to engage intellectually with the admittedly vague aspirations to social justice in the Proclamation. It was radical feminists who tried to kick-start initiatives for children, most notably St Ultan's Hospital.[40]

A more modest proposal concerned playgrounds. During the Great War the squares of the city had been opened to all its citizens, and now a group of women trade unionists began a campaign to reopen them as badly needed playgrounds for the children of the tenements. They met with a firm refusal. The Law Agent of Dublin Corporation advised that it would take an act of Parliament to open Rutland, Mountjoy, Merrion and Fitzwilliam Squares. Helena Molony of the Irish Women Workers' Union, who led a deputation to Dublin Corporation with Helen Chenevix, said they had no objections to Rutland Square remaining closed, as the Rotunda Hospital 'was doing very good work,' but children in the slums were in urgent need of safe recreational spaces. Councillor Hanna Sheehy Skeffington (Sinn Féin) then proposed that the matter be referred to the Public Health Committee and suggested that a decree by Dáil Éireann might get over the problem of an act of Parliament.[41] But the Dáil was preoccupied with the Treaty and its repercussions, and the notion of playgrounds for tenement children would become one more experiment in social progress buried by civil war.

Chapter 5 ∾

'YOU WOULD NOT SHOOT ME, CHRISTY'

Six days before the anti-Treaty IRA raid on Sir Henry Robinson's house at Ballybrack, the last President of the Dáil Éireann government, Arthur Griffith, died of a cerebral haemorrhage. His death made little difference to the prosecution of the Civil War, other than increasing further Michael Collins's freedom of action. The two men had barely been on speaking terms since the election pact Collins made with de Valera in May.

By now the Civil War was won in military terms and would increasingly become a policing operation, but the anti-Treaty IRA retained its capacity to seriously disrupt the economy, as it demonstrated when it disconnected all ten transatlantic telegraph cables at the beginning of August. Only four lines now operated between Britain and North America, and Irish traffic had to go through Penzance, adding to the congestion. The *Irish Times* urged the government to 'strain every nerve to curtail the wicked campaign of destruction.'[1]

Whether Collins undertook his tour of Munster to negotiate an end to the fighting or simply as a tour of inspection and to make a triumphal visit home has remained a matter of conjecture. He was certainly maintaining pressure on Republicans to accept the new state as a *fait accompli*. One of his last executive acts before heading south was to push through the 'oath of fidelity', which required every public servant to sign an undertaking that

I have not taken part with [*sic*], or aided or abetted in any way whatsoever the forces in revolt against the Irish Provisional Government and I promise to be faithful to that government and give no aid or support of any kind to those who are engaged in conflict against the authority of that government.[2]

Nevertheless his death at Bealnablath, between Macroom and Bandon, transformed the political climate in which the war was taking place. It not only embittered the conflict but, ironically, would ultimately isolate the hard core of pro-Treaty commanders who prosecuted it to a ruthless conclusion from their own government as well as from their former comrades in arms. The seeds of the 1924 army mutiny were being sown as well as the long-term bitter legacy of fratricidal strife.

The death of Michael Collins also personified the triumphant return of localism to Irish politics. Since 1913 the momentum of the Irish Revolution had been driven from Dublin. The election of the second Dáil in May 1921 was the culmination of this process. The only candidates were those approved by Sinn Féin.[3] The Republic had become a one-party state.

With the return of localism, TDs had to begin taking cognisance of constituents' feelings and of sectional interests as well as national ones if they wanted to be re-elected. Collins may have considered the Treaty a stepping-stone in a dynamic process towards the Republic, but his death came near to turning it into a tombstone in the coming decades as far as social change was concerned. The emerging political parties of the new state exhibited all the conservative tendencies of the old Irish Party without having to engage, as it had, with progressive elements in British society. Sectional groups in the new Dáil, such as the farmers, were deeply conservative, and the Labour Party leadership, instinctively cautious and knowing it lacked the social and economic weight to be a decisive force in a property-owning peasant democracy, was more adept at adapting to circumstances than at changing them.

If the Corkman had to make the long journey home to meet his death,[4] Arthur Griffith had only to go as far as St Vincent's Hospital in St Stephen's Green. Although he had been in bad health for months, Griffith's death on 12 August came as a shock to the public. His chief role since the Treaty had been to preside over the burial of the Dáil Éireann institutions, while Collins had been central to creating those of the new state.

It is hard to imagine two more different individuals. Collins was a boisterous, ruthlessly ambitious 'man of action', deeply attached to his rural roots, while Griffith was the quintessential Dubliner, short, pugnacious, and more interested in winning the argument than in wielding the power that flowed from victory. Now they were united in death as martyrs to the new state. The state funerals of both men were demonstrations of strength, with every member of the cabinet following the gun carriages and a massive military presence. Press reports put the crowds at as much as 400,000, which would have made them larger than those for the 1916 hero Thomas Ashe, the Cork martyr Terence MacSwiney or Dublin's late Catholic archbishop, William Walsh; but such estimates were intended as public markers of political significance rather than literal head counts.

Collins gave the oration at Griffith's funeral, and Mulcahy gave that at Collins's graveside, marking symbolically the central role the National Army was playing in the formation of the new state. The expressions of regret were more unstinted in the case of Griffith, especially from the *Irish Times,* the voice of Southern unionism.

He, more than any other man, persuaded Dáil Éireann to ratify the Treaty, brought the Treaty's merits home to the electors and created the situation which finds a vast majority of the Irish people on the side of settlement ... This newspaper, and those who think with it, supported the British government when it was at war with Sinn Féin. Now that it has made its peace with Sinn Féin the loyalists of Southern Ireland have accepted the new arrangement. Their place is in Ireland. They desire to serve her, and they only ask that for Ireland's sake they shall receive full, unfettered opportunities of service. All Southern loyalists will mourn Griffith's untimely death. They respected him as a brave man who forgot 'at once in peace, the injuries of war.'

It attributed Griffith's relatively early death at the age of fifty-one to 'the selfishness and wickedness of fellow-Irishmen.'

The *Irish Independent* was equally effusive and had no need to engage in any apologia. It said that 'never perhaps has the passing of an Irish leader created such feelings of profound sorrow.' Both newspapers made much of the condolences sent by King George v and the British Prime Minister, David Lloyd George.[5]

The death of Collins ten days later was even more unexpected and dramatic. The *Irish Times* editorial stated nervously that 'we are still too close to the event to realise fully what it means to the future of our country.' Nevertheless it did acknowledge that 'no man tried so hard as General Collins to save Ireland from civil war,' and that he was 'Ireland's most popular leader and popular man.' The paper's London correspondent commented frankly that 'it would be affectation to say that the feeling in regard to it was the same in quality to that evoked by the death of Mr. Griffith. Nevertheless there is a very general regret that he should have been removed at this critical juncture.'[6]

The *Irish Independent,* which scooped its unionist rival by having news of Collins's death in its edition of 23 August, also published a far more detailed report the next day.

Its coverage of Collins's last moments by a 'special correspondent', under a centre-page pen portrait, describes the fatal ambush in lachrymose tones and concludes by describing the dying man's last moments after the firing ended:

The general is still conscious and makes a motion to speak. To General [Emmet] Dalton he says in broken murmurs: 'LET THE DUBLIN BRIGADE BURY ME.'
    After a short lapse once more he speaks, only two words, yet they draw away the veil and, as nothing else in all his life manifest the greatness and nobility of that passing soul. 'FORGIVE THEM,' he said and with that prayer of forgiveness on his lips he breathed his last, and his great soul passed on its way to the All-Just Judge.

However, it is unlikely that Collins was able to say anything after the catastrophic head wound he had suffered, and Dalton never verified these apocryphal words.[7] They probably emanated from a press briefing the National Army's press officer, Major-General Piaras Béaslaí, gave journalists that emphasised the greatness of the fallen leader, his affinity with the Dublin Brigade and the pettiness of his opponents. Béaslaí would later write a two-volume hagiographical life of Collins.

——

Despite the crowds and the outpouring of grief, normality inexorably reasserted itself. The Horse Show continued during Griffith's funeral, as did the annual Liffey swim, deferred because of the battle for Dublin in July; and Clery's took advantage of the huge crowds at the Collins funeral to reopen its renovated department store in O'Connell Street. It was heralded by a spectacular advertisement that covered the front page of the *Irish Independent*. A muscular image of 'Industry' and statuesque 'Commerce', clad in what presumably passed for ancient Irish garb, supported the image of the pristine new edifice that replaced the warehouse in Lower Abbey Street that had served as temporary accommodation since the 1916 Rising. The advertisement assured readers that Clery's was now

> the largest establishment of its kind in the country ... Throughout the many trials and tribulations which have beset us since 1916, we have maintained unimpaired the efficiency of our great organisation, which handles the products of the world as well as the manufactures of our own country.[8]

That champion of industry and normality, the Irish Labour Party and Trade Union Congress, could not afford to buy full-page newspaper advertisements to publicise its concern at the delays in having Dáil Éireann called. Its own conference, convened on 7 August in the Mansion House, was overshadowed by the deaths of Griffith and Collins. The death of Collins in particular led to further delays in having the new Dáil convened, even though, as one delegate, Cormac Breathnach of the Irish National Teachers' Organisation, put it, the present government had no constitutional right for making civil war in the interval between the holding of the General Election and the assembling of An Dáil. Constitutionally the Dáil came to an end on June 30th, and, therefore, the Dáil Ministry [government] should have fallen … The people who are now running the country are merely individuals.[9]

The delegates voted for the new Dáil to convene by 26 August or Labour's seventeen deputies would resign *en masse*, further reducing the Provisional Government's legitimacy and that of the new Dáil, which had already lost four deputies during the Civil War: Collins, Griffith, Cathal Brugha and Harry Boland, a Dublin tailor and a leading figure on the anti-Treaty side who had been shot dead on 31 July by National Army soldiers at the Grand Hotel in Skerries in controversial circumstances. However, the Labour leadership did not demur when the slightly unconstitutional Provisional Government announced that the Dáil would finally convene on 9 September.

——

When it did convene, the new Dáil was confronted with a new crisis: a strike in the postal service. As we have seen (chapter 2), unions had been on the defensive since 1921, fighting a rearguard action against pay cuts, redundancies and the consequent fall in membership. The impact was now encroaching on public servants, as the new government and the local authorities sought to trim budgets to meet the growing mountain of compensation claims, to pay for essential repairs to infrastructure and to find the wages for a rapidly expanding National Army.

Even before the Treaty was signed some members of Dublin Corporation were suggesting the need to cut its own pay bill. On 9 January 1922 the leader of the Municipal Reform Association, Alderman James Hubbard Clark, proposed cutting the wages of all employees and abolishing war bonuses. However, the motion was ruled out of order on the advice of the Law Agent.[10]

The postal strike on 10 September came after the Provisional Government unilaterally imposed pay cuts on employees and was the first major industrial challenge to the new state. It showed how its creation was converting erstwhile revolutionaries into pillars of the establishment. The Postmaster-General, J. J. Walsh, had been a Post Office clerk until his revolutionary activities earned him the sack. He had the distinction of leading a small group of Hibernian Rifles, the paramilitary group set up by the Ancient Order of Hibernians, into the GPO in April 1916, which earned him a death sentence, subsequently commuted, and helped secure him a seat representing Cork in the first Dáil.

The new Secretary of the Ministry of Posts and Telegraphs, P. S. O'Hegarty, was almost a carbon copy of Walsh. Like Walsh, he was a former Post Office clerk and had also worked in London, where they knew each other through the IRB and, like so many figures in the new Free State establishment, became Collins loyalists. Like Collins too they believed the Treaty to be 'the better of two bad alternatives,' and, like many poachers-turned-gamekeepers, proved unrelenting in enforcing the new dispensation. Walsh's enthusiasm for the use of Irish had already led to the gibe that it was less important to know Irish than to know 'Welsh' to get a civil service post. The new satirical magazine *Dublin Opinion* published a cartoon entitled 'The night the Treaty was signed,' showing armies of Cork men sprinting up the Dublin road in pursuit of government jobs. The appearance of the magazine was a vote of confidence in the new state and a very public reassertion of the old cynicism about politics that had been buried during the 'four glorious years' that followed 1916.

The Provisional Government certainly took a cynical view of the postal workers. At the opening of talks to avert the strike in February it issued a statement that it stood 'for the payment of a fair wage to all its employees' but could not allow any section to take advantage of the current transfer of power 'to entrench itself at the expense of the public.'[11] It was agreed to set up a Commission of Inquiry into Post Office Wages and Conditions, to be chaired by Senator James Douglas, a Quaker businessman and trustee of the Irish White Cross. Other members included Sir Thomas Grattan Esmonde, a pro-Treaty TD, Thomas J. O'Connell, a Labour TD and general secretary of the INTO, and Luke Duffy of the Irish Union of Distributive Workers and Clerks.

The commission was the brainchild of Collins, and he more or less appointed it by diktat, in the face of opposition from the Ministry of Finance.[12] It demonstrated once more his extensive power network throughout Irish society and his capacity to stretch the system beyond its usual limitations. It was effectually a replacement for the Whitley Commission system that negotiated public-service pay and conditions in Britain.

The commission came up with a proposed compromise in May, but with the outbreak of civil war the Provisional Government withdrew from the process, and by September there was no Collins to massage a compromise. The strike began at 6 p.m. on 10 September when telephone operators withdrew from the central telephone exchange in Crown Alley, Dublin. The reaction of the Provisional Government was immediate and savage. It not only rejected any compromise on pay cuts but denied the right of postal workers to go on strike and promptly hired strike-breakers. 'Few civil servants would have conceived of ever going on strike,' Martin Maguire, the historian of the public service, has pointed out, 'but to be told that the right to strike was expressly denied them by their employer was a shock. Nor had it been forgotten that the same politicians had applauded strikes by civil servants in support of Irish political prisoners in April 1920.'[13]

On the first evening of the dispute a National Army officer fired over the heads of pickets outside the telephone exchange, and when the strikers responded with mass pickets outside post offices more than ninety members of the Irish Postal Union and its British counterpart, the Union of Postal Workers, were arrested by the DMP, although the latter protested that the picketers were doing nothing illegal. One constable was dismissed for refusing to carry out what he regarded as an illegal order. The strike committee urged members to 'conduct themselves with dignity and restraint ... so that we may retain the respect and support of the public in our just fight for a living wage.'[14]

Walsh was far more belligerent than Collins, and there was a collective feeling in the cabinet that the outbreak of civil war strengthened its hand in dealing with unions.[15] In his memoirs, *Recollections of a Rebel*, Walsh wrote dismissively that

the Post Office staff, which had never dared to say 'boo' while the British were here, took strike action before we had time to get into our stride. We could scarcely help feeling aggrieved at what we considered a stab in the back, and in particular, observing that [though] the Postal Workers' Organisation covered the thirty-two counties, the strike was confined to the twenty-six.

The men who resent this wrecking policy are those who were loyal to this country during the past four or five years. The men who were trying to stampede this big postal organisation into a strike say that for 30 years they have agitated with the English, but they never struck.[16]

It was the first significant occasion on which the National Army undertook what were essentially police duties in the Civil War. While this would later happen in rural areas, it reflected the unwillingness of the Dublin Metropolitan Police to engage in the mass intimidation of pickets. In one of the most serious incidents, on 17 September 1922, a man and three women picketers were fired on as they left Crown Alley and were walking through Merchants' Arch to the quays. One of the women, Olive Flood, had a lucky escape when one of the bullets struck her leg and was deflected by a suspender belt. Armoured cars ran through picket lines, and knuckle-dusters were used by soldiers on occasion. Similar attacks were made in provincial centres, particularly Limerick, while 'flying columns' of strike-breakers were given military protection.

Because of the delays in summoning the new Dáil, the start of the postal strike the very next day meant it would adversely affect relations between the new regime and the Labour Party from the beginnings of this infant democracy. Thomas Johnson asked for standing orders to be suspended to allow the discussion of a motion that repudiated a statement by Kevin O'Higgins, Minister for Home Affairs, declaring that the Provisional Government 'does not recognise the right of Civil Servants to strike.' In a fine speech defending the right to collective bargaining and the associated right to strike, Johnson asked if the government 'think that the workers of this country are going to accept the position which

places one section of the workers obviously and clearly in the category of slaves?'
The deputy leader of the party, Cathal O'Shannon, a former member of Sinn Féin
and the IRB, warned that 'all the guns and all the power and all the force in Ireland
is not going to make the whole working class in Ireland lie down when the right
to strike is challenged.'

But the issues were equally fundamental for the government, and O'Higgins
told the Dáil that

> no State, with any regard for its own safety, can admit the right of the
> servants of the Executive to withdraw their labour at pleasure. They have the
> right to resign; they have no right to strike ... The Civil Servant occupies an
> intermediate position as between the members of an army or police force and
> industrial workers. In one sense the discipline is not so rigid; in another sense
> certain recognised rights of industrial workers are denied, and must be denied,
> if the State will preserve itself.[17]

The Labour motion was defeated by 51 votes to 24.

The only cabinet member to show any insight into the nature of the dispute was
Joe McGrath, a former ITGWU officer and Collins confidant. Even so, it was only
when it looked as if postal workers might be joined by railway workers resisting
pay cuts and the spectre of a general strike arose that the government decided
to offer the terms it had withdrawn in the summer negotiations. This allowed
Senator Douglas's commission, assisted by McGrath and Johnson, to negotiate
an agreement by which the strikers would return to work. In fact figures for the
cost of living would have justified sharper cuts, and similar reductions had already
been accepted by British postal workers, who had not gone on strike.[18]

An important element in the negotiated return to work on 30 September was
that there would be no victimisation of strikers. Unfortunately, Walsh continued to
display vindictiveness towards union activists, and much of the next fifteen months
would be taken up with disciplinary hearings and appeals.[19] Nevertheless postal
workers had secured the right to strike and a new unity that led to the amalgamation
of the Irish Postal Union and Postal Workers' Union in the new Post Office Workers'
Union in 1923. Three weeks of industrial strife had at least ensured that civil servants
would eventually be regarded on the government's spectrum of industrial relations
as nearer to private-sector workers than to soldiers or policemen.

————

None of these concerns had any visible effect on the thinking of the leadership of
the anti-Treaty IRA, which had no political or military strategy beyond seeking to
make the Free State ungovernable. They did maintain quite an effective propaganda

machine, which challenged the government's legitimacy from the outbreak of hostilities to the bitter end of the Civil War, but it rarely referred to bread-and-butter issues, such as rates of pay or the right to strike. It was largely the work of Erskine Childers and Joe MacDonagh, two leading figures in the pre-Truce struggle who brought considerable expertise in journalism and business, respectively, to the operation, but they were not attuned politically to the prevailing mood of a public sick of war and disruption.

The first issue of *Poblacht na hÉireann: War News* was published on Wednesday 28 June, the 'Seventh Year of the Republic.' Appearing as soon as the attack on the Four Courts began, it was a poster rather than a newspaper, printed on one side so that it could be slapped up on walls or notice-boards. It tried to appear daily and in fact managed 175 issues by 16 March 1923, six weeks before the IRA ceased operations, an average of one issue every 1½ days. Only two issues were mimeographed, including number 175.[20] It managed to produce a special Christmas supplement and some 'stop press' editions, beginning on 16 November, when it announced the arrest and forthcoming trial of Erskine Childers. It also published his speech to the military tribunal that sentenced him to death, and similar items that were heavily censored in the national press.

Besides members of the IRA and Fianna Éireann it had other sympathisers who distributed it, including possibly Father Albert Bibby and Father Dominic O'Connor, the two Capuchin priests who had stayed with the Four Courts garrison throughout the bombardment, tending the sick and giving the last sacraments.[21]

It has to be remembered that, despite their espousal of the right to free speech, the anti-Treaty forces were not averse to denying it to others, including the *Freeman's Journal*, which in early 1922 published the proceedings of the IRA convention in March and was itself reduced to mimeographed production for no less than fifteen issues after its presses were smashed by IRA Volunteers. It only returned to normal production on 25 April, just in time to report on the general strike against militarism. In Cork the *Cork Examiner* and other papers were subjected to censorship by the anti-Treaty IRA during the brief 'Munster Republic' that was even more severe than that of the Free State.

The first issue of *Poblacht na hÉireann*, on 28 June 1922, announced dramatically that Tom Ennis, a Collins loyalist and former commander of the 2nd Battalion of the Dublin Brigade, had demanded the surrender of the Four Courts at 3:40 a.m. and had opened fire at 4:07 a.m. The main item was a brief statement from Rory O'Connor, declaring that 'THE BOYS ARE GLORIOUS AND WE WILL FIGHT FOR THE REPUBLIC TO THE END.' It called on all citizens to defend 'your Republic' and denounced the National Army as 'traitors and mercenaries in Irish uniforms paid, equipped and armed by England,' with artillery 'borrowed from Churchill.' The paper was factually accurate and maintained its fevered tenor throughout the coming months.

The second issue, on 29 June, contained tersely written news briefs, including an interview with de Valera lamenting that the Provisional Government had yielded to British pressure to attack 'the best and bravest of our nation.' At the bottom of the page Paddy O'Daly, another Collins loyalist, was denounced for ignoring protests by the Red Cross over his shelling of the hospital section in the Four Courts. It claimed that a convoy of ten RIC lorries had been delivered to 'FS Officers' in Dublin Castle earlier that day and that joint foot patrols of British and Free State troops were taking place in the south inner city.

The following issue repeated the allegation of joint Free State and British army patrols in Dublin and said that Free State soldiers were using 'the Tower of St Michan's Protestant Church and the Protestant Medical Mission as sniping posts against the soldiers of the Irish Republic.' It asked whether this constituted civilised warfare and, 'if not, will the Irish People tolerate it?' The same issue reported that King George V was disbanding the Irish regiments of the British army 'because they could not be reliable in operating against their fellow countrymen.' In any case 'he has a good substitute in the new Royal Irish Republican Army of Beggars Bush who are not so squeamish.'[22]

Besides *Poblacht na hÉireann* there was a plethora of underground material, mimeographed, typewritten or printed on small presses for distribution around the city; some of the pamphlets were produced in Britain. Each additional blow to the Republican cause fuelled the frenetic energy of the writers with a mixture of anger and fear, humour and outrage, as the reaction to the deaths of Cathal Brugha and Harry Boland shows. One leaflet adopted a traditional, reverential approach and was entitled 'In Memory of Cathal Brugha and Harry Boland and their many brave comrades who have fallen in defence of the Irish Republic.' It contrasts the pageantry that accompanied the state funerals of Griffith and Collins with the relatively low-key obsequies for the Republic's martyrs.

> Not for these, O Eire,
> Not for these, or thee.
> Pipers, trumpeters, blazing loud,
> The throbbing drums and colours flying,
> And the long drawn muffled roar of the crowd
> The voice of the human race:
>
> Theirs it is to inherit
> Fame of a finer grace,
> In the self-renewing spirit
> And the untameable heart,
> Ever defeated, yet undefeated,
> Of thy remembering race.

By contrast there was this raw piece of doggerel:

> Who killed Cathal Brugha?
> 'I,' said Mick Collins with a toss of his head
> ''Tis well he is dead
> 'I killed Cathal Brugha.'

> Who killed Cathal Brugha?
> 'I,' said Mulcahy
> 'But our friendship's not ended
> 'The killing was splendid
> 'I killed Cathal Brugha.'

> Who killed Cathal Brugha?
> 'We,' said the guards
> 'With the kindest regards
> 'His blood's on our banners
> 'We taught the fool manners
> 'We killed Cathal Brugha.'[23]

Children followed the examples set by their elders with rhymes such as

> What's the news, what's the news?
> De Valera's pawned his shoes
> To buy ammunition for his men.
> They were eating currant buns
> When they heard the Free State guns
> And all the dirty cowards ran away.[24]

They also imitated them in other ways. Fifteen boys appeared in Dublin District Court on Tuesday 10 October 1922 charged with causing £3 10s worth of damage to the grounds of St Mark's Church (Church of Ireland) in Great Brunswick Street (Pearse Street) as well as breaking gas lamps valued at 16s. Rev. John Carson said the boys had knocked down a portion of wall, pulled up shrubs and broken a gas lamp during their fight. The arresting officer said they were 'engaged in mimic warfare, on one side of republicans and the other of Free Staters. They were throwing stones at each other.' The magistrate said he could not understand families allowing their children to take part in 'such desperate practices.' The parents of each boy were ordered to pay 6s 2d in compensation and provide bail of £5 to keep the peace for two years. The boys were put on probation for the same period.[25]

———

The Republicans had always been more effective on the propaganda front than in their military endeavours during the War of Independence, and now their reverses saw them reopen another area of operations in which they had enjoyed considerable success: the prisons. However, they would not receive the same general sympathy available during the War of Independence as, unlike the British forces, almost every member of the National Army killed in the Civil War had a family and friends within the new state.

When three of the women most closely identified with the Republican prisoners' issue—Charlotte Despard, Maud Gonne MacBride and Hanna Sheehy Skeffington—interrupted the debate on the new Free State constitution on 20 September they were hissed by other members of the public in the visitors' gallery of the Dáil.[26] After their removal the Labour Party leader, Thomas Johnson, and the new state's Minister for Foreign Affairs, Desmond Fitzgerald, apologised to the Dáil for the interruption and explained that the ladies had been told they could not interrupt the debate. Cosgrave accepted their explanations and said, 'It was possible that a person, particularly a lady, might lose control through emotion, but what occurred that day appeared to be a concerted movement on the part of the three persons responsible.' The third deputy who had provided them with tickets was the Lord Mayor, Laurence O'Neill, who, unabashed, agreed to receive a deputation on behalf of the city council a few days later.

Meanwhile a Prisoners' Defence Association was established at a meeting in the Mansion House presided over by another veteran suffrage and Republican campaigner, Helena Molony. Charlotte Despard proposed the motion establishing the new organisation, and Father Kevin O'Farrelly from Mount Argus Church in Harold's Cross gave a vivid account of a visit he had just made to Wellington Barracks to see a prisoner, Fergus Murphy. The priest had difficulty gaining access to the prison, where the medical officer told him that Murphy had a slight scalp wound and did not need a priest. When pressed for more information the doctor said, 'My duty is to dress their wounds ... not listen to their complaints.' It was only when Father O'Farrelly pointed out that if he was not allowed to see Murphy it would only confirm reports that the prisoner had been tortured and was now critically ill that he was permitted to look for him across the barbed wire. When a soldier called for Murphy, prisoners shouted, 'You did for him!' Eventually Murphy emerged from the press of bodies. Father O'Farrelly told the Mansion House crowd that

> as he drew near, I had a sickening feeling, because I had never before seen a man after torture. His head, from the eyes and ears upwards, was heavily bandaged. His eyes were blacked and twitching with pain. His face on both sides of the nose was also black. His right cheek was terribly swollen. I asked him what had happened him. He motioned to the Intelligence Department and said, 'They took me down there last night and left me as you see me.'[27]

A colleague of Father O'Farrelly, Father Joseph Smith, had already written to the newspapers about the incident, and it was raised in the Dáil by a Labour deputy, Thomas O'Connell, who demanded an inquiry into allegations that prisoners were being tortured. The veteran Dublin labour leader William O'Brien said he knew innocent people, let alone prisoners, who had been ill-treated before being released, and the independent deputies Alfie Byrne and Laurence O'Neill supported the call. Cosgrave dismissed the allegations as propaganda and said that Father O'Farrelly's colleague was not an impartial observer.[28]

––––

The prisoners' issue had already proved divisive for the Corporation (see chapter 4) and proved even more so now. The same formidable trio of women who disrupted the proceedings of the Dáil presented their case in the council chamber on 9 October. On this occasion the public gallery was filled with supporters, almost all of them 'women and girls,' according to the *Irish Times*. Charlotte Despard presented a letter from the anti-Treaty TD and city alderman Seán T. O'Kelly. She then described the plight of between six thousand and seven thousand prisoners in Free State custody. She claimed that some prisoners were being tortured and expressed particular concern for those in Wellington Barracks. Living conditions there were a health hazard, with 145 prisoners sharing three wash-basins. There was an open latrine, and raw sewage overflowed into the prisoners' compound. At Mountjoy she said prisoners could have a bath only once every six weeks because of the overcrowding, and she called on the Corporation to assert its authority in the city.

Jennie Wyse Power, a founder-member of Sinn Féin and prominent pro-Treaty councillor, rose to speak. She had supported the call by a majority of the Corporation in July for the men who surrendered at the Four Courts to be treated as prisoners of war, but this failed to win her a hearing now, and her voice was drowned by calls to 'Sit down.' Alderman William O'Brien, leader of the main Labour faction on the Corporation, who had been one of the architects of the movement's alliance with Sinn Féin and the IRA in the War of Independence, called on the Lord Mayor to have the public gallery cleared. He was the next to be heckled, with a cry that 'You were in jail and you were glad to get out of it.'

Surprisingly, it was Sir Andrew Beattie, a veteran unionist and now member of the Municipal Reform Association, who secured a hearing when the question was asked about what the visiting justices of the peace were doing to inspect prison conditions. He pointed out that the election of visiting justices had been put off for a year, but there was nothing to stop the retiring justices—himself included—seeking visiting rights. The last time he had visited Mountjoy it was 'in good order.' The Government had a difficult task, but the men in prison should be 'brought to justice. If found guilty let them get their sentence, but if they were innocent why should they not be set free?'

There were claims from the gallery that Dr M. J. Russell, the city's Medical Superintendent, had been refused admission to Kilmainham Prison, which was once more being used to house political prisoners. This brought the councillors a brief reprieve. When Dr Russell appeared, to loud applause from the public gallery, it was to confirm that he had called to Kilmainham and had spoken to the deputy governor, who assured him that complaints were being attended to. Dr Russell told the Corporation he had no right of entry to government premises, even in connection with serious health or sanitary issues.

An anti-Treaty councillor, Laurence Raul, called for an inter-party committee to inquire into conditions in the prisons, but Alderman James Hubbard Clark— like Sir Andrew Beattie a former unionist and now the leader of the MRA— declined a nomination to the committee, as did an MRA colleague, Michael Medlar, who added that he 'did not believe there was anything to inquire into. It was all propaganda.'

Uproar ensued, with cries of 'Traitor' and 'Sit down.' Hubbard Clark then sought to calm things by proposing that the Corporation call on the Provisional Government to investigate the complaints. Unfortunately, in seconding the motion a pro-Treaty Sinn Féin councillor, George Lyons, said, 'I don't know why this delegation came near us, or organised a gang to shout us down.' This time the Lord Mayor had to ask Maud Gonne MacBride to appeal for calm. She climbed onto a chair to call for quiet but received no thanks from Lyons. 'He had gone to the prisons to try and get first-hand information on the matter,' and, he added, in a side swipe at Maud Gonne MacBride,

> he had as much right as any foreigner to talk about this matter in his native country. He had himself a nephew in prison. He did not live in St Stephen's Green. He had lived in the slums and he had worked in the slums. He went into houses and took down from the mouths of mothers and wives and sisters of prisoners their complaints. He had also visited the mothers and widows of the murdered soldiers of Ireland [uproar in gallery]. The council had been taken for a political stunt.

John Lawlor of Trades Council Labour said it was unfair to call the deputation 'an organised gang'. Some had lost sons, and the sons of others were in prison. When people came to see them in such circumstances the Corporation 'could not expect them to be like saints.' The leader of Lawlor's group, the union veteran P. T. Daly, said the Corporation should demand the right to inspect all the prisons in the city, but he 'would not lend himself to the sufferings of the prisoners being used for political purposes.'

On that note a compromise was reached, with Hubbard Clark and Medlar agreeing at last to serve on the committee to investigate the plight of the prisoners, alongside Alderman Kathleen Clarke, the leading anti-Treayite on the Corporation.[29]

The committee would publicise conditions in the prison, but it was at the price of even poorer relations with the government. The mediating influence of Laurence O'Neill, who knew Cosgrave well, was lost when he was incapacitated by illness for the rest of the year.

When the Corporation next debated the prisoners issue, on 24 October, Alfie Byrne presided. A report from Dr Russell showed that he had not been as successful as Father O'Farrell in gaining access to Wellington Barracks, nor had the committee itself. Byrne, who was its chairman, now reported that he had had a conversation with Cosgrave on 13 October in which the latter insisted that there was no ill-treatment of prisoners. There was 'some overcrowding ... but that was not the fault of the Government.'

Alderman Thomas O'Reilly (Republican Labour), who did not allow the fact that he was the largest slum landlord on the Corporation to temper his outrage, said he was appalled by reports of conditions in Wellington Barracks. He demanded that members of the Corporation who were TDs raise the issue 'through the alleged Dáil—not the Dáil, but the alleged Dáil.' This brought applause from the public gallery, where members of the Prisoners' Defence Association had once more appeared in force, having been admitted on promising again not to interrupt proceedings and then heckling any speaker whose contribution they did not like.

The leader of the Trades Council Labour group, P. T. Daly, who also chaired the Public Health Committee, said the Corporation had no right to enter government buildings in the city, but there had never been an objection by the British when concern had been expressed about conditions in the past, even at Fron Goch in Wales, where insurgents had been interned after the 1916 Rising. He said that the British authorities had recognised the value of such visits in improving the material conditions, mental health and even discipline among prisoners.

But it was clear from M. J. Moran's contribution that there was no appetite for pursuing the issue further among many councillors, especially as they did not believe there was 'anything wrong' in the prisons, which provoked more heckling.

One step the Corporation did take was to give half pay to the families of Republican prisoners who were employees of the city. A similar scheme had existed for men who volunteered to join the British army during the First World War, and some employees who were imprisoned or were on the run during the War of Independence received full pay. This decision would lead the Minister for

Finance, Ernest Blythe, to instruct the Corporation in early 1923 to discontinue the practice or face financial sanctions, provoking another row with the government that was as bitter as any with Dublin Castle in earlier times.[30] (See chapter 8.)

———

As their numbers grew, the issue of the prisoners would have an increasingly polarising effect on opinion in Dublin, and the country at large. Those opposed to the Treaty from the outset would secure growing support from prisoners' families as well as those concerned about humanitarian and civil liberties issues, including supporters of the Treaty.

Meanwhile the growing level of atrocity on each side fed the flames of fratricide. On the same day that the Corporation met, an inquest began into the deaths of three young Republicans. Edwin Hughes (aged seventeen), Brendan Holohan (also seventeen) and Joseph Rogers (sixteen) went out on the night of Friday 6 October with a bottle of paste and a bundle of posters to put up around the streets of Drumcondra, where they lived. The bodies of Hughes and Holohan were discovered next morning near the village of Red Cow in west Co. Dublin and that of Joseph Rogers in a quarry nearby. Hughes had been shot through the heart and Holohan in the back of the head. Both young men had other wounds to the abdomen, torso and limbs. When Rogers was found the overcoat he was wearing was 'saturated with blood.' He had sixteen wounds, including three to the head. One bullet had struck him through the nose, another through the right jaw and the third in the back of the head. Any one of these could have been the fatal shot, yet Dr V. Lee, medical officer at the nearby army camp in Tallaght, who examined the bodies, found that Rogers was 'slightly warm', and the local parish priest had administered the sacraments shortly beforehand, as he thought the youth might still be alive.

Lawyers for the dead boys' families made a determined effort at the inquest to have the jury bring in a verdict of murder against Commandant Charles Dalton, a National Army officer whose brother Emmet was one of the commanders who played a leading role in the attack on the Four Courts in July and in the capture of Cork the following month and had been with Collins at Bealnablath. Charlie Dalton had worked as a member of IRA intelligence in the War of Independence. The brothers were well known in Drumcondra, having grown up a few streets away from the dead youths.

The inquest attracted great public interest and showed how intimate and local the violence was becoming in Dublin. It also exposed the gulf in perceptions of political legitimacy that now existed between combatants.

The victims' youth inevitably attracted public sympathy. Edwin Hughes was an engineering student, Joseph Rogers an apprentice car mechanic, 'a child in years but a man in stature,' said one of the families' solicitors, Michael Comyn, and Brendan Holohan was a clerk in Arnott's who had won a first-class exhibition (scholarship) at middle grade but clearly lacked the means to continue his studies. All three were members of the IRA, Holohan a 'private' who had joined only a week earlier. Despite their youth, the other two had been active in the War of Independence as members of Fianna Éireann.[31]

Comyn led what in effect became the prosecution team on behalf of the families. His own sympathies were firmly anti-Treaty. He came from Ballyvaghan, Co. Clare, where his family had been active in the Land League. He had become a militant nationalist and had numbered the veteran Fenian John O'Leary and 1916 leaders Tom Clarke and Patrick Pearse among his friends. He would go on to advise Éamon de Valera on the land annuities dispute in the 1930s.[32] He had taken the test case on behalf of Cork prisoners sentenced to death by British courts-martial the previous year. As we have seen (chapter 1), it proved a legal failure but had ultimately saved their lives. As an opponent of the Treaty he had provided shelter to men on the run, including Erskine Childers. He could therefore have faced prosecution himself under the Army Emergency Powers Resolution, which made aiding and abetting the Republican forces a crime.

Hughes appears to have been the moving spirit behind the decision to go postering that Friday night. He had a typewriter and printing press in his parents' house in Clonliffe Road. His mother, who supported him in his activities, told the inquest that her son had been a member of the 'Republican Army since his childhood, as was also his brother.' He volunteered to put up the posters after a young Cumann na mBan member, Jennie O'Toole, told her senior officer, Julia Gordon, that she was afraid to go out again after being assaulted on the previous two Saturdays.

The three youths set out at about 10:30 p.m. on Friday. Unfortunately for them, Leah Sandross, who lived opposite Hughes, was being dropped home by her fiancé, Captain Nicholas Tobin of the National Army, just as the lads began their flyposting mission. Sandross and Tobin had spent the evening at the theatre with a Commandant O'Connell. On the way home they had been given a lift by Charlie Dalton in an open-topped Lancia touring car, a National Army vehicle that he intended using to arrest Republican suspects in the city that night. Nicholas Tobin was a brother of Liam Tobin, Collins's former deputy director of intelligence, who was now serving with Emmet Dalton in Cork.

This account of the innocuous, if improper, use of a military vehicle illustrates the intimate and privileged world of the new Free State officer corps. The evidence was strongly contested on both sides. After leaving Leah Sandross home, the officers certainly stopped and questioned two or three young men at the corner of Clonliffe Road and Jones's Road a hundred yards away. According to some accounts, they arrested the youths, seized their posters and retrieved two revolvers from the tail of a trench coat one of them was wearing.[33] They maintained that they had arrested four other men that night and taken them to Wellington Barracks for questioning, and that all four prisoners had been subsequently released. None of the men arrested was armed but were found to have copies of *Poblacht na hÉireann* on them. Three men subsequently appeared at the inquest to testify that they had been arrested and released in the early hours of Saturday morning. Their names were not disclosed in court, to protect them from reprisals.[34]

Captain Stephen Murphy, an intelligence officer at Wellington Barracks who interrogated the men, gave times for their arrival that ruled out Dalton and his companions being in the vicinity of Red Cow at the time local people heard the shots that killed the three youths. On the other hand, eyewitnesses to the arrests, including Leah Sandross and a CID detective, Charles Murphy, gave evidence that strongly suggests that the three youths had been stopped and that at least one of them was carrying guns. A witness at Red Cow described a vehicle similar to that used by Charlie Dalton in the vicinity at the time shots were heard.

The truth will probably never be definitively established. It took the jury only three-quarters of an hour to return their verdict that the three youths died 'from gunshot wounds inflicted by a person, or persons, unknown.' The jury were clearly unmoved by the posters that festooned the exterior walls of the temporary coroner's court in Clondalkin when it opened that morning declaring 'The Republic lives' and 'Perjurers beware.'

What is indisputable are the very different world views that now existed within the previously united ranks of militant nationalism. The Provisional Government was so determined to prevent itself being put on trial over the deaths of the three youths that its legal representative, John O'Byrne, made it clear that he was not there to protect Charlie Dalton, who hired T. M. Healy to represent him. O'Byrne had been even more engaged as a lawyer in the separatist cause than Comyn. He was a legal adviser to the Irish delegation in the Treaty negotiations and then became a member of the committee established by Michael Collins to draft the Constitution of the Irish Free State.[35]

Timothy Healy was one of the ablest and longest-serving nationalist lawyers of his day and certainly the most controversial. Widely credited with the destruction of Parnell, he had made his accommodation, albeit reluctantly, with Sinn Féin and would shortly be appointed first Governor-General of the Irish Free State.[36] In defending Dalton he sought to expose the flawed thinking behind the demand for the officer's indictment. He had a difficult task, as some of the evidence—a scream in the night, a fusillade of shots from the quarry where young Rogers was found, the medical evidence of wanton brutality and possible torture—was harrowing.

Comyn had resorted to the sort of rhetoric that had been successful in securing murder verdicts from juries confronted with the victims of Crown forces little more than a year previously. 'There is murder here, the murder of these noble young boys,' whose 'only crime had been to volunteer to put up posters after a young girl had been intimidated out of doing so,' he said. He

> was there to assist the Coroner and the jury in the vindication of human liberty and the sanctity of human life. In the sad condition of the country they were the only tribunal to which appeal could be made. The jurors represented the people and their voice was the voice of the people. The narrative he would submit would be one of chivalry and devotion on the part of these noble young boys—one that would make the Red Cow quarry a place of pilgrimage, where altars would be raised to these heroic boys who died that a little girl might be saved from injury and insult.

Healy's defence was more oblique. He challenged the legitimacy of the proceedings by arguing that the coroner's court had no legal standing in the interregnum that now existed between the end of direct British rule and the establishment of the Irish Free State, as the Treaty did not come into effect until one year after its signing, namely on 6 December 1922. He further argued that the existing legislation required all witnesses to have their summons served by the RIC; their successors, the Civic Guard, had no legal jurisdiction to do so.

This cut no ice with the coroner or the lawyers representing the next of kin, who insisted that the court was covered by the British legislation. While Healy lost the argument, it helped him win his case with the jury, for he now sought to draw the argument away from evidence 'drenched with innuendo' to wider issues of public concern, above all the preservation of order. He pointed out that there were no inquests being held for Free State soldiers.

> There was no inquest on Michael Collins. But an attempt was made the moment anyone connected with those who started the civil war was injured … to resort to the King's courts. The Coroner was sitting as the King's Coroner. The jurors were summoned as the King's jurors and the witnesses brought there came on warrants signed by the Coroner by virtue of the office he held in the King's name.

He said his client had 'no hand, act or part in this transaction' and that the prisoners he had taken were 'alive and well and in court.' The youths who died, 'who could not have been more than eight or nine years of age when the Great War started,' had been living through a time 'plied with stories of war, battle and bloodshed, so that human life seemed no longer to weigh in the scales of conscience.' Nor were the posters they intended putting up that night ordinary anti-government posters. They declared:

To all whom it concerns

Any person employed in the Free State forces in uniform or mufti found loitering in the vicinity of Drumcondra on or after Sunday, October 8th, 1922, shall be shot at sight. This warning applies to the murder gang, otherwise known as the military intelligence and so-called CID men. Also any person giving information to or helping the same.

Signed Irish Republican Defence Association, Drumcondra Branch.

Warning—Any person found disfiguring or destroying this notice should be drastically dealt with.

Dalton was a local man, and if he had seen the notices he could well have read them as notice of his own forthcoming execution. It was not that Healy particularly wished to draw attention to that point but rather to the general lethal intent of the dead youths. Annie Hughes, the mother of Edwin, inadvertently assisted him by admitting that both her sons were members of the IRA. She stated that Edwin must have been one of the suspects arrested that night, because independent witnesses had described one of them as lame or limping, and her son had 'wrenched his foot … while engaged in the cause which he had at heart.' She confirmed that Republican material, including the poster in the name of the Irish Republican Defence Association, had been produced in the house.

The hearing certainly took its toll on her. When she reminded Healy under cross-examination that he was there himself as a 'King's counsel' it drew laughter from the body of the court, and although it was at Healy's expense she lost her composure. 'You may have the pretence of gentlemen,' she told the court, 'but you are not men. It has cost me a great deal to come here and try to keep myself up vindicating my boy. If you had to go through the same ordeal as I have you would find something else to laugh at.' She then burst into tears.

The officers giving evidence were made of sterner stuff and may have been buoyed up by the presence of a large number of National Army personnel in the court. When Captain Stephen Murphy corroborated the evidence of his fellow-officers that they had delivered prisoners to him about the time the youths were being shot in Clondalkin, Comyn asked him, 'How long are you in the Army?' Murphy retorted, 'I am in the IRA before you applied for the Solicitor-Generalship,' which drew applause from the body of the court.

The exchanges grew more heated. When Comyn asked him what he considered seditious literature, Murphy replied: 'Anything in the nature of propaganda against the state.'

Comyn: Against the Free State?
Murphy: Against the National Army.
Comyn: Would documents against the Irish Republican Army be seditious?
Murphy: We are the Irish Republican Army.

When Comyn argued that no inquest was required on Michael Collins because he had died in battle, a voice from the body of the court roared, 'You are a liar.' These were men as committed as their opponents to their belief that they were the true inheritors of the Fenian tradition and militant nationalism.

Alexander Lynn underlined these differences, and also the shaky constitutional edifice of the new state, when he said he had a brief for the 'GHQ of the IRA.' When the coroner protested that no-one could appear in his court representing 'an illegal association of men engaged in national revolt against the … government,' Lynn replied that the army that his learned colleague John O'Byrne represented had no legal existence either. No army could be raised except by a special act of Parliament, and 'the National Army is no army at all.' O'Byrne said he did not represent any army but the Provisional Government. The coroner decided that the issues were beyond his remit and that his only task was to ascertain the cause of death of the three youths.

Summing up his case, Healy returned to the argument that the other side had started the Civil War and, invoking the rhetoric of his former leader, Charles Stewart Parnell, asked the jury, 'Once you begin battle and bloodshed, what man can place boundaries to the march of extermination?'

The speedy verdict of the jurors confirmed his judgement that there would be little sympathy for those seen as the initiators of the Civil War. Of course it could be argued that the Civil War had been initiated by the assault on the Four Courts by the National Army; but it was the continued refusal of the anti-Treaty forces to accept the outcome of the conventional conflict that rendered men of substance, such as the Clondalkin jurors, increasingly tolerant of the onward 'march of extermination' by the National Army, legal or not, if it ended the mayhem.

In the long run, the failure to hold an inquest into the death of Collins and of other National Army personnel was a serious miscalculation by the Provisional Government. As T. M. Healy had pointed out, it conferred premier rights to victimhood on those opposed to the Treaty, something they would exploit for decades to come.

———

The references at the inquest, and by Charlotte Despard in her address to Dublin Corporation, to men being interrogated in Wellington Barracks reflected growing disquiet about the activities of Military Intelligence. It was in fact only half the intelligence network Michael Collins had set up in the city. The other half had an even more unsavoury reputation.

Figures such as Charlie Dalton, who had been part of Collins's intelligence-gathering operations in the War of Independence, now operated through Military Intelligence, but many of the operatives who carried out the assassinations or attacks on British forces, based on information provided by men such as Dalton, were attached to the Criminal Investigation Department, based at Oriel House, at the corner of Westland Row and Fenian Street. Collins's deputy head of intelligence in the IRA, Liam Tobin, was given responsibility for both groups, but on 8 August Collins decided to split their structures, with army officers returning from Oriel House to Wellington Barracks and other military posts while the men remaining in Oriel House purportedly concentrated on armed criminal gangs and detective work. Apart from a few former moles in Dublin Castle, such as David Neligan, their capacity for the latter duty was limited, and unlikely to improve, given their contempt for the DMP detectives they had been killing before the Truce. The feeling was reciprocated; and both looked down on the Republican Police, which had usually been made up of the most expendable IRA Volunteers.

Although Oriel House was brought technically under civilian control, the minister responsible was Joe McGrath, another close confidant of Collins. Whether this was an example of Collins's tendency to micro-manage and control as many parts of government as possible or a genuine attempt to civilianise Oriel House and make it an Irish 'Scotland Yard', as some senior military personnel thought, we shall never know, because a fortnight later he was dead. Given his capacity for extending his reach into every crevice of the regime, however, it is hard to believe that his sole concern was to make Oriel House more amenable to the formal state structures.

After Collins's death McGrath was seconded to the army to head all intelligence operations. Under his direction Oriel House personnel continued their heavy involvement in tracking down, interrogating and in some cases torturing and killing suspects.

Its operations were extended in November to include a Protective Officers' Corps that was dedicated to guarding ministers, important government supporters, public buildings and some commercial premises. A Citizens' Defence Force followed, which included about a hundred British ex-servicemen as well as former IRA Volunteers and some women. Its driving force was Henry Harrison, who typified some of the more colourful constitutional nationalists who came to the aid of the Free State. From a wealthy unionist background, he converted to Home Rule and became Parnell's secretary in the final phase of the latter's career. He was also close to Parnell's successor, John Redmond. He became a banker but in March 1915, at the age of forty-seven, he joined the British army and on a number of occasions was decorated for bravery. After the war he gravitated towards Sinn Féin, defending its policies at the Kildare Street Club, and in 1920 he became secretary to the Irish Dominion League, founded by Sir Horace Plunkett to champion what became the political outcome of the War of Independence. When the Civil War broke out he offered his services to the Irish Free State as a private soldier; instead he was appointed supervisor of the Citizens' Defence Force at Oriel House.[37]

Ernest Blythe explained the rationale behind the Citizens' Defence Force, and indeed the Oriel House enterprise, by recalling that

at one stage during the Civil War, when groups of Irregulars carrying revolvers made attacks unexpectedly on people and buildings, and it proved impossible to deal with them by ordinary methods, Henry Harrison volunteered to organise a system of armed civilian patrols. He got together a number of men whom he could trust and, armed with revolvers, they patrolled certain areas where they thought they were likely to meet similar groups of Irregulars. I believe that they did on occasion effect contact and exchange shots with Irregular groups. Kevin O'Higgins was the Minister directly in touch with Henry Harrison, and I remember that for a time, at any rate, he was satisfied that Harrison's patrols were serving a useful purpose and proving very disturbing to marauding Irregulars.[38]

The accretion of the Citizens' Defence Force brought the total CID strength to 350, of whom about 140 were for use against Republicans. Oriel House also ran a number of agents in the enemy's ranks. The director, Staff Captain Pat Moynihan, had worked as an investigator in the Rotunda Rink mail centre, which had replaced the GPO after it was destroyed in the 1916 Rising. His job was to detect theft and missing mail, and he used his position to intercept sensitive correspondence for Collins.

Moynihan carried out other undercover work, including posing as 'George Moreland' to rent the premises at 10 Upper Abbey Street where Collins's Squad was based in the War of Independence. He acquired other premises as arms dumps, including the stables at Brook's Hotel, where the kerosene for burning down the Custom House in 1921 was stored.[39] Like members of the Squad, his experience fighting the British gave him an intimate knowledge of the IRA network and tactics in Dublin, and he had a good record for detecting crime within the Post Office. He denied that prisoners were tortured in Oriel House during the Civil War and said in defence of its interrogation methods that they were 'at least as humane as that form at present extensively used in America and known as the Third Degree.' He argued that the fear inspired by the very name of Oriel House caused many suspects to break, without any pressure being applied to them beyond the prospect of a visit to the premises.

By the time the Civil War ended the CID would have netted five hundred prisoners and many weapons and have built up a bank of files on two thousand individuals.[40] This probably made it the most effective counter-insurgency unit working for the Free State.

Joseph O'Connor, commander of the 4th Battalion of the Dublin Brigade and one of the few experienced senior anti-Treaty officers still at liberty, planned an attack on Oriel House in the autumn of 1922. Access through a manhole was used to plant four mines in the basement of the building, but only one exploded when it was detonated on 23 October, and the main entrance hall absorbed most of the blast, which shattered shop windows in Lincoln Place. Seven civilians were injured by flying glass. IRA Volunteers outside fired fifty or sixty rounds at the building but made no attempt to enter it, beating a retreat once CID members began returning fire. Meanwhile Moynihan had gone into the basement and cut the wires on the three unexploded bombs with a scissors.

No-one was hit in this exchange, but four IRA Volunteers were captured subsequently and became the first Republicans to be executed under the new Army Emergency Powers Resolution, which made it a capital offence to be caught in possession of arms or to participate in attacks on the National Army.[41]

Undeterred, O'Connor ordered another attack on the building by members of G Company of the 4th Battalion, in spite of the increased security. A machine-gun had been posted on the first landing covering the front door, and the plan was to send two Volunteers into the hall on the pretext of offering information and then kill or disable the machine-gunner. The shots would be the signal for twenty more Volunteers outside to join the attack. But the Volunteers sent in to dispose of the machine-gunner missed, so that when the rest of the assault party rushed in they were met by a hail of fire. They beat a hasty retreat.

O'Connor himself was not to enjoy his freedom for long. Like many anti-Treaty Volunteers, he continued to work at his day job, as a rates collector for Dublin Corporation, as he had a family to support. While his job meant he could keep on the move around the city, he had to sign in occasionally at the office, and his luck ran out not long after he ordered the second attack on Oriel House. 'As I was signing the Attendance Book in the City Rates Office … I felt a gun being stuck in my back and I instantly knew that the game was up.' He was then taken to Wellington Barracks.[42]

Despite being the centre of Military Intelligence, Wellington Barracks was also a regular army post, serving as headquarters for the 2nd Eastern Division, whose main theatre of operations was Dublin and the surrounding counties. Discipline was lax, and it proved possible to bribe guards to slip messages out; but the same indiscipline could also be a disadvantage, as O'Connor discovered after an attack on the complex on 8 November, when IRA volunteers armed with rifles, a Lewis machine gun and Thompson sub-machine guns opened fire on the garrison at their morning parade from surrounding rooftops. About a hundred soldiers, most of them unarmed, thought it was practice firing until they saw bullets ricocheting off the parade ground and ran for cover. 'It seemed as if marbles were being rained down from an immense height,' one soldier told reporters. Sustained fire lasted about five minutes. One soldier was killed and up to twenty-two wounded. Two IRA Volunteers were killed in the follow-up operation—at least one of them after he was taken prisoner—and fourteen suspects were arrested.[43]

As usual, there were non-combatant casualties. William Warren of Leinster Place, a helper at McGuirk's butcher's shop in Harold's Cross, was killed by a shot in the chest, as was the horse pulling the delivery van. The driver, Peter Burke from New Street, was hit above the heart but survived. According to the *Irish Times* he exhibited 'great bravery' by carrying Warren to safety. John Dorney, a historian of the Civil War in Dublin, considers that the attack was the most effective by the IRA in the city during the conflict and attributes the low number of deaths from a range of about fifty yards to 'the paucity of military training in the Anti-Treaty IRA.'

The Republicans made their escape through Kimmage and Crumlin, carrying two badly wounded comrades. They were pursued by National Army personnel, who later claimed to have killed two of them in a fire-fight. Some veterans of the War of Independence now serving as senior members of the National Army said a similar attack had been discussed during the War of Independence but rejected on the grounds that opening fire on unarmed soldiers on parade was 'too dirty'.[44]

Joe O'Connor and other prisoners, including the four men captured at Oriel House, heard the gunfire. 'It was a good sharp fight,' he said,

> but when it was ended our turn came. We were crowded into the Gymnasium and the door locked. Some Staters got outside the north door with sub-machine guns and fired through the wooden door … A strong inside iron bolt deflected the bullets. Only for this the casualties amongst the 250 prisoners would have been very great, but as it was not more than half a dozen were wounded.[45]

Frank Sherwin, a Fianna Éireann member who had joined the National Army briefly at the start of the Civil War but then joined the anti-Treaty IRA, was among a group of young Republicans lifted from a house nearby in the immediate aftermath of the attack. In his memoir, *Independent and Unrepentant*, he wrote: 'We were marched to Wellington Barracks, about a mile away. Some of the people on the street shouted and jeered at us. Perhaps they knew some of the soldiers who had been shot that morning.' He was brought into the Intelligence Department, where Joe Dolan, an old Squad member, interrogated him. Sherwin says he was kicked and punched, 'my clothes were dragged off me until I was naked … I was lashed for about twenty minutes.' The next day he was pistol-whipped, and the following day they set to again, hitting him across the head with a revolver, poking him with wires and a bayonet, thrusting a rifle muzzle into his mouth and threatening to cut his throat with a razor.

By the time he was thrown back in with the other prisoners 'my face was swollen, my nose was broken, several teeth were missing and I had cuts and lumps on my head, with bruises all over my body. I could not stand or move for nine days.' He never recovered the full use of his right arm.[46]

James Spain, a 22-year-old upholsterer, was less fortunate. *Poblacht na hÉireann* described him as a lieutenant in the IRA. He was badly wounded in the leg during the retreat from the attack on Wellington barracks. He lived locally, but never made it home. He was pursued by a National Army patrol with a Lancia armoured car. Limping badly, he approached a Mrs Doleman, who was feeding her hens in Donore Road, and said, 'For God's sake let me in! Jesus, Mary and Joseph help me, if they get me they'll shoot me!' She let him in and then fled into the yard, to be met by a patrol entering by her back gate. They rushed passed her into the house. The last words she heard the young man say were either, 'You would not shoot me, Christy?' or 'Don't shoot me!' According to *Poblacht na hÉireann,* one of the arresting party knew Spain well and had previously threatened to kill him. The prisoner was taken around the corner to Susan Terrace, where a Miss O'Byrne was standing on her doorstep looking out for a funeral. Spain was marched up the street in front of the armoured car. As the group approached, she closed the door. Shortly afterwards she heard shots.

Spain was hit twice in the head, once in the abdomen and once in each knee; a shot behind the left ear may have been a *coup de grâce*. An anonymous National Army witness at the inquest said that Spain might have been with, or in the vicinity of, a group of armed men who attacked the patrol and could have been hit when the armoured car returned their fire. He was certainly known to some of his pursuers, as he had previously been taken prisoner and escaped. No witnesses to his actual death were produced. The jury returned a verdict that he was shot by soldiers acting in pursuit of their duty.[47]

———

November was a busy month for the anti-Treaty IRA in Dublin, which showed a capacity for destruction that extended beyond purely military targets. Income tax offices were attacked, as they had been in the War of Independence, because they were vulnerable and an attack on them struck a potentially damaging blow at the infrastructure of the new state. On 3 November offices were raided in O'Connell Street, Gardiner Street, Adelaide Road and Upper Merrion Street as well as the home of a tax inspector in Morehampton Road. Members of the staff were held at gunpoint while documents were set on fire. On the same day armed men took records from the excise bonded stores in Bonham Street. Further raids took place on 22 November when two income tax district offices at the Mercantile Buildings in Nassau Street were sprinkled with petrol, but the raiders fled when a lorryload of National Army soldiers arrived.[48]

More successful was a raid on the temporary central post office at the Rotunda Rink in Parnell Square. The rink, which had its own claim to fame as the venue of the inaugural meeting of the Irish Volunteers in November 1913, was robbed by armed raiders on Friday 3 November 1922. The following day the watchman was approached by a couple of men seeking access to the building and claiming to be 'Oriel House men'. When he remained sceptical they held him up at gunpoint while twelve Volunteers set the complex alight. It covered almost 150,000 square feet, but it was constructed mainly of wood, and the Fire Brigade was powerless to halt the blaze. The Banba Hall across the square was converted into a temporary sorting office, but the disruption to services was significant. Ironically, the armed guard placed on the premises during the postal strike in September had been removed afterwards as a concession to the strikers.[49]

Railways were becoming another soft target, where the damage wrought far outweighed the risk of capture or injury. Liffey Junction Station at Phibsborough was attacked the following Tuesday, 7 November 1922. When the raiders failed to set it on fire they seized a cattle train that had arrived in the station at 6:55 p.m., decoupled the engine, stoked the furnace and sent it hurtling down the three miles of track to the LNWR station at the North Wall. Not alone the engine but eleven wagons on the track were badly damaged when it collided with them. Miraculously, no-one was hurt, and the wagons prevented the engine from mounting the platform or colliding with a munitions wagon twenty yards away.

Early on 9 November armed men blocked the track with stones at Killiney and seized the station. When a goods train heading from Bray to the city arrived, the driver and fireman were forced at gunpoint 'to put on steam' and to jump off. As the engine began to pick up speed Patrick O'Toole, an elderly milesman (who inspected lines and carried out minor repairs) came across the blockage on the line and hurried towards the station to raise the alarm,

but before I reached it I saw what appeared to be a goods train approaching me. I showed the red light and stood in the centre of the line waiting for the train to pull up. It showed no signs of slackening and when it was almost abreast of me I noticed that it had no wagons or driver. It passed me at a rather slow rate. I dropped my lamp and coat and boarded the footplate. In doing this I hurt my knee and remained clinging to the cab rails of the engine for a few seconds. Using all my strength I pulled myself onto the footplate and managed to shut off the steam.

O'Toole was given a bonus by the directors of the Dublin and South-Eastern Railway for 'the commendable effort he made.'[50]

Similar attacks were made on other trains, and signal boxes were set on fire around the city. One of the worst incidents that winter was on a passenger train from Connacht that was seized at Liffey Junction en route for Broadstone. IRA Volunteers doused several of the carriages with petrol and forced the driver to start up the engine and send it headlong into the terminus, with many of the passengers still on board. At the last minute the driver, M. Glynn, ignored the gunmen's threats and boarded the train again by jumping onto the footplate. He managed to divert the train into a siding and bring it to a halt, but not before a number of passengers had been injured in jumping from the blazing carriages. Glynn was presented with £50 by the Great Midland and Western Railway for his bravery. When the Ministry of Finance enquired about a recognition of Glynn's bravery the general manager of the MGWR replied that he thought the driver 'has already been sufficiently rewarded' but that a letter of thanks from President Cosgrave 'would be greatly appreciated.'[51]

Meanwhile the anti-Treaty IRA ratcheted up its campaign in the west, mounting large-scale attacks on towns ranging from Drumshanbo, Co. Leitrim, to Killorglin, Co. Kerry. The rapid military successes of the opening stages of the Civil War were now in danger of being negated by guerrilla activity on an unprecedented scale.

On 27 September the Provisional Government introduced martial law, although it was pointed out by critics, including Thomas Johnson of the Labour Party, that they were doing little more than retrospectively sanctioning the increasingly brutal acts of elements in the National Army. The Army Emergency Powers Resolution was as legally dubious as some of the practices it endorsed.

———

The primary task of the third Dáil was to draw up a constitution for the Irish Free State so that the terms of the Treaty could be implemented and legislation duly enacted from 6 December 1922 onwards for the newest dominion within the British Empire. The Army Emergency Powers Resolution never reached the statute book, yet it gave the army primary responsibility for establishing law and order and setting up military courts with power to arrest, detain and sentence to death citizens found guilty of a range of offences, including 'taking part in or aiding or abetting any attack upon or using force against the National Forces.' These courts could deal with cases of 'looting, arson, destruction, seizure, unlawful possession or removal of, or damage to any public or private property,' unlawful possession 'of any bomb or article in the nature of a bomb, or any dynamite, gelignite, or other explosive substance, or any revolver, rifle, gun, or other firearm, or lethal weapon, or any ammunition for such firearm.' It even made any breach of general orders or regulations introduced by 'the Army Authorities' an offence punishable by death or penal servitude 'for any period of imprisonment' or a fine 'of any amount, either with or without imprisonment of any person found guilty by such Court or Committee, of any of the offences aforesaid.'

The army was given control over all firearms in the state and had power to intern 'any person taken prisoner, arrested or detained by the National Forces,' with the extraordinary provision that they could be imprisoned outside as well as inside the ironically named Free State. In the Dáil debate, when the Labour deputy Cathal O'Shannon asked if the government intended sending prisoners to the Congo, a government deputy, Dr Pat McCartan, riposted: 'Have some respect for the nation, if you have none for yourselves.'[52] In fact the government was actively considering both St Helena and Lambay Island. However, the British government would not oblige in the first case, while cost, an inadequate water supply and the anticipated 'most strenuous opposition' of the owner, the Honourable Cecil Baring, ruled out the second.[53]

Inevitably the measure led to accusations that it was more draconian than any legislation introduced by the British. But the IRA was reverting to the tactics of the War of Independence with far more weaponry and personnel than in that conflict, and the Provisional Government did not possess the resources and resultant wide margins of tolerance for failure that were available to its British predecessor. Defeat for ministers might mean forfeiting not only office but their lives as well. In proposing the motion, Cosgrave said it was necessary because 'the Irregulars'' armed opposition to the National Army ... is an attempt to overthrow Parliament, and it is a direct challenge to the authority of the people.' He encapsulated the basic issue quite neatly.

One of the reasons put forward for this armed opposition is that the Treaty was accepted under duress, and the question naturally arises as to whether or not the people had a right under the circumstances to accept the Treaty. It was open to them to accept war if that was the alternative; but the minority in the country had no right to say that the people were bound to accept war, or bound to accept their opinions. [This] particular rebellion ... attempts to create a new order in the community. Highwaymen loot and commandeer property, and raid and destroy to such an extent that in certain places people's means of livelihood are practically destroyed.[54]

It was a Dublin shopkeeper speaking, but the Free State was a nation of farmers and shopkeepers.

One of the few deputies representing men and women with little or no property was the Labour Party leader, Thomas Johnson, who challenged the legal basis for the motion and voiced a widely held concern about 'setting up ... a military dictatorship' by 'an army of novices' that had the 'power of life and death over civilians and over soldiers without public trial.' Like many people, Johnson had personal knowledge of the excesses of some National Army members. He cited the case of Michael Neville, an IRA Volunteer from Lisdoonvarna, whose remains were lying in the Pro-Cathedral that day with a Cumann na mBan guard of honour after being found dead in Killester Graveyard.[55]

> A certain man was taken out of his place of employment, taken into the country, and shot. An ordinary murder, motive unknown, one might say. He lies in the Morgue; his friends come to visit him; they pray, and military forces come up in lorries and armoured cars and arrest these men and denounce them, and threaten them, and say: 'If that man had not ever handled a gun, he would not have lain where he is.' That is what happened in the case of this man Neville.

Cathal O'Shannon protested that 'exceptional qualities' were required to perform the task the Government was assigning to

> these young men—and most of them are young men—[who] have not the training, the ability or the experience in decisions, involving big questions of law, constitutionalism and everything else. They are not fit to be the judges in courts that have power of life and death over tens of thousands and hundreds of thousands of people in this country.

He pointed out that deputies did not yet have copies of the army regulations under which these men would be operating and recounted another example of the excesses being indulged in by the National Army from his own constituency.

> To my eternal shame and horror as an Irish citizen I looked to-day on the hands of a man, who was two hours a prisoner, and on his arm are branded two letters. He told me these letters were branded by National troops, in the town of Drogheda. No charge was made against him at all. He told me there were two or three other prisoners who were branded there too. I shall never vote that the power of life and death shall be put into the hands of the officers who ought to have been controlling these four or five soldiers who did that act.

Darrell Figgis also voiced concern about the motion; but it was a signatory of the Treaty, George Gavan Duffy, who was the only deputy to vote with the Labour Party in opposing it. He had already resigned as Minister for Foreign Affairs over the abolition of the Dáil courts. At first he had intended voting for the motion, but he was dismayed at the reaction of Cosgrave and his fellow-ministers, including Gavan Duffy's own replacement, Desmond Fitzgerald, and their responses to criticism. It culminated in an exchange between Gavan Duffy and Cosgrave just before the vote was taken when the former sought to establish what rights citizens had who were to be arraigned before the military.

Duffy: Are they prisoners of war or military prisoners?
Cosgrave: Largely they are people whose mental balance is bad.

The motion was passed by 48 votes to 18.[56]

————

The adoption of this resolution was followed by a two-week period of grace during which Republicans could surrender their weapons and return to civilian life. On 10 October the Catholic hierarchy issued a pastoral letter urging Republicans to 'take advantage of the Government's present offer, and make peace with their own country.' The guerrilla war being carried on by the Irregulars 'is without moral sanction; and therefore the killing of National Soldiers in the course of it is murder before God.' The seizure of property and attacks on the country's infrastructure were acts of robbery and wanton destruction; all those engaging in such activities were contravening the bishops' instructions and thereby could not absolve their sins through confession or be admitted to Holy Communion.

Any priest who gave moral succour to those in arms against the Provisional Government were 'guilty of the gravest scandal' and would have their religious faculties withdrawn. One of these would be Father Albert Bibby, who had been with the Four Courts and the 'Block' garrisons in the opening stages of the Civil War.[57]

There were few defections from Republican ranks, and some men who did 'sign out' resumed military activities, including two of the last Volunteers executed in 1923. (See chapter 9.) It certainly had little effect on the IRA campaign, which continued unabated.

It was not until 17 November that the four men arrested in the aftermath of the attack on Oriel House on 23 October were executed. These were James Fisher, an eighteen-year-old who worked in Ruddell's cigarette factory, Richard Twohig, a 21-year-old who worked at the Inchicore works of the GSWR, and John Gaffney and Peter Cassidy, both aged twenty-one, who worked in Dublin Corporation's electric lighting department. All four had been living at home with their parents. In Twohig's case his mother was a war widow, his father having died in the Great War, and he was the principal breadwinner, with a younger brother and three sisters. Fisher and Twohig, members of the 2nd Battalion of the anti-Treaty Dublin Brigade, were arrested on the day of the attack, while Cassidy and Gaffney were lifted on 27 and 28 October, respectively. All four were arrested on the street and brought to Wellington Barracks for interrogation. They were subsequently court-martialled at the barracks in the days immediately preceding the attack on soldiers on parade there. They were transferred to Kilmainham Prison, where they were shot. According to one account,

the firing party and the Officer in Charge were all young and somewhat raw.
They naturally disliked what they had to do and were somewhat upset. Three of
the young men to be executed were killed instantly. The fourth was not, though
he was providentially rendered unconscious. It therefore became the unenviable
duty of the Officer in Charge to administer the coup de grace with his revolver.

He added that the officer

acted for a moment as if he were going to order the man to be taken to hospital.
He recovered his poise, however, and the execution was completed.[58]

It is possible that the four Volunteers were chosen for execution because their target
had been Oriel House. However, it could equally have had to do with the arrest
on 9 November of Erskine Childers, one of the most hated anti-Treaty figures
among members of the Provisional Government. They may have wanted to create
a pretext for executing a prominent opponent on the relatively less serious charge
of unlawful possession of a firearm by setting a precedent with four ordinary
working-class Volunteers.[59] Whatever the reason, a majority of the cabinet had
concluded that executions were inevitable if the Civil War was to be brought to
a successful conclusion well before Childers' death. The first 'inkling' that Cahir
Davitt, the recently appointed Judge Advocate-General of the National Army, had
that this was the case came from Ernest Blythe, Minister for Local Government, at
a social gathering of ministers and senior officials in September.[60]

In the course of conversation about the state of the country Blythe remarked
that sooner or later drastic action would have to be taken to put an end to a
state of affairs which, if it were allowed to continue indefinitely, would result
in national ruin … I asked him what he meant by 'drastic action.' He said
that, 'when any Irregulars were cornered they seldom if ever fought it out but
usually surrendered tamely, knowing that the worst that could happen them
was a period of internment during which they would be freely supported at the
expense of the State. There was … no element of deterrent effect in this. I asked
did he envisage a policy of military courts and executions, and he said he did.

Davitt warned of the danger of creating martyrs.

Several of those present joined in the discussion which, like most political
arguments in this country, was warm, interesting, and of course entirely
inconclusive. I went home quite convinced that my worst fears were about to
be realised.[61]

Blythe and most of his colleagues feared that the Civil War

> might be brought to an end by negotiations. Individual Commanders in various areas, instead of pursuing the war with full vigour as they ought to have done, were inclined to try to make contact with their opposite numbers and enter upon discussions. This seems to have extended ... right through the top ranks of the Army. One cabinet meeting took place at which it was decided that nobody on behalf of the Government would negotiate any more ... until the Irregular forces surrendered. General Mulcahy was present at the meeting and apparently agreed in full with the decision, though he had already on his own account made an arrangement to meet Mr. de Valera. As far as we could learn afterwards, Mulcahy went straight out of the cabinet meeting, got into his car at the door of Government Buildings and drove to a rendezvous with Mr. de Valera. Nothing came of the conversations which took place between them and quite possibly the other Ministers would never have heard of the meeting but for the fact that a Father McGuinness ... who was Provincial or General of the Carmelites and who had brought about the meeting, wished to publish a statement in the Press about it.

When Mulcahy admitted to his colleagues that the meeting took place Blythe recalled that

> there was a dead silence for what seemed to be minutes. All of us realised that the only thing that it was proper to say was that General Mulcahy must hand in his resignation. [But] in view of the state of affairs generally, and in view of the way in which the Government was cut off from the Army, none of us felt that we could make that demand. When the silence had lasted so long that the Cabinet meeting seemed on the point of becoming rather like a Quaker prayer meeting, Mr. Cosgrave said, 'That's all,' got up and left his chair, and all of us left the room without a single word of comment on General Mulcahy's disclosure. Personally, I may say that the whole incident affected my mind very deeply in regard to General Mulcahy, and I never had full confidence in him afterwards.

Worse for the civilian government than a continuation of the war was the prospect of a return to the Truce conditions, when military fiefdoms proliferated and instability reigned. Despite mounting a very public defence of the National Army, the cabinet was not alone unhappy with Mulcahy's stance but alarmed by the behaviour of some senior commanders, such as Paddy O'Daly, one of the Collins loyalists who had ensured the defeat of the Republican forces in Dublin and was now in command in Co. Kerry.

Yet the government's action in passing the Army Emergency Powers Resolution ensured in effect even more brutal action by the National Army, which would draw a line in blood between them and their former comrades. 'We decided on committees of officers [to try prisoners],' Blythe said, 'because the procedure for courts-martial was so strict and so cumbersome.' Government backbenchers usually kept their criticism of ministers for meetings held behind closed doors, and there was general support for the introduction of military tribunals, until they came to be implemented. When Blythe announced that 'three young fellows who were caught with guns somewhere in County Dublin' had been sentenced to death, 'I noticed dismay on several faces.' He recalled, somewhat cruelly:

> Pádraig Ó Máille, whose face was very large and fat, sat directly in front of me and I remember that as he listened to the news, his whole visage shook like a blancmange. There were some appeals to the Government to let the young men off, but they came from a small minority of the Party.[62]

Unlike the 'three young fellows' from 'somewhere in County Dublin' (who were actually four in number and all from the city), there was extensive lobbying on behalf of Erskine Childers. There was undoubtedly much personal animus against the 'damned Englishman,' as Arthur Griffith had dubbed him and whom Blythe confessed that 'many of us thought … responsible for the actual occurrence of the Civil War.' Yet the Provisional Government displayed an impartiality that would have been commendable in other circumstances in deciding that a former member of the British and later Republican establishment should not be treated more favourably than 'young people with no influence and with no knowledge of affairs, who had been caught with guns just before Childers, [and] had been sent before the firing squad.'[63]

Chapter 6 ⟿

'I KNELT ON ONE KNEE TO PRAY FOR COURAGE; THEN I SAT ON THE END OF THE BED, REVOLVER IN MY HAND, LISTENING IN THE DARKNESS'

Almost as big a blow to the Republican cause as the capture of Erskine Childers had been that of Ernie O'Malley on 4 November 1922. O'Malley had been operating from the home of the Humphreys family in Aylesbury Road. Ellen Humphreys was a sister of Michael O'Rahilly, who had helped found the Irish Volunteers and had been killed in the 1916 Rising. The National Army found it politically embarrassing to raid such houses and in the process provide propaganda material for the enemy.[1]

As assistant chief of staff of the anti-Treaty IRA, O'Malley spent six frustrating weeks there, working in an office built behind a walk-in wardrobe with a false back to it, 'acting in the capacity of a third class clerk issuing orders which could not be carried out.' He was looking forward to a transfer to Connacht to co-ordinate operations in the west when the raid took place. It may have been triggered by Ellen Humphreys' insistence that he acquire a suit (at her expense), as she felt his bedraggled appearance was 'unbecoming to an Assistant Chief of Staff.'

It was following his return from a fitting that the house was raided. Her daughter Sighle knocked on the door of his bedroom at 7:30 next morning to warn him that 'the Staters are coming in the gate.' He dressed quickly, pulling on his trousers and coat over his pyjamas, collected some important documents, loaded his revolver and took out a hand grenade. 'I knelt on one knee to pray for courage; then I sat on the end of the bed, revolver in my hand, listening in the darkness.' He found himself dwelling on 'what Ferdia wore' on the day he fought Cú Chulainn at the ford and his rage as he prepared to fight the man who, unknown to him, was his son. It was a peculiarly idiosyncratic, Pearsean yet very characteristic way for republicans of O'Malley's generation and intellectual bent to see themselves as they prepared for battle.

It did not take long for the soldiers to find him. A rifle butt splintered the false panelling, then the door began to give way. O'Malley was reluctant to throw his grenade in among the raiders, for fear that Ellen Humphreys or one of the other women might be in the room, but then he realised that the enemy might toss one of their own grenades into the darkness. 'A heavy crash, the door swung open and a hand appeared,' he wrote later. 'I fired twice; once at the hand, then below and right at what might have been a body, and there was a cry of pain.'

As he came out of the room he saw the soldiers 'scrambling out of the hall like frightened sheep.' A face began to emerge from a doorway and he fired again, shooting Ellen Humphreys' sister Annie O'Rahilly through the chin. Mrs Humphreys helped him pull her sister onto a bed. O'Malley recalled long afterwards:

> 'Never mind her now,' Mrs Humphreys said to me, as I remained near the bed, feeling helpless and distressed. 'She's not badly hurt. Think of yourself,' and she smiled. Mrs Humphreys was as calm and as sweet faced as when pouring tea at breakfast. Miss O'Rahilly tried to smile also.

They were joined by Ellen Humphreys' daughter Sighle, who said waspishly of the raiders, 'They're brave, aren't they? And you should have seen them run away.' But the soldiers were firing now at the house from all sides as O'Malley agonised over what to do. When he heard voices downstairs he threw the grenade.

> There was a stampede and a rush for the front door. Men huddled, crouching as they ran. I did not fire as they were too frightened but I watched their panic in a strange kind of detached wonderment. Soon the hall was empty, only the unexploded grenade remained below in the centre of the floor. Evidently the cap was defective.

Having lost his most effective weapon and any hope of escape, O'Malley picked up a rifle and returned fire for a time, as did Sighle Humphreys. During the siege Mrs Humphreys only lost her composure once, with a burst of indignation at the 'Staters' for refusing to allow an ambulance through to attend to her wounded sister. Eventually O'Malley attempted to fight his way out of the house but collapsed on the lawn in a hail of bullets.[2]

———

O'Malley's capture was a coup for the Provisional Government but would make no real difference to the desultory war going on in Dublin, where the anti-Treaty forces made up for the lack of any strategic direction with the frequency of their attacks. Sunday 11 November 1922, Remembrance Day, was a reminder of how far the balance of forces had swung against them. Dublin was the only dominion capital where there was no official ceremony to mark the end of the Great War and all those who had fallen, 'but an astonishing number of Flanders poppies were worn' in aid of Earl Haig's fund for ex-servicemen and their dependants, the *Irish Times* reported.

> Women sellers with high piled trays made their appearance in Grafton Street and other places soon after nine o'clock and were literally besieged. Stocks were cleared and replenished time and again, and soon everybody seemed to be wearing poppies. In popular tea rooms and theatres in the afternoon fully 90 per cent of people 'remembered.'

In those churches that held memorial services, Catholic as well as Protestant, the majority of worshippers wore mourning clothes, and many carried wreaths for family members who had died. Only at Trinity College, where the great bell tolled as the provost and other luminaries gathered in the chapel and flags flew at half mast, was there a sour note to the proceedings. As recalled by Wilmot Irwin, a Southern unionist who left his office in nearby Foster Place to observe events, the students poured

> out of their lecture rooms and attempted to imitate the feat of the Auxies the year before in bringing all traffic to a standstill for the two minutes silence at 11 a.m. They swarmed across the roadway, forming a kind of circle, holding hands. All traffic came to a standstill. Not quite. With about a minute to go, a car carrying a Civic Guard inspector with a uniformed Guard driver came along from the Grafton Street direction, pulled up, and hooted loudly for free passage. The students ignored the interruption. The driver let out the clutch and attempted to drive through the silent cordon. Silent no longer, however. Angry shouts of 'Pull them out!' rent the air, and the two guards would have been plucked from the car but for the timely intervention of one of the Bank of Ireland Free State Guard, who, with a drawn revolver forced a passage for the car ... amidst the curses and jeers of the students, who thereupon proceeded to give a lusty rendering of 'God Save the King.' None of the newspapers reported the incident, which impressed me very much at the time.[3]

There was a more discreet but effective commemoration of the old regime at Marlborough Barracks (McKee Barracks) and Phoenix Park Barracks, where full-dress military parades were held. When the guns roared out their salute to commemorate the Great War dead it was a sombre reminder to all the denizens of the city that the British garrison had not yet departed.[4] There were no attempts by Republicans to disrupt proceedings or to contest the streets with loyalists, as they had done in previous years. Indeed the main topic of conversation seemed to be whether Andrew Bonar Law, Edward Carson's old ally in the Ulster Unionists' revolt against the third Government of Ireland Bill, would honour the Treaty provisions after the British general election in four days' time, which the Tories were expected to win.[5]

———

A more potent if mundane threat was the growing public unrest over profiteering, real or imagined. The pending postal workers' dispute provided the trigger for the collection of economic data on the cost of living, and a Prices Commission was established in the autumn of 1922. Not only were postal workers by far the largest bloc of state employees but for months the wider trade union movement had been claiming that Irish workers paid more for essential items than their British counterparts as a reason for resisting any cuts.

Up to 1921 the British government's *Labour Gazette* had been relied upon by employers, unions and state bodies for data that could provide an agreed basis for pay negotiations. The new Ministry of Economic Affairs now began to collect its own information, and the figures turned out to be almost identical to those in Britain. Using July 1914 as the base month, it was found that inflation had fallen significantly since the end of the Great War, but in March 1922 it was still 91 per cent higher than in 1914 and in June 1922 this had only fallen to 85 per cent. Crucially, from the viewpoint of the Provisional Government and the employers, inflation was falling faster in Ireland than in Britain, thanks in part to the collapse in prices for agricultural goods.[6]

But if Irish exporters were being paid less, consumers were not benefiting at home. An essential commodity such as bread was 1d a pound dearer in Dublin than in London. The bakeries said this was because of higher wages, with Irish workers being paid 94s for a 46-hour week, compared with 60s for a 48-hour week in London.[7] There were calls for a Consumers' Council to be set up, and Dublin Corporation demanded a Prices Commission.[8]

Although there was scepticism in government circles about the existence of organised profiteering and the practicality of controlling prices, it was accepted that it was important 'to ascertain the facts ... Public opinion can then be left to digest the facts and to propose measures for dealing with them.' It was hardly leading from the front, but, significantly, provision was made for labour and employer representation on the commission, or commissions, if local investigations of conditions were required. The measure, introduced by the Minister for Industry and Commerce, Joe McGrath, and seconded by Ernest Blythe, was welcomed by the Labour Party, the Farmers' Party and independents. One of the latter, Darrell Figgis, expressed the hope that no-one selling items under investigation would be appointed to the new body. Only Sir James Craig, representing the University of Dublin constituency, expressed scepticism, and he angered Labour deputies when he said that 'if the working men could get their pint of porter at a decent price they would not object to their wages being reduced.' Most of them, he claimed, drank three or four pints a night, 'and there was a lessening of moral fibre in the country ... from the effects of the war.'[9]

The government was certainly keen to be seen to be acting on the issue, with an initial delay in June being attributed to the outbreak of fighting in Dublin. The Northern Ireland government had already established a Prices Commission, and McGrath's departmental files contained press cuttings of Dublin Corporation meetings calling for price controls, as well as coverage of parliamentary debates on the high cost of living. A former finance officer for the ITGWU, as well as a TD for Dublin, McGrath was well aware of the importance of being seen to be sympathetic to the plight of consumers. He ignored the advice of civil servants to hold hearings in private. They feared that witnesses would either feel inhibited or else be tempted to play to the gallery. He also ignored their advice about appointing an independent chairman or giving the commission power to compel witnesses to attend and give evidence. From his standpoint the most important objective was to be seen to be addressing a pressing public concern.

The chairman, Professor Joseph Whelehan, was a pro-Treaty member of Sinn Féin representing Galway. Sir James Craig, the Trinity College academic so concerned about the price of the pint, was also a member, as were representatives of the business community, such as William Hewat and Michael Moran, and the trade unionists Thomas Farren and William O'Brien. All were well known to McGrath. The ballast was composed of civil servants and government supporters, such as Councillor Margaret McGarry and Ernest Blythe's wife, Annie.[10] The one truly independent-minded member was Darrell Figgis.

The commission's brief was restricted to basic items: bread, flour, milk, meat, potatoes, porter and stout, coal, and tobacco. Yet despite the widespread outrage at profiteering only twenty witnesses appeared to give evidence, and they were of highly variable quality. This was less than two witnesses for each of the sixteen public notices published at a cost of £113 10s 9d, or just under £5 per head, twice the average weekly wage of many workers.[11]

The evidence of many individual witnesses was purely anecdotal. A handful of middle-class shoppers complained that even traders regarded as free of the profiteering taint were putting up their prices, because 'everybody else is doing it.' Working-class customers were more likely to shop around, and Moore Street dealers were believed to offer the best bargains, followed by shops in their near vicinity. But the bulk of witnesses were trade associations and trade unions, sometimes acting in concert. Drink remained near the top of the agenda at the early meetings, because the Retail Purveyors', Family Grocers' and Off-Licence Holders' Association, the Licensed Grocers' and Vintners' Protection Association and the Irish National Union of Vintners', Grocers' and Allied Trades' Assistants all refused to give evidence before the commission, the latter for fear of undermining their employers, thus fuelling popular suspicion that price-fixing was indeed going on.[12]

Not surprisingly, the commission's findings were inconclusive, and its members reported that 'no proper conclusions can be reached unless we are endowed with statutory powers.' It recommended that retailers be required to display prices publicly and then asked for the dissolution of the commission 'as at present constituted.'[13]

The most telling findings were delivered in a separate note by Figgis. As well as supporting the general contention that the commission should have the power to compel witnesses to attend, he argued that it should be given resources for carrying out its own investigations rather than relying on the evidence of voluntary witnesses. At the same time he believed enough evidence had been given to demonstrate that

> very large profits were being charged by certain trades. But it was also clear that some of these traders were barely able to maintain a livelihood. The large percentage of profit ... had become necessary because of the large number of persons competing with each other for the same business within a very small area ... It is usually supposed that great competition will reduce prices, whereas so far as distribution is concerned, excessive competition means that there are many to share a limited amount of business, and that each of the many must, therefore, in order to live, increase his or her profits in order to make a livelihood.
>
> I have therefore been driven to the conclusion that the higher rate of living in Ireland, by comparison with England, is due to the fact that there is a higher percentage of persons dependent on distributive profits rather than on production. Any country in which so large a percentage of the population is engaged, as in Ireland, in the distributive trade must necessarily ... be more expensive to live in. The only real way to mend this fault is to create productive employment, in which to draw off those who are now engaged in, or dependent on, merely distributive profits.[14]

———

While the commission did not address the fundamental questions raised by Figgis, it certainly provided a lot of information on prices.[15] It first looked at flour, the main component of Dubliners' staple diet. The commission was unable to come to any conclusions about profiteering because of the lack of co-operation from millers and bakers, but the latter did provide figures from chartered accountants that showed that their profit on a 4 lb loaf costing 10½d was only a third of a penny. The retail profit margin, by contrast, was ten times that amount.

These figures must be treated with caution. Real margins were undoubtedly greater than stated, because 20 per cent of loaves were imported at prices much lower than bread baked in the city. The Master Bakers declined to give information on the cost of these 'outside' loaves or evidence that loaves were being sold anywhere in the city for less than the standard 5¼d for a 2lb loaf and 10½d for a 4 lb loaf. Nevertheless the partial information provided does bear out Figgis's contentions about the flaws in the market, as does the fact that 85 per cent of the flour used was imported.

Further supporting evidence came from the Dublin and District Co-Operative Society, which said it could lower its prices if it had more customers. There was indirect evidence of price-fixing, in that bread was slightly cheaper in parts of Co. Dublin where competition existed from local non-unionised family bakeries. Dubliners therefore had the worst of all worlds: too many bakeries to achieve economies of scale, a degree of hidden price-fixing and a mass of small traders who needed high profit margins to survive. The only working-class beneficiaries from this system were unionised bakery workers, whose negotiating power allowed them to secure pay increases well ahead of the cost of living.

The commission's recommendations were limited to proposing that customers be made aware that 'outside' loaves were available, and that these should be sold at a lower price. However, it could not say how much less in the absence of more detailed information. It also called for the current retail price, which incorporated a delivery charge of 1½d on a 4lb loaf and ¾d on a 2lb loaf, to be reduced by those amounts for customers buying bread across the counter.

More useful in determining the effect of inflation on the economy than the findings of the commission are the figures, albeit selective, for the cost of the various components provided by the Master Bakers in the manufacture of a loaf.

Table of prices, Dublin, 1914–22 (November)[16]

	1914	1922	Increase
Flour (sack)	27s to 28s	45s 5d	55%
Yeast (pound)	26s	80s	110%
Rice flour (sack)	20s	40s	100%
Coke (ton)	19s 6d	45s	131%
Gas (cubic feet)	3s 6d	6s 9d	93%
Electric power (unit)	1¼d	3½d	180%
Electric light (unit)	3½d	9d	134%
Oats (14-stone barrel)	10s	18s	80%
Hay (hundredweight)	4s	8s	100%
Bran (hundredweight)	7s	9s	29%
Horseshoeing (set)	5s	12s	140%
City rates	10s 9½d	20s 4d	88%
Insurance			200%
Repairs and renewals			150%
Bread (4-lb loaf)	6d	10½d	75%

Wages, 1914 (54-hour week) and 1922 (46-hour week)

	1914	1922	Increase
Table hands	34s	94s	177%
Ovensmen	43s	106s 6d	148%
Others	28s	70s	150%
Van-drivers	25s	81s	195%

———

It says something for the centrality of porter and stout in the Dublin working man's diet that it took precedence over milk in the commission's findings. 'Porter and stout could not be regarded as luxuries for a working man but part of his diet,' the general president of the ITGWU, Tom Foran, told the commission. He had once believed that higher prices might limit consumption but now accepted that for 'men working on the quays at uncertain hours, custom had had the effect of having porter and stout regarded as sustaining foods.' He could have added postal workers, sailors, carters and fishermen to the list of shift workers. Evidence was heard that stout and porter, whether sold by the bottle or as draught, varied greatly in price. A pint of porter was usually 8d in Dublin and a bottle of stout was also 8d. Bottles of stout were usually 7d in the north of England and as cheap as 6d in London. A pint of Guinness xx could be had for 6d in Manchester, whereas a pint of Guinness was 10d in Lucan and Leixlip. In Cork and Mallow, however, draught was 9d and a bottle was 6d or 7d.

The Retail Purveyors', Family Grocers' and Off-Licence Holders' Association, the Licensed Grocers' and Vintners' Protection Association and the Irish National Union of Vintners', Grocers' and Allied Trades' Assistants once more refused to give evidence, or even to return questionnaires. They were joined in this policy of non-cooperation by Arthur Guinness, Son and Company Ltd, the Irish Maltsters' Association and the Irish Brewers' Association. The Barley Growers' Association, however, did give evidence, claiming that the prices its members received were only 10 per cent more in 1922 than in 1914, while a 32-gallon barrel of Guinness had increased in price by 109 per cent, net of excise. The malt-producers had a similar tale and said that, as Guinness's provided virtually the only market for malt, the company determined the price.

Once these aggrieved parties broke ranks the Licensed Grocers' and Vintners' Protection Association relented and gave evidence, although it expressed concern about divulging 'trade secrets'. It said that the price of draught porter, stout and xx stout had all risen by about 396 per cent between 1914 and 1922 but their mark-up had remained fairly constant, at between 35 and 48 per cent, depending on the product. Over the same period commercial rates had doubled, as had lighting bills, as a result of the exigencies of war and fuel shortages. The cost of coal had risen 150 per cent, painting, repairs and breakages by 170 per cent, insurance by 61 per cent and wages by 185 per cent.

They further claimed that consumption had dropped by half since 1914 as a result of the extra duties imposed by the British government. The Irish National Union of Vintners', Grocers' and Allied Trades' Assistants disputed some of the evidence given by the employers on such matters as breakages and staffing levels but accepted that when it secured large pay increases for its members during a strike in the first quarter of 1920 one of the clauses required the union to 'co-operate with the employers in maintaining prices.' When asked about the morality of such an agreement to maintain prices at high levels a union representative asked, in turn, 'Who is to judge if they are unreasonably high?'[17]

Public disquiet over the price of a bottle of stout was such that the commission decided to have sample batches of half a dozen bottles of Guinness bought at eight premises around the city and have the contents measured. At six premises the price charged was 7d and in the remaining two it was 8d, but the commission found that the content was significantly less than claimed by the publicans and that each gallon of Guinness would yield on average 15½ bottles rather than the 14 claimed by the Protection Society. This increased the profit margin, based on mark-up, from the maximum of 48 per cent claimed by publicans to between 54 and 112 per cent. As farm prices on malt and barley had fallen since 1921 and the price of stout had not, the commission concluded that real profit margins were even higher. It recommended standardising the size of bottles for stout and a retail price of 6d, whether consumed on or off the premises. The maximum price of draught porter should be 6½d a pint, and the maximum charged for draught stout should be 9d.

———

Milk was the cheapest form of protein available to Dubliners and the most important for babies and young children. The price of a quart (two pints) was 8d in most dairies and milk bars in Dublin. A few sold it at 7d, making it less than half the price of a pint of beer. As with the publicans, members of the Dublin Cowkeepers' Association, the main suppliers of milk to the city, refused to fill out questionnaires, although representatives gave oral evidence. They said that the vast majority of members did not keep accounts and therefore could not supply the information requested in written form.

A Co. Wicklow farmer giving evidence on behalf of the Irish Farmers' Association said he supplied milk to the Dublin market at 10d a gallon in May 1922, which doubled in price to 1s 8d by September. On that basis the retail mark-up was between 150 and 300 per cent. Yet the Dublin Union (workhouse) said it had to pay between 1s 5d and 2s a gallon in the winter of 1922/3 and that some of the cheapest milk came from the provinces, despite the extra cost of rail freight. This suggested that bulk orders were providing no benefits to ratepayers, fuelling popular perceptions of price-fixing and corruption in the administration of the workhouse. Some of the cheapest and best milk was produced by Albert Agricultural College in Glasnevin, which sold it for 5d a quart, but the entire output went to the Infant Aid Society and the National Women's Health Association.

The only commercial operator to provide detailed accounts was the Lucan Dairy Company, which produced milk at 4d a quart in the winter of 1922/3 and sold it for 8d. The manager told the commission that it cut the price to customers to 7d a quart (which included home delivery) 'but did not gain a single customer from doing so.' He believed that 'the Dublin public does not appreciate cheap milk.'

Not surprisingly, the lack of information from the Cowkeepers' Association meant that the commission lacked the information needed to come to any firm conclusions other than noting the strong *prima facie* case for high mark-ups. 'We strongly recommend that a Commission, endowed with statutory powers, should be established by the Government to inquire into the cost of milk in Dublin,' it said. It also proposed that, as in the case of bread, customers should not have to pay a 'delivery' charge when buying milk across the counter. This would reduce prices by 1d a pint or 2d a quart.

Potatoes were the other staple food investigated. Again there was reluctance by suppliers, other than farmers, to provide evidence. There had been manipulation of the market during the First World War, and on one occasion the British army had released supplies to combat profiteering.[18] A Co. Dublin farmer claimed it cost £7 a ton to produce potatoes but he realised only £5 8s on them. 'There were too many middlemen in the trade ... and not a decent living in it for anybody,' he told the commission. A Dundalk farmer said it cost him only £4 4s to produce a ton of potatoes but the cost of bagging, storage and, above all, transport wiped out any potential profit. Rail freight cost 11s 9d a ton, and it cost another 6s a ton to transport potatoes from Amiens Street (Connolly Station) to the Corporation market. Consumers were charged 10d a stone, or the equivalent of £6 13s 4d a ton.

The Smithfield Factors' Association, whose twenty members controlled the trade and were as reticent as other business bodies about disclosing details of their financial transactions, said they worked off a commission of between 5 and 6¼ per cent when selling produce for farmers, but they operated mainly as wholesale merchants. They claimed that competition was 'very keen' with other merchants who dealt directly with farmers.

However, the Dublin and District Co-operative Society once more provided a dissenting voice. It said that it made a gross profit of 18 per cent on potato sales. Like the farmers, its representative said there were far too many middlemen, and it had made several attempts to bring producers and consumers together but had always been defeated by vested interests. In the absence of sufficient evidence, the commission made no recommendations other than reiterating its call for statutory powers to compel witnesses to attend and give evidence, and for price lists to be displayed.

The commissions established in Cork and Waterford proved even less successful than the main body in Dublin. The Cork committee issued 174 questionnaires, of which 13 were returned. Only seventeen members of the 'purchasing public' gave evidence. The Cork Workers' Council decided to boycott the proceedings, as it was not represented on the local committee; it even continued the boycott after a member was nominated. The only trade union submission came from the Clonakilty Branch of the ITGWU. Consequently, the Cork committee reported 'an utter lack of public interest and deplores the absence of statutory powers.'

The Waterford committee elicited so little interest and information that it did not even feel qualified to endorse the general report. Committees established in other towns made no reports at all.[19]

The lack of interest in the issue is perhaps understandable, given the disturbed state of the country, but political interference also subverted the work of the commission. An interdepartmental committee involving the Ministries of Finance, Agriculture, Economic Affairs and Labour insisted that the findings of the commission be sent to the various departments for 'correction'. The interdepartmental committee would be deciding 'whether any undue advantage is being taken of the general body of consumers and, if that be the case, to the adoption of appropriate remedies.'[20] The low level of public interest in the commission's work probably deprived it of any potential countervailing mandate to the civil servants.

In the event, the corrections made were minute, but the commission of elected public representatives had been put in its place by the senior civil servants and, as we have seen, the commission recommended its own dissolution.

―――

Nevertheless, the publication of the commission's findings at the end of 1922 offered shoppers the first comprehensive survey of prices since the end of British rule. It showed that food prices were more than 88 per cent higher in March 1922 than in July 1914 and that clothing was 92 per cent higher. Fuel and light had the sharpest increase, of 117 per cent, and rents the least, of 27 per cent. 'Sundries' had risen by 97 per cent, bringing the average increase 'for all Items' to 87 per cent. It also showed that prices were falling quite dramatically from their peak of 240 per cent at the end of the Great War, during which most public servants had been given war bonuses of 130 per cent of basic pay. This bonus had continued to increase automatically with basic pay to keep incomes in line with those of private-sector workers during the post-war boom. But the review of prices now showed that this bonus should be cut to 85 per cent by mid-1922 if it was to track falling prices. In the United Kingdom the fall in the cost of living had been much less but it still warranted a cut in the war bonus to 105 per cent. The Commission's report and the corrections from the interdepartmental committee were thus heralding further wage cuts and reductions in government spending, including old-age pensions, the main welfare burden on the exchequer.[21]

The report made some interesting comparisons about household spending habits in the Free State compared with the United Kingdom. In both countries the proportion of family income spent on food and rent had fallen while that spent on clothing, on fuel and light and on sundries had risen, suggesting significantly higher disposable incomes. But the greatest differential was in rents, with people in the United Kingdom paying a higher proportion of their income on shelter.

Proportion of household expenditure spent on essentials, Irish Free State and United Kingdom, 1914 and 1922[22]

	Irish Free State		United Kingdom	
	July 1914	June 1922	July 1914	July 1922
Food	56%	57%	60%	59%
Clothing	17%	18%	12%	16%
Rent	8%	5%	16%	13%
Fuel and light	7%	7%	8%	8%
Sundries	12%	13%	4%	4%

Like its other members, Darrell Figgis did not profit politically by his involvement in the short-lived Prices Commission or from his erudite analysis of the problem, any more than he did from playing a leading role in the drafting of the Constitution of the Irish Free State that summer. Without the support of Collins, who had appointed him to the constitution's drafting committee, or the patronage of Arthur Griffith, who had realised his potential and secured him the vice-presidency of Sinn Féin in 1922, Figgis seemed destined to self-destruct. He was a brilliant polemicist and political analyst but was also arrogant and combative. In June 1922 he had won more than 15,000 votes in Co. Dublin because the electorate was outraged at the action of Robert Briscoe and his accomplices in attacking Figgis in his home and terrorising his wife. By August 1923 Figgis struggled to win the last of eight seats, his vote shrinking to less than 3,000. In the Dáil many deputies would walk out when he rose to speak. In November 1924 his wife, Millie, would shoot herself with a revolver given to her by Michael Collins in the aftermath of the 1922 pre-election attack.

Either shortly before or after this incident Figgis had become involved in a relationship with a dancing instructor, Rita North. She died in October 1925 of septicaemia contracted during a botched abortion in London. At the inquest Figgis testified that he was unaware that she was pregnant until she came to him, already dying. He gassed himself afterwards in a rented room in London.

It was a sad end for one of modern Ireland's architects. He had played a leading role in pivotal events reaching back to the Howth gun-running in 1914.[23] He must be ranked among the remarkable generation of independent thinkers, including Pearse and Connolly, who were destined to lay the foundations of the new state but were spirits too original to be permitted across its threshold.

———

One positive benefit of the Civil War in Dublin was that it helped ease unemployment. Recruitment to the National Army appears to have been far more popular than to the British army during the First World War. For instance, between August 1914 and December 1918, 115 men from the traffic department and permanent way division of the Great Southern and Western Railway enlisted in the British army. By comparison, 120 men from the same departments enlisted in the National Army during the nine months of the Civil War. Although half the National Army were ex-servicemen, only fifteen of this sample served in both armies. Unlike 1914, when the GSWR was reluctant to lose men, by 1921 it had a labour surplus. The economy in decline meant less business, and the withdrawal of British military control meant an end to government subsidies and the automatic sanctioning of fare increases to offset rising labour costs.

Dublin Port and Docks Board was another body that encouraged employees to join the National Army. It abolished 275 jobs in 1922, the largest number in its history. Of the men laid off, 52 joined the National Army, compared with only 15 who had joined the British forces during the war.[24] Other push factors were pay cuts, complemented by longer working hours for those who remained.

The employers' offensive was punctuated by a series of strikes in late 1922 as unions resisted the changes, inflicting still further reductions in real income.[25] Another reason for the influx of men into the National Army was that 48 of the 52 men involved were working for the Port and Docks Board on what was in effect a short-term relief project for pre-Truce IRA members. On 18 May 1922 the board accepted a proposal from Joe McGrath, as Minister for Labour, that the government would provide 60 per cent of the wages on the construction of a spur wharf in Alexandra Basin. The money was made available on condition that half the jobs went to IRA Volunteers and half to men previously employed by the board. The minister said that the names of IRA members would be supplied through the labour exchange but the final selection would be made by the relevant Port and Docks Board manager or supervisor, to make sure no unsuitable individuals were appointed. In the event that not all the vacancies could be filled in this way the ITGWU should be asked to fill the vacancies.

McGrath was pushing an open door. Two men who would serve on the Prices Commission, Alderman James Moran of the Municipal Reform Association and William Hewat, were also members of the Port and Docks Board, as was McGrath's former employer in the ITGWU, its general treasurer, Alderman William O'Brien. Moran praised the proposal as far more flexible than previous schemes put forward by the British government for the employment of ex-servicemen, while Hewat—a director of three firms that were involved in the Dublin Lockout of 1913—went so far as to suggest that his former protagonist from that era, William O'Brien, be appointed to a special subcommittee to oversee the scheme.

The scheme was of particular interest to members of the 2nd Battalion of the Dublin Brigade, which was based in the area and was the most pro-Treaty unit in the city. All the Volunteers hired under the scheme were labourers, and the great majority left the Port and Docks Board to join the National Army in July 1922 immediately after the Civil War broke out. Among them was Patrick Ennis junior, brother of Tom Ennis, who was now commander of the National Army's 2nd Eastern Division, with overall command of the Free State forces in Dublin. Tom Ennis had worked as a labourer and then a scavenger for the Port and Docks Board, where his father, Patrick Ennis senior, was a clerk. When Ennis was interned for his part in the 1916 Rising he was sacked. On his release he rose gradually through the ranks of the 2nd Battalion, serving his apprenticeship as a founder-member of Collins's Squad. He was among the quartet of gunmen who killed Detective-Sergeant Patrick Smyth, the first member of the DMP Detective Division to die in 1919. He took a leading part in the Bloody Sunday assassinations in November 1921 and, as officer commanding the 2nd Battalion, was Oscar Traynor's second in command during the burning of the Custom House in May 1921.[26]

In spite of all this he was still listed as a general labourer in the port, then a checker, and drew his wages every week. How much work he did is debatable, but it is unlikely that any employer in the city would sack him. A Collins loyalist, Ennis owed his promotion as commander of the 2nd Eastern Division to his record as a gunman and the decision of so many of his superiors, including Traynor, to oppose the Treaty. By the end of the Civil War he would be a major-general, after which his association with the Collins cabal that had facilitated his rise would lead to his involvement in the army mutiny of 1924 and subsequent resignation.

Not all the Volunteers employed by Dublin Port and Docks Board that year joined the National Army, although it looks as if the great majority did. At least one took the anti-Treaty side; he was sacked by the board on the day after he was arrested by his former comrades on suspicion of IRA membership.[27]

There were 13,000 republicans interned in the Civil War, not all of whom would have been militarily active, compared with 55,000 members of the National Army and 150,000 ex-servicemen from the British armed forces. Perhaps as many as a fifth of all British ex-servicemen joined the National Army. An interesting but relatively small number served in the British army and the anti-Treaty IRA, most notably Tom Barry, who wrote a fine if much-contested memoir. Republicans certainly made up in vociferousness for their lack of numbers, but then many of them were highly articulate as well as politically motivated. They also came primarily from a middle-class or lower middle-class background. Members of the British and Free State forces, apart from the officer class, came overwhelmingly from the urban working poor and unemployed. They left comparatively little by way of memorabilia and even less in the form of memoirs.

In recent years there has been a resurgence of interest in the fate of these ex-servicemen, some of it driven by guilt at their being 'forgotten' for much of the twentieth century, but the picture is more complex than one of past neglect redeemed by rehabilitation in the national pantheon of victims and heroes. For a start, the problems of British ex-servicemen were extensively aired in the 1920s, and a perception of widespread discrimination against them led to the establishment by the Free State government of a Committee on Claims of British Ex-Servicemen in 1927.[28] Certainly unemployment was higher for ex-servicemen than for many workers, and there was undoubtedly a discriminatory element in this. But discrimination tended to cut both ways: it could operate in favour of ex-servicemen as well as against them. The factors involved were often local and personal and sometimes flew in the face of directives or policy at the national or departmental level by both the British and Free State governments.

Nor should it be forgotten that many Irish recruits were unskilled and either unemployed or casually employed before they joined the British army or navy. This was especially the case in Dublin, where 30,000 men were recruited, and they were therefore more at risk of unemployment again when the Great War ended, especially once the post-war boom collapsed in 1921.

Health was another important factor in an era when most work was manual and often imposed a heavy burden on even the most able-bodied. Companies that gave men leave to join the armed forces usually stipulated that their job would be kept open provided they were capable of performing the same tasks after the war.

Some companies, such as the GSWR and Guinness, would go to considerable lengths to facilitate men. For instance, three amputees were given jobs as level crossing keepers by the GSWR, and twenty-seven men who enlisted from the locomotive department were re-employed before the war's end, as they were no longer fit for military service. Another sixty-five were taken back at the Inchicore works by April 1919, of whom five suffered from various disabilities, including a labourer with a missing forearm and another labourer with heart disease. These men all kept their original positions and pay grades.

Reallocation to lighter work usually meant a reduction in pay, but soldiers who had been injured would be receiving an army pension. These varied in amount according to the degree of disability, but most British army pensions ranged from 3s 6d to 27s 6d a week. The loss of a forearm, for instance, was worth 15s a week. But not all war disabilities were that obvious. A painter who returned to the GSWR works had no eyelashes on his right eye because of a chronic skin disease and suffered from infections and inflammation when exposed to dust and turpentine fumes. A former member of the Dublin Fusiliers, William Hiskey, had enlisted on 5 May 1915. His mother had received 5s a week from the GSWR as a dependant; on his return from military service he applied to be reinstated as a wagon-shop labourer at the Inchicore works but was refused because he had TB. After six months in Crooksling Sanatorium he was taken back, only for the GSWR to discover that he still suffered from pulmonary tuberculosis and had defective eyesight.

The greatest concern of the company was not so much finding work for such men but running the risk of subsequent claims by them or their dependants in the event of early death or forced retirement. Eventually the problem was resolved by the GSWR continuing to employ some ex-servicemen under a separate insurance scheme, with a guarantee from the British government that it would cover additional costs. However, as Hiskey's case demonstrated, there were complications with some medical conditions. In March 1919 a GSWR company doctor, W. G. Gibson, notified the insurers that the company would no longer take back men with lung or heart diseases. He also expressed concern about other veterans. 'Partly maimed or unfit persons are much more liable to meet with accidents than the ordinary sound and healthy employees. Also it took them longer to become fully productive.' There was still no problem with men who were 'perfectly fit' resuming work or those with disabilities that did not interfere seriously with their duties, such as Ed McDonnell, a porter at the North Wall, who suffered from deafness in the right ear 'due to concussion from bursting shells'; Joseph Kearns, a porter at Kingsbridge Station with partial loss of power in his right hand; or Michael Phelan, a porter in Cork with deformity of his right forearm caused by compound fractures resulting from shrapnel.[29] In a few cases the company even provided early-retirement pensions or gratuities.

As the railway historian Peter Rigney has pointed out in his study of returning ex-servicemen, many accounts stress the negative experience, but

> this does not reflect the experience of staff of the GS&WR, which fulfilled the arrangements for servicemen more generously than intended in 1914, while allocating more than half of all post-armistice vacancies to other ex-servicemen. The GS&WR and the other railway companies were among the first to erect commemorative public plaques for those of their staff who died during the conflict.[30]

——

Guinness's brewery was even more active in looking after employees who joined the colours. It had issued a circular in August 1914 informing employees that it would facilitate as many of those as possible aged between nineteen and thirty-five who wished to enlist. More than 650 did so, of whom 104 were killed.[31] Every employee received half pay while serving in the armed forces, costing the firm £76,669 12s 6d between August 1914 and December 1919, when there were still fourteen men awaiting demobilisation.[32] All thirty-seven widows were treated generously, which was easily done, as there were so few.[33] Some employees had returned already, having been declared unfit for further military service. In anticipation of similar cases the company made arrangements to deal with 'a certain number of men who will at any rate for a time be only fit for light work.'[34]

At first the company treated cases individually, for fear of setting precedents, but in December a former labourer in the brewhouse, Andrew Ryan, returned to the company after three years suffering from 'neurasthenia following shell wounds to the head.' He was considered 'unlikely to be able to work for some time.' He had twelve years' previous service with the company and had a wife and four children to support. Knowing it would face a wave of similar cases, the company decided to leave him on half pay, as if he was still in the British army, until his condition was diagnosed.

From then on every ex-serviceman deemed unfit to resume work was left on half pay until he was either considered able to return to work or placed on sickness benefit. As with the GSWR, payments from the Guinness-approved benefit society were integrated with the British Ministry of Pensions scheme for ex-servicemen, thus reducing the financial liability on the firm. But many of the men taken back were suffering from serious injuries or disabilities. In the racking department, for instance, twenty-seven men were employed, of whom sixteen had bullet or shrapnel injuries, or both, mainly to the head, limbs and hips. One man had shrapnel lodged in his abdomen. Two men suffered from the long-term effects of gas poisoning, two from long-term non-combat injuries sustained on active service; one man had lost an eye and another the use of an eye. One man suffered from shell shock, one from trench foot, one from frostbite, one from severe concussion of the brain, one from nephritis caused by shell shock, one from epilepsy, one from gastritis and nervous debility, one from malaria and one from deafness. Some of the men suffered from more than one of these conditions. Nevertheless the company not only took back these former employees but recruited another 694 ex-servicemen, 259 of them on a temporary basis and some suffering from disabilities.

In October 1922 each department was asked to establish how many men were 'suffering from wounds or disablement caused by the war, stating their length of service, nature of disablement, the work which they are doing at present, and whether you consider them suitable for their present occupation.' Several men considered unfit as a result of this cull had been recruited since the end of the war.[35] Every man over whom there was a question mark had to undergo a medical examination, and those who failed it were let go. Men with pre-1914 service were given an allowance by the firm that would bring their war pension up to their full wage. Those recruited after 1918 received nothing.[36] Patriotism had its limits.

Despite its reputation as a staunchly unionist firm, Guinness took back not only employees demobilised by the National Army after the Civil War but at least some anti-Treaty IRA Volunteers as well. On 29 March 1923 Charles Dempsey, who had been employed as a messenger in the Offices Department, reapplied for his job following eight months as an internee in the Curragh. He had been released the previous day after signing the declaration that he would not take up arms again against the Free State. His manager said that Dempsey, who had been taken prisoner in September 1922, had a large family and had served in the South African War and in the Royal Naval Sick Berth Reserve from 1914 to 1918. He was not only re-employed but was given four weeks' pay 'for the period absent,' the same standard gratuity given to returning National Army men.[37]

Like the GSWR, Guinness remembered its war dead every 11 November, not alone in the brewery but elsewhere, such as at the Victoria Quay depot, with two minutes' silence. British army and navy reservists were also facilitated in taking annual holidays to coincide with annual training rosters.

———

Of course not all ex-servicemen were fortunate enough to be returning to companies as paternalist or as loyalist in sentiment as the GSWR or Guinness. One of the least fortunate groups of ex-servicemen were those returning in the hope of receiving holdings under the Irish Land (Provision for Soldiers and Sailors) Act (1919). County committees were requested by the Department of Agriculture and Technical Instruction to ensure that instructors paid special attention to these smallholders, but only 181 had been dealt with by September 1921. Not only was the funding inadequate but some applicants were unable to engage in heavy manual work because of injuries or ill-health incurred in the war. In 1923 the new Free State government abolished all special categories of people eligible for consideration under the Land Purchase schemes, including ex-servicemen. Although funds continued to be provided, a significant portion of the land had to go to local people with uneconomic holdings. It was generally accepted that any other arrangement would breed hostility towards the ex-servicemen.

By 1928 some 360 ex-servicemen had been accommodated on holdings averaging 28 acres, while 356 existing smallholders received grants of land averaging 14.35 acres. This was, if anything, positive discrimination in favour of the ex-servicemen. If the Committee on Claims of British Ex-Servicemen subsequently found that the annuities on many of these smallholdings were too high to make them viable, it suggests that the problems of land resettlement ran deeper than official prejudices for or against ex-servicemen.[38]

As we have seen (chapter 2), all houses financed by the Irish Sailors' and Soldiers' Land Trust in estates such as Killester and Pembroke went to ex-servicemen, as did most of the jobs in building them. If this seemed like a housing paradise to other Dubliners, the rents charged were too high for many tenants, leading to rent strikes and evictions. The high rents, equivalent to a week's wages for many blue-collar and white-collar workers, meant that the great majority of ex-servicemen who were either unemployed or in low-wage jobs had to rely on Dublin Corporation for accommodation. The efforts of the British government, therefore, to house ex-servicemen may look impressive compared with assistance to aspiring smallholders—2,626 as opposed to 360—but it still constituted a drop in an ocean of misery.

If Killester, with 465 houses, was by far the largest development in the Free State, Dublin Corporation, impoverished as it was, had still managed to house 547 ex-servicemen and their families by 1925. Ex-servicemen were understandably angry at the failure of the British government to honour promises made on recruiting platforms that those who joined up would return to decent homes and smallholdings. Telling them that the promises were not binding, as they had never been enshrined in legislation, did nothing to assuage the sense of betrayal, and this registered with the committee, which included a retired senior British officer, Brigadier-General Robert Browne-Clayton DSO, a Great War veteran from an old ascendancy family in Co. Carlow.[39] Not surprisingly, the committee found that 'the amount of money provided by the British Government was inadequate to provide satisfactory housing accommodation for British ex-servicemen in the Free State.' Nevertheless the Sailors' and Soldiers' Land Trust made a very significant contribution to renewing the social housing stock of the country nationally between 1922 and 1928. While 4,128 new housing units were built by the local authorities, of which 2,436 were in Dublin (60 per cent), the trust built 1,927, of which only 526 (27 per cent) were in Dublin city and county. The committee found some justification for allegations of favouritism, and when it asked the trust about the imbalance that favoured Munster the trustees said they were so struck by the appalling housing conditions in Cork and Limerick that they decided to allocate 40 extra houses to the former and 18 to Limerick, compared with 15 to Dublin.[40]

————

Allegations of discrimination against ex-servicemen in the labour market were another contentious issue, with associations representing war veterans drawing attention to an unemployment rate of up to 46 per cent. Republicans responded by pointing to the favouritism shown towards British veterans by companies such as Guinness and the railways as well as the civil service, compared with hostility by many employers towards IRA members.

There were elements of truth in both cases. As we have seen, Oscar Traynor told Dublin Corporation in January 1922 that unemployment among Volunteers active in the War of Independence was as high as 40 per cent. (See chapter 2.) This would rise for those who took the anti-Treaty side until Fianna Fáil came to power; then it was their turn to benefit from the new political dispensation.

The departure of the Auxiliaries created a power vacuum on the streets of Dublin in early 1922 that exasperated businessmen such as William Hewat, president of Dublin Chamber of Commerce. During the Truce he admitted to 'fear of violence, fear your life's work may be destroyed before your eyes.' (*Courtesy of National Library of Ireland*)

An army in the making, or in transition? Richard Mulcahy, chief of staff of the Irish Volunteers, accompanied by his deputy, Eoin O'Duffy, arrives at Beggarsbush Barracks to inspect what would become the first unit of the National Army, under Paddy O'Daly, who had commanded the 'Squad' during the War of Independence. Mulcahy is still wearing a Volunteer uniform, which would soon be worn only by their opponents in the anti-Treaty IRA. O'Duffy appears to be in civilian clothes. (© *Bettmann/Corbis*)

Belfast refugees were exploited for propaganda purposes by opponents of the Treaty but received little practical assistance from either side. They were urged to go back and 'fight their corner.' (©*Hulton-Deutsch Collection/Corbis*)

British soldiers on duty at the Hibernian Bank in the centre of Dublin. Meanwhile National Army troops protected the Bank of Ireland, which became the Provisional Government's banker in January 1922. Anti-Treaty forces occupied symbols of British power such as the Four Courts, but their opponents guarded the funds needed for waging war. (© *Walshe/Topical Press Agency/Getty Images*)

National Army soldiers arriving at Ferguson's garage in Lower Baggot Street to prevent anti-Treaty forces confiscating vehicles. They arrested Leo Henderson, director of the Belfast boycott. When Ernie O'Malley seized Lieutenant-General J.J. 'Ginger' O'Connell, assistant chief of staff of the National Army, in retaliation, it triggered the Civil War. The Belfast boycott enabled the anti-Treaty forces to dominate the streets, but it also reinforced partitionist mentalities and was a challenge to public order that the Free State authorities could not ignore indefinitely. (*Courtesy of Dublin City Public Libraries and Archive © Dublin City Council*)

'The noise went on all day with very little impression on the Four Courts,' Sir Neville Macready, officer commanding British forces in Ireland, would recall a few months later, 'but with much amusement and interest to the inhabitants of Dublin, who lined up on either bank of the Liffey about a hundred yards east and west of the battle, being kept in their places by policemen in the same way as at a festival or a Lord Mayor's Show.' (© *Bettmann/Corbis*)

Guests evacuate the Edinburgh Hotel as fighting becomes widespread in O'Connell Street. Almost three hundred employees found themselves out of work as a result of hotels being taken over by anti-Treaty forces. (*Courtesy of Dublin City Public Libraries and Archive © Dublin City Council*)

Father Albert Bibby arriving to minister to the spiritual needs of the anti-Treaty forces in O'Connell Street. He organised religious services in the 'Block' in O'Connell Street at the height of the fighting, even recruiting some who were not Catholics, such as Robert Barton, to participate in recitations of the Rosary. Father Albert was later exiled to England and had his religious faculties withdrawn by the Catholic hierarchy, which stood firmly behind the new Free State authorities. (*Courtesy of National Library of Ireland*)

Armoured cars and artillery enabled the National Army to dominate the conventional fighting in Dublin. Here two armoured cars engage the anti-Treaty garrison in the Hammam Hotel in O'Connell Street at close range. It was in one such exchange that 'Todd' Andrews, serving next door in the Dublin Tramways offices, was wounded. (*Courtesy of Dublin City Public Libraries and Archive © Dublin City Council*)

National Army soldiers fire a field gun from behind armoured cars on the corner of Henry Street at anti-Treaty positions in the 'Block'. The popular mood in the city was with the Provisional Government. The National Army had plenty of encouragement from bystanders, who even pointed out 'irregular' snipers. (*Courtesy of National Library of Ireland*)

Dublin Fire Brigade tackles a fire at the YMCA headquarters as fighting rages around them in O'Connell Street. Crossfire between the National Army and anti-Treaty IRA frequently forced the fire brigade to suspend operations. During the siege of the Four Courts three members were seriously wounded while trying to contain the fires. (*Courtesy of National Library of Ireland*)

Medical care for combatants was good, with hospitals and trained staff in close proximity to the conflict. Here casualties are treated on the spot. (© *Topical Press Agency/Getty Images*)

Members of the St John Ambulance Brigade carry an injured woman to safety.
Red Cross insignia were frequently used by anti-Treaty forces in Dublin,
particularly by members of Cumann na mBan, in transporting weapons or
evading arrest when strongpoints were overrun. Ernie O'Malley later wrote
that 'all thought it legitimate for us to abuse the Red Cross, but for no one else.'
(© *Underwood & Underwood/Corbis*)

Children imitate their elders, with war games between 'Staters' and 'Rebels'
replacing cowboys and Indians. Some youngsters appeared in the magistrates'
courts when 'hostilities' got out of hand. (*Courtesy of Dublin City Public
Libraries and Archive © Dublin City Council*)

National Army reservists, pre-Truce Volunteers still in civilian clothes, guard a bread van. While such measures kept food supplies flowing during the chaotic first week of the Civil War in Dublin, the government did nothing to control prices. (*Courtesy of Dublin City Public Libraries and Archive © Dublin City Council*)

The funerals of anti-Treaty leaders, such as that of Cathal Brugha on 10 July 1922, were attended by much smaller crowds than those that turned out to mourn Griffith and Collins. (*Courtesy of Dublin City Public Libraries and Archive © Dublin City Council*)

Crowds outside Trinity College wait for the funeral cortege of Michael Collins to pass in August 1922. The funerals of Arthur Griffith and Michael Collins were used to sanctify the role of both as builders of an independent Irish state and as victims of irreconcilable 'destructionites'. (*Courtesy of National Library of Ireland*)

Seán Collins accompanies his brother's remains to Glasnevin Cemetery, surrounded by officers of the Dublin Guard, who took a proprietorial interest in their dead commander. They regarded Michael Collins as their political and spiritual leader. The occasion was made a massive display of strength by the National Army, much as the British army had done when the remains of officers killed by Collins's men on Bloody Sunday, 1920, were escorted through the city to Dublin port for burial in Britain. (*Courtesy of National Library of Ireland*)

'Father, forgive them, for they know not what they do.'

Sean Cole, Alf. Colley
Boy Scouts of the FIANNA
Murdered Aug 26. 1922.

'Father, forgive them, for they know not what they do': Seán Cole, a 19-year-old electrician, and Alfred Colley, a 21-year-old tinsmith, senior members of Fianna Éireann, had both been shot four times when their bodies were found at Yellow Lane, Santry, on 27 August 1922. It is not clear who killed them, but evidence at the inquest suggested that they knew and trusted the men who abducted them. The circumstances of their deaths were similar to those of three other young republicans killed near Red Cow in October 1922. All were adopted as martyrs by the anti-Treaty forces. (*Courtesy of Dublin City Public Libraries and Archive © Dublin City Council*)

A demonstration of the unemployed in Dublin on 9 September 1922. Despite the fighting, public meetings and demonstrations remained an integral part of political life in the capital. Increasing economic hardship led the infant Communist Party to launch the unemployed movement, but it made little headway when the political environment was dominated by the politics of Civil War. (*© TopFoto*)

Maud Gonne (centre), with Mrs Barry Delaney, writer, and Annie MacSwiney, a sister of Terence MacSwiney (on the right), outside Mountjoy Prison with a picture of the Blessed Virgin and Infant Jesus. Civil War hunger strikes generated much less support for republican prisoners than in the War of Independence. Most people put a premium on peace at any price. (© *Hulton-Deutsch Collection/Corbis*)

Opponents of the Treaty were often denied the opportunity to bury their dead. Here mourners mark the executions of the Four Courts commanders—Richard Barrett, Joseph McKelvey, Liam Mellows and Rory O'Connor—in December 1922 with a march through the city to Glasnevin Cemetery. Men were reluctant to attend such events for fear of arrest. First interred in Mountjoy, Richard Barrett's body was not released for reburial until November 1924. (*Courtesy of National Library of Ireland*)

Many civilians gathered to say goodbye to evacuating British soldiers on the North Wall in December 1922, while attacks continued on what *Poblacht na hÉireann: War News* denounced as the 'Royal Irish Republican Army' in the city centre. The British retained significant forces in the city until they were confident that the Free State would win the Civil War. Half the officers and men who joined the National Army had formerly served in the British army. (*Courtesy of National Library of Ireland*)

Dublin's street dealers never missed an opportunity for business. Here women sell fruit to departing members of the British garrison before they boarded ship for what proved a rough crossing of the Irish Sea. (*Courtesy of National Library of Ireland*)

General Emmet Dalton (left) and General Tom Ennis en route to capture Cork on the *Lady Wicklow* after they played a leading role in the defeat of the anti-Treaty forces in Dublin. Like many members of the military cabal that grew up around Collins during the War of Independence, both men found themselves politically adrift after his death and later had difficulty adjusting to civilian life in the new state they had helped create.

The interior of Sir Horace Plunkett's home, Kilteragh House, after he was burnt out by anti-Treaty IRA volunteers under the left-wing republican George Gilmore in February 1922. Plunkett, the founder of the Irish co-operative movement, was selected because he was a Freemason and a member of the Free State Senate. At the time of the attack he was researching new agricultural techniques in the United States to improve the productivity of Irish farms. (© *Walshe/Topical Press Agency/Hulton Archive/Getty Images*)

To the Electors of Dublin City (South)

Standing as the Republican Candidate for this Constituency, I wish, respectfully, to put the following points before the electors for their consideration:—

1. The Irish Republic was established by the free votes of the Irish People and cannot be disestablished by a British Act of Parliament. As a member of the Irish Republican Army I took an Oath of Allegiance to that Republic, and I have kept that Oath.

2. When the Republican Government is functioning freely in Ireland, it will mean more than a mere change in the name or the form of Government. It will mean a definite improvement in the conditions under which the people live. The Republican Party is pledged to the following principles:—

(a) The protection of our industries by the imposition of adequate tariffs.

(b) It is the first duty of the Government to provide work for the people, particularly in time of economic depression, as at present.

(c) It is the duty of the Government to ensure that proper wages are paid in all industries and trades, and that no class is compelled, by force of circumstances, to live in a condition of deprivation.

(d) All men are born equal and free, and in order to ensure equal opportunities to all a system of free education, with a proper system of scholarship, should be introduced in the schools. These are not election promises, made to be broken. These are definite principles to which the Republican Party, and I, as their candidate, pledge our support.

A vote against the Republic is a vote for the continuance of the present chaotic condition.

A vote for the Republic is a vote of Peace and ordered progress. The electors must choose between those alternatives.

I have no doubt that the sound commonsense of the Dublin people will assert itself, and that they will declare, in no uncertain manner, for

National Unity and absolute Independence

Published and issued by Joseph Clarke, 110 St. Stephen's Green, Dublin, Agent for Seán Lemass, and printed by the Wood Printing Works, Ltd., Fleet Street, Dublin.

Seán Lemass's election leaflet 'To the Electors of Dublin City (South)' in 1924 stressed bread-and-butter issues and even asserted that 'a vote for the Republic is a vote for Peace,' in contrast to the bombast of much anti-Treaty propaganda. The horrific death of his brother Noel was an important factor in winning public sympathy for an army that always benefited politically from its defeats rather than from its successes. (*Courtesy of Dublin City Public Libraries and Archive © Dublin City Council*)

Clientelism was deeply embedded in the Irish political psyche, and it would remain so into the future.

———

As soon as the war ended, the British government ensured that Ireland was involved in the drive to find employment for demobilised soldiers and making the United Kingdom a 'land fit for heroes.' This aim was not helped by mass demobilisation. In 1919 ex-servicemen flooded the labour market. Nevertheless, such bodies as the Department of Agriculture and Technical Instruction adopted the legislation so enthusiastically that they usually exceeded the official requirement for three-quarters of vacancies to be filled by ex-servicemen wherever possible. The DATI itself achieved 100 per cent in some areas. One of the largest public-service employers, it took on ex-servicemen as temporary clerks. This was a favoured option throughout the public sector, as it meant that literate and numerate men too debilitated by war service for other work would be able to perform the tasks required.[41] The DATI told the government that

> preference is given in every case to men who have served with the colours. In this connection ... no candidate other than ex-servicemen has been appointed to a clerkship in the Department; and approximately 70 ex-servicemen are at present employed in a temporary clerical capacity.[42]

There was a similar policy regarding technical staff. All six veterinary inspectors, and four technical appointees in the Fisheries Board, were ex-servicemen. All but one of the fifteen members of the crew of the *Helga,* which had shelled Dublin in the 1916 Rising when pressed into military service, were ex-servicemen. At the limnological laboratory on Lough Derg six of the seven employees were ex-servicemen. At Portandhu, Co. Antrim, ten of the twelve employees were ex-servicemen; the exceptions were the foreman and a carpenter. There was an identical arrangement at Knockadoon, Co. Cork, where all employees were ex-servicemen except for the foreman and carpenter. The DATI assured the government that this discriminatory recruitment policy would continue to be departmental policy.

It adopted a similar approach to maintenance and training grants. These were specifically tailored for ex-servicemen, with the aim of restoring to the labour market 'as soon as possible the supply of men with higher general scientific, professional and business attainments whom the nation needs for every profession and industry.' It added that 'the scheme applies equally to officers, warrant officers, non-commissioned officers and men of like standing, who have educational qualifications [similar] to those usually possessed by officers.' Under the scheme, academic or training fees of up to £50 a year were available, and maintenance grants of £75. A married man could receive up to £200 per year, plus £24 for each child under sixteen, up to a maximum of four. However, men over thirty were eligible only under exceptional circumstances, as it was considered that anyone who was that old and would have been eligible for entry to university or a profession would already have qualified before the war. There were also Lord Kitchener Memorial Scholarships for the sons of ex-servicemen; the department said that a lot of these had been granted but gave no numbers.

However, very few Dubliners benefited under these schemes. The vast majority of grants went to applicants from a farming background, with the area around Enniscorthy particularly favoured, for some reason. The rural bias was inevitable, given the DATI's remit and the overwhelmingly agricultural nature of the economy, but the capital's educational institutions did play a prominent role when it came to training. Successful candidates attended courses in the Royal College of Science, the Royal Veterinary College, the City of Dublin Technical Schools, Pembroke Technical School, the Royal Botanic Gardens and Albert Agricultural College. A fortunate few attended the Metropolitan School of Art. For those who had not attained the educational qualifications 'usually possessed by officers' there were courses in motor engineering at the technical school in Ringsend. In Belfast there were courses in printing and in boot and shoe repairs, while in rural areas courses were run in such subjects as estate carpentry, harness-making, blacksmith's helper, poultry-rearing, orchard maintenance, beekeeping, and butter and cheese-making.

Of 677 applications received up to 1 July 1922, 482 were approved, 188 rejected and 7 withdrawn. Applicants who withdrew or were rejected were referred to the Ministry of Labour for consideration on other courses. The amounts spent on such courses were also considerable, coming to more than £17,300 in the year ending 31 March 1920 and almost £40,000 in the year ending 31 March 1921.[43]

Ex-servicemen received preferential treatment not only in recruitment practices but in career prospects. In a memorandum of 18 August 1921 a DATI departmental head, Dr Smith, said that seven ex-servicemen had been made permanent out of twenty-six men given temporary clerkships. One of these permanent clerks had moved to another civil service department, where he 'was preferentially promoted to the second division. One (an ex-officer) was given special leave.' The temporary clerks were 'given ... preference over other temporary officers of the Branch of the Department for overtime and Taskwork.'[44] One of the returning officers who received a scholarship to study engineering and was appointed a temporary clerk with the Board of Works was Captain Emmet Dalton of the Royal Dublin Fusiliers, who went on to become Director of Training with the IRA and a major-general in the National Army.

Voluntary bodies also provided support in various forms to war veterans. The Irish Committee of the Red Cross, for instance, donated a cardiograph machine to Mercer's Hospital in September 1921, on condition that it be made available to ex-servicemen free of charge. The Clarendon Evening School ran classes for ex-servicemen who had literacy or numeracy problems.[45]

———

However, this benign climate did not last long. Even before the position of the Provisional Government was regularised on 6 December 1922 and the Irish Free State came formally into being, the long-term employment prospects of some ex-servicemen in the public sector had become uncertain. John Kavanagh, a clerk in the Royal Barracks (Collins Barracks), claimed that he was dismissed on 29 June 'in consequence of the change of government.' He had joined the Connaught Rangers in 1907 as a regular and had been discharged as medically unfit in December 1917, with a pension of 8s a week. After losing his job in 1922 he applied to various employers but found it 'impossible to obtain work due to the relentless murder campaign of the Sinn Féiners ... against loyal Government employees.' He subsequently emigrated to New Zealand and then to Australia, working on the roads and clearing brush until his health gave out. Moving to London in 1926, he made a claim to the Irish Grants Committee in London. But there are problems with his claim. Firstly, the attacks on other ex-servicemen working as civilian clerks that he cites as evidence that his life was at risk in 1922 occurred during the War of Independence.[46] Secondly, his reference from the Army Service Corps is either a poor copy of a lost original or a forgery. Finally, he provides no information on his wife and other dependants. His claim was eligible only if he could show that he had suffered loss as a direct result of his service to the Crown.

This inevitably encouraged men to portray themselves as victims and to think in those terms. It also led to the perpetuation of such bodies as the Dublin Municipal Ex-Servicemen and Dependants' Association, which the British Legion had hoped to replace. The association constantly campaigned against discrimination in order to justify its own existence. Nor did the secretary of the association lend credibility to the cause. He was John Saturninus Kelly, a former 'Labour Home-Ruler' who lost his seat on the Corporation in 1914. He had founded the Irish Railway Workers' Trade Union, generally regarded as a 'scab' organisation, which was never accepted into membership of the Irish Trade Union Congress, and he had the distinction of being the only leader of an Irish union to support the British war effort. It was widely believed that his union was financed by the railway companies, and there was certainly a strong mercenary streak in all Kelly's activities. He volunteered his services to the War Office and the Admiralty in early 1915 and worked as a 'civil recruiting agent' in the Dublin area until the war ended. He stood in the 1918 election as an Irish Party candidate for the Liberties, where he was trounced by Joe McGrath of Sinn Féin.

In his new capacity as secretary of the Ex-Servicemen and Dependants' Association, Kelly made a submission to the Committee on Ex-Servicemen's Complaints, drawing attention to the decision of the Corporation to abolish the war bonus for employees who had joined up. These men would have received half pay during the war, as did other local authority employees, but the loss of the war bonus affected them badly and was unfair, because the cut was not imposed on other employees who had not actually participated in the war.[47]

As we have seen, the withdrawal of British forces seriously affected businesses dependent on their custom, and many closed. (See chapter 1.) The same fate awaited some employees of the armed forces, and Kelly compiled a number of cases for the Committee on Ex-Servicemen's Complaints, including the following:

- A. J. Stafford, who lived in Chelmsford Avenue, Ranelagh, had worked as a clerk in the Army Ordnance Department since October 1914 but was let go less than two weeks before Christmas 1922, as his services were not required by the new National Army.
- Edward Gaffney of Ossory Road, North Strand, had twenty-one years' service with the Ordnance Department as an assistant foreman for the Barracks and Hospital. The Ex-Servicemen's Committee was informed that he was 'discharged in 1922 owing to change of Government. Is absolutely destitute. Willing to take any kind of employment. Not a British Ex-Serviceman.'
- H. G. Greene of St Claire Villas, Bray, had served in the Great War from August 1914 to May 1915, when he had his right foot amputated. He was discharged in March 1916. He was one of the ex-servicemen given preferential treatment by the DATI, being appointed to the Board of Fisheries. On 22 December 1922, two days before Christmas, he 'lost employment owing to change of Government … preference [given] to National Army's men.'
- Andrew Dunne of Rehoboth Road had worked for eight years as a civilian clerk in the Royal Engineers office at British Army HQ in Parkgate and had lost his job on their departure. In 1928 the committee was informed that 'he is now 66 years of age and absolutely penniless.'
- E. Toomey of Annesley Avenue sought compensation from the Ex-Servicemen's Committee for loss of employment as a carpenter at Beggarsbush Barracks and Ship Street Barracks but failed to supply dates.

Complaints related to changes in salary structures as well as jobs. For instance, W. H. Heron was re-engaged as a temporary valuer at the Valuation Office after being discharged from the British army, only to find he was locked in to his old pay scale, with a ceiling of £240 a year, compared with the new one that began at £240 15s and went up to £300. This was a continuing source of grievance throughout the public service, which was resolved in Britain by the report of the Southborough Committee in 1923, but that was too late for men like Heron who found themselves living in the Free State, where there was little sympathy from younger, nationalist-minded civil servants, more concerned with creating a level playing-field for the permanent staff than with accommodating relics of an old system they perceived as based on favouritism and rewarding loyalty to the Crown.[48]

Many Great War veterans were let go by the Post Office after the 1922 strike and again in 1927 because of government cut-backs. Naturally they felt it was because of their past military service in the Great War.[49] This should have been a rich vein for Kelly to tap, but he was as unsuccessful in this venture as in all the others he had undertaken. The cases of discrimination he compiled were all dismissed in the High Court by 1926. His services do not appear to have been engaged by any postal workers after the 1927 purge.

Regarding public employment generally, there were proportionately more *prima facie* cases of discrimination in other garrison towns than in Dublin, which suggests that the capital remained as benign an urban environment as could be expected for ex-servicemen outside Belfast and its environs. Nevertheless there was too much anecdotal evidence of hostility towards ex-servicemen seeking employment for it to be dismissed out of hand by the Government Committee on Complaints of Ex-Servicemen.

A far more impressive representative of the ex-servicemen than Kelly was Captain William Archer Redmond DSO, son of the former leader of the Irish Party and representative of the Non-Permanent Government Clerks' Association. Their argument was based on general principles rather than individual cases. The association contended that the government had failed to recognise the 'moral right' of ex-servicemen in the civil service to a 'special degree of security.' It had not provided any compensation to those who were dismissed, in contravention of article 10 of the Treaty, which promised civil servants who retired terms no less favourable than those in the Government of Ireland Act; and, most importantly, the selection procedures for new permanent posts were stacked against them.

This was the nub of the problem. Ex-servicemen in temporary posts could be let go at between one week's and one month's notice, depending on where they were employed, but they were not entitled to compensation. They could become permanent civil servants only by competing with school-leavers, National Army men and other applicants for posts. Most of these were much younger, and had a knowledge of Irish, when 10 per cent was added to marks for answers in Irish and there were further bonus marks for National Army service.[50] There were no bonus points for past experience in the job or a candidate's actual performance in filling temporary posts. The Ministry of Finance accepted, in response to queries from the commission, that of 658 ex-servicemen employed as temporary civil servants in 1922 only 158 remained by July 1927.[51] It had no information on what had happened to the other 500, and although some may have been made permanent, it was generally accepted that recruitment to the permanent civil service was on nothing like the scale of 60 per cent achieved in the United Kingdom.[52]

The Non-Permanent Government Clerks' Association complained that ex-servicemen dismissed from the civil service found it 'practically impossible' to secure other jobs through local labour exchanges, because even there preference was given to National Army members. Some were even told it was their own fault for not joining up to defend the Free State in the Civil War, yet many claimed they had been refused permission to enlist, as their services were needed in their departments.[53] The Committee on Claims of British Ex-Servicemen found that the position of these temporary civil servants

> is undoubtedly difficult and we have had a great deal of evidence of the hardships endured by those men consequent on unemployment. Many of them certainly suffered by the change of policy in the Civil Service consequent on the setting up of the Irish Free State. In the British civil service ex-Servicemen were first in order of preference for absorption into the permanent service and last for dismissal, whereas, in the Irish Free State Civil Service, another class, ex-members of the National Forces, had certain limited advantages in examinations and had a preference for retention when discharges became necessary. The British Government could afford relief by compensation, or by opportunities hitherto denied these men of re-entering the British Civil Service. It is not for us to say whether any measures are possible or not.[54]

It was advice the British government chose to ignore.

If British ex-servicemen in the Irish civil service had reason to resent their treatment by the Free State establishment, they also had a just grievance against their former employers in London. This is clear from individual submissions made to the committee. Of 539 complaints, 337 related to war pensions, 67 to land and housing issues and 17 to miscellaneous grievances, for which the British government and its agencies were responsible. A further 17 complaints related to loss of employment owing to the British evacuation. The number of cases relating to discrimination by the Free State government was 42, all of them relating to former temporary civil servants. There were a further 39 claims of discrimination in obtaining employment or social welfare benefits against the Free State. In other words, 84 per cent of grievances related to the British government.

Complaints against British and Free State governments[55]

Against the British government

War pensions:	337
Land and housing:	67
Loss of employment resulting from British evacuation:	17
Miscellaneous grants, such as War Bounty and King's Fund:	17
Total:	438

Against the Free State government

Discrimination against temporary civil servants:	42
Discrimination in other areas of employment or welfare benefits:	39
Total:	81

————

Positive discrimination in favour of demobilised National Army members extended well beyond the civil service to all publicly funded jobs. Not alone were National Army soldiers with dependants put ahead of all civilian applicants, including British ex-servicemen, but so were National Army members without dependants, reflecting the policy adopted by the British government in 1919. As half those serving in the National Army were British war veterans, at least some of them must have benefited from this form of positive discrimination.

As evidence of the widespread distress experienced by ex-servicemen in the early years of the Free State, the British Legion said it had spent £36,800 in maintenance payments to veterans up to the end of 1927.[56] This was not a particularly large sum. The Society of St Vincent de Paul spent as much in 1919, a bad year financially, and well over £60,000 in almost every year subsequently, including some disbursements to ex-servicemen. The Committee on Claims of British Ex-Servicemen later reported that

> the British Legion accepted that there is no discrimination against British ex-servicemen in connection with employment on Road, Relief etc., Schemes, but alleged that in the choosing of men for labour locally, there was often discrimination by the Foreman of Works against British ex-Servicemen. It is obviously impossible to frame regulations to guard against such incidents.[57]

Figures supplied to the committee by the Ministry of Local Government and Public Health for the seventeen months ending 30 April 1928 showed that the average number of men employed each month on relief schemes and paid out of the rates or government grants was 17,674, of whom only 1,740 (10 per cent) were former members of the National Army. The average number on schemes paid for solely from government grants was 8,008, of whom 1,316 (16 per cent) were former members of the National Army. While the relative differences were significant, the committee accepted that the total numbers employed 'on road or other schemes is so small that there appears to be no real foundation for the complaint.'[58]

The reality was that independence came at a price for all, including public servants, who were mainly based in Dublin. What few of them envisaged in 1922 was that pay rates in the Free State would not keep pace with those in Britain, and one of the less reasonable complaints of some ex-servicemen was that an exception should be made for them. They wanted permanent Irish civil service jobs on British rates of pay.

That there was discrimination was undeniable, but, as the committee pointed out,

> ex-servicemen in the Irish Free State form a small proportion of the population and a large number do not belong to any Organisation owing, *inter alia,* to being scattered over wide geographical areas. On the other hand, in Great Britain ex-servicemen comprise a far larger proportion of the population and owing to concentration in industrial centres are in a much better position to form organisations.[59]

The committee also accepted that, 'compared with ex-servicemen in Great Britain, ex-servicemen in the Irish Free State were at a disadvantage owing to the disturbed state of the country in the years from 1918 to 1923.'

While the findings of the committee hardly reflect well on the new regime, at least the Free State investigated the issue of institutional discrimination, unlike its counterpart in Northern Ireland. The Stormont government not only failed to investigate allegations of discrimination against its Catholic minority but saw those discriminatory practices as a vindication of its own legitimacy. In 1928 the Northern Ireland government even introduced an Unemployment Insurance Act that precluded anyone who had not been resident in the United Kingdom for at least three years from access to unemployment or other benefits, thus becoming the only part of the United Kingdom to discriminate against British ex-servicemen who decided to leave the Free State.[60]

––––

The Committee on Complaints of Ex-Servicemen decided to hold its deliberations in private, including submissions from representative bodies and individual ex-servicemen. While this may have facilitated more frankness on the part of witnesses, it also fuelled anecdotal accounts that served the cause of such groups as the Southern Irish Loyalist Relief Association and its Unionist allies in the House of Commons in claims for compensation. On occasion they used the plight of ex-servicemen to promote their own concerns and to suggest that they were the same.[61] The reticence of the committee also left unanswered the charges by William Redmond that were largely responsible for its establishment. In a celebrated outburst to the Waterford Branch of the British Legion in 1927 he said that

> the position in which ex-servicemen were placed was a deplorable one. Many a time in the Dáil he had endeavoured to do something towards securing at least fair play and equality of citizenship for his comrades of the Great War, but, unfortunately, for one reason or another, the Government—probably because a man took a man's part in the Great War, or an Irishman took an Irishman's part—thought he should not be treated as an ordinary, self-respecting, honest Irishman, and that a differentiation should be made in regard to him. That was a state of affairs which must not continue.

He then took to task Kevin O'Higgins, Minister for Justice and Vice-President of the Free State government, over his rejection of a proposal to build a cenotaph to commemorate the dead of the Great War in Merrion Square, facing Leinster House. This was 'in spite of the fact that Mr. O'Higgins had one brother who served in the Army and another in the Navy.' The Minister had 'gone out of his way to be particularly obnoxious to the 120,000 ex-servicemen surviving in the Free State, as well as 50,000 dead.' Redmond would 'describe it as the Merrion Street mentality, a remarkable mentality, which no just nationalist would tolerate or condone. It was pure spleen, not unmixed with a certain amount of jealousy.'[62]

Redmond's reaction to O'Higgins's rejection of the proposal to commemorate the dead of the Great War at the seat of government says as much about the blind spots in the political outlook of former Irish Party supporters and the British Legion as it does about the Free State government. As Anne Dolan has pointed out, O'Higgins was probably more inclined than most to favour Redmond's proposal, but the Free State's rulers could not afford to cut themselves adrift from the separatist tradition from which they still ultimately drew their legitimacy. The British Legion and ex-servicemen in general would have to make do with Edwin Lutyens's magnificent memorial garden in 'the wilds of Islandbridge.'[63]

The '50,000 dead' became the accepted figure for those who died, and it was frequently invoked to contrast the sacrifice of ex-servicemen with their subsequent treatment. The British Legion was vocal in publicising the exposure of ex-servicemen to mass unemployment, 'betrayal' and 'actual starvation'. This was, regrettably, true, but it was the general condition of the urban working poor, from whose ranks most of these men were drawn. If there was no plan to rescue them there was no conspiracy either to penalise them. The committee's report suited no-one and was ignored, thus saving the Free State government embarrassment and leaving Redmond and the British Legion with a drum to beat at the political establishments in Dublin and London.[64]

Chapter 7 ⌒

'THE SOCIAL GOSPEL OF THE GERMAN JEW, KARL MARX, WAS HERE, INSTALLED IN IRELAND'S PLACE OF HONOUR'

The new regime felt its isolation keenly in the autumn of 1922. It emulated its British predecessor by imposing an oath of fidelity on all civil servants, including those who transferred from Dáil Éireann. This was certainly needed. Insubordination and absence from work were quite marked in government offices. Even some messengers refused to carry out orders because they said the Provisional Government lacked legitimacy.

The new regime reacted, as Martin Maguire has said, 'in an echo of ... the Easter 1916 Rising.' Civil servants 'were compelled to give an account of their movements on the days after June 27th and the outbreak of the Civil War.'[1] When Dr Conn Murphy, a founder-member of the Gaelic League and of the Civil Service Alliance as well as a long-standing IRB member, socialist, contributor to Jim Larkin's *Irish Worker* during the 1913 Lockout and friend of James Connolly, wrote a letter to the newspapers criticising the behaviour of National Army soldiers who raided his house, he was dismissed. All efforts at reinstatement failed.

He was probably not helped by the representations of Áine Ceannt, widow of another friend and executed 1916 signatory, Éamonn Ceannt, nor by his own letter to the Minister for Local Government, Ernest Blythe, yet another friend, in which he expressed outrage that his family had been terrorised by 'an organised murder gang, the members of which are at present employed and paid by the Provisional

Government.' Past service counted for little when the new regime was fighting for its life.[2]

Another old comrade and fellow-contributor to the *Irish Worker* was Séamus Hughes, who had made an even longer pilgrimage than Murphy, one from working-class seminarian to socialist, trade union leader, Irish Volunteer and now secretary of a new political party that the government was setting up, to be called Cumann na nGaedheal. Hughes had been a precocious child. The son of a baker, he won a series of prizes at the O'Connell Schools, a breeding-ground for rebels, and in 1897 he entered the Dominican novitiate at Coublevie in the foothills of the French Alps. This coincided with an anti-clerical drive by the French government that saw Hughes return to Ireland and decide that he had no religious vocation. Nevertheless his sojourn in France left him with fluent French and Italian, a good musical education, a sonorous 'priestly voice', love of physical exercise and 'an otherworldliness evinced in a detachment from money or power.'[3] These would prove mixed blessings. He taught French at the Dominican College in Newbridge (Droichead Nua) and at Enniscorthy Christian Brothers' School, then worked part-time for the Gaelic League and later as a clerk for an egg and poultry merchants' company in Dublin, Carlton Brothers in Halston Street.

All the time he immersed himself in the Irish cultural movement. He played hurling as goalkeeper with Ard-Chraobh, the Gaelic League team that won several Dublin championships, and he was awarded the 'Irish tenor' gold medal at the 1912 Feis Cheoil. He was in popular demand at public concerts, where his rendition of the 'Marseillaise' was particularly well received, and in December 1914 he gave the first public performance of Peadar Kearney's 'The Soldier's Song' at Clontarf Town Hall. He wrote music to turn verses from writers as varied as Thomas Davis, Douglas Hyde and James Connolly into songs. Among them was the tune for Connolly's 'The Watchword of Labour', which became the anthem of the Irish Labour Party.

Inducted, like so many sports and language enthusiasts, into the IRB, Hughes joined the Irish Volunteers and became quartermaster of the 2nd Battalion in Dublin, was involved in the Howth gun-running of 1914, was a member of the garrison in Jacob's factory in Bishop Street in the 1916 Rising and in prison became a close friend of the Volunteers' first chief of staff, Eoin MacNeill.[4] He had written extensively for the radical press, including the *Irish Worker* during the 1913 Lockout, and on his release in 1917 became financial and correspondence secretary of the ITGWU. He played a major role in its revival, working closely with the general president, Tom Foran, and William O'Brien.

A more worldly and canny infighter might have consolidated his position in the leadership of the ITGWU, and no-one doubted his intelligence, ability or capacity for hard work; instead he was used by O'Brien to help defeat the latter's main rival in the trade union movement, P. T. Daly, after which O'Brien dispensed with

Hughes's services as part of the process of consolidating his own position. The experience left Hughes disillusioned with socialism as well as with the trade union movement. He had grown increasingly sceptical about reports from Russia and about the growing influence of James Connolly's son, Roddy, in the Socialist Party of Ireland, which changed its name to the Communist Party of Ireland shortly after Hughes left.

What Hughes objected to most was not an excess of revolutionary fervour but a lack of democracy. Despite their differences, he chose Roddy Connolly's revived *Workers' Republic* (a title closely associated with Connolly's father) as the platform for an attack on the ITGWU leadership. The occasion was a strike by clerical workers in May 1922, all of them well known to Hughes. He accused the leadership of the union and the Labour Party of suffering from the 'deadly disease' of 'bureaucracy'. He accused the president of the ITGWU, Tom Foran, and O'Brien, now general treasurer, of destroying the personal independence of the 'splendid staff with whose aid the union was built up after the debacle of 1916.' He claimed that Foran stood for a 'Dublin union', supplemented by a 'convenient number' of provincial tributary branches, while O'Brien 'would like the ITGWU to be broadly national in scope ... on condition, however, that he should hold the strings himself.' The members and staff of the union must have 'pliant knees ... or get out.' The number of organisers had been reduced from twenty-one to six 'by all the art known to capitalists and a few others that can only be learned in the trade union bureaucracy world.'

Hughes lamented 'the glorious possibilities of an exceptional situation wasted and lost for personal ends.' If the 'mandarins in Parnell Square'[5] had yielded 'to the repeated demands of the branches for greater authority in local affairs by the establishment of district councils ... the country would have been covered with a network of labour bodies elected on an occupational basis and available for all industrial, co-operative, and political work of local and national import.' The union could more effectively have resisted job and pay cuts, while the Labour Party 'would not have been reduced to the necessity of flirting for power with political leaders.' The 'refusal of the ITGWU executive to decentralise and expand when the labour wave was at its highest was the greatest betrayal of working class interests in Irish history.'[6]

It was no wonder that the infant Communist Party was willing to provide a former union bureaucrat with a platform for such comments, and there was certainly some truth in them, but there was also a strong element of wishful thinking. Whatever the failings of Foran and O'Brien, the primary reason for the reduction in union staff was the fall in union membership, and the primary reason for that was the economic crisis, aggravated by civil war. Union membership had reached a peak at somewhere between 120,000 and 130,000 in 1920 but fell to 69,500 in 1921, rising briefly to 82,000 in 1922 before resuming its downward march. This reflected the fall in total union membership among affiliates of the ITUC from 229,000 to 183,000 over the same period.

Nor could the ITGWU leadership be accused of lack of support for members, with strike pay reaching a peak of £128,724 in 1923; this was equivalent to more than 150 per cent of its rapidly dwindling annual income, a position that was clearly unsustainable.[7]

Perhaps an opportunity was lost in 1921 to build a more democratic union, but the structures for doing so were there, and it was Hughes, ideally placed to fight that battle, who was either unable or unwilling to do so. Interestingly, at no point did he argue that a more democratic or dynamic union would have led to a socialist revolution.

After leaving the ITGWU Hughes went to work for the Irish Co-operative Clothing Manufacturing Society in Abbey Street, with which the union had strong links. The co-operative flourished with the public mania for import substitution and enjoyed the general good will towards co-operative ventures that accompanied the rise of Sinn Féin. It made and sold men's and women's clothing, with clerical garments 'a speciality'. Poor management and defective workmanship would kill the venture, but Hughes had nothing to do with either, as he was seconded to Eoin MacNeill's staff at the Irish Race Convention in Paris in January 1922.

Envisaged as a means of maximising the support of the Irish diaspora for the independence struggle, the convention decided to press ahead despite the Truce and subsequent deep divisions that emerged from the Treaty debate. These ensured that the convention would be the first and last of its kind. For Hughes it cemented his friendship with MacNeill, and confirmed him in his dislike of de Valera. At one point it looked as if he might be appointed secretary to the convention, but the split ensured that there was no secretariat. He returned to throw himself, like many Dublin IRB men, into working to ensure that the Treaty was passed.[8]

It was in this capacity that Hughes's efficiency, enthusiasm and commitment secured him a place on the election subcommittee established by Collins before the June election. Following victory, Hughes was appointed to a 'general and election committee' that took on the complementary tasks of building popular support for the Provisional Government and creating a political party that could become its election and policy vehicle. It was in this context that Hughes proposed a civil defence organisation to act in support of the National Army.[9] Ernest Blythe, Minister for Local Government, whom Hughes knew well from Gaelic League days, wrote back confirming interest in the idea from both the government and army headquarters. The original idea was that members of the civil defence organisation, who would carry identity cards but were not to be armed, would report on 'criminal affairs, robberies, raids, hold-ups, murders etc.' to the new CID in Oriel House and on 'military matters, snipers, dumps, ambushes etc.' to army headquarters in Portobello Barracks. Thomas Morrissey, Hughes's biographer, believes Hughes had no further involvement in what would become the Civil Defence Force. Blythe probably thought him too fastidious for such work, and they had a ready-made substitute in Henry Harrison. Nevertheless the association with Oriel House would prove fatal to Hughes's subsequent short political career.

Of more immediate consequence was a meeting on 7 September 1922 at which Blythe brought a deputation from the pro-Treaty parliamentary group to meet the general and election committee of the proto-party, and it was agreed to establish a 'political organisation' that 'would work through the Treaty towards a united and distinctively Gaelic Ireland.' Hughes became a member of the five-man committee charged with drafting a constitution for the new party, under the chairmanship of Blythe. Between then and the adoption of the final draft on 10 November, Hughes was in his element, and much of the sentiment contained in the new party's objects bears his intellectual imprint.

> To carry on the national tradition; to utilise the powers of government now in the hands of the Irish people for the fullest development of the nation's heritage, economic, cultural and political; to achieve the political unity of Ireland and to fuse the divergent elements of the nation into one harmonious whole inspired by a common sentiment of citizenship and justice.

The objects included the promotion of Irish and developing Irish manufactures. In a more radical section it sought 'to make the whole soil of Ireland available for the use of the people by completing land purchase and dividing up the idle ranches into economic holdings,' as well as financing 'a national scheme of housing.'[10]

On 13 October 1922 Hughes used the opportunity of addressing the Catholic Truth Society's annual conference in the Mansion House to expand on his new social thinking. He went much further in his speech than in the *Workers' Republic* article five months earlier. The conference came three days after the Catholic hierarchy's pastoral letter condemning opposition to the Provisional Government (see chapter 5), and it was used to mount a counter-attack on the elements threatening 'moral anarchy'. The phrase was used by another speaker, Rev. P. J. Gannon SJ. 'At present they had young sons and daughters of liberty everywhere, unamenable to any authority, parental, ecclesiastical, civil, human or divine,' he complained. After denouncing the Belfast pogroms and deploring Orange mobs that turned Catholics into 'human torches' he said the Church had no right to be complacent in the South. The 'get rich quick' people were making

> enormous profits by catering for the most humiliating weaknesses of mankind in novels, magazines, theatre, music hall, cinema and dancing saloon. The designers of women's costumes follow suit and fashion becomes the hand maiden of Belial ... For almost a century they had seen a vast international

propaganda at work denying man's right to private property. The result was not doctrinaire communism. It is practical communism, that is to say highway robbery.[11]

Hughes followed Gannon with a paper on 'community rule versus class dictatorship,' in which he told the audience that

> they owed it to their self-respect as Christians, but still more to the great institution of the Church to face resolutely those evils which were playing such havoc with the people ... Class rule was a grave evil, whether it be a veiled dictatorship of a propertied minority or the avowed rule of a proletarian majority. The social gospel of the German Jew, Karl Marx was here, installed in Ireland's place of honour. Officially the Labour movement had no connection with Communism, [but] the Labour chiefs were teaching their followers to think of themselves as a nation within a nation, a people apart, whose interests were diametrically opposed to the interests of everyone else.

He then explained his own concept of community rule, which

> would render it impossible for any one element or type of individual to override the human rights of any other section of citizens, and which would make it easy for a minority to assert its rightful claims in an effective manner. In such an order of society all classes would share the power and responsibility of government, and have guaranteed to them in return free access to the necessaries of life—food, clothing and shelter. [If] the ultimate object of the Labour movement was the welfare and happiness of its members, then Labour in Ireland must get ready to re-export Karl Marx to Palestine or Russia ... There was no future for the working man as such, except as a factor of economic democracy. There was no hope for Labour's success until it dropped the pursuit of the will-o-the-wisp called power, and settled down to its own job, the concrete problems of scientific reconstruction.

Hughes wanted the labour movement to revert to its nineteenth-century role of purely trade union activity while still denouncing capitalism, which allowed

> the strong [to] crush out the weak, and were not thousands of Irish Catholics now without food, clothing or shelter? That was the result of our commercial system, but that system was not from God—it was from man and non-Catholic man at that. The organised community must dictate industrial policy while leaving the onus for carrying out such policy on the operatives engaged in the industries concerned.

If Hughes appeared to be advocating some form of workers' control in an oblique way, he identified financiers as the villains rather than employers. He called on the Government

> to appoint a Commission, on which the Government, Labour, and the Church would be represented, whose function would be to carry out a social survey to get and collect information on ... occupations of the people; incomes; property held; living conditions; physical and educational fitness; charitable institutions and benefit societies.[12]

In many ways Hughes was seeking to enlist Catholic social thinking on corporatism to provide workers with a more central role in the organisation of society, and he found some sympathy from the Catholic hierarchy and laity, who were already beginning to provide so many of the social services required in the new Free State. The departure of the British was welcomed by the hierarchy not least because it removed the threat of an interventionist, secular regime. For the same reason it remorselessly opposed the advocates of secularism, from anti-clerical republicans to communists. Hughes had found his niche.

He was supported by Rev. Dr Peter Coffey, who lectured on philosophy at Maynooth and argued that James Connolly's teachings were compatible with Catholicism. A leading figure on the management committee of the Catholic Truth Society, Coffey praised Hughes's 'thoughtful and valuable contribution towards a right solution of the social and economic question.' The Free State offered an opportunity

> to replace the old party system of government by a more rational business-like system. It was on economic conditions and economic forces that our future physical and social well being was going to depend. The Irish people could go terribly astray unless two things could be clearly proved to them—first, that the actual class war between employed and employers was not only un-Christian, but downright foolish and idiotic; and, secondly, that there was another and alternative line of action, the line of quite friendly and intelligent co-operation ...
>
> The present industrial and commercial system was equally indefensible from the social and the Christian point of view. It was up to organised Labour to table a national substitute, and in the effort to get it adopted Labour was entitled to, and would receive, immense help from all other elements in society that were conscious of the defects of the present system.

Coffey accepted the contention of the leaders of organised labour that workers' wages were falling, 'but they were wrong in saying that the employers could afford to give a higher wage without raising the prices of the products. The employers, on their side, were … wrong in saying that the wage ought not to rise when prices rise, for the wage worker must live.' Like Hughes, he depicted the financiers as the villains.

> The employers and the employed alike were the victims of a banking and financial system, which, of its very nature, tended to paralyse industry, to throw the workers out of employment and to make it impossible for the employers— that is the owners and administrators of plant, machinery and processes—to keep the industrial machine going.

He advocated a 'social credit' movement to replace the banks (a position that probably cost him promotion to the professorship of ethics in the university in 1929).

The only speaker at the conference to criticise Hughes's paper was William Davin, general secretary of the Railway Clerks' Association and a newly elected Labour TD for Laois-Offaly. He said he did not share 'the pessimism of Mr Hughes,' but he devoted most of his time to denying that communism had any influence within the Labour Party. Nor had he much faith in 'long winded Commissions.' Bishop McKenna, on the other hand, in a vote of thanks to Hughes, warned that 'Marxism is destructive of human liberty. It not only reduces men to the status of beasts in the field, but it also destroyed their deep and spiritual interests.' He was less convinced of the efficacy of the reorganisation of society along the lines advocated by Hughes but, unlike Davin, he felt it would be 'a function of the proposed Commission … to elucidate that.'[13]

Not surprisingly, Hughes's erstwhile comrades were not impressed by his conversion. The following issue of the *Voice of Labour*, the journal of the ITGWU, referred to Hughes as a 'one time member of the Socialist Party of Ireland' who was now warning workers of the pitfalls of following the teachings of Connolly and Larkin. It said that it little thought that the first public denunciation of James Connolly should come from 'a former disciple and an ex-official of' the union to which the martyred labour leader 'had devoted so much of his precious time and clear thinking.'[14] In fairness to Hughes it must be said that he had never claimed to be a Marxist, but his change of direction was indicative of a new political trajectory being pursued by a significant element within the revolutionary elite that had led the struggle for independence.

———

Although Hughes was not involved in the Free State's military effort, and had not been active in the Irish Volunteers since 1916, apart from some intelligence-gathering activities, like many prominent figures he faced the risk of more lethal attacks than those in the columns of the *Voice of Labour*. Unlike some government ministers, he did not move into Government Buildings but he did spend many nights in his office at 5 Parnell Square, a former dentist's surgery. It was a relatively short distance to his home in Drumcondra, where his wife, Josephine, would leave a light on in the hall overnight if it was unsafe to enter. Suspicious activity by a female caller suspected of being a Republican spy caused Hughes and his wife not to attend the Holy Communion of their daughter Clora in October 1922, and on the evening beforehand there was a bomb attack on the office in Parnell Square.

The execution of the four Volunteers who attacked Oriel House in November increased the stakes. Not only ministers but TDs who had voted for the Army Emergency Powers Resolution, or 'Murder Bill', as Republicans dubbed it, were declared legitimate targets by the anti-Treaty IRA. On 7 December two of those TDs, Brigadier-General Seán Hales and Pádraig Ó Máille, Deputy Speaker of the Dáil, were shot in an opportunist attack in Dublin. Hales died, and Ó Máille was seriously wounded.

The next day four leading Republicans taken prisoner when the Four Courts fell—Dick Barrett, Joe McKelvey, Liam Mellows and Rory O'Connor—were shot in Mountjoy Prison in retaliation. Many local authorities passed motions condemning the executions, but when Dublin Corporation met on 11 December the motion of sympathy passed tendered its 'sincere sympathy to the parents and relatives of the late ... Seán Hales' as well as those of the Republican leaders.

Councillors also rejected a proposal that the dependants of Corporation employees who were in hospital or had been interned 'during the recent disturbances' should receive half pay. The motion was only narrowly defeated, by 17 votes to 15; it might have been passed if some anti-Treaty councillors on the run or in state custody, such as Joe Clarke and Joseph MacDonagh, had been able to vote. Most of the Labour councillors of both factions supported the payments to families, but a solid block of MRA and pro-Treaty Sinn Féin councillors blocked it.

The Corporation's Law Officer, Ignatius Rice, accepted that 'in 1916, and since, the law has been strained to its utmost in favour of persons interned, and in some cases, even to convicted prisoners,' but he warned that under the new Free State regime there was a danger that the surcharge on the rates might not be reimbursed as it had been by the Local Government Board under British rule. He did point out that some employees in hospital because of the 'disturbances' might be eligible for sickness pay.[15] Meanwhile payments continued to at least some employees on the run.

The prisoners issue remained a divisive one for the council. A poorly attended meeting on 20 November agreed to establish public sittings at the Mansion House to hear complaints from prisoners and their relatives every Monday, Wednesday and Friday evening, which all councillors could attend but few did, even when one of their own, Joe Clarke, a veteran of the battle of Mount Street Bridge in 1916, sent in a letter complaining of his treatment in custody. Clarke wrote that he had been pulled off his bicycle and arrested by CID men in Capel Street on 8 November. One of his captors

> threatened me with his revolver and said he would make me tell where the Republic [*Poblacht na hÉireann*] was printed and the whereabouts of Austin Stack. I was driven to Mountjoy ... Then I was taken to Portobello Barracks. I was then interrogated by an IO [intelligence officer] who beat me around the room with his revolver. He struck me several times with the butt and muzzle. He said he would make me tell where the Republic was printed. He also said he would make it hot for me if I sent out information about the way he ill-treated me.
>
> I was then taken to Wellington Barracks about 5.30; here myself and nine others were lined up and brought in one by one to the torture room.

The hunt for the offices of *Poblacht na hÉireann* seems to have taken up a lot of CID time. At 11:15 p.m. on 10 November a number of newsboys were arrested outside the Theatre Royal in Hawkins Street, where they had been selling copies. They were taken up into the gallery when the audience left and beaten for about twenty minutes because they refused to say who the distributor was. All their money, the proceeds of their day's sales, was taken.

Clarke was also questioned about people who frequented the Sinn Féin offices at 23 Suffolk Street, where he worked as secretary. His interrogators, Frank Bolster and Joe Dolan, both former Squad members, 'twisted my arms, kicked me on the legs and body, tore my moustache off with a pliers and scissors, a razor and some other torture instrument.' He said Dolan did 'most of the torture' and threatened him with a hot iron 'if I did not inform on my comrades.' Bolster 'said I would be shot.' Clarke added that all his money—more than £6—a fountain pen and a knife were taken and not returned. All the other prisoners received similar treatment; one of them, John Lawlor, had been so badly beaten that Clarke understood he had been taken to hospital.[16]

The committee wrote to Cosgrave on 14 November demanding safe conduct for witnesses to its hearings. On the 15th Cosgrave's secretary replied that the council had no right to hold a sworn inquiry and that if it persisted in holding such hearings 'the matter will be referred to the Chief State Solicitor with a view to advising on a prosecution.' It was decided to proceed regardless, but the meeting adjourned briefly as a mark of respect to Councillor Clarke,[17] before reconvening half an hour later to discuss the possibility of a smallpox outbreak in the city following reports of cases in Glasgow. It was decided to make chicken pox a notifiable disease for six months in case of the misdiagnosis of smallpox. The Corporation also decided to discourage the importing of second-hand clothes from Scotland while the smallpox threat remained.[18] As in the War of Independence, the routine misery of life in the city had to be managed, as well as the impositions of Civil War.

At the next meeting, on 4 December 1922, a motion of 'sincere sympathy' was passed 'to the parents and relatives of the late Joseph Spooner, Patrick Farrelly and John Murphy, recently executed.' These three Volunteers had been arrested in Erne Street on 30 October in possession of a revolver and three bombs following another unsuccessful attack on Oriel House. They were shot exactly two weeks after the first four Volunteers executed in the city. It was in the wake of these executions that the Council agreed to print and circulate the evidence being collected at the Mansion House hearings into the 'alleged ill-treatment of prisoners.'

Meanwhile Dublin's civilians continued to be shot out of hand in the cross-fire between combatants. As councillors debated the plight of prisoners on the evening of 4 December a young woman was shot dead and three other people seriously injured in a gun battle between the anti-Treaty IRA and the National Army. The dead woman was Angela Bridgeman, a 23-year-old waiter in the Mont Clare Hotel. She was hit by a bullet under the eye and died instantly as the open-top tram she was travelling on passed a National Army patrol near the National Children's Hospital in Harcourt Street. Two other women passengers were shot in the legs and a man was bit by a bomb splinter in the spine. An *Irish Times* reporter who was on the tram told readers next day that

the people on the top of the car threw themselves flat on the floor, and stayed there huddled together while the shots were flying. I saw a Crossley tender behind us. The soldiers had dismounted and, using the tender as cover, were firing at the attackers. I could see flashes from their rifles. The attackers seemed to be on the rooftops, and, to judge by the position of the wounded, it was their shots that struck the people on the tramcar.

The car had stopped, and we were held between the two fires. Suddenly a man in front of me shouted, 'Oh, I'm gone ...' Then one of the women—most of the passengers were women—shrieked, 'My God, I am hit!' and began to cry and moan. Then another woman screamed. Some of them became hysterical. We could hear screaming in the interior of the tram. On the top of the car they were praying and crying.

A man who had been collecting for the Holles Street Cancer Hospital—probably a medical student—crawled along the top to the wounded and, with the assistance of some of the other men passengers, did what he could, even while the firing lasted, but it was very little that could be done in that cramped and crowded space, with the bullets flying around. It was queer to see the medical student in his white robe, mask, and false moustache trying to comfort and aid the injured people.

It seemed as if it was an hour before the shots eased, and we risked raising our heads. There was a fair light at that point, and the wounded man was carried downstairs by some of the other men. He was brought to a dentist's close at hand.

The conductor rang the bell to start the car, and several people shouted to him to wait until the wounded were removed. 'We must get out of danger first,' said the conductor. 'Are you going to let the woman die?' he was asked. But it was easy to sympathise with his point of view, and there is little doubt that the first thought in the minds of virtually all the passengers was to get out of the danger zone.

The car stopped in a few yards, and one of the women was carried into the National Children's Hospital. The other casualties were taken to Vincent's Hospital. At that point I did not know that one of the women was dead, and I think nobody did. She must have died almost instantaneously.[19]

Meanwhile in the Mansion House some councillors were doing what little they could to address the crisis. James Gately, a former Irish Party supporter and now an independent nationalist, proposed a motion, seconded by P. T. Daly, leader of the Trades Council faction of Labour,

that as unemployment and consequent distress are certain to be largely increased during the present winter and early spring, it behoves this Council to take measures that may to some extent meet such threatened extension of misery and want:

We, therefore, respectfully suggest to the Provisional Government to have passed by Dáil Éireann an Emergency Decree requiring all ground owners to have removed all debris within the ruined spaces within the city, and in the case of failure, to give the Borough Council of Dublin power to enter on such spaces and carry out this work, charging the costs of same to such owner as neglects or refuses to have such work done. Work to be started at earliest possible date.

It was passed unanimously. In a city pockmarked by slaughterhouses, dairies and piggeries, the additional hazard of derelict sites that were sometimes used by the anti-Treaty IRA for ambushes certainly needed attention, but it also demonstrated the lack of real power the city fathers had to deal with the dangers confronting citizens.[20]

———

The next motion was much more contentious. It came from the Finance Committee and proposed giving a pension to employees who had to retire for reasons of health or age amounting to two-thirds of their final salary averaged over three years. Alderman J. Hubbard Clark, leader of the Municipal Reform Association, proposed that it be referred back, saying that 'the legislature [House of Commons] never contemplated that every employee should be superannuated on the highest scale.' He also objected to pensions being calculated on the basis of 'a temporary bonus equivalent to the wage itself.' This was the 'war bonus' introduced in a wide range of occupations in 1917 to deal with widespread industrial unrest caused by wartime inflation. As it was worth 130 per cent of basic pay for low to middle earners, such as labourers, craft workers and clerical grades, it added substantially to the pensions bill.[21]

Hubbard Clark had been advocating the abolition of war bonuses for over a year. As we have seen, as early as 9 January 1922 he had proposed that war bonuses for salaried staff be reduced by half. (See chapter 5.) He had been supported by Andrew Beattie, another former Unionist who had joined the MRA, and they wanted to halve the war bonus for wage-earners as well.

Both proposals were ruled out of order on the advice of the Law Agent.[22] Now, when the Town Clerk pointed out that the legislation did not provide for reductions in pensions, only for the maximum that could be set, a horrified Hubbard Clark said, 'Well, I object [to] every Tom, Dick and Harry getting the maximum.' Some of those on the list were between forty and forty-five. 'The man who came into the service at the fag end of his life was not entitled to the maximum'. Nevertheless the report was adopted by a comfortable majority.

The onward march of labour, or at least its cost to the ratepayers, was not to be halted. By the end of the Civil War there were 2,877 Corporation employees, being paid a total of £652,213 a year, compared with 2,345 paid £401,660 at the beginning of the War of Independence. This was an increase in numbers of 23 per cent and an increase in wages of 62 per cent.

Employees of Dublin Corporation, 1919 and 1923

	31 March 1919		31 March 1923	
	Number	Total pay	Number	Total pay
Overseers	35	£7,026	44	£11,204
Foremen	37	£7,297	31	£8,380
Assistant foremen	4	£781	7	£1,717
Timekeepers	16	£3,231	16	£4,102
Assistant timekeepers	5	£794	5	£1,111
Measurers	2	£408	2	£529
Assistant measurers	1	£175	1	£220
Class III employees	322	£53,370	323	£71,348

Tradesmen	259	£48,099	353	£79,473
Labourers	1,092	£154,087	1,482	£287,717
Officials, officers, clerks, etc.	393	£107,861	401	£148,595
Fire Brigade	44	£7,248	50	£12,729
Nurses, probationers, domestic staff, TB Committee	37	£3,418	43	£4,507
Miscellaneous charwomen, office cleaners, etc.	98	£12,865	119	£20,581
Total	2,345	£401,660	2,877	£652,213

There was no acrimony about nominating Corporation members for the new Free State Senate, although Alderman Kathleen Clarke left the chamber before the vote was taken, in case her presence might 'be taken to imply recognition of partition and the degradation of the country from the independence proclaimed and sealed by blood in 1916.' There was inter-party agreement on the nominations. They included the only Unionist, William McCarthy, and the leading woman member of Sinn Féin to take the pro-Treaty side, Jennie Wyse Power.[23]

That civil relations could be maintained in such circumstances was a tribute to Corporation members. This was evidenced by the decision in late November to publish the allegations of ill-treatment of Republican prisoners in Free State custody, although government supporters were clearly embarrassed at the prospect. Another example was the measured vote of sympathy for the Four Courts leaders shot in Mountjoy Prison in retaliation for the killing of Seán Hales. On the night before the vote was taken the homes of two TDs and a senior civil servant, as well as the business premises of Jennie Wyse Power, were subjected to incendiary attacks.

The worst incident involved the family of Captain Seán McGarry, a former city councillor and former president of the IRB, who was now a TD and National Army officer. He was not at home in 37 Philipsburg Avenue that Sunday evening when a group of five or six armed men called to the house. They ejected his mother-in-law and sister-in-law onto the street before sprinkling petrol through the kitchen, sitting-room and hall and setting fire to the house. They ignored pleas from the women that McGarry's wife, Tomasina, was upstairs with her children and slammed the front door shut to make sure no-one could enter or leave the premises. Tomasina McGarry, her two sons and handicapped daughter were rescued by Sergeant Smith of the DMP and two local men. One boy survived unscathed, but Tomasina and her other two children suffered serious burns. Seven-year-old Emmet died five days later in Temple Street Children's Hospital 'after much suffering.'[24] The IRA defended its action, blaming the fire brigade for not responding in time, but the brigade was very busy that night.

The other TD whose premises were attacked was J. J. Walsh, the Postmaster-General who had confronted the postal workers in September. (See chapter 5.) His newspaper, stationery and tobacco shop was tailor-made for incendiaries and, like the McGarrys' house, was completely destroyed.

Senator Jennie Wyse Power was more fortunate. Only one of the three incendiary bombs thrown at her Irish Farm Produce Shop in Camden Street exploded, 'shattering the big plate glass window, which fell in fragments into the street,' but the fire brigade successfully doused the flames. Wyse Power's previous shop in Henry Street had been looted and then destroyed by British artillery in the 1916 Rising.

The other target was the home of Michael McDunphy, yet another IRB veteran, who was Assistant Secretary to the Free State government. It was in Clonliffe Road, not far from the McGarrys' house. Confronted by armed men, McDunphy asked for time to put his affairs in order before they shot him[25]; instead they began dousing the premises in petrol, sprinkling McDunphy and his wife in the process. Fortunately the fire brigade's response was faster than at Philipsburg Avenue, and the fire at the McDunphys' house was quickly put out.

The death of one McGarry child and severe injuries to another, and their mother, were largely forgotten in the uproar over the executions of the Four Courts prisoners.[26] Nor was the IRA finished with McGarry, destroying his electrical fittings business in St Andrew's Street the following month.

The attacks on the McDunphys and the McGarrys, who lived in the same general area, showed that Hughes was right to be concerned for his safety. Even more worrying was the death of Séamus Dwyer. Dwyer was almost a mirror image of Hughes on the right wing of the national movement. While Hughes's father was from the working class and his precocious son had been a trade union activist and socialist, Dwyer's father was a prosperous provisions merchant in Lower Baggot Street. All four sons went to Blackrock College, but instead of going on to university Séamus opened a high-class spirit and grocery shop in Rathmines Terrace, where he lived over the shop with his wife. Hughes's interest in public affairs led him into the ITGWU, Gaelic League and GAA, while Dwyer became vice-president of the Family Grocers' and Purveyors' Association, a member of the Committee of Management of the New Ireland Assurance Society and of the Robin Hood Golf Club. He joined Sinn Féin and was a founder-member of the Cuala group, which sought to widen the organisation's appeal in the most middle-class and unionist-minded constituency in Dublin. Other members of the group included his fellow-businessman Joe MacDonagh, brother of the executed 1916 signatory Thomas MacDonagh; Áine Ceannt, widow of another signatory, Éamonn Ceannt; Hanna Sheehy Skeffington, widow of yet another 1916 martyr; Cahir Davitt, a barrister and son of the founder of the Land League, Michael Davitt; and Dr Kathleen Lynn, probably the most politically radical member. They narrowly failed to secure the election of the Sinn Féin candidate, P. J. Little, losing the seat to Sir Maurice Dockrell, the only Unionist elected to the House of Commons in 1918 outside of Ulster and Trinity College.

Dwyer was Little's election agent, and in the 1920 municipal elections Sinn Féin almost secured a majority on Rathmines Urban District Council. Dwyer was not able to take his own seat because of a technicality, but he served as an intelligence officer in the 4th Battalion of the Dublin Brigade in the War of Independence. His social circle, which included Sir James MacMahon, Under-Secretary in Dublin Castle, Sir Henry Robinson, Vice-President of the Local Government Board, and members of the Kildare Street Club, gave him access to sensitive information, and he reported directly to Michael Collins, briefing him on official thinking as well as relations between members of the old guard, such as Robinson, and Sir John Anderson's new team brought over from London to clean up the administration and develop links with the rebels that would ultimately lead to the Truce in July 1921.

Dwyer was elected to the second Dáil in May 1921 and voted for the Treaty. He was unsuccessful in the election to the third Dáil, where he was running alongside much stronger pro-Treaty candidates, such as Desmond Fitzgerald, George Gavan Duffy, Michael Derham and the independent Darrell Figgis as well as Thomas Johnson, leader of the Labour Party. Like Hughes, Dwyer committed himself to the new regime, but while Hughes was essentially an intellectual with considerable organisational talents Dwyer appears to have combined political activity with continuing involvement in intelligence work. At least that appears to have been the perception among Republican activists, who associated him with the Citizens' Defence Force to a much greater degree than Hughes. In fact Dwyer was fatally associated anecdotally with illegal executions of Republican activists by Oriel House gunmen.

Remarkably, Henry Harrison, the actual 'supervisor' of the CDF, does not appear to have come to the attention of the IRA at all.[27] A major weakness of anti-Treaty IRA intelligence, now that the guiding hand of Collins was absent, was an inability to look beyond familiar foes within the Unionist establishment and the usual suspects within the ranks of former comrades. Nor was its leadership able to pool information efficiently or think strategically. Instead the anti-Treaty IRA decided that Dwyer was 'not an ordinary shop keeper; he had been doing undercover work with the Citizens' Protection Association for the Staters, laying traps and having activists arrested and at least one volunteer Tony O'Reilly from Celbridge, executed.'[28] O'Reilly had deserted from the National Army, joined the IRA and been taken prisoner in Co. Kildare. He was subsequently tried by court-martial and shot in Kilmainham Prison in January 1923. This was the normal fate of deserters taken in arms fighting for the enemy, and it is hard to fathom how Dwyer could have been involved in any way with his execution. A possible source of such information may have been one of his shop assistants, a member of the 4th Battalion who supported the anti-Treaty forces.

In any case, a man running a grocery shop is a vulnerable target, and Dwyer appears to have taken no precautions against assassination, which suggests that he was not in fact involved in the sort of deadly activities his opponents thought he was. At 4:50 p.m. on 20 December 1922, with four shopping days left to Christmas, Dwyer stood behind the bacon counter talking to customers when a young man of small, athletic build entered and asked for him. One of the assistants indicated his employer to the caller, who walked up to Dwyer and said, 'I've got a note for you.' As Dwyer extended his hand to receive it, the young man 'whipped out a revolver and fired two shots at what was virtually point blank range.' Dwyer's assailant ran out into Rathmines Road in the gathering gloom, pursued by a customer and Walter Foley, Dwyer's shop manager, who vaulted the counter to join the chase. They were joined by a DMP constable, Maurice Aherne, who had been on traffic duty a short distance away. Aherne had been a member of Collins's intelligence network within the DMP in the War of Independence and almost certainly knew Dwyer.

The gunman cut through a lane into Church Avenue and lost his pursuers in the winter gloom.[29] Dwyer was dead on admission to the Meath Hospital, shot through the heart. He left a widow, Maria, who was in their flat over the shop at the time. They had no children.

Dwyer's killer, Bobby Bonfield, may well have made his way home to Ranelagh that evening. A dental student, he came, like Dwyer, from a comfortable middle-class background but was almost a generation younger. Among his friends had been Kevin Barry, the iconic medical student hanged by the British in the War of Independence, and the sons of the Minister for Education in the Free State government, Eoin MacNeill, one of whom, Brian, had been killed fighting against the National Army at Lislahelly, Co. Sligo.[30] They were all part of a young revolutionary elite who could have looked forward to rewarding careers under the new regime if they so chose.

Dwyer received what was in reality, if not formally, a state funeral on 23 December 1922, with a military guard of honour as it passed through Rathmines. It paused outside Lissenfield House, the residence of General Mulcahy at the rear of Portobello Barracks, where a number of senior officers joined the funeral procession. A few weeks earlier Francis Power, a 22-year-old fellow-student with Bonfield, had been shot dead on that very spot in an unsuccessful attempt to assassinate Mulcahy. Among the mourners had been Dwyer and Bonfield's former superiors in the pre-Truce 4th Battalion, including Commandant F. X. Coghlan, who had argued so bitterly with Todd Andrews over the latter's raid on an arms dump.[31] All the businesses along the street closed, and many houses had their blinds drawn.

Bonfield managed to survive almost to the end of the Civil War, but his luck finally ran out on 30 March 1922, Holy Thursday. He was on his way to McCarthy's newspaper shop in Lower Leeson Street, which was a dump and letter drop for the IRA, when at about 5 p.m. he encountered W. T. Cosgrave with his bodyguard at St Stephen's Green. Cosgrave was on his way to church, but that did not inhibit his bodyguards, who seized Bonfield and took him in the general direction of Oriel House. Next day his body was discovered at Red Cow, where the remains of Edwin Hughes, Brendan Holohan and Joseph Rogers had been found six months earlier.

If Cosgrave had any concerns about the legality of what his escort was planning he does not appear to have voiced them, but he had already sanctioned many executions through the Army Emergency Powers Resolution passed by the Dáil in September 1922. When Republicans denounced it as the 'Murder Bill' they were not exaggerating, for once.[32]

The anti-Treaty forces had not yet finished with Dwyer's shop. On 29 April 1923 it suffered collateral damage when Edward Lee's drapery store beside it was blown up. Lee was one of the leading survivors of the old liberal Unionist establishment in Dublin, and this group was targeted as relentlessly as other pillars of the Free State establishment in the city. Former Unionists and Redmondites nominated to the Free State Senate at the end of 1922 were denounced in *Poblacht na hÉireann* as 'imperialists', with particular attention being drawn to Freemasons in their ranks, such as the Earl of Dunraven, Lord Glenavy, the Marquis of Headfort, the Earl of Kerry, Sir Horace Plunkett and General Sir Bryan Mahon—who had commanded the 10th (Irish) Division of the British army in the First World War and was the most politically adept commander of British forces in Ireland after the 1916 Rising—as well as Andrew Jameson, who played an important role in financing the republican administration in City Hall during the War of Independence and facilitated secret negotiations for the Truce in 1921.[33]

The Freemasons featured as strongly in anti-Treaty demonology as that other secret oath-bound organisation, the IRB. Meanwhile the death of Dwyer saw Séamus Hughes co-opted to the Provisional Standing Committee of Cumann na nGaedheal, to take his place in planning for the forthcoming inaugural convention on 26 April, three days before Dwyer's shop suffered collateral damage during the attack on Lee's.[34]

––––

Not surprisingly, 1922 had been the worst year in the history of Dublin Fire Brigade, with 474 calls, 382 fires and 90 false alarms, of which 61 were malicious. As in previous years, the majority of fires, 262, were 'slight', involving a financial loss of less than £50. There were 39 fires classified as 'medium' involving damage of between

£50 and £500. That left only 28 fires recording losses of £500 or more, but some of the losses claimed were very large, and the total value of the property endangered was even greater. The chief fire officer, John Myers, put the actual loss at £134,158, but this still compared badly with an annual average of £37,418 over the previous twelve years.[35] This figure does not include £2½ million in damage sustained in the 1916 Rising, most of it caused by the British artillery bombardment; nor does it include the total value of property lost in the city during the conventional phase of the Civil War, which was estimated at between £3 million and £4 million. But on this occasion the British exchequer would not be footing the bill.

The first building seriously damaged at the outbreak of the Civil War was the head office of the Orange Order in Rutland Square (Parnell Square), when the departing Republican garrison set it on fire. Far worse in financial terms was the damage caused to the Four Courts and surrounding buildings during the siege that followed. It was impossible for the fire brigade to operate effectively in such conditions and it was a miracle that only three firemen were injured. Elsewhere the holes made in the walls of the fortified buildings Republicans occupied to ease internal communications also facilitated the rapid spread of fires.

Barricades proved another threat, not alone in obstructing fire engines and ambulances but in setting fire to adjoining buildings when combustible material used in their construction, such as furniture, was set alight. Altogether, twenty-one major buildings in O'Connell Street were destroyed in the fighting and almost sixty others badly damaged. If the Irish Times bewailed the loss of a dozen hotels in Dublin during the earlier warfare up to the Truce, it could add the Gresham, Hammam, Granville, Crown and Edinburgh Hotels to the tally. The head office of the Dublin United Tramways Company, Sackville Club, YMCA, Hibernian Bible Society and Catholic Truth Society were counted among the ruins. Another conflagration was averted only when gallons of whiskey and other spirits were removed from Gilbey's and from Findlater's before the flames reached them.

One building that came through the fighting unscathed was St Mary's Pro-Cathedral in Marlborough Street. The fire brigade regularly doused the walls with water to make sure the fires in nearby buildings did not cause any damage. Its venerable neighbour, St Thomas's, which served a declining working-class Church of Ireland congregation, was not so lucky and was completely destroyed.[36]

Some idea of the conditions in which Dublin firemen worked is given by this extract from the chief fire officer's report for 1922 covering the week of fighting in Sackville Street (O'Connell Street):

Brigade on arrival was directed to the YMCA building, 43 Upper Sackville Street. I found the building strongly barricaded and, after failing to procure an entrance, resorted to playing two jets from hydrants through the upper windows from the street. In the meantime an aerial ladder from C Station

[Buckingham Street] was extended ... as a water tower. The prolonged rifle and machine gun fire grew intense and bullets came dangerously near, a number striking the escape. We had to take cover, and our attempts had only the effect of temporarily allaying the outbreak. The extended ladder had to be abandoned, and next morning when firing had quietened down [the] Station Officer and the men in Buckingham Street recovered it.

On July 5th at 12.19 p.m. called to conflagration involving northern end of Sackville Street. All sections ordered out. Motor from Central Station under Lieutenant Power and Station Officer Kelly stopped by armoured car at corner of Marlborough and Gloucester Streets and held for thirty minutes. Seizing the first opportunity two lines laid down into Thomas Lane were working right between the cross-fire ... The greatest danger was from ricocheting bullets and at one time we had to abandon our appliances and take cover.[37]

Apart from the Pro-Cathedral, little respect was shown by combatants for property or lives during the intensive city-centre fighting that followed the fall of the Four Courts, although neither side was slow to complain about infringements of their own rights by the enemy. Nor were individual firemen always neutral in the conflict. Joe Connolly, whose brother Seán had been a captain in the Irish Citizen Army and the first insurgent shot dead in the 1916 Rising, also served in the Citizen Army and helped wounded Republicans evade capture by spiriting them away in fire brigade ambulances. So did other firemen, such as James McKeown and James Markey.

When the IRA resorted to guerrilla warfare the fire brigade remained in the firing line. Many of the malicious hoax calls made over the coming weeks were to divert the brigade from intended Republican targets, such as income tax offices, the Rotunda Rink sorting office, railway signal boxes and the homes or businesses of government ministers, TDs and supporters, adding still further to the burden borne by the service.[38]

Towards the end of the year P. T. Daly, leader of Trades Council Labour, and another trade unionist, Michael Brohoon, proposed that, in recognition of their 'heroic efforts to save human life and protect the citizens during the recent war in Dublin,' the Corporation should consider establishing a Dublin Fire Brigademen's Widows' and Orphans' Pension Fund. It was agreed by 15 votes to 11, the opposition coming as usual from those staunch defenders of the ratepayer, the Municipal Reform Association and its independent allies.

Daly also proposed a motion thanking the St John Ambulance Brigade for its 'heroic efforts', seconded this time by another trade unionist, Councillor John Farren. Daly proposed that the government make provision in the next year's budget estimates for £300 to be given to the brigade each year. This 'small tribute of appreciation' was defeated, by 17 votes to 9.[39]

Chapter 8 ⌒

'PAUDEEN ... WHEN YOU ARE COMING UP TO SHOOT ME, WON'T YOU BRING ME A DRINK'

The nearest thing to normality in Dublin as the new year broke was the January sales. Forrest's of Grafton Street and Wicklow Street offered customers 'All-fur Coats in Beaver and Seal, Coney, Musquash etc. Clearing at Half Price,' which still left skunk stoles at 20 guineas (£21) and a beaver coat in the 'latest short style' at 23 guineas (£24 3s).[1] Its main rival, Brown Thomas, was offering fur coats from 15 guineas (£15 15s). McGuire's in Merrion Row was offering women's fur-lined coats for only 35s and men's overcoats from 18s 11d. Hickey's in North Earl Street offered seal-fur coats for 5 guineas (£5 5s), while Clery's, which had barely reopened its O'Connell Street premises in time for Christmas, made no attempt to compete at the upper end of the market. Edward Lee's chain of stores offered a discount of 10 per cent on all purchases of £1 or more.

The same newspapers carried advertisements for the National Army. It was growing at the rate of 1,000 men a week and would reach a strength of over 55,000 in 1923. With the new Civic Guard still in its infancy, the army was responsible for policing most of the country outside Dublin, where the Dublin Metropolitan Police continued to operate. A significant part of this expanded role was the protection of property, of employers in general, and farmers in particular, from industrial unrest. In the south-east the fight against pay cuts that followed the abolition of the Agricultural Wages Boards was especially bitter, with 'soviets' being established, factory occupations taking place and even occasional sniping at 'scabs'. National Army troops smashed strikes and other forms of protest, much as they had done during the postal dispute, when the DMP proved half-hearted in its efforts to break the picket lines.

Because the Irish Volunteers had been a locally based militia, both the anti-Treaty IRA and National Army had officers drawn from Volunteer ranks who often had close ties to farming and business families in their command areas. By June 1923 the National Army would formalise its role in combating rural unrest with the establishment of the Special Infantry Corps.[2] This received a significant infusion of personnel from the Railway Maintenance, Repair and Protection Corps. On 24 July 1923, when the 3,097-strong RMRPC was disbanded, 13 officers and 550 other ranks were transferred to the Special Infantry Corps. This was the largest redeployment of members to any other unit, apart from the Corps of Engineers.[3]

The RMRPC was one of the shortest-lived but most successful units in the history of the National Army. It was also the first to be presented with its own colours (regimental flag), in June 1923.[4] Its disbanding shortly afterwards was a tribute to its success in combating the anti-Treaty IRA, which had made the destruction of the railway network a cornerstone of its strategy of plunging the Free State into disorder.

The corps originated in the chaos that engulfed the railways from early 1922 onwards. Attacks on the railway network began before the Civil War with the reactivation of the Belfast boycott. This saw not only trains stopped and goods seized but an increase in theft and armed robbery from railway stations and depots. Between 1 February and 27 June 1922 there were 683 incidents, although only twelve raids were reported in Dublin, most of which were for tools and materials.

Only three Dublin raids seemed directly related to the boycott. In one the contents of a wagon were removed and destroyed on the North Wall; in another, fourteen bales of blankets were seized at Kingsbridge for use by Belfast refugees; and in the third, thirteen bottles of Bushmills whiskey, eleven bottles of Coleraine whiskey and eight ounces of Gallaher's tobacco were seized at Amiens Street Station. Their destination is unknown, but a receipt for the confiscated goods was left on behalf of the 'Director of Boycott, Four Courts Barracks.'[5]

As we have seen, the onset of civil war saw these attacks raised to a new level, with trains not alone raided but derailed, carriages set on fire and bridges blown up. In the first two weeks of July there were 118 serious incidents. Again, very few of them were in Dublin. One incident, however, was a portent for the future when the engine cylinders on a newly commissioned armoured train were broken in the workshop at Inchicore, seriously delaying its completion.[6]

The first firm to feel the brunt of the railway war was the lowly Dublin and Blessington Steam Tramway when Ernie O'Malley and the South Tipperary men assembled a column in the area it served in order to relieve the pressure on Oscar Traynor's forces in Dublin. What happened shows in microcosm what awaited railwaymen and passengers in the coming months.

On Saturday 1 July 1922 the 7:15 p.m. train from Poulaphouca to Terenure was held up by armed men at the Embankment Station in Corbally. Passengers were transferred to the incoming train from Terenure while the Poulaphouca train was used to shuttle anti-Treaty forces from Crooksling up to Blessington. The crew were held overnight and were then used to continue the shuttle service on Sunday. Eventually they were allowed to take the engine back to Terenure, while the carriages remained in Blessington. The company ran no services that day but tried to resume services on the Monday with a mixed goods and passenger train. While this was allowed to reach Blessington, a consignment of bread was seized, and about half the milk consignment due to make the return journey to Dublin was requisitioned by O'Malley's thirsty men. No further trains were run that day.

On Tuesday and Wednesday the company risked two trains each day but they carried no foodstuffs. The second train on Wednesday was commandeered to resume moving anti-Treaty forces between Crooksling and Blessington. Telephone communication from the Embankment that day was cut, and on Thursday the company ran a train to Blessington, only to have it hijacked and the crew forced to derail three wagons for use as a barricade. No trains ran on Friday but a limited service was resumed over the weekend as far as Brittas. A full service was resumed subsequently. Besides the damage to rolling stock and the loss of customers' goods, the company had coal regularly commandeered from its trains by O'Malley's men.[7]

The Dublin and Lucan Steam Tramway was the next to be attacked, and the track carrying trains across the Malahide Estuary was also damaged. This situation would soon replicate itself around the country, and further disruption occurred when National Army units began raiding railway stores for equipment. On 17 August 1922 Richard Mulcahy had to issue an order forbidding the practice and requiring the return of all items removed.

Total collapse of the railway network seemed imminent. Nor were the railways in a sufficiently sound financial condition to withstand losses, whatever the source. Many of the local lines, such as those to Blessington and Lucan, had always relied on British government subsidies. From the end of 1916, when the military took control of the national network, this applied in effect to the large companies as well. One of the benefits of state control was that wartime inflation could be met by a combination of exchequer subsidies and fare increases approved by London. The end of British military control in 1921 led to pay cuts and industrial unrest. (See chapter 2.) By the end of 1922 even the GSWR was running at a loss and no longer paying a dividend to shareholders. Despite the pay cuts only the mainline companies—the GSWR, the Great Northern, the Dublin and South-East and the Midland and Great Western—were in a position to pay the reduced rates. Joe McGrath, in his capacity as Minister for Industry and Commerce, told the Dáil on 3 January 1923 that the GSWR alone would have an operating deficit of £10,384 a week that year, or £15,177 if fixed charges and interest on debentures were included.[8]

There were still forty-five separate railway companies in operation, with twenty-eight boards of management, most of them with no hope of recovering commercial viability. They were matched by twenty-eight trade unions and trades councils representing the workers, for railways were among the most organised industries in the country. But even highly organised workers could not defy economic gravity. In October 1922 the two main railway unions, the National Union of Railwaymen and the ITGWU, struck for a restoration of working hours and wages. This followed a partial restoration of both for engine-drivers and firemen as the GSWR began running more trains. However, the engines were only pulling half the rolling stock used before the outbreak of civil war, so there was no extra work for other traffic staff.

The whole system ground to a halt with up to 1,000 men on strike at the North Wall and Kingsbridge and 1,400 laid off at the Inchicore works as a result. The unions in Dublin had closed down railway traffic to the south-west without derailing a single train or blowing up a single bridge.

Fortunately the strategic implications were lost on the anti-Treaty forces. On the other hand Joe McGrath was acutely aware of the consequences that a 'complete stoppage' of services would have, and, combining as he did the roles of Minister for Labour, Minister for Industry and Commerce and Director of Intelligence, he had the means and the capacity to deal deal with them. As with so many things in those chaotic weeks,

most of the instructions with regard to the Corps were given verbally without confirmation afterwards on paper … Three things, however, were very clearly understood by all concerned:—

That the railways were to be opened up and kept open at all costs.

That the railway men were to be enlisted [in the National Army] and made do the work of opening and protecting the lines in the greatest possible number.

Railway rates and conditions were to be offered [to the enlisted men].

For this and without authorisation from GHQ but on verbal authority from the Minister of Industry and Commerce it was decided to organise a Corps through the Trades Union Organisation and not through the Railway Companies. Frequent meetings were held between the Corps Commander and the leading Trade Union Officials which eventually resulted in gaining the whole hearted support of the National Union of Railwaymen, and the leading Trade Union Officials of this Union were induced to join the Corps and undertake Recruiting duties. When one remembers that the Transport Union [ITGWU] was bitterly opposed to the scheme on the plea that it was a dodge by the Government to torpedo Trades Unionism, the scores and scores of questions with regard to service conditions asked by the other Unions can be imagined. No undertaking, however, was given which was outside Railway conditions, and no undertaking of any kind, even within these limits, was given in writing outside the Corps Attestation Papers.[9]

The terms even included the payment of national insurance contributions for many members of the Railway Corps, making them unique among National Army personnel. A meeting took place subsequently with the employers to rubberstamp the agreement.[10]

The Railway Maintenance, Repair and Protection Corps was formally established on 8 November 1922. It had a proposed complement of 42 officers and 939 other ranks and an upper limit of 2,000 personnel.[11] By the following weekend the strike was over and railway workers were being armed not to establish a socialist republic, as some within the more radical ranks of the trade union movement and the anti-Treaty IRA wished, but to defend their livelihoods.

Although the new corps was part of the National Army it was autonomous for practical purposes. Its commander was Colonel Charles Russell, who had been serving as second in command of the Air Corps and doubling as a reconnaissance pilot. Like other central figures in the Free State military hierarchy, he displayed a happy knack for multi-tasking and adaptability, including a combination of military management skills and those needed for negotiating with the trade unions. As with many units of the National Army, life in the new corps was little easier for its members than for their IRA opponents. Russell recalled later that

> every boot, every uniform, every cap and every gun that I drew ... I drew with the greatest difficulty. There was no appreciation at all of the difficulties in commanding a corps and there was no assistance from the Supplies Organisation to make sure that you had enough supplies ... The thing was so bad at times that I was really ashamed to inspect the men. Their feet were out of their boots; they were verminous and they had no change of clothing and no overcoats.[12]

Not all trade unionists were happy at these developments, least of all the largest one, the ITGWU. On 4 December 1922, the same day that Angela Bridgeman was shot dead in Harcourt Street and Dublin Corporation debated the ill-treatment of Republican prisoners, a conference of railway unions was held in the Mansion House to discuss the establishment of the RMRPC and the growing practice of workers employed in other capacities being attested by the National Army. This did not convert the relatively few clerical and manual workers employed in barracks into soldiers but it did subject them to military discipline, something that the many British ex-servicemen employed on a temporary basis would have been well used to.

It came as a surprise to most of the ILP&TUC leaders that the British-based National Union of Railwaymen had agreed to the creation of the Maintenance

Corps and the induction of so many members into the military, but they had to accept it as a *fait accompli*. When the ILP&TUC subsequently met General Mulcahy in his role as Minister for Defence he said it had been necessary to put everyone working in army barracks and camps under military discipline while the war lasted. He promised the deputation that union officials would be issued with permits for access to military installations to represent members, although this often proved difficult. Nor did it prevent officials being detained on occasion when army officers attempted to pressure them into calling off strikes, especially in areas where 'soviets' and agricultural unrest were involved. McGrath's name does not appear to have featured in the discussions with the ILP&TUC, but no-one contradicted Mulcahy when he said it was the railway workers themselves who had offered to join the National Army to protect their livelihood.[13]

During the War of Independence the munitions strike had not only severely hampered the movement of British troops but almost brought the country to a standstill, hence the decision to end it after six months. Now the railway workers who had defied the British forces, at considerable risk to their own lives, to protect the IRA were being attacked by that same organisation. This was certainly how the men saw it. A large NUR meeting at Ballybrophy, Co. Laois, on the Dublin–Cork line, unanimously condemned 'the policy of destruction adopted by the irregular forces.' It did so as a

> branch of Irish railwaymen whose members … took a prominent part in the fight for our country's emancipation.
>   The burning of our old and historic buildings, the destruction of railways, signal cabins etc., the dislocation of all industries that are the wealth of the people will not, in our opinion, obtain freedom for our country, but bring unemployment to the worker and loss to the community; nor can these acts be called patriotic or defended from a military point of view.

It called on 'the Government and the irregular forces to arrange a Truce to the present deadly conflict of brother against brother, neighbour against neighbour.' They needed 'to repair the damage caused by the present fratricidal madness of misdirected patriotism.'[14]

The difference between the munitions strike, which had denied the use of the railways to the British through industrial action, and the IRA campaign was that the latter aimed at destroying the railway infrastructure. Many railway workers were passionately attached to their engines. 'Good work could be had from the worst of engines, provided they had the right crew for the job,' wrote one seasoned observer, while another said, 'I verily believe that they thought more of their old engines than their wives.'[15]

These attacks not only forced the National Army to deploy troops guarding the railway network but closed down businesses and brought some provincial towns to the brink of starvation in the winter of 1922/3. It began in earnest with the destruction of the bridge at Mallow on 9 August 1922 as Cork, the capital of the 'Munster Republic', fell to a seaborne invasion under Emmet Dalton. It cut off the south-west from the rest of the country in a spectacular start to the railway campaign. It was the weapon of a militarily spent force but it had a near-fatal nihilistic capacity. As Liam Deasy, one of the senior anti-Treaty IRA officers involved in the Mallow operation, put it, 'the fight could go on indefinitely, in so far as our destructive policy was concerned.' More thoughtful than most of his colleagues, Deasy also realised that such a struggle would eventually result in losses 'so great that ... England, will be called on to intervene and possibly be welcomed with more enthusiasm than was displayed on her departure.'[16] The creation of the RMRPC would eventually counter that strategy, as the only way to combat its patrols, backed by armoured trains and armoured cars mounted on the railway tracks, was by assembling anti-Treaty IRA Volunteers in such large numbers that it left them susceptible to counter-attack by conventional forces.

Despite these problems the British government was confident enough of eventual victory by the Free State to withdraw its last units from Dublin on 15 December 1922. A curious mixture of middle-class unionists, war veterans and working-class Dubliners gave 'the friendliest of farewells' to the British troops. At Eden Quay, Wilmot Irwin, whose grandfather had served in the East Yorkshire Regiment, found himself in the company of 'hundreds of other well-wishers' to see them off. The mood was celebratory. All the old Southern Irish regiments, including the Dublin Fusiliers, had already been disbanded, so the departing garrison was a mixture of English and Welsh infantry contingents.

> It was the Lancashires and the Berkshires which swept into view, headed by a band. I recall the tune well—an old melody from *The Runaway Girl* entitled Soldiers in the Park. The words rose involuntarily to my lips as the khaki columns swung past on their way to the North Wall ... but I was in no mood for singing. A military lorry rolled by with the following legend chalked on its side. 'Goodbye, dear old dirty Dublin.'
>
> My heart was too full for words. Blindly I reached up with scores of other hands to shake the gloved fist of a British officer in an armoured car slowly driving past to enable him to shake every proffered hand. He did not miss one. Even after forty years I am moved with emotion to think of it. A Free State armoured car with a lorry of green-clad soldiers, presumably acting as escorts

put in a brief appearance. They were loudly hissed and hooted by the crowd. I think they understood our emotions. They smiled sheepishly and passed on. At all events they were the victors.[17]

On the North Wall, dealers sold the men fruit and local people posed for photographs with them before they embarked on a very stormy passage back to England. Of course the operation meant a welcome overtime bonus for dockers just before Christmas. The officer commanding British forces, Sir Neville Macready, found the atmosphere in the city a curious one.

> Among the crowd, which was considerable, many men and women cheered continuously as they waved small Union Jacks, and all, including Free State officers in their slate green uniforms, saluted the regimental colours as they passed. A strong detachment of the Legion of Irish Ex-Servicemen was present, who very kindly gave me a badge of their association as a memento. At the docks the crowd was so dense that it was with difficulty that the last battalion got through. The utmost good humour was shown by the crowd … many hats even being raised when the band on the last troopship struck up the National Anthem as she moved slowly away.

The only untoward incident as far as Macready was concerned came at the beginning of the operation when he handed over command of the Royal Barracks, already renamed after Michael Collins, to Mulcahy. The Minister for Defence and commander in chief told the Free State garrison arrayed before them that 'the incubus of occupation that has lain as a heavy load on our country for years has been removed this morning.' Macready seems to have taken the reference personally. Nor was he too pleased with some of the next day's newspapers, where his photograph with Admiral Fox, commander of the Royal Navy contingent taking the troops home, carried the headline 'Two gallant Irishmen.' A week later Macready, the man who had resisted Churchill's demand to attack the Four Courts in June and had lent Emmet Dalton the guns to do the job instead, was rewarded with a baronetcy.[18] Unofficial wars in Ireland did not warrant anything more.

While crowds celebrated the departure of British troops at the North Wall, the Civil War continued in the city. Private Paddy Fitzgerald, a 24-year-old member of the Engineers Corps, was shot dead in Granby Row that evening near his home in Bolton Street. He was off duty and unarmed at the time. So was Private Michael O'Connor, a 21-year-old from Letterkenny who served as a clerk in the Marlborough Hall garrison in Glasnevin. He was talking to friends at the Parnell Monument and was seriously wounded. The bullet that passed through his right thigh hit a thirteen-year-old girl standing behind him, Eveleen Stephenson of Ballybough, in the left foot. There were also ambushes on National Army patrols in other parts of the city that evening, including Oriel House, but no casualties resulted.

The flurry of activity may have been provoked by the British evacuation, or possibly by news that seven IRA Volunteers had been executed in Kildare the previous Tuesday. It was the largest batch of executions during the Civil War. The victims consisted of three labourers and four railway workers who had been involved in attacks on the railway network, derailing engines and firing on troop transports.[19] In contrast to the three thousand railwaymen in the RMRPC, some of their comrades put the Republic before their livelihood.

––––

Many Dublin city councillors found it difficult to reconcile long-held political aspirations with the practical problems they now confronted in the city. The price of gas continued to rise, despite the dire economic situation. A thousand cubic feet now cost 6s 9d in Dublin, compared with 3s 9d in Belfast. A review of prices had been held by the Board of Trade in London in 1921 but the Corporation had boycotted the proceedings, as it had declared its allegiance to Dáil Éireann in 1920. Now Dubliners were paying the price. The Corporation belatedly sought support from the southern townships for an inquiry.

Meanwhile the war was never far away. On the day the Corporation discussed gas prices, an ambush on a National Army patrol in O'Connell Street left one man seriously wounded by bomb splinters and several women injured when they fell and were trampled by the panic-stricken crowd. Two Crossley tenders had been carrying troops northwards when anti-Treaty IRA Volunteers opened fire from the ruins of the 'Block' on the east side of the street. Two bombs were then thrown from the CYMS ruins on the west side. These 'exploded with deafening detonations between the two vehicles.' The *Irish Independent* reported that

> terrifying scenes followed. Men, women and children ran in all directions for safety, crowding into doorways, flinging themselves flat on the ground; many were thrown down and trampled in the stampede. Bicycles, parcels of every description, hats, sticks and umbrellas lay in wild confusion on the footpaths, and in the roadway, even motor cars were deserted by their terrified occupants.
>
> Amongst those caught in the rush were women with perambulators, and at one point a woman with a baby in her arms was seen lying on the ground for safety, whilst a little boy, who accompanied her, in terrified tones, implored some of the crowd to save his mother.
>
> Above the din could be heard the rattle of gun fire and the screams of women. Horses on the neighbouring hazard [cab stand] took fright, and ran away, adding to the confusion.

The only combatant reported injured was a National Army soldier, whose forehead was grazed by a bomb splinter. The anti-Treaty IRA's proclivity to use hand grenades dated from the War of Independence and almost invariably caused more civilian casualties than military ones, as the devices either bounced off the trucks they were aimed at or missed them altogether. On this occasion the recipient was John Whelan, a 29-year-old commercial traveller. His right shin was shattered by bomb fragments, while his right foot was struck by another and a bullet passed through his left foot.[20]

Nor did Republicans abandon open political activity in the city centre. On the Sunday after the ambush the Prisoners' Defence Association held a rally in Upper O'Connell Street at the site of the Hibernian Bible Society, now a charred relic. About 1,500 people gathered to hear the speakers, who included Maud Gonne MacBride, Charlotte Despard and Helena Molony. Madeleine ffrench-Mullen was in full flow when a National Army tender and armoured car arrived. The officer in charge stepped out of the armoured car and ordered the crowd to disperse. A man tried to grab his revolver, which went off, shooting the hat from a bystander. A voice in the crowd cried, 'Come on, boys, we'll disarm them,' and there was a rush by women as well as men to seize the weapons from the soldiers in the tender. Shots rang out, some of them probably fired by anti-Treaty IRA Volunteers from the ruins of the Bible Society, and the crowd dispersed only after the Vickers machine-gunner on the armoured car fired a burst over their heads. Seventeen-year-old Lilly Bennett was left dying on the pavement, while two men and a sixteen-year-old boy were wounded.

Michael Comyn, who represented the three youths killed at Red Cow, appeared for the Prisoners' Defence Association at the inquest into Lilly Bennett's death and again sought to pin responsibility on the National Army, but the bullet retrieved from the dead girl's body was a 9 mm automatic round, rather than the .45 and .303 rounds used by the soldiers. The jury found that her death was caused by 'some person or persons unknown' and added a rider that public warnings should be issued before meetings were suppressed.

The same evening that Lilly Bennett died four young men were blown to pieces beside Blackhorse Bridge on the Naas Road at Inchicore. A woman living nearby noticed a large group coming out of a field 'in answer to a whistle' at about 8:15 p.m. 'They were all bunched together as if they were carrying something, but I could not see what it was because of the darkness,' she told an *Irish Independent* reporter. 'Then suddenly, as I stood at the door, a terrible big flare of light burst up from the ground into the air with a red flame, and spread out like a great fire.' Three Volunteers were killed instantly and a fourth, 22-year-old Thomas Whelan, an engine-cleaner at the Inchicore railway works, was found lying behind the wall, having lost most of his right leg. He was rushed to Dr Steevens' Hospital, where he told the DMP he had been shot. He died shortly after an operation to amputate the remains of the mutilated limb. The remains of the other men were scattered along the Naas Road.

Among the first witnesses on the scene were members of a National Army unit returning to their base in Baldonnel after patrolling the city. Their vehicle was probably the intended target of the mine, and they saw the flash. The first remains they came upon belonged to a 22-year-old, Volunteer Bernard Curtis, another engine-cleaner at the Inchicore works. His upper torso was lying on the road, the right arm missing and brains protruding through the skull. Blood was 'gushing from the base of the chest,' according to one soldier. The body of Volunteer Patrick Egan, a nineteen-year-old goods clerk at Kingsbridge Station, was so badly mutilated that his brother could not identify him. Half the head and all his limbs were missing.

The fourth fatality was Thomas Maguire, a fitter from Phibsborough and the only dead man not employed by the GSWR. He too had lost both arms from the shoulder joints and his trunk was blown away below the chest, suggesting that he had been carrying the mine with Curtis and Egan when it exploded. There were certainly other Volunteers involved, and 'there was a thick trail of blood along the road leading to the country, apparently made by a badly wounded man as he moved away.' Rifles and bandoliers were found a short distance away at what was probably the intended ambush site.

When Patrick Moynihan, the head of the CID, arrived, he said the mine was similar to the ones planted at Oriel House and he thought it likely that the switch was accidentally triggered when the device was being lifted over the wall. The wall itself was splattered with human remains, and local people helped the ambulance service retrieve body parts from a wide area.[21]

Not only did city councillors and aldermen have to live, like their fellow-citizens, with the daily prospect of this unbidden mayhem but they had to weigh the rights of the Republican prisoners and those protesting on their behalf against the need of the general populace to be protected from anti-Treaty IRA Volunteers still active on the streets of the capital. It was a debate complicated by the fact that some of those in custody were members of the City Council. Joseph MacDonagh was a member of both Dublin City Council and Rathmines Urban District Council. A former director of the Belfast boycott, MacDonagh had been acting Minister for Labour in the Dáil Éireann government. A former customs officer forced to retire over his brother's involvement in the 1916 Rising, he quickly became a leading figure in the militant nationalist movement. He was headmaster briefly of Patrick Pearse's school, St Enda's, and then went into private practice as an income tax expert, quipping that by recovering thousands of pounds for clients he inflicted greater damage on the British government than any other living Irishman. He also became a partner in an insurance brokerage with W. T. Cosgrave, but he was far more radical in his politics than Cosgrave, or most other Sinn Féin TDs for that matter. He was imprisoned several times, on the first occasion with Thomas Ashe in 1917. When Ashe died after being forcibly fed on hunger strike, MacDonagh was a key witness at the inquest. As acting Minister for Labour during Constance Markievicz's imprisonment he actively promoted workers' co-operatives and helped establish the Irish Engineering, Shipbuilding and Foundry Workers' Trade Union. He proved a 'relentless and efficient' director of the Belfast boycott and spent much of his time on the run disguised as a priest. Bitterly opposed to the Treaty, he brought his management flair to the new task of distributing *Poblacht na hÉireann.*

Arrested on 30 September 1922, MacDonagh fell seriously ill with acute appendicitis in Mountjoy Prison but refused to 'sign out' and promise never to take up arms against the Free State again. Transferred eventually to the Mater Misericordiae Private Nursing Home, he died forty-eight hours later, on Christmas Day, from peritonitis.[22] His funeral at Glasnevin had a large if overwhelmingly partisan attendance, made up of Republicans still at liberty, many of them women, including Margaret Pearse, Kathleen Lynn and Madeleine ffrench-Mullen. There was also a large uniformed contingent from Cumann na mBan, but no members of the city council are reported as present. Even during the War of Independence aldermen and councillors attended funerals regardless of the political complexion of the deceased, but then there had been no attacks on councillors, their homes or families by former comrades.

———

However, the practice of making provision for the families of Corporation employees on the run or interned persisted, despite the Law Agent's misgivings. As he had anticipated, when the Corporation met on 19 February 1923 there were two letters regarding prisoners. One was from General Mulcahy warning council members that half pay for internees and their families must cease, on pain of arrest; the other was from the Minister for Home Affairs, Ernest Blythe, notifying members that failure to comply with the instruction to cease payments to internees would mean the suspension of all housing grants.[23]

A third letter informed the Corporation that the municipal elections that should have been held in January would be deferred until June.[24] This piece of correspondence was the first in a series announcing the postponement of local government elections, which continued until after Dublin Corporation was abolished in 1924. No doubt some councillors were glad they would not have to face the electorate. There had been no election since 1920, and vacancies since had been filled through co-options.

The contents of all three letters were noted for the moment. Whatever about the practicability of making individual councillors, most of whom supported the government, liable for the payments to internees, the letter from Blythe posed a serious threat to the ambitious housing programme that the council was preparing to embark upon after a decade of upheaval had frustrated previous initiatives.

Before the outbreak of the First World War, Dublin had attracted a great deal of attention from town planners, thanks in large part to the pre-war Viceroy, Lord Aberdeen, and his wife, Ishbel, who came to regard the city as the potential 'geo-technic capital' of Britain and Ireland.[25] Now it was the capital of a new Irish state instead, which had been plunged into civil war, and the prospects of major planning initiatives were greatly dimmed.

This was not enough to discourage some of the original pioneers, such as Ernest Albert Aston, a former inspector with the Local Government Board and an engineer-turned-journalist and champion of urban renewal. On 14 December he gave a talk to the Engineering and Scientific Association at University College, where the proposals of the Greater Dublin Reconstruction Movement were 'exhibited and discussed.' Aston had recruited figures from across the political spectrum to the organisation, including Senator James Moran from the MRA group on Dublin Corporation, Seán McGarry TD, and Lady Aberdeen herself, a leading advocate of housing and health reform. The proposals were based on a plan prepared by Abercrombie and Kelly, the Liverpool firm of architects that won the first prize for town planning at the 1914 Civic Exhibition in Dublin. Many of the proposals, such as the transfer of the GPO to the scorched shell of the Custom House, the conversion of the old GPO to a new head office for the Corporation and the moving of the Oireachtas to the Royal Hospital in Kilmainham never came to fruition, but the Greater Dublin Reconstruction Movement did breathe new life into the cause of urban planning, which had been ground down by a decade of war, revolution and industrial strife. It also revived the long-lost cause of slum clearance.

By 1922 the number of Dubliners in urgent need of rehousing had risen to 60,000. The population density in the city was now 96 people per acre, rather than the 75 per acre recommended by public health experts. Reducing the density would require not only more local housing units but more land on which to build them and more ratepayers to finance them. This meant extending the city's boundaries to Crumlin and Cabra, absorbing the wealthy southern townships and encouraging more private housing developments in such middle-class areas as Drumcondra and Clontarf. When that veteran public representative Alfie Byrne, a survivor from the glory days of the Irish Party, asked Blythe in the Dáil if he was aware 'that many thousands of Dublin citizens are now sheltering in rat-infested basements of slum property and whether he is now in a position to state the Government's Housing Policy for the year 1923/4,' Blythe bluntly stated that the estimates for the current year could not 'provide further state aid for municipal schemes owing to the prevailing unsettled conditions and the heavy financial deficits.'[26]

Byrne was as aware as Blythe that no funds were available, whether or not the Corporation persisted in helping internees and their families, but he also knew there were votes in housing.

———

Law and order was the priority of the Provisional Government and its Free State successor. As was often the case, it was Kevin O'Higgins who provided the clearest view on the situation from Government Buildings. As early as October 1922 there were plans to intern twelve thousand prisoners,[27] more than double the number under British rule for the whole country. As the British had discovered, belatedly, internment could be very useful in bringing about military success but left a bitter residue for the future. O'Higgins was very much focused on the present. He told his colleagues:

> We are dealing with anarchy under cover of a political banner.
> A great deal of support that the Irregulars are receiving comes from people who have vested interests in chaotic conditions—people who are (*a*) in possession and enjoyment of property (land or chattels) which is not legally theirs, or (*b*) people who owe money, whether shop debts, Land Commission Annuities, or rent, or (*c*) people who are at present engaged in illegal, but profitable concerns (e.g. poteen making). To these people the Irregulars are now champions and defenders—if they were forced to disgorge, the Irregulars' halo would disappear.

O'Higgins called for the army, as the main arm of the state in most areas, to take complaints against its own members seriously if it wanted to secure the support of the law-abiding majority of the population. On a more general level he advised colleagues that 'propaganda should be improved immediately, should not be predominantly a war propaganda. It should be propaganda in Civics, not a hymn of Hate, but an appeal to reason and decent instincts.' He singled out 'Clergy, doctors, lawyers, Bank Managers, Farmers Unions' for attention. 'A special type of reasoned propaganda addressed to branches of Labour Unions, would also be desirable.' He concluded that the 'Government' is simply a Committee with a mandate to make … life and property safe and vindicate the legal rights of their fellow citizens.' The emphasis on political action was necessary because 'the writ of this committee is running limp in most counties, and is not running at all in many despite the fact that it has 30,000 armed servants at its disposal.'[28]

His colleague Eoin MacNeill, whose son Brian had died after a running fight with National Army soldiers in Co. Sligo the previous month, gave an even more brutal assessment of the situation. 'The Irregulars have acted very intelligently. Defeated on what we may call the military front, they have shifted their whole campaign to the Sabotage front.' He advised giving priority to the execution of the culprits. 'This should be done now and on a sufficient scale to strike terror into the plunderers and destructionites.'[29] For MacNeill, anything less would make the death of his own son a meaningless tragedy.

––––

There undoubtedly was massive social unrest, although not all of it could be laid at the door of 'destructionites,' as the deployment of the Special Infantry Corps demonstrated. Indeed in the latter case hundreds of armed railway workers in Free State uniforms were in effect being used to suppress strikes by fellow-workers throughout the country. It was also true that hundreds of Circuit Court and High Court orders were left unexecuted, particularly in the south and west, but not in Dublin.

The Civil War largely petered out in Dublin after Christmas 1922.[30] This made the plight of the prisoners a particularly fraught issue, as the necessity for internment was no longer so apparent in the city. Not only that but Dublin, as in the War of Independence, accounted for more prisoners than anywhere else, with 847 out of the 5,582 still being held at the end of 1923 coming from the city, closely followed by Cork, with 813. After that the figures drop dramatically. While the Curragh was the main place of detention, Mountjoy Prison held the largest prison population after Port Laoise. Camps at Gormanston, Co. Meath, and Baldonnel, Co. Dublin, held well over a thousand more. All the women prisoners were held in Dublin, and clashes with the prison authorities, ranging from riots to hunger strikes, received far more coverage when they took place in the capital.

Meanwhile the Corporation's decision to proceed with its inquiry into the treatment of these prisoners continued to provide evidence of serious ill-treatment, particularly during initial periods of arrest and detention. Staff Captain Frank Bolster, who led the attack on the anti-Treaty forces in the Orange hall and Fowler Hall at the outbreak of the Civil War, featured repeatedly in signed statements collected from IRA prisoners in Dublin, as did Wellington Barracks, where he was based.[31] James Kelly of the 1st Battalion said that when he was arrested on Tuesday 15 August 1922 and taken to Wellington Barracks, Bolster was in charge of the interrogation and 'made a furious onslaught on me calling me a "murderer" and threatening to shoot me, but he was ably assisted by his confederates, all of whom bashed me about.' Kelly knew Bolster, who 'sneered' at him for a limp he had from being wounded in the fighting in July and 'made a vile and dastardly insinuation as to the cause of my disability.' It was another former Squad member, Jim Slattery, who rescued Kelly from Bolster's clutches, only for the prisoner to find himself confined in a cell for the next two days, not even allowed out to use the toilet.

The pattern of interrogation was always the same: beatings about the head and body, interspersed with breaks when men were told to prepare themselves for execution. In some cases guns were discharged at close range beside their heads, presumably loaded with blanks.

Some men were obvious suspects, such as James Kelly or Thomas McCarthy, a member of the 4th Battalion's Active Service Unit. McCarthy had been arrested at 11 p.m. on Friday 1 September 1922, 'my revolver being found on a young lady in my company, which she was carrying under orders from my O/C.' Others, such as Christopher Ferguson, a fireman in the GSWR and ITGWU activist, were simply suspected of IRA membership but suffered similar treatment. McCarthy was 'taken all around the city as a hostage and made stand up, while another prisoner and Free State troops kept under cover.' He was taken to the old cemetery in Church Avenue, Drumcondra,

> and interrogated about what men took part with me in certain ambushes … When I refused this information one of the C.I.D. men fired a shot right through my hair over my left ear. They put me in the car again and took me under machine gun fire … right through the 'Dardanelles' [Aungier Street] up to Wellington Barracks.

McCarthy was repeatedly beaten and told he would be shot at 11:30 the next morning. 'The CID man told me to prepare and to say my prayers. I told him to go ahead, as I was not in a state of mortal sin.' Instead McCarthy was left in his cell until 5:30 p.m., when he was taken with three other prisoners for interrogation by 'CID men … and a Lieutenant in uniform.' Again McCarthy refused to give information. 'I was caught by the throat, and my head banged against the wall. I was put into a corner and my face bashed right and left, my lips were burst inside and my teeth all loosened.' He was punched repeatedly in the stomach and then given a respite while another prisoner received the same treatment, before being beaten again.

This pattern continued through the weekend until a commandant, hearing his screams, came into the interrogation room with 'a civilian' and ordered that McCarthy be put in a cell. The 'murder gang' tried to interrogate him again but were turned away by the sergeant of the guard, who then had him 'hidden away' in another cell. He told McCarthy 'they would plug me all right' if they could. The next day he was transferred to an internment camp with the other prisoners.[32]

Christy Ferguson, an apprentice boilermaker, was arrested on Tuesday 15 August after shouting 'Up the Republic!' in response to some repartee at the Inchicore railway works, where sabotage was a problem. Unfortunately he was overheard and was brought for interrogation by an intelligence officer, who

> said 'I'll give you up the *** Republic, you *** little Robert Emmet.' He then struck me with his clenched fists several times and asked me for the name of my Company Captain, which I refused, then he gripped me by the hair and banged my head against the wall again and again. I was told to get on my knees and say my prayers as I was going to be shot, no sooner had I begun than I was seized by the shirt which was torn open and the cocked revolver thrust inside my chest [sic]. Then a shot went off right beside my head. I was told it was a blank but the next one should be death for me, while a fusillade of foul names was directed at me all the while. Then another shot was fired and I was beaten about the head and face with clenched fists until the Sergeant of the Guard intervened and told these men, who were his superior officers that he would tolerate it no longer and forced them to desist. I was then removed to solitary confinement in a cell 11-and-a-half feet by eight-and-a-half feet, whither four others were brought the following day, Wednesday, and the five of us left there herded together until Thursday at 7 p.m. and only allowed to the lavatory at meal times. I am only a boy of eighteen years of age and was no match for these bullies but I refused to give them any information and defied them to shoot me.[33]

Another GSWR employee, James Kelly (no relation of the IRA officer interrogated), was arrested by the CID on the same day as Ferguson after it was reported 'that I advocated refusal of men to light fires on Troop Trains—at a Transport Workers meeting that never took place.' His treatment was almost identical to that dealt out to Ferguson, and he was also transferred to prison the following day. He was also 'threatened with death' if he told anyone about his treatment.[34]

Nor was hostility to the prisoners confined to officers and veterans of Collins's old intelligence network. When a Dublin Fire Brigade ambulance collected casualties from an ambush in Lucan on Saturday 9 September the crew found three 'Free Staters and one Republican' at the local barracks, the terminology indicating clearly where their own sympathies lay.

> The three wounded Free Staters were carried out into the ambulance which was then directed to start for Dublin. One of the ambulance men asked about the fourth man, and was told that he was not being brought. He then said to a Free State soldier that there was plenty of room in the ambulance ... The soldier's reply was that the wounded [Volunteer] was a die-hard (using a filthy expression) and that he could stop there.
>
> The ambulance man then pointed out that it was their duty to take all wounded to hospital, there being no distinction under the Red Cross ... One of

the slightly wounded Free Staters in the ambulance overhearing the discussion outside, called out 'none of the *** die-hards will come into this ambulance with us. If he's put in, we'll finish him off on the road to Dublin' …

It was not until 5 o'clock on the afternoon of the following day that this man … whose leg is badly broken was removed to Dublin. He is in Wellington Barracks, in which place also, there is no proper hospital for dealing with a serious case.

The Fire Brigade witness, Austin McDonald, complained that

the victim of this outrage is a Dublin man, that the Fire Brigade ambulance which was not allowed to take him is paid for by Dublin ratepayers, and that the Free Staters who occupied it, as well as those who prevented its proper use were paid gunmen from the provinces.[35]

The transfer journeys, usually in National Army vehicles, could also be an ordeal, especially as prisoners were sometimes used as hostages if travelling through areas where the anti-Treaty IRA was active. But perhaps the worst journey of all was the voyage of the LNWR steamship *Arvonia*. After being used as a troop transport in the capture of Cork, on Wednesday 30 August 1922 it was sent to Limerick to collect 550 Republican prisoners and transport them to Dublin.[36] It arrived the following evening in Dublin Bay 'after a very severe journey.' According to a message smuggled ashore while it lay in the bay,

the men were ordered below the deck by Staff Captain Bolster who drove them below at the point of a revolver, saying he would shoot them before the end of the journey.

The prisoners are now confined in the lower cabin for the past three days and nights, without air, exercise or sufficient food. The portholes are closed thereby preventing ventilation of any kind. The majority of men are on hunger strike for some days previous to their leaving Limerick, and most of them are now suffering swelling of the lower joints caused by insufficiency of air, exercise and want of proper diet, and more especially overheating of the place. It is providential that an epidemic has not broken out, considering that the lavatories, insufficient in number, are without water except for a few hours per day.

No sleeping accommodation of any kind is provided, and consequently the men are compelled to crowd together on the floor.

Most of the men are in a semi-conscious condition, especially the men whose wounds have not been dressed for the past week; and 50 or more Fianna boys, whose ages are from 12 and upwards, are now lying physically wrecked and in a prostrate condition denied all medical treatment by Captain Bolster.

The only food consisted of 'tea and bread twice daily.'[37]

The *Arvonia* lay in Dublin Bay until 9 September, discharging prisoners in batches at the North Wall, where special trains took them to the internment camps. An undated report submitted to the Dublin City Council inquiry claimed that twenty-seven injured prisoners, two of them in a critical condition, had been among those brought ashore.

> The prisoners on board are suffering severely from rheumatism, and an epidemic of scabies has broken out. The condition of the ship is filthy ... A party in a rowing boat approached the *Arvonia* and asked permission to send comforts to the prisoners. They were fired on by order of Lieutenant Bolster.[38]

A more serious incident occurred on Saturday 2 September when a motorboat approached the vessel and the sentry opened fire on the occupants, hitting 45-year-old Michael Garland in the right thigh and 13-year-old William Smyth in both legs. There is no indication that either was involved with any Republican organisation. Garland, a gentleman of means living in Howth, had taken the motorboat over to view the *Arvonia* where it was moored in Scotsman's Bay. The engine of the boat may have drowned out the sentry's voice when he ordered them away. Garland was taken, along with his young companion, on board the British destroyer *Vivacious* nearby to be given emergency medical treatment before being landed at Dún Laoghaire and then taken to the Royal City of Dublin Hospital in Baggot Street.[39]

Even when prisoners reached their place of detention they were far from safe, especially in the chaotic early stages of the Civil War, when the Free State government was overwhelmed with administrative problems. Its ambition to intern opponents far exceeded its capacity to do so efficiently, let alone humanely. The most comprehensive summary of the situation was compiled by Hanna Sheehy Skeffington, who had collected many of the statements of ill-treatment from prisoners. She pointed to the lack of uniformity in conditions and policies between holding centres; the lack of access by prisoners to association with each other; the fact that there was no communication with the outside world through visitors or letters; the absence of books, newspapers and food parcels; the denial of the right to elect their own officers or representatives for dealing with the prison authorities; the denial of access to the Dublin medical officer; and the absence of 'dry canteens' where prisoners could buy food. In some centres compulsory labour was also enforced, and she pointed out that the British authorities had not made labour compulsory and had honoured most of the rights the new Irish state was denying its internees.

> To sum up, the prisoners (now over 6,000 as admitted by the Government) are, while deprived of prisoner of war treatment on the one hand, on the other hand

are treated as military prisoners for purposes of punishment, while ordinary untried and uncharged civilians are denied the ordinary privileges of untried prisoners and kept under military custody, even their legal representatives being denied access to them.[40]

The changing public mood can be seen with Ernie O'Malley's family. Although originally from Co. Mayo, the family were jobbing 'Castle Catholics.' Ernie's father, Luke Malley, was a first-class clerk at the offices of the Congested Districts Board in Dublin by the time Ernie became a pupil (like Séamus Hughes) at the O'Connell Schools. He won a Dublin Corporation scholarship in 1915, and his son has speculated that he might have followed his older brother Frank into the Dublin Fusiliers if the 1916 Rising had not occurred. A younger brother, Albert, served in the Connaught Rangers. Neither of them returned to Ireland, but his three youngest brothers fell under Ernie's influence, despite their parents' disapproval, and joined the Republican movement. Like him, they took the anti-Treaty side. It was the death of Charles fighting with the anti-Treaty forces in O'Connell Street in July 1922 that was the turning-point for their parents. O'Malley's son writes:

> When Charles O'Malley was killed, the attitude of the Malley parents started to change.
>   Luke still implored his children not to become involved in the struggle or do anything foolish, but at least he and his wife, Marion, better understood for what their own children were willing to fight and die. During the course of the Civil War the Malley parents, who hitherto had been the epitome of the new middle class establishment were ostracised by their neighbours because of their children's anti-Treaty activities. With one child dead for his cause, several others interned, Ernie an anti-Treaty hero and an elected Republican TD, the Malley household had changed dramatically. In late 1923, in a letter to Mrs Erskine Childers, Mrs Luke Malley even signed herself Marion K. O'Malley.[41]

———

Republican prisoners were far from passive. As in the past, many of them took the war to the enemy, with attempted escapes, hunger strikes and other forms of protest. These were as much for public consumption and propaganda purposes as for continuing the fight behind bars. Prison struggles had been one of the most potent means of mobilising public support between 1916 and 1921.

Few prisoners understood the nature of this struggle as well as Peadar O'Donnell, one of the first brought to Mountjoy after being taken prisoner in the Four Courts. He soon found himself tunnelling through the wall of his cell in D Wing to link up with his comrades.

So we moved through one opening after another until we reached an alcove leading out on the corridor.

Prisoners were streaming out in a cheering throng while down below guards were bellowing and whirling revolvers. An officer came on the scene and blew a whistle but we all cheered and his words were lost. Suddenly rifle shots rang out and bullets cut through the air while there was a general rush for the shelter of the alcoves.[42]

One prisoner was wounded, and the prisoners began hurling abuse at the guards, who began arguing among themselves. The prisoners erected a barricade inside the gate that led from their wing into the central 'Circle' or prison well. They refused to allow warders or military guards inside the wing and organised their own orderlies to keep it clean and distribute food from the prison kitchen.

O'Donnell's wing faced the North Circular Road and, as most of the prisoners were Dubliners, there were soon large crowds gathering outside every day. Prisoners smashed the windows to hear messages from the crowd and to shout back their answers. 'It was extraordinary how amid the chorus of bellowing one could aim words at a special person in the throng and snatch a reply,' O'Donnell recalled, although as a Donegal man he knew virtually no-one apart from his wife, Lil, who was a nurse in the nearby Mater Hospital and a member of Cumann na mBan. When things were quiet the prisoners could hear the crackle of rifle fire, the clatter of machine guns and the boom of artillery as fighting continued in the city centre.[43]

This intercourse with friends and relations continued for a fortnight, with messages being tied on bricks and thrown from the windows. The prison's acting governor, Dermot O'Hegarty, had more or less lost control of the wings by now, but on 12 July a tunnel was discovered and he used it as an opportunity to assert himself. On the 14th he ordered the prisoners to withdraw from the windows or he would order the soldiers to open fire. Some soldiers baulked at the order, and O'Hegarty had to bring in Joe Dolan, one of Collins's Squad members now based in Wellington Barracks, to do the job.

When the deadline came at 12:45 p.m., Dolan ordered his men to open fire. The first volleys were aimed high, but once the faces disappeared from the windows he ordered his men to fire through them into the cells.[44] Two prisoners suffered flesh wounds from ricochets. The pattern had been set for future engagement.

Pádraig O'Keeffe, former secretary of Sinn Féin and one of the few pro-Treaty TDs to lose his seat in the 1922 general election, was seconded from the National Army to become deputy governor of Mountjoy. He was a small man (known by the nickname Paudeen, which he hated) with a short temper but he established a rapport with the prisoners that was beyond O'Hegarty, who returned to headquarters as director of organisation, a post he had held during the War of

Independence. Mountjoy was very much seen as a career backwater by military men, and O'Keeffe had two governors appointed over him in almost as many months. Philip Cosgrave, brother of W. T., was made governor on 4 September 1922. A veteran of the War of Independence, this 'unassuming, compassionate, and selfless man' was ill-equipped to be a prison governor. In effect, O'Keeffe continued running the prison.

O'Donnell says that the chorus of 'Paudeens' at lights out was as unpleasant 'as a nail scratching on tin.' Sometimes O'Keeffe would react by firing blindly into the wings, to cheers; but on one particular evening he asked one of his anonymous tormentors, 'What the hell's wrong with you?'

> 'Take me up a drink,' the voice replied.
> 'Be Jaysus, if I go up I'll shoot you.'
> After a brief silence the cry 'Paudeen' answered him again.
> 'What is it now?' O'Keeffe demanded.
> 'When you are coming up to shoot me, won't you bring me a drink.'

————

Work began on another tunnel, but it was soon discovered. Instead Lil O'Donnell organised arms to be smuggled into Mountjoy by National Army soldiers sympathetic to the prisoners. These included explosives and items of an officer's uniform as part of a plan for a mass break-out.[45]

Meanwhile, contact with Republicans on the outside carried other risks, not all of them military. On 22 September the *Irish Times* and *Irish Independent* published the contents of three documents that Liam Mellows had sent to Austin Stack and Ernie O'Malley for consideration by the Republican leadership.[46] These would become known subsequently as his 'Notes from Mountjoy' and would prove central to the ideology of socialist republicanism over the next ninety years. Copies appear to have been sent out separately, and one of these consignments was intercepted by the Free State authorities. Copies were given to the press on 21 September. (This was the day that the anti-Treaty TD Séamus Devins and Eoin MacNeill's son Brian were among nine IRA volunteers killed in controversial circumstances during a running battle with the National Army in Co. Sligo.)

The *Irish Times* published a summary of the material under a matter-of-fact headline 'Anti-Treaty programme.' However, the *Irish Independent* quoted the documents in full, under the headline 'Views of a leader of Irregulars,' with subheadings such as 'Communistic republic,' 'Danger to Catholicism' and 'Is a class war contemplated?' In case readers still missed the point it added an explanatory comment from the Government Publicity Department. This identified the writer, 'LOM,' as 'Liam Ó Maoilíosa, Liam Mellows, one of the real leaders of the Anti-Treaty Party.' It described the documents as a 'plan for the "Republic".'

> The 'Republican policy' ... consists avowedly and solely of a policy proposed in the *Workers Republic,* the organ of a small number of persons in Dublin known as the Communist Party. This programme, the author proposes, is to be made appear to be the same as the Social Programme of Dáil Éireann (January, 1919) translated into something definite.

A core element of Mellows's plan was the creation of a Provisional Republican Government, to distinguish it from the Provisional Government of the Free State, which would not be superseded by the Free State executive until 6 December 1922, when the Treaty with Britain came into force. The Provisional Government's Publicity Department emphasised the fact that even Mellows accepted that his proposed republican government would only be able to function, if at all, 'in a most limited way.'

> Much less would it be able to establish the proposed Communistic system in Ireland or in any part of Ireland. The purpose of the new 'Republican' programme is to be dangled before the eyes of the landless men, the unemployed, the 'thousands of people' whom 'starvation is facing,' so that the situation may be utilised for the Republic.[47]

Mellows was certainly keen for his proposals to be well aired, although not with the spin now put on them by the enemy. Like many of his compatriots, he still nursed the expectation that the British government would intervene at some point if they thought the Free State could not win the war. In such a situation he believed a Republican Provisional Government would provide a better rallying-point for the people than its Free State equivalent.

Even more importantly, as he had told Ernie O'Malley, Mellows saw the formation of a government as a means of bringing politics back into the Civil War arena, 'otherwise it becomes a fight between individuals.' He was critical of the Republican propaganda machine, arguing that a recitation of violent incidents or atrocities actually strengthened the Free State's claim that it was fighting to establish peace and stability.[48]

Contrary to the impression given by the government's Publicity Department, Mellows's Notes were longer and more wide-ranging than the *Workers' Republic* editorial on which they were partly based; but the essential concepts were certainly drawn from it. The editorial had posed the question, 'What will attract the masses to support the Republicans?' It pointed out that at present the Free State offers them more economic and social advantages. At the moment it seems as if the Labour Party, representative of the masses, can find salvation in the Free State ... Once you show the masses that Republicanism in Ireland will bring them definite and concrete advantages in their economic and social life, in their day-to-day life, then they will consider that the Republic is worth 'fighting for still further after all.'[49]

Mellows recrafted this as:

We should certainly keep Irish Labour for the Republic; it will possibly be the biggest factor on our side. Anything that would prevent Irish Labour becoming Imperialist and respectable will help the republic. Johnson, O'Brien, O'Shannon and Co., it will interest you to know that when they called on us in the Four Courts last May they (particularly Johnson) remarked that no effort had been made by an Dáil to put its Democratic Programme into execution. In our efforts to win back public support to the Republic we are forced to recognise— whether we like it or not—that the commercial interest so-called—money and the gombeenman—are on the side of the Treaty, because the Treaty means Imperialism and England. We are back to Tone—and it is just as well—relying on that great body 'the men of no property.' The 'stake in the country' people were never with the Republic.[50]

He uses the Communist Party programme, without acknowledging it, as a handy summary of the main political demands he believes Republicans should be making to garner support. These include placing industry under the control of the state, for the workers' and farmers' benefit.

All transport, railways, canals etc., will be operated by the state—the Republican State—for the benefit of the workers and farmers. All banks will be operated by the State for the benefit of Industry and Agriculture, not for the purpose of profit-making by loans, mortgages etc. That the lands of the aristocracy (who support the Free State and the British connection) will be seized and divided amongst those who can and will operate for the Nation's benefit etc.[51]

Mellows believed that the issue of confiscating 'demesnes and ranches' was already being examined by the anti-Treaty IRA Executive, when in fact it was no more than at the discussion level among Republican 'politicians', such as P. J. Ruttledge and Tom Derrig, who were little better regarded by many Republican military activists than their Free State counterparts.

Ernie O'Malley, who was seeking guidance from the chief of staff of the anti-Treaty IRA, Liam Lynch, had taken it upon himself to 'write to certain individuals in the Labour Organisation' to ask that 'railway men refrain from handling military stores or driving troop trains.' He hoped they would see that this would avoid 'the destruction of railways and will consequently cause unemployment in their ranks and general inconvenience to the public and that responsibility will be theirs.'[52]

Apart from failing to anticipate that Joe McGrath would come up with an alternative solution to the problem by arming the railway workers to protect the railway network, and with it their jobs, O'Malley and Lynch failed to take account of the changed public mood. When O'Malley reported on his failure to convince the railway workers to reactivate the weapon of the munitions strike used against the British, Lynch could only 'wonder how they can reconcile their present attitude with all their "gas" about a Workers' Republic.' It was clear that neither man had followed the proceedings of the two ILP&TUC conferences in February and August 1922, both of which had been widely reported in the press. In its report for 1922 the ILP&TUC National Executive condemned the Provisional Government for 'seizures, arrests, etc. which practically drove the whole political Republican Party into giving active support' for the IRA. But, it added,

> two rival Governments cannot exercise power in the same area without a clash. And not only do we consider the political claims of the Republican Party to be irrational, but their method of warfare is such as must be strongly denounced. Ambushes in the city streets, the destruction of bridges, railway tracks, and buildings are tantamount to a war upon the people, as these acts are certain to hurt the civilian population more than they damage the opposing military forces.[53]

Lynch asked O'Malley for 'a copy of that suggested Democratic Republican [sic] Programme,' apparently unaware that it had been adopted by Dáil Éireann in 1919 as one of the foundation documents of the Republic he had been defending for the previous four years.[54] While Mellows was certainly right in seeing the need for a Republican government to provide a political focus for opposition to the Free State, his suggestion that propaganda efforts should concentrate on emphasising 'Dev's work in America' during the War of Independence and the publication of a short biography of Cathal Brugha were of little relevance to the realities facing the populace.

The most telling example of how out of touch opponents of the Treaty were with the popular mood was the section of his notes on 'Food Control'. He predicted, correctly, that the

> obstruction of roads, railways and communications will be intensified; towns will feel it the worst. Some plan of rationing will have to be thought out and some person (a Labour man for preference) put in control. If the Republic is to

win out against the Free State and British we will have to face the idea of people suffering many privations ... As a matter of fact, Ireland suffered nothing (comparatively speaking) either during the Great War or our war. English people (and English women) cheerfully put up with severe deprivations and we Irish think our Cause worth putting up with anything. But do we? Judging by the whines and grumbles, one is tempted sometimes to say 'Certainly not.'[55]

Men such as Liam Deasy on the outside could see where the strategy of destruction was leading, but until the death of Liam Lynch and his replacement by Frank Aiken, who was close to de Valera, there would be no reprieve for militant Republicans, or anyone else.

——

The enforced idleness of imprisonment may have given leaders such as Mellows and O'Donnell an opportunity to discuss future political strategy, however detached from reality; but the constant preoccupation of all the inmates was escape. The most serious incident in Mountjoy Prison was on 10 October 1922 when a mass break-out was attempted from c Wing, where senior figures such as Richard Barrett, Liam Mellows, Rory O'Connor, Joseph McKelvey, Peadar O'Donnell and Andy Cooney were confined. Like Ernie O'Malley, Cooney was a former medical student and a member of GHQ Staff in the War of Independence. Unlike O'Malley, he had been offered a senior command in the National Army, only to have the offer withdrawn after it was decided that he was politically 'unreliable'.

He had been elected officer commanding c Wing and was in overall charge of the attempted escape. This took place at about 8:45 a.m.[56] when trays of food were being brought up for breakfast from the kitchen in the basement, where it was prepared by the small number of civilian prisoners remaining in Mountjoy. Ordinary criminals were often used as servants when it came to supplying the needs of the political prisoners, a role no-one seemed to question, least of all the men carrying out these tasks.

By now the occupants of c Wing had secured three revolvers and a limited amount of ammunition and explosives. However, these were not enough for what proved an extremely foolhardy escape attempt. The opportunity arose because one of the military policemen on duty was still in the kitchen, another had gone for his breakfast, and the gate between the Circle, which linked all the wings together, and the adjoining guardroom may have been left open.

Once the gate into c Wing was opened to deliver the food, the remaining military police on duty were rushed by the prisoners, with cries of 'Hands up!' When they failed to do so one military policeman, James Kearns, was shot. The other, James Gallagher, fired and then ran for the gate out of the Circle. He was shot by one of the prisoners as he reached it. Overhead, Privates Thomas Gaffney and William Wilson, stationed on the middle and top landings, respectively, opened fire on the prisoners below. Gaffney was shot dead by one of the prisoners and Wilson incapacitated by a knee wound.

The plan had been to overpower the soldiers and military police in the Circle and then rush the guardroom, capturing more weapons and gaining access to the six remaining gates that had to be negotiated to reach the outside. The gunfire had ruled out the possibility of reaching the main gate, but the capture of the guardroom itself might still have been achieved if two soldiers, Daniel Sweetman and Laurence Coffey, had not rushed out and opened fire. Coffey said afterwards that he deliberately aimed wide.

The prisoners retreated into the wing as O'Keeffe arrived with reinforcements. He ordered all the prisoners out on parade and in the process, whether deliberately or not, lessened considerably the prospect of any individual being identified as killing the three dead soldiers, not to mention wounding three others during the exchanges. Many of the garrison were frightened and resentful. O'Donnell said, 'We were surrounded by the angriest set of soldiers I had seen.' Lieutenant Henry Mangan, known as 'Hammer' among the prisoners, told the soldiers around him loudly, 'We will plug every man we find with a gun.'

Cooney partially defused the situation by walking up to O'Keeffe, who was surrounded by officers, and saying, 'I take full responsibility for all this.'

'Well, be Jasus, Cooney, you're a man. Come on,' O'Keeffe said, and marched him off.

In the subsequent search of c Wing, Mangan found Peadar Breslin, former quartermaster of the Dublin Brigade, either dead or dying in one of the cells. He had been shot through the eye and was being tended by Richard Barrett. A revolver with three empty cartridges lay nearby. Another prisoner, Seán Harbourne, had been wounded. In the search two more revolvers were recovered, along with a small amount of ammunition, a Mills hand grenade and two small mines, one ready for use. Rory O'Connor, an engineer by profession, was made to disarm the mine. O'Donnell recalled O'Keeffe returning to the wing. He

thought he detected a grin on [Joe] McKelvey; he ordered him to be dragged away to the basement. Paudeen certainly excelled himself in his flow of abuse that day but I believe it was his way of restraining his underlings. He let them work off steam and gave them some consolation from the abuse he piled [on us].

The inquests into the deaths of the four dead men were held next day. The jury brought in almost identical verdicts in each case, that death was due to 'shock and haemorrhage caused by bullets fired by some person or persons unknown.'

A government inquiry was held from 14 to 16 October by Commandant-General Seán Ó Murthuile and the former governor, Commandant-General Dermot O'Hegarty. Both men were senior IRB figures who had played a leading role in reorganising the Volunteers after 1916 and knew all the main protagonists well. This did not prevent them coming to some harsh conclusions about the prisoners and the need to regain control of the prison's three wings, although O'Hegarty omitted to mention that the problem had arisen during his own term as governor. They were scathing in their principal findings, that

> Police Officer Kearns and Gallagher[57] and Private Gaffney were murdered, and that Private Wilson was seriously injured by prisoners from 'C' Wing. We are satisfied that prisoners Richard Barrett and Peadar Breslin took part in the murder, though it may not be possible to obtain a conviction on the evidence. We are also satisfied that the following prisoners were privy to the occurrence and to the preparation thereof, viz. Roderic [i.e. Rory] O'Connor, Andrew Cooney, Cathal O'Hagan, Andrew Doyle and Patrick Mooney. The murder was [a] particularly cold blooded and wanton one inasmuch as the prisoners, if they had intended to shoot the men, were too cowardly to go on with the attempt. There can be no doubt that the revolvers in the possession of the prisoners was supplied from within with the assistance of some members of the civil or military staff at the prison. It has not been possible to trace the offender.

Barrett was named by a civilian remand prisoner, Patrick O'Neill, as one of the armed men involved in the break-out. Ó Murthuile and O'Hegarty advised the government to send papers to the Legal Officer to see if the statements given to them could be the basis for a prosecution. Whether the men making them had been cautioned in advance that their statements might be used in this way is far from clear. All the members of the Prison Council had accepted responsibility for the break-out, rather than leaving Cooney as the sole culprit, and must have been aware of the possible consequences. The report found that no blame was attached to 'Officers of the prison, but we are of opinion that the prisoners should be submitted to more rigorous discipline.'

The other main findings were that prisoners should be locked up at night, two to a cell, and 'at any other time when this may be desirable'; searches should be conducted of all prisoners and all wings at least once a fortnight; records should be kept of prisoners' possessions and of their behaviour, with breaches of prison discipline punishable by solitary confinement and a punishment diet; all parcels should be prohibited except items of clothing; and post cards provided by the prison authorities should be the only written communications permitted, the contents limited 'to statements regarding health etc.' No newspapers should be allowed, and the presence of prisoners' representatives at the distribution of food should end. Finally,

> instructions to the police and guard to fire wide to frighten prisoners [should] be withdrawn, and that orders be issued that prisoners disobeying certain regulations [unspecified] be fired at; that, if it is necessary to fire at a prisoner, the shot should be fired to hit.

Improvements were also proposed to the security procedures.

> All civilian warders in direct contact with prisoners should be searched before going on duty. The keys to the entrance door and gate to the 'Circle' should be held by a Policeman stationed outside. An armed soldier should be on duty outside the Guard Room at all times, and four Police Officers should be on duty in the 'Circle' whenever the gate is opened. The prison guards should be changed at least once a month, outside walls and exercise areas should be inspected daily before prisoners are allowed out for exercise.

Privates Sweetman and Coffey, who had stemmed the rush by the prisoners in the Circle, were singled out for praise. 'Their promptitude probably saved the guardroom.'

————

The situation in Mountjoy settled down, and Peadar O'Donnell recalled that Ethel Voynich's novel *The Gadfly* was being widely read in C Wing as winter descended.[58] 'It is a tale of Italian revolution with a ghastly execution,' O'Donnell wrote. 'And on McKelvey this book made such a deep impression that he often ... expressed the hope that if he ever had to face a firing party his killing would be more efficiently carried out.' He was still reading this revolutionary romance on the morning of 7 December.

The 'Murder Act', as Republicans called the Army Emergency Powers Resolution, had been passed at the end of September but had not been enforced until the execution of the four young IRA members on 17 November after the attack on Oriel House. (See chapter 5). However, it was the execution of Erskine Childers on 24 November that shocked the IRA leadership. On the next day *Poblacht na hÉireann* published the names of all the 'Murder Members' of the third Dáil who voted for it and declared they would each be held to account. On 4 December it published an open letter from the IRA chief of staff, Liam Lynch, on behalf of the Army Council, to the 'Speaker of the Provisional "Parliament" of Southern Ireland,' putting them on notice that, next to the members of your 'Provisional Government' every member of your body who voted for this resolution by which you pretend to make legal the murder of soldiers is equally guilty. We therefore give you and each member of your body due notice that unless your army recognises the rules of warfare in future we shall adopt very drastic measures to protect our forces.

The same issue carried a warning to the Labour Party leader, Tom Johnson, that

the continued participation of your Party in the proceedings of this illegal Parliament can only be construed by us as an intentional co-operation with enemy forces in the murder of our soldiers, a great proportion of whom are drawn from the ranks of Labour.[59]

This attack ignored the fact that the Labour Party had opposed the Emergency Powers Resolution and had provided the only coherent parliamentary opposition to the Free State government. But it was not really at odds with Liam Mellows's advocacy of 'keep[ing] Irish Labour for the Republic.' The key word in that phrase is 'Irish'. Peadar O'Donnell, who was a former ITGWU organiser and exercised a powerful influence on Mellows, saw Johnson and most of the ILP&TUC leaders as reformists who were blocking a realignment of Labour with the Republic. Although he was not personally motivated by anti-English feeling, O'Donnell was not above exploiting crude nationalism for his own purposes. Johnson was an English socialist born and bred, whose job as a commercial traveller had first brought him to Ireland. An article by O'Donnell published in the Communist Party paper, the *Workers' Republic,* on 26 August 1922 illustrates this approach well.

It is England's devilish luck that at a moment when Irish Labour is faced with a situation of tremendous possibilities, the dominating influence on the National Executive should be an imperial English mind ... Johnson is a very excellent, able man but he is a reactionary leader.

O'Donnell appealed to Labour's militants to deal with Johnson and his like. 'The duty of the Irish Citizen Army is plain. Tom Johnson must be deported. Deport him.'[60] The rest of the Labour Party's National Executive he dismissed as 'just a collection of Imperial toadies.'

The problem was that there was no significant counterforce to Johnson and his 'toadies'. The Irish Citizen Army had shrunk to an insignificant auxiliary of the pro-Treaty IRA. It was natural for instinctive radicals such as Mellows and O'Malley to follow O'Donnell's advice on relations with the labour movement, but it is much harder to understand the latter's misreading of the situation. It was partly a result of being isolated from the outside world in Mountjoy Prison; but O'Donnell and the broad trade union mainstream within the Labour Party would remain antithetical for decades to come.

Meanwhile the opportunist shooting dead of Seán Hales TD and the wounding of Pádraig Ó Máille, Deputy Speaker of the third Dáil, by two Dublin Volunteers on 7 December was a significant escalation of the retaliatory spiral that had become the Irish Civil War. The shooting of unarmed off-duty National Army members had become common practice, as had that of anti-Treaty IRA Volunteers being taken prisoner. Hales was still a serving soldier as well as a TD, like several of his Dáil colleagues. Although he was the only Cork Brigade commander to support the Treaty, he was widely respected, and his brother Tom was a leading figure in the anti-Treaty forces. It was wrongly assumed that Lynch had authorised the attack, but it was perfectly natural for ordinary Volunteers to assume it was open season on figures such as Hales on the strength of the article in *Poblacht na hÉireann* and Lynch's statements.

Nor were the imprisoned Republican leaders in Mountjoy Prison particularly shocked. When O'Donnell met Richard Barrett at the head of the stairs on C Wing that evening he said 'something to the effect that it was a pity that some person more poisonous than he had not been got.' Barrett replied, 'Ah, shag him. Why did he join them?' The main interest of the men in the wing was the escape tunnel they were excavating. O'Donnell remembered playing a few 'really keen' rubbers of bridge in the afternoon and chairing a discussion that evening on 'Women in industry: equal pay for equal work?'

When Paudeen O'Keeffe arrived with an escort to collect Barrett, McKelvey, Mellows and O'Connor it seemed no more than a routine transfer. 'They were just told to dress and pack their belongings.' It was only when they had been taken off the wing and put in individual cells that they were each presented with a document informing them that they would be shot in the morning, as a reprisal for the death of Seán Hales.

The executions were supposed to take place early, before the other prisoners rose, because 8 December was the Feast of the Assumption and the more devout inmates would be attending 7:30 Mass. But there was a problem. None of the condemned men would recant their unholy war against the Free State, and without it the prison chaplain would not hear their confessions and administer the sacraments. Mellows was the most obdurate. In his last letter to his mother he wrote:

I have had the chaplain to see me. It is sad but I cannot agree to accept the Bishop's Pastoral. My conscience is clear, thank God. With the old Gaodhals I believe that those who die for Ireland have no need of prayer.

In the end the chaplain at Wellington Barracks, a convinced but not 'fanatical' supporter of the Free State, came over to sort out an understanding with each man in turn. Mellows was the last and most difficult prisoner to come to an understanding with, but eventually the Mountjoy chaplain went to obtain the viaticum from the chapel. However, either accidentally or deliberately he locked himself in the sacristy and they had some difficulty getting the key from Paudeen O'Keeffe, who had been anaesthetising his emotions with drink.

The executions were every bit as bad as McKelvey had feared after reading *The Gadfly*. When the firing squad had finished it took nine revolver shots by the officer in charge to despatch the four men.[61]

———

The number of women Republican activists arrested in the Civil War was far less than of men but they posed problems for the Free State government out of all proportion to their numbers. The split in Cumann na mBan paralleled that in the IRA. On 12 March 1922 a meeting of pro-Treaty members in the Mansion House established Cumann na Saoirse 'to assist in the return at the forthcoming elections of candidates who accept the Treaty, as a step towards the complete independence of Ireland.' Councillor Jennie Wyse Power, who presided, said: 'An idea had gone abroad that all women were against the Treaty. Their presence showed that in the City of Dublin there were women who saw that the course they proposed to adopt was the right one from the national point of view.'[62] Nevertheless, it was the opponents of the Treaty who seized the initiative.

When the Civil War broke out, members of Cumann na mBan not only sheltered anti-Treaty IRA members and acted as couriers and nurses but took part in hostilities. In Dublin they were particularly active in bringing arms into the country from a network set up by Constance Markievicz in Scotland. On 8 September 1922 Richard Mulcahy proposed converting Kilmainham Prison into a women's prison for those 'found assisting the irregulars ... in any military activity or violation of the Red Cross.'[63] However, the General Prisons Board insisted that it be renovated first and, as it was still being used as a transit centre for male prisoners, this work took much longer than expected.

When Ellen Humphreys was arrested on 4 November with her daughter Sighle and sister-in-law Nancy O'Rahilly after the capture of Ernie O'Malley they were brought to Mountjoy, where they were put in the hospital section of B Wing. They were joined three days later by Máire Comerford, who had been arrested in possession of a revolver. Put in the same cell as Sighle Humphreys, Comerford smashed it up 'barehanded', resulting in parcels and letters for all the women prisoners being stopped. As Ann Matthews has shown, the female prison agenda was very much driven by militants such as Comerford. They also appear to have developed factions behind prison bars long before the men, had gone on hunger strike and, as we have seen, were supported by the very active Prisoners' Defence League established by Maud Gonne MacBride, Charlotte Despard and other veterans of earlier struggles. Mary MacSwiney, sister of the Republican martyr Terence MacSwiney, was the first woman prisoner to go on hunger strike in protest at her imprisonment. Richard Mulcahy had a water bed delivered to Mountjoy for her, and on 27 November she was released, after twenty-three days. Like other Republican prisoners, she had been denied the sacraments under the bishops' pastoral letter but her confession was heard and she received holy communion and the last rites because of her deteriorating health just before she was released, which gave her 'a sense of victory over both the government and the church.'[64]

Women prisoners were sent to Dublin from other parts of the country, and on 29 November interned women were granted political status and allowed to run the wing themselves, despite the previous experience with the men in Mountjoy. Prisoners with funds could buy food, tobacco and books, while the National Army undertook to clothe poorer women and male inmates through the Prisoners' Department of the Adjutant-General's Office. Matthews says that some women prisoners, including Lily O'Brennan, sent their laundry home for the family servants to wash. She also sent out her false teeth for repair, but over time even O'Brennan washed her own clothes as items began to go missing.[65]

In December the women formed a prisoners' council, with Margaret Buckley from Cork as OC, but this did not prevent a split into an 'aggressive' faction on the top landing and a majority group that opted for peaceful co-existence. They united, however, in their campaign to receive religious sacraments denied to them by prison chaplains carrying out the bishops' instructions. 'In the days that followed our religion was our bulwark, our food, our stay,' Margaret Buckley later wrote.

> Though denied the sacraments by human agency, we were in close communion with God; nobody could deny us access to Him; and often during the dark nights in the lonely cells, when the black fingers of despair clutched at our hearts, we cried to Him, and then the dawn would peep in through the prison bars, shyly at first and [then] boldly until the glory of the Resurrection enveloped us, and we began another day with renewed courage and renewed hope.

There was even an 'officer commanding prayers,' Ellen Humphreys. On release many of these women felt it keenly when they went to Mass and the priest passed them by at the communion rail. From respectable middle-class backgrounds, they felt deeply humiliated by such treatment, and Paudeen O'Keeffe, sensitive to their feelings, sent civilian women prisoners to clean their cells for them.[66] The gap between the two groups was enormous. Ordinary women prisoners could not understand why the internees went on hunger strike over conditions. Margaret Buckley concluded that, 'poor creatures, their vision was circumscribed by their animal feelings; that is possibly why they were there at all.'[67]

By the end of January, Kilmainham Prison was finally brought into use and forty-two of the fifty-three women in Mountjoy were transferred there. Women convicts cooked the food and delivered it to internee orderlies. Tea was delivered in a bucket, and internees dipped mugs into it. Each prisoner could send and receive one letter a week. There were no visitors, but prisoners had access to the exercise yard from 11 a.m. until 1 p.m. and from 4 p.m. to 6 p.m. The number of women in custody rose to eighty-six, but a higher proportion of them than of male prisoners seem to have signed the form of undertaking issued by the government promising not to take arms against the Free State. Some of the signatories, of both sexes, subsequently broke their parole.

Classes in Irish, French and German were organised at Mountjoy. Craft classes produced souvenirs, embroidery and knitted items. Family and friends outside were allowed to send in parcels of food, such as eggs and bacon, 'and, almost without exception, the first parcel contained rosary beads.'

Kilmainham was a much older, grimmer complex than Mountjoy, and life there took its toll on inmates. When Hannah Moynihan from Tralee was arrested with her sisters Cis and Jo Power for producing a Republican newsletter, the *Invincible,* they were brought by first-class train to Dublin and then by army lorry from Kingsbridge to Kilmainham. As they stood in the entrance hall,

suddenly a shrill voice addressed us from we knew not where 'are you prisoners?' We timidly answered 'yes.' In still shriller tones the voice said 'Up the Republic' … We saw two wild eyes glaring through the grating of the door, which we presumed was the entrance to the main jail. Our hearts sank when a few minutes later Deputy [Governor] Ryan opened that same door to let us enter. 'God,' said Sis 'are we to join that hysterical woman?' The deputy overheard and hastened to reassure us. 'No … you won't join her until the morning, but don't let that thought disturb you, you'll all be hysterical by then.[68]

In March 1923 the British government deported hundreds of men and sixty-six women to Ireland who were suspected of aiding the anti-Treaty forces. The Anne Devlin Branch of Cumann na mBan in Glasgow had been particularly active, under the direction of Constance Markievicz. Even before the deportations two members had been arrested on a trip to Dublin and questioned about the whereabouts of Joe Robinson, the senior anti-Treaty IRA officer in Scotland at the time and a brother of the Tipperary TD and anti-Treaty leader Séamus Robinson. The women were brought up the Dublin Mountains and told they would be shot if they kept refusing to tell ... where Robinson was hiding ... Three times they stopped the lorry, got their guns, made the two girls kneel, and asked them to say their prayers, as they would shoot them when they would count to the number ten. The girls remained silent kneeling on the Dublin Mountains; eventually they dragged them to their feet and threw them up on the lorry. They brought them back to the city and locked them in Kilmainham Gaol at 4 a.m.[69]

They were then sent back to Glasgow, with the threat that they would be shot if they ever returned, but they continued to smuggle arms until they were deported and incarcerated in Mountjoy.

———

Conditions in both prisons deteriorated as the number of women internees rose, sparking a round of protests and retaliation by the authorities, leading to a withdrawal of privileges. By late March 1923 there were fifty-one prisoners in Mountjoy and 220 in Kilmainham. Hannah Moynihan and her sisters were dismayed when ninety-one women in Kilmainham voted to go on hunger strike from 23 March, and she wondered 'is one justified dying for letters and parcels?' On the 29th the Free State government tried to break the deadlock by restoring privileges as an Easter gesture of good will, but in April a more protracted hunger strike took place involving Nellie Ryan, Richard Mulcahy's sister-in-law, who had been arrested in Wexford with documents and was accused of 'endeavouring to seduce a soldier of the National Army to act in a treacherous manner by ... establishing a line of communications between irregular forces.'

On 10 April, Maud Gonne MacBride was interned in Kilmainham and went on hunger strike. She had been continuing her campaign for prisoners, who still included her son, Seán MacBride, when she was arrested at the offices of the *Irish Citizen* with her daughter, Iseult, and other women painting banners 'for seditious demonstrations.' Her arrest inevitably attracted widespread interest and outrage. W. B. Yeats wrote to Cosgrave calling for her release on the grounds that 'she is 57 and cannot be expected to stand the same strain as a younger woman.' Charlotte Despard, the sister of Field-Marshal Sir John French, also wrote protesting at Gonne's arrest. Lord Glenavy made similar representations on behalf of another hunger-striker, Kathleen Costello, pleading her 'delicate' health. Her only offence had been the possession of copies of *Poblacht na hÉireann*. Dr Patrick McCartan, a senior figure in Sinn Féin and the IRB as well as a Pro-Treaty TD, made further representations on her behalf.[70]

On 27 April there began the transfer of all the women prisoners to the old North Dublin Union complex at Grangegorman. It provided far better accommodation than Mountjoy or Kilmainham, but the women refused to move and had to be dragged from the landings. They protested at being strip-searched by female warders, and when soldiers were ordered in, the confrontations became violent. Máire Comerford subsequently had to have stitches to her head and Mary MacDermott had a broken wrist. MacDermott managed to smuggle a letter out, which was published in the *Daily Herald*, suggesting that the strip-searching was not as extreme as claimed. A subsequent inquiry by the Prisoners' Department of the Adjutant-General's Office claimed that MacDermott had attacked one of her searchers and, far from being stripped, 'her coat and blouse were simply opened.' It claimed that 'the women were moved in a manner that was as gentle as was compatible with efficiency. But if you consider that the prisoners had to be dragged or carried down two flights of stairs, you will realise that gentleness was not very possible.'[71]

As soon as the women arrived at Grangegorman, battle was joined over such issues as the number of beds per dormitory. The Cumann na mBan council decided to put what it considered surplus beds out in the yard, which meant newcomers sleeping in the open. Fortunately, female warders allowed the new arrivals to dry clothes in their quarters after a wet night. The open-plan accommodation also created privacy issues, which allowed Cumann na mBan prisoners far more freedom from supervision than male internees had, and on the night of 6 May nineteen of them escaped over the wall into Broadstone Railway Station. Most were soon recaptured, but Máire Comerford was one of those who managed to remain at liberty.

By then the Civil War was over and a gradual release of women prisoners began. This did not prevent further protests and hunger strikes over conditions and the slow rate of release of internees. Even after Mulcahy announced on 21 September 1923 that all women prisoners would be released there was a last hunger strike, to coincide with that by male internees. Unlike the women, the men had gone on hunger strike because they had not been given assurances that they would all be released. The women prisoners divided on whether or not to participate in the men's hunger strike. There were four main groups: those who still saw hunger strikes as a means of continuing the war by other means, those who thought they should strike on their own behalf to demand immediate release, those who thought there was no moral basis for such extreme action, and those who would accept a majority decision. After a heated debate on 24 October, 51 of the 86 women in Grangegorman went on hunger strike.[72]

The government responded by beginning to release women who were not on hunger strike, and by 13 November the strike was down to just eight women. Ironically, Constance Markievicz had returned from Scotland and was arrested after speaking at a public meeting in Aungier Street. She joined the hunger strike thirty-six hours before it was called off when the men's protest ended on the 23rd. The last four women, including Markievicz, were released on 15 December, and on

11 January the North Dublin Union complex was transferred to Grangegorman Mental Hospital. Unfortunately there were no funds for renovating the buildings, and the management arrangements at Grangegorman were later thrown into confusion when Dublin Corporation was abolished in May 1924, with the hospital's further development becoming yet another casualty of the Civil War.

Although far fewer women were interned than men—a total of 645 between November 1922 and November 1923,[73] as opposed to 11,480 men in July 1923 alone[74]—their treatment attracted proportionately more attention. The fact that they were women, and the majority from impeccable middle-class backgrounds—such as Ellen Humphreys, widow of Michael O'Rahilly, and Albina Broderick, sister of the Earl of Midleton—was certainly exploited by Republican propagandists. Reporting on the release of Mary MacSwiney, *Poblacht na hÉireann* ascribed it to 'the outburst of popular indignation at her torture ... on hunger strike under conditions more harsh than her brother Terence was kept [in] by his English jailers.' Nor could most of the women detained be shown to be actively involved in military activity; instead it was when they were involved in propaganda work and fund-raising for such bodies as the Republican Prisoners' Defence Fund that they were arrested.[75] The Free State authorities recognised that this work was far more effective in sustaining the Republican cause than any number of shootings or bombings.

The women were more combative than the male prisoners in protesting at their conditions, but then the treatment visited on them for protesting was far less brutal. They traded intelligently on their femininity and on traditional male attitudes to embarrass the Free State authorities. They were helped by the fact that many of them were related to members of the new Free State establishment, including Richard Mulcahy, W. B. Yeats and Lord Glenavy. Whereas former friendships seem to have militated against male prisoners, or in some cases may even have contributed to their execution, such as those of Erskine Childers, Rory O'Connor and Liam Mellows, it had the opposite effect where women were concerned. Rough justice was something men dealt out to other men but was not visited on women—at least not outside the home, but domestic violence was one of the many taboo subjects in the new state, which protected the perpetrator rather than the victim. The combination of publicity and what was acceptable public male behaviour combined to make the prisons perhaps the one area of Irish life where feminists could score victories, however little they affected the lives of ordinary women outside.

———

One group of prisoners who did not receive any publicity or special treatment, good, bad or indifferent, were civilian inmates. Fortunately for all concerned, the numbers in Dublin had shrunk since before 1914. There were only 237 inmates for Mountjoy's 900 cells at the beginning of 1922.[76] Progressive British legislation had drastically reduced the number of offences for which imprisonment was a penalty. Many of the young men from deprived areas of the city who made up the bulk of the prison population in normal times had joined the British army between 1914 and 1918, when the largest group of male offenders was military deserters and absentees.[77] These were routinely sent back to their units. Ironically, the general breakdown in law and order from 1916 onwards because of political unrest meant that the apprehension and imprisonment of ordinary criminals was no longer a policing priority.[78]

Unlike Republican prisoners and their families, there was little public sympathy and few funds available to help this group. The General Prisons Board gave £3 5s to prisoners on discharge and discretionary clothes and boots. In 1922, thirty-one pairs of boots and 175 other articles of clothing were distributed to 197 prisoners who left Mountjoy Prison. These were supplemented by the Catholic Male Prisoners' Aid Committee, but it could only provide items worth £1 4s 6d in 1922, compared with a hardly extravagant £8 13s 9d in 1921. More important was the committee's follow-up work with the men, most of whom were aged between twenty and forty-five, were married and had families. In some cases their needs were simple, such as retrieving clothes from the pawnshop so that they could seek work. In other cases more sustained support was required. In one instance the family of a fifty-year-old man received a weekly grant for forty-six weeks while he sought work in England; but such extended help was rare.

A more common problem was arrears of rent. The Prisoners' Aid Committee would intercede with landlords, especially if the prisoner or former prisoner had children. Landlords would accept reduced payments in some cases rather than go to the trouble of an eviction. Sometimes employers willing to take on former prisoners would look for incentives. One shopkeeper sent a 26-year-old farm labourer, who had just served twelve months' imprisonment for housebreaking, to the committee to acquire suitable clothing to make him fit to serve behind a counter.

Quite a few soldiers and ex-servicemen were among those helped, including veterans of the Great War from England and Scotland. Nor were such applicants always what they claimed to be. One 33-year-old ex-serviceman, who was married with two children, on completing eighteen months' imprisonment for larceny was sent 'a complete outfit, including boots.' He never had the chance to wear them, as a National Army escort turned up to take him into custody for military offences on the morning of his discharge. He may have left one army but had omitted to mention that he had joined another.

On the other hand a National Army member sentenced to four years' imprisonment for larceny handed over 'all his civilian clothes and boots' for use by the Prisoners' Aid Committee. 'His offer was most gratefully received.'

Inevitably the failure rate for interventions was high. A 27-year-old packer and ex-soldier, married with five children, with three convictions for larceny, admitted that drink was the cause of his 'downfall'. He was given help after agreeing to go to confession and taking a life pledge to abstain from alcohol. 'His home was visited no less than 14 times. At the time of last visit, there was ample proof that the promise given to visitors had not been carried out.'

Nor were all prisoners from a deprived background. A 32-year-old boilermaker, married with two children, obtained help in paying arrears of union dues to resume employment only to return for more assistance.

> This man was brought up by his parents in a most religious atmosphere, surrounded by every comfort. Some time after marriage he began a downward moral career. It is only too evident that his promises of a return to the straight road ... were made only for the purposes of deception.

And yet there were successes. A 24-year-old bank clerk unable to 'get even labouring work' after his release was found employment in 'one of the colonies,' and six months later the chaplain there reported 'that every promise made by this young man has been kept.'[79]

The most depressing aspect of these cases is that they failed to change much in character over the next few years. Unemployment, drink and debt were the lot of most discharged prisoners, characterising in an aggravated form the problems faced by thousands of other poor Dubliners.

Chapter 9 ∾

'PEOPLE THOUGHT IT WAS COURAGEOUS TO TAKE A GUN OR A MINE AND USE IT, BUT IT REQUIRED MORE COURAGE TO SPEAK THE TRUTH'

While the plight of the new state's twelve thousand political prisoners rightly attracted public concern in the Civil War years, those other guests of the state, the inmates of the workhouses and county homes, were largely ignored, except when allegations of corruption were being investigated or an increase in the charge on the rates was being debated.

The old workhouse system was replaced in most of the country by the county homes during this period, but in the capital the South Dublin Union survived. Between 1920 and 1924 it dealt with 37,518 cases, and the number of inmates remained stubbornly high.[1] The operation of the institution was a standing scandal. Successive auditors' reports revealed flagrant breaches of accounts procedures and a failure to meet statutory obligations. For instance, the half-yearly audit to 31 March 1920 showed an increase of £500 in expenditure on tobacco and snuff, although the number of inmates had fallen by 102. Temporary staff, who made up 30 per cent of the total, were paid out of the petty cash book; there were no proper procedures for contracting in goods and services; thirty-four pigs had been omitted from the farm stocktaking; and the inmates' property book was missing, allegedly destroyed by the British army during a raid. The auditor, Francis Barnard, described the coal records for the previous six months as 'in a chaotic condition and the figures therein are in the majority of cases utterly valueless.'[2]

Even the returns for the number and age of residents were unreliable. Ages were a particular problem, as some residents who had claimed they were old-age pensioners before entering the workhouse now made a declaration that they were younger—by up to ten years in some instances. Inadequate birth records had led to large numbers of Irish people claiming the old-age pension, so that when the scheme was introduced in 1912 they accounted for 27 per cent of all claimants in the United Kingdom.[3] On the positive side, the introduction of the pension was the first major step away from the Poor Law system. Between 1916 and 1919 the number of 'aged and infirm' admissions to the Dublin workhouses fell from 30 per cent of inmates to 20 per cent, at a time when the total workhouse population fell from 4,800 to 3,500, thus accounting for most of the decrease. This meant that more old people were living in the community, at a lower cost to the ratepayer, not only because residential care, even by workhouse standards, was more costly than outdoor relief (entitlement to money or other benefits without having to enter the workhouse) but because the old-age pension came out of British exchequer returns. Those elderly citizens who did enter the workhouse now found that they had to contribute to their upkeep from their pension.

Apparently there were no penalties for false declarations, but neither were receipts issued for contributions received from pensioners who were inmates.

The records for outdoor relief were equally poor, filled with 'superfluous' observations rather than 'salient facts,' according to Barnard. The amounts paid out in 1920 had increased by 48 per cent on the same period in 1918–19 and now absorbed 30 per cent of the total workhouse budget. This might have been partly due to the forced closure of the North Dublin Union at the end of 1918, when the British army took it over as winter quarters for part of the Dublin garrison and some former inmates were transferred to outdoor relief rather than the South Dublin Union premises in James's Street.[4] However, the opportunity to make savings and to rationalise services with the forced amalgamation of the two institutions was not only missed but attracted much criticism because of the large redundancy payments granted to surplus employees; and an investigation into the disposal of furniture and other irregularities further blackened an already besmirched reputation.[5]

Workers were also well paid relative to other employments. When John Colbert was appointed school principal in March 1919 he had a salary scale of £150–200, plus a war bonus of £92 8s a year. The Board sought to justify it subsequently on the grounds of the merger of the Cabra and Pelletstown schools after the forced amalgamation of the North Dublin and South Dublin Unions. The Local Government Board was unimpressed. In a letter to the Board of Guardians (governors) in June 1920 it pointed out that 'if Mr. Colbert had been appointed as principal teacher of an ordinary national school with an average attendance of from ten to 19 pupils he would be entitled to ... £64 per annum, War Bonus, which, at the present time amounts to £75 per annum and a residual capitation fee of 5s on average attendance.' Colbert had fourteen pupils, so that as the principal of an ordinary school he could have earned no more than £142 10s a year—a difference of between £100 and £150 per year.[6]

Better records appear to have been kept for the half year ending 30 September 1920, but these showed further anomalies. Returns for outdoor relief revealed twenty-two cases in which payments were illegal, as those helped were eligible only if they had entered the workhouse. However, Barnard decided that, given that it was more economical to provide claimants with outdoor relief, and more beneficial to the social status of the family, 'in an attempt to relieve the present pernicious system, I have allowed such expenditure.'

In another case, involving Dr Richard Hayes, a veteran of the Battle of Ashbourne in 1916 and a former Sinn Féin joint director of public health with Dr Kathleen Lynn, it was found that he was being paid more than £500 a year as a dispensary doctor, although he had not been legally appointed. The reason was his refusal to furnish the Local Government Board with a declaration that he would 'not engage in conspiracy and rebellion against the Government while he was drawing a salary from public funds.' Dr Hayes was now an ardent supporter of the Free State, and the auditor decided to give retrospective approval to the payments.

There was a great deal of retrospection in all the workhouse accounts, for the simple reason that they had not been properly audited for two years. Nor were the problems restricted to poor bookkeeping or corruption. The decision by Dublin Corporation to recognise Dáil Éireann in 1920 meant the withdrawal of much British exchequer funding, while the Rathdown Union, which also refused to recognise British rule, decided to solve the problem by referring applicants from its catchment area in south Co. Dublin to the South Dublin Union. By March 1921, when the accounts of the South Dublin Union were once more submitted for audit, the operating deficit was £11,196.[7]

If the disruption caused by 1916 and its aftermath adversely affected the finances of the South Dublin Union it also provided conditions in which corruption flourished. The situation was aggravated by the fact that the Board of Guardians, who were all elected, took a regular role in administering the Union. Not only were all members of the permanent staff appointed by them but the temporary staff held their positions entirely at the discretion of the Guardians. On the other hand, recipients of aid and their families were of course voters. The staff was highly unionised and was able to lobby guardians directly as well as through their unions and the Dublin Trades Council. Some guardians may have wanted reform, if only to assuage the concern of the ratepayers and wider electorate, but they had fears that any corruption uncovered could affect their own political careers. Relieving officers, who dispensed more than £2,600 a week to low-income families, were almost immune from investigation, because they were ideally placed to canvass support for Board members running for re-election or for membership of the Corporation and Dáil. In January 1923, in a rare case of disciplinary action against an employee, the Guardians dismissed one relieving officer after 101 of the 230 cases he was handling were struck out, and relief for some of his clients was reduced. Other relieving officers had to repay money not properly accounted for.[8]

These rare efforts by the Guardians to reform the South Dublin Union sometimes revealed other anomalies in the political economy of the city. For instance, when they decided to tender competitively for 3,000 tons of American coal in September 1922, local coal merchants offered prices of 34s 9d to 42s a ton, compared with British tenders of 21s 9d to 27s a ton. The Board of Guardians opted for J. Crean of Liverpool, which proffered the second-cheapest bid of 22s 9d a ton. Crean's offered to ship it for 4s 3d a ton, bringing the price to 27s. The Guardians agreed to the transport charges provided the coal was shipped by Heiton's, one of the leading Dublin coal companies, which had offered to supply the coal at 35s 7d a ton. Heiton's was also permitted to charge 9s 4d a ton for bringing the coal from the ship to the South Dublin Union, making the total price 36s 4d. This was agreed, because the standard cost of unloading and delivering coal in the city was 17s 8d a ton.

It appears that the Board agreed unanimously to buy the coal in Liverpool before factoring in additional transport costs, so that it ended up paying 7d a ton more than if it had accepted Heiton's bid in the first place. This typifies the poor decision-making processes, which increased suspicions of corruption. The high cost of transporting the coal from the ship to James's Street also supports the analysis of inflation offered by Darrell Figgis in his minority report from the Prices Commission, which showed that Dublin suffered from an excess of competition in the supply and distribution of basic goods. (See chapter 6.)

The costly blunders by the Board of Guardians, inefficiencies in the provision of services and outright corruption were deeply resented by ratepayers, who saw the Poor Rate (that portion of the rates allocated to relief of the poor) increase from as little as 1s 10½d[9] in 1914 to 4s 10¾d by 1923, an increase of 157 per cent.

The South Dublin Union was becoming an embarrassing administrative anomaly in the Free State. By 1922 the workhouses outside Dublin had been generally consolidated into one county home and one hospital for each local authority. Services had been radically reduced, and as many inmates as possible had been put on outdoor relief. Further savings were achieved by cutting staff levels; previously some institutions had more employees than inmates. The breakdown of British rule in much of the countryside and the financial crises facing local authorities after the withdrawal of exchequer subsidies created an opportunity for councils dominated by Sinn Féin and supported by the IRA to wield the axe more drastically than in normal times.

This was not possible in Dublin. The poor were too numerous, the workhouse trade unions too strong, the forces of the Crown too powerful and Sinn Féin too reliant on Labour support in dominating the city council for such draconian solutions to be applied. Besides, the closure of workhouses in nearby districts, such as Dunshaughlin, Co. Meath, and Rathdown, in south Co. Dublin, saw more applicants flooding into the city, not to mention Belfast refugees. The reorganisation forced on the city by the British army's occupation of the North Dublin Union saw young and old, mothers with children, beggars, 'lunatics and idiots' thrown together, while Pelletstown on the Navan Road became home to unmarried mothers and their children. As we have seen, this soon fell under the direction of St Patrick's Guild. (See chapter 4.)

The dislocation of local government by the political and economic crisis that engulfed the Free State would lead to hundreds of private tragedies emanating from such institutions in the years ahead. But perhaps the most potent factor at work was the lack of any comprehensive plan to replace the Poor Law system with something better. Instead, everything was dealt with ad hoc. Undoubtedly the greatest setback was the collapse of the contributory national insurance scheme introduced by the British government on the eve of the First World War. As unemployment soared, temporary unemployment relief was introduced by the British authorities in 1919. Inadequate though it was, Republican Labour rejected the call by Sinn Féin in Dublin to boycott the system, as no substitute was on offer to take its place. Nor was there any prospect of extending the medical benefits available under that scheme in Britain to post-war Ireland. Ironically, while John Redmond had successfully blocked the extension to Ireland of medical benefits under the British social insurance scheme before 1914, one of the obligations that the Free State had to meet under the financial settlement in 1922 was the employment of almost seven hundred doctors to provide treatment for British ex-servicemen here.

Ironically, workers fortunate enough to be in Irish trade unions that provided health insurance were protected after the establishment of the Free State, but Irish workers in British unions were not; members were compelled to switch to an Irish insurer if they wanted to retain cover. Rather than see trade unionists forced to join commercial schemes, such as Hibernian Insurance, the ILP&TUC established its own society, the Irish Trade Union Congress Health Insurance Society. It began business on 2 July 1923 with 8,108 members in twenty-seven unions—a reminder of how fragmented the movement remained. 'The larger question of the amalgamation of all Trade Union Societies is, of course, one of considerable complexity and importance, and will require to be considered in the future,' the ILP&TUC annual report said. The Labour Party in the Dáil managed to secure provision for trade unionists who were in other insurance societies to switch their benefits to the new one if they wished.[10] This was the sort of useful amendment to legislation that significantly improved people's lives, but it rarely registered with trade union voters, let alone the wider public.

Once the Free State government was officially established, on 7 December 1922— the same day that Deputy Seán Hales was killed—the balance of forces changed rapidly. It was obvious that the Poor Law system, now restricted to Dublin and Cork (where it operated more efficiently), had to go. On 30 April 1923 a government inquiry got under way into the South Dublin Union, conducted by Séamus MacLysaght, a Local Government Board inspector.[11] By now the Union was spending £320,000 a year and employing four hundred people. It had also inherited a debt of £20,000 from the previous Board, which it had replaced in April 1920. The majority of the new Board were Sinn Féin members, but any reforming fervour seems to have ebbed fairly early. By 1923 MacLysaght found that only 25 of the 72 members attended meetings regularly and only 15 of these 'showed a devotion to duty worthy of mention.' Of the rest he said that 'for any practical purpose their concern for the poor and the ratepayers was negligible.' The auditor, Francis Barnard, had drawn attention to defects in the accounts procedures 'again and again ... and very little has been done to remedy these matters.' Contracts had been 'poorly handled,' and goods had been accepted into the stores that should have been 'immediately rejected.'

By 1924 outdoor relief far exceeded all other expenditure, and MacLysaght expressed concern that information supplied by relieving officers was unreliable in the few instances he had investigated. Despite the partial purge in early 1923 he was convinced that more discrepancies would be found if a systematic investigation was carried out. Irregularities had been uncovered in almost ninety cases, ranging in value from 4s to £82. 'Since Relieving Officers are directly concerned with about two-thirds [of] the entire Expenditure of the Union by way of relief inside and outside the house,' MacLysaght stated, 'every effort should be made to procure the services of first class officials.' He proposed that two superintendent inspectors of relieving officers be appointed, as 'the Guardians of themselves cannot show any appreciable results in this direction.'

He was even more scathing of the network of twenty-six medical dispensaries attached to the South Dublin Union, which were run by local general practitioners. 'With few exceptions I found the Dispensaries in a dirty condition and in many cases the houses are altogether unsuitable.' All but one were in need of basic repairs. Notice-boards were neglected, and none had fires lit in the surgeries, although it was October and patients often had to strip to be examined. Windows were, without exception, dirty, as were all the measure glasses, and there was a general absence of brushes and other cleaning utensils.

> In a City Dispensary a little girl picked up a piece of dirty paper from the floor to use as a cork for a bottle the compounder had handed her. Though this Compounder had been doing duty for two weeks he had not yet troubled to find out if a supply of Cork was available. The Porter, following my inquiries, immediately opened a drawer full of corks.

Medicines were 'thrown about in an untidy manner. Poison presses were not locked in many cases and large paper bags containing powders ... were generally left open and exposed and the powder scattered about.' There were depleted stocks of some essential medicines, and 'two midwives I had occasion to meet presented an untidy appearance.' MacLysaght had to point out to a doctor at the Clondalkin dispensary that patients' interests had to come before the experiments he was conducting on them. Attendance by porters at dispensaries was poor, and in one case a doctor did not turn up to meet MacLysaght.

One of the areas that caused him most concern was child welfare, particularly that of babies and young children boarded out, 'at nurse' or being adopted. High mortality rates among such children were causing mounting public concern.

> The evidence shows that an actual system of baby farming has been indulged in and this applies principally to the child that is adopted for an immediate monetary consideration. The homes where six babies died in two weeks is painfully illustrative of this. The unregistered Nursing Home is an equally grave danger and the practice of boarding children by Voluntary Societies in unhealthy and dirty areas should be immediately discontinued.
>
> I would suggest that the Voluntary Societies dealing with child welfare, together with those responsible for the management and control of the Union should hold a conference to see how best the interest of the child may be protected from all the evil influences with which it is already threatened. There would appear to be a serious need of legislation under which Nursing Homes, private or otherwise, would be compelled to register before accepting the care of any child. This is an essential step and severe penalties should attach to non-compliance therewith. Children are, in some cases, merely got 'rid' of, and the methods used are to evade criminal prosecution. This is first perpetrated by the mother in giving the child to unsuitable foster parents and secondly by the person who receives a lump sum for its supposed care and maintenance. It is a reflection on the whole administration and calls for immediate and decisive remedies.

The supervision of employees was described as 'defective', with no justification for higher rates paid to such groups as tradesmen than those prevailing in the city. No records were kept of materials taken from stores, no time sheets retained, no clock-in system maintained, and the clerk of works had no authority over employees. MacLysaght said that 'the value of a good officer cannot be overestimated,' but there was scant regard for the qualifications, character or previous experience of those appointed. There was not even a medical examination in many cases. In the two years under review he pointed out that 23,981 days had been lost in sickness leave by the four hundred employees—an average of sixty days each—and £7,305 paid for hiring substitutes. In most cases it was the same individuals who were continually absent,

> giving rise to a certain amount of suspicion. While appointments are made with an enthusiasm not experienced in any other … administration there is, if anything, a disinclination to order dismissals or suspensions … It would appear that every official is a law unto himself.

He noted that the great majority of the seventy-two guardians attended meetings only when there were appointments to be made. He was satisfied that the Master, Matron and doctors in the establishment had no real authority, and the Guardians' 'indifference' to complaints led to 'a spirit of insubordination'. He cited examples of a tradesman 'dragging' at his work, a wardmaster dismissed after serious allegations were proved against him only to be reappointed, and a cook retained although she could not cook. He also criticised the Matron for not spending enough time supervising the staff and the clerk of works for 'not being fully conversant with all matters pertaining to his position.' He found that the Master 'took the line of least resistance' with problems. Hygiene in the wards was poor, and far too many inmates were from outside Dublin. He concluded that

> the affairs of the Dublin Union are not managed, they are merely transacted. A quarter century of this process has led to the clogging up of the machinery which at any time may lead to decided hardship for the ratepayers. Coupled with the provision of defective services to the poor.[12]

The government dissolved the board on 21 November; the decision evoked no opposition. When the Board of Guardians met to discuss the findings of the report only eleven members turned up, and only eight supported a vote of confidence in the staff.

Number of cases dealt with by South Dublin Union, 1920–24

Sick adults	12,918
Sick children	1,763
Healthy adults	5,628
Healthy children	6,667
Aged and infirm	7,037
'Lunatics and idiots'	2,251
Mothers living with infant children	1,254
Total	37,518

Outdoor relief in South Dublin Union, 1920–23

	Payments	Cases	People	Average payment per person
September 1920	£52,869	5,279	10,408	£5.08
March 1921	£52,457	5,087	9,966	£5.26
September 1921	£55,206	5,132	9,967	£5.54
March 1922	£60,474	5,095	10,317	£5.86
September 1922	£58,515	5,346	10,890	£5.37
September 1923	£69,017	5,625	11,673	£5.91

Dublin Union: State of houses, percentage changes, 1920–24 (summer)

	July 1920	July 1921	1920–21	July 1922	1921–22	July 1923	1922–3	July 1924	1923–4	1920–24	1922–4
Sick adults	1,330	1,212	–8.8%	1,063	–12.3%	1,100	+3.5%	1,102	+0.2%	–17.1%	+3.7%
Sick children	168	191	+13.7%	174	–8.9%	162	–6.9%	169	+4.3%	–0.6%	–2.9%
Aged and infirm*	739	604	–18.3%	601	–0.5%	534	–11.1%	529	–0.9%	–28.4%	–12.0%
Healthy adults	557	554	–0.5%	518	–6.5%	444	–14.3%	404	–9.0%	–27.5%	–22.0%
Healthy children	655	617	–5.8	629	+1.9	611	–2.9	523	–14.4	–20.2	–16.7
Lunatics and idiots	137	353	+157.7	356	+0.8	353	–0.8	373	+5.7	+172.3	+.4.8
Mothers living with infant children	107	127	+18.7	122	–3.9	130	+6.6	109	–16.2	+.1.87	–10.7
Total	3,693	3,658	–0.9	3,463	–5.3	3,334	–3.7	3,209	–3.7	–13.1	–7.3

*First week in July each year.

Dublin Union: State of houses, percentage changes, 1920–24 (winter)

	Dec. 1920	Dec. 1921	Dec. 1922	Dec. 1923	Dec. 1924	Change
Sick adults	1,245	1,225	1,083	1,105	1,146	–6%
Sick children	192	184	162	153	129	–30%
Aged and infirm	639	611	577	539	420	–31%
Healthy adults	617	515	488	455	485	–6%
Healthy children	636	625	597	591	433	–31%
Lunatics and idiots	340	341	354	359	367	+8%
Mothers living with infant children	140	107	109	108	110	+3%
Total	3,809	3,608	3,370	3,310	3,090	–14%

*Last week in December each year.

Meanwhile the war in the city was sputtering to a close. Just after Christmas 1922 Denis McCullagh, a former president of the IRB and one of the architects of militant nationalism, had his music shop in Dawson Street destroyed by a land mine because of his support for the Free State. He was a refugee from Belfast, where his business making uilleann pipes had been a casualty of the sectarian conflict in the city.

The anti-Treaty IRA had also hit on a new tactic for dealing with Free State supporters. On 29 January 1923 Senator Oliver St John Gogarty was kidnapped. A prominent surgeon and man of letters, he was a long-standing Sinn Féin supporter, had attended Arthur Griffith in his last illness and had embalmed the body of Michael Collins. He was also a strong swimmer and he escaped his captors by jumping into the Liffey at Islandbridge. He moved his practice temporarily to London, although he regularly commuted to Dublin to attend the Senate. When Republicans offered to allow him to resume his medical practice if he resigned from the Senate he told the *Freeman's Journal* that 'he had no intention of betraying the Government. As to his practice, it would be continued where there was no party which included decoying and kidnapping medical men in its resistance to civilisation.'[13]

The latter stages of the Civil War do not seem to have been marked by the type of unofficial reprisals in Dublin that marred the reputation of the National Army in other parts of the country, although many of the abuses in the south-west were the work of the Dublin Guard. As in the War of Independence, a tighter rein on soldiers by proximity to headquarters, along with a profusion of potential witnesses on city streets, were probably inhibiting factors. Nor was the curfew weapon used. However, there were plenty of official reprisals, and at times Kevin O'Higgins showed himself willing to consider more ruthless measures even than GHQ. Having taken the plunge on 8 December by voting for the execution of the Four Courts commanders, who included one who had been best man at O'Higgins's wedding, Rory O'Connor, he went on to advocate dealing with 'middle class Irregular families' by putting them out of their homes and closing their businesses. Mulcahy and O'Hegarty argued that it would take too many soldiers to enforce such an order, and besides, 'our people have more property for destruction than the Irregulars have.'[14]

The presence of thousands of Republican prisoners in custody provided a readier means of retaliation. By the end of the year prisoners sentenced to death in some areas, such as Co. Kerry, were in effect hostages, who would be executed if there was a resurgence of anti-Treaty IRA activity.

Oliver St John Gogarty's athletic prowess may well have been a blessing in disguise for his captors. When Senator John Bagwell was kidnapped the following day and his house in Co. Tipperary burned to the ground a government proclamation announced that if he was not released within forty-eight hours 'punitive action' would be taken against the kidnappers' associates in custody. Bagwell was released. While the practice of executing prisoners as a reprisal for anti-Treaty IRA actions was barbaric, it was proving effective.

Twenty-five of the eighty-one executions carried out during the Civil War took place in Dublin.[15] Apart from the high level of anti-Treaty IRA activity there, it was easier to convene courts-martial in the city. While most public interest and criticism of the system concentrated on the courts-martial, which tried 140 cases, there was an ancillary committee system that processed 1,039. Far from automatically convicting prisoners, the committees acquitted 54 per cent of those coming before them. Only sixty-four prisoners were eventually executed, or 4½ per cent of the total number of cases processed. The committee system was introduced at battalion level at the end of 1922, and in January thirty-four men were shot, the highest total for any month; but it also took the focus off Dublin, where the bulk of executions had been taking place until then. In February 1922 there was only one execution after Liam Deasy, the deputy chief of staff, issued an appeal for a ceasefire while he was under sentence of death. When de Valera followed this with a suggestion that the concept of 'external association' might be explored again he received a public rebuke from Liam Lynch, demonstrating clearly where the power lay in the anti-Treaty ranks. It was not until Lynch's death in a skirmish with National Army troops on 10 April, followed by the capture of Austin Stack with a memorandum calling for an immediate end to armed resistance, that the prospect of a unilateral anti-Treaty IRA ceasefire began to emerge.[16]

The war lingered on in the south and west, but in Dublin it was all but over. The last Volunteer executed in the capital was James O'Rourke, on 13 March 1923, for taking part in an attack on Local Government offices set up in Jury's Hotel, at the corner of College Green and Anglesey Street. In the attack, which took place on 21 February, O'Rourke was seriously wounded in the head during an exchange of fire with the National Army. He was convicted of unauthorised possession of a revolver and three rounds of ammunition, rather than participating in the attack, probably because it was much easier to secure a conviction on possession, which also carried the death penalty. Two women were arrested nearby with arms and ammunition, but neither was charged.[17] During the entire conflict no woman was charged with a capital offence.

In all, well over a hundred men were sentenced to death and eighty-one executed through the committee and court-martial systems. By far the greatest number of cases involved unauthorised possession of firearms or bombs. Other convictions came a long way behind, with armed robberies exceeding participation in armed attacks on the National Army. In Dublin sixteen men were executed for unlawful possession of weapons or explosives, while another four were 'administrative reprisals' involving the execution of Richard Barrett, Joseph McKelvey, Liam Mellows and Rory O'Connor. The remaining five were National Army soldiers who had deserted to the IRA and joined the North Kildare Flying Column.

The whole column of twenty-two men had been captured, along with their weapons, in a two-hour battle at Grangewilliam House, near Leixlip. The success of the National Army operation was largely due to the rapid arrival of reinforcements from Dublin under Mick McDonnell, Frank Saurin and Frank Traynor, all veterans of Collins's intelligence campaign in the War of Independence. The senior ranks of the National Army were riddled with such men, including Liam Tobin, in charge of Army Intelligence, Tom Ennis, first commander of the 2nd Eastern Division in Dublin, and Paddy O'Daly, pursuing a ruthless counter-insurgency campaign in Co. Kerry. They brought the same brutal approach to their work as they did in the fight against the British on the streets of the capital. As Stephen Murphy said at the Red Cow inquests, such men considered themselves to be the real IRA and guardians of the Fenian tradition. With Collins dead, the only man most of them looked to for political direction was Joe McGrath.

Meanwhile the capture of the North Kildare column was regarded as a significant victory. Only one National Army soldier, a local man from Kilcock called Moran, was killed in the encounter. It was a sign of wilting Republican morale that members of the captured column, including eventually its commander, Patrick Mullany, signed the declaration not to take up arms again against the Free State. Nevertheless Mullany was sentenced to four years' imprisonment.

The National Army prisoners were in a very different category: they had not alone deserted but had gone over to the enemy. None of the men was from Dublin, nor do they appear to have participated in the War of Independence or held any strong political views before their fatal decision to change sides.[18] This did not deter Republican propagandists from looking into their souls and declaring:

> You saw that you were ranged in arms on the side of the Empire against the ancient and undefeated cause of Ireland. Then your eyes were opened. You saw that by treachery and falsehood you had been betrayed; and like honourable men you returned to your old allegiance ... For this you were executed. For this you died.[19]

Joe McGrath responded in kind. In a graveside oration for Divisional Commandant Austin McCurtin and another War of Independence veteran killed in an ambush in north Tipperary he said the 'leader of the Irregulars who, having shot the Officers with expanding bullets, cried "Mercy, we are all Irish", had once stood guard over him (McGrath) in Arbour Hill Barracks in 1920. Referring to McCurtin and his comrade, McGrath added that 'It was hard to think that men with such records— one of them had led a column for three years—should meet death at the hands of men who, when the fight with England was on, were not in the Bearna Baoghail.' He paid tribute to the 'extraordinary forbearance' of the soldiers and 'hoped it would continue.'[20]

There was no question of releasing prisoners simply because the new IRA chief of staff, Frank Aiken, suspended offensive operations on 30 April. De Valera, as

President of the Republican government, issued a proclamation on the same day outlining six principles on the basis of which his government was prepared to negotiate with the Free State government. The essential one was a recognition that

> the ultimate court of appeal for deciding disputed questions of national expediency and policy is the people of Ireland ... not because the decision is necessarily right or just or permanent, but because acceptance of this rule makes for peace, order and unity in national action, and is the democratic alternative to arbitrament by force.[21]

It was the first indication that some, at least, on the anti-Treaty side were willing to accept the democratic process.

———

A fortnight earlier Seán O'Casey's *Shadow of a Gunman* was performed for the first time at the Abbey Theatre. O'Casey had long parted company with the nationalist and labour ideologues of his youth, although not with his socialist ideals. In fact it was his adherence to these that led him to observe in a letter to Lennox Robinson that

> every thinker has a contempt—more or less—for organised opinion; but he may have a decided regard for organised action. I know Republican philosophers who have a supreme contempt for the organised opinion of the Free State, but who have, when bullets are flying about, a wholesome regard for that opinion in action.[22]

O'Casey had been struggling for years to have a script accepted by the Abbey, and his new offering came at a time when it caught the public mood of revulsion at the seemingly endless cycle of political violence, the desperate need of the theatre for government support and the government's need for a propaganda vehicle that transcended routine denunciations of the 'Irregulars'. *The Shadow of a Gunman* did far more than that: it lethally lampooned the other side. When Seumas Shields, one of the main characters, is reminded that he once 'believed in nothing but the gun' he replies, 'Ay, when there wasn't a gun in the country; I've a different opinion now when there's nothing but guns in the country.'

The play did not secure immediate government funds for the Abbey, although it would soon become the first 'national theatre' in the English-speaking world to do so, but it did pull in the audiences. It came just as the Irish dramatic renaissance was pronounced dead by St John Irvine in his weekly column in the *Observer*. The play has Shields and his fellow-lodger Donal Davoren posing as dangerous revolutionaries who persuade a young woman, Minnie Powell, to hide a bag of grenades when Auxiliaries raid the tenement house where they all live. She is subsequently shot trying to escape after the cache is found.

Almost alone of the Dublin theatres, the Abbey had defied an order by the anti-Treaty IRA to close in March 1923 as a mark of respect for the Republican prisoners who had been executed. Now a National Army guard was placed on the building as the new play was performed. One of its directors, W. B. Yeats, already had a bodyguard as a member of the new Free State Senate, and his fellow-director Lady Augusta Gregory arrived at the theatre to find a National Army soldier helping one of the actors into a Black and Tan uniform and showing him how to hold a revolver correctly. Precautions had to be taken not only to screen the audience as they arrived but to let them know that the reverberations of bombs and bullets were stage devices rather than the real thing outside on the street.

By 1926, when the last of O'Casey's revolutionary trilogy, *The Plough and the Stars,* was performed and the Abbey had finally secured its state subsidy, Republican activists had recovered enough confidence and organisation to disrupt performances, with Kevin Barry's sister Elgin, Dorothy Macardle and Hanna Sheehy Skeffington among protesters on behalf of the 'widows, sisters, daughters and supporters of the men who fought in the Easter Rising.' It did not stop the bookings breaking all the Abbey's records.

There could be no meeting of minds between O'Casey, the iconoclastic communist playwright, and Hanna Sheehy Skeffington, widow of a former comrade and herself a formidable campaigner for social change, although both believed the Irish Free State had betrayed the revolutionary aspirations of their generation. She denounced the 'supposedly national theatre' that 'helped to make Easter Week, and that now in its subsidised, sleek old age jeers at its former enthusiasms.' O'Casey declared that her 'tearful remembrance' of Easter Week and all it stood for

> make me sick. Some men can't even get a job. Mrs. Skeffington is certainly not dumb, but she appears both blind and deaf to all the things that are happening around her. Is the Ireland that is pouring to the picture houses, to the dance halls, to the football matches remembering with tear dimmed eyes all that Easter Week stands for?

She responded sharply that the Ireland O'Casey invoked is 'the Ireland that sits comfortably in the Abbey stalls and applauds Mr. O'Casey's play. It is the Ireland of the garrison, which sung twenty years ago "God Save the King".'[23]

————

On a more constructive note, Thomas Johnson, a TD for Co. Dublin and leader of the Labour Party in the third Dáil, had welcomed de Valera's 'six principles' for ending the Civil War. He expressed the 'hope that his statement would mean that spasmodic action by small bodies or parties would cease, and that if individuals persisted in committing outrages they would be punished with the approval of both sides in the present conflict.' He also called on the Free State government to respond 'by ordering a cessation of activities—raids and arrests—by the military and CID.'

De Valera's initiative came a few days before the first convention of Cumann na nGaedheal, the new party sponsored by the Free State government. Séamus Hughes was heavily involved in organising it and brought to the task much experience from his years in the ITGWU; but as a colleague, Frank O'Reilly, put it, 'we were a shell, not an organisation, and out of touch with what was going on.'[24] Having just won the war, and determined not to lose control of a conflict that had already cost the Free State £30 million in damage to the economy and another £17 million in prosecuting military operations, O'Higgins took the lead in telling members that if the government had been compelled to do unpopular things they were done in the national interest. His advice to the people was 'Obey your own laws.'

The press was barred from the proceedings in the Mansion House. The programme adopted was one that many anti-Treatyites could subscribe to: developing to its fullest 'the nation's heritage—political, cultural, and economic'; securing the unity of Ireland, fostering the Irish language, games, art 'and every element of national culture'; promoting agriculture and fisheries; stimulating and safeguarding 'suitable manufacturing industries'; providing for 'a national scheme of housing, urban and rural'; and substituting 'as far as possible for the unemployment dole national schemes of useful work, including arterial drainage, reafforestation, and the improvement of roads and waterways.' It proposed securing 'the fullest opportunities of educational advancement for every section of the community.' It even proposed further land distribution 'by utilising the depopulated grass lands,' in accordance with a 'broad national plan.' At a public rally in the Mansion House afterwards Cosgrave admitted that 'the government had not solved the housing question, and they had not solved the land question, but they were able to hand over to their successors a National Army of which the nation was justly proud.' (Applause.)[25]

De Valera approached two members of the Senate, Andrew Jameson and James Douglas, to open up an avenue for peace talks. Jameson, a leading figure among Southern unionists, had helped prepare the way for the Truce in 1921, while Douglas, a Quaker, had been involved in the White Cross. Both had become close associates of Collins, and, as we have seen, Douglas mediated in the bitter postal dispute of 1922. Nothing came of the exchanges, with Cosgrave describing de Valera's exposition of his six principles as 'a long and wordy document inviting debate where none is possible.'[26]

At least the exchange was followed by an end to the executions. The last three took place on 2 May 1923 in Tuam, Co. Galway. A group of Volunteers suspected of participating in local arson attacks had been stopped on 21 April in Carmody Street, Ennis, in the heart of de Valera's own constituency, by a National Army search party. In the ensuing gun battle Private Stephen Canty was shot dead. Four of the Volunteers were captured shortly afterwards. Two of them, Christopher Quinn and William Shaughnessy, had shot Canty, and the third man executed, Patrick O'Mahony, had previously been released after signing the declaration not to take up arms again. Shaughnessy had also signed the declaration as far back as September 1922 and had then resumed the fight. The fourth prisoner, John O'Leary, had his death sentence commuted to ten years' penal servitude.

On 24 May 1923, Aiken ordered a complete ceasefire and told units to dump their arms. De Valera issued his valedictory address of consolation to the 'Legion of the Rearguard' to accompany it. But the National Army sweeps continued unabated. Ernie O'Malley later recalled that

> areas never before visited, now swarmed with troops and round-ups took place in mountainy areas where troops had found it difficult or impossible to get through before. Our men who wished to avoid capture were hunted like foxes. They could not offer any resistance, and if they went home they were arrested and suffered very often at the hands of their captors. 'On the run' was now no misnomer. Some of them who were put amongst us said they had never travelled so fast, or so long before, with their 'caps in their fists' as they said.[27]

On 1 August the Public Safety (Emergency Powers) Act was passed, enabling the Free State government to detain internees indefinitely, and on 8 August the Garda Síochána (Temporary Provisions) Act was passed, incorporating the Civic Guard in the new legislation. On the next day, determined to appear active on social questions, the government passed the Land Act, which accelerated the transfer of unpurchased holdings from landlord to tenant though leaving the knotty problem of arrears on land annuities unresolved. Nevertheless, with the war won the government felt confident enough to call a general election and to replace the third Dáil, or 'Constituent Assembly', with the new state's first regularly constituted parliament.

On 16 August de Valera was arrested while addressing a public meeting in Ennis and so became one of the many Republican prisoners running for election. The result boosted Republican morale. The number of seats had been increased from 128 in June 1922 to 153, yet the new Cumann na nGaedheal party of the outgoing government managed only to increase its representation from 58 seats to 63, while the Republican representation increased from 36 to 44. Eighteen of these were won by prisoners, including Ernie O'Malley, who was elected in north Co. Dublin. By contrast, the Labour Party lost every seat in Dublin city and county except that of its leader, Tom Johnson.

The labour movement was embroiled in its own civil war between Jim Larkin, who had recently returned from a nine-year sojourn in America, and the men he had left in charge of the ITGWU, now the country's largest union. The Labour vote halved, but the vagaries of proportional representation in large constituencies meant that the number of Labour deputies only fell from 17 to 14. This still left it with one seat less than the Farmers. It was ironic that the party that had done most in the third Dáil to oppose the violation of civil liberties and to defend Republican prisoners was now in a weaker position than ever before to defend workers' interests as social and economic issues began to receive more attention.[28]

———

As early as June 1923 the Free State government began releasing prisoners, and the numbers gradually fell. In July, Moira Connolly, a daughter of the 1916 Labour martyr James Connolly, took a case of *habeas corpus* to the Court of Appeal on behalf of her sister, Nora Connolly O'Brien, who was interned in the North Dublin Union. The case was brought on the grounds that internment was no longer necessary, because the National Army had won the Civil War. Ironically, the contents of a captured document from the new anti-Treaty IRA chief of staff, Frank Aiken, accepting that the war was over and expressing the opinion that 'if we have to fight another war with the Staters, it will have to be short and sweet,' helped clinch the judges' decision to grant Connolly her writ of *habeas corpus,* along with an application for another prisoner, Éamonn Donnelly.

The court granted the applications on 1 August. That night the government rushed a new Public Safety (Emergency Powers) Act through the Dáil, restoring its right to suspend *habeas corpus,* but it also set up new procedures to begin releasing those they considered the least dangerous prisoners. At first pressure was applied by demanding that prisoners sign the declaration renouncing armed resistance to the state, prison discipline was tightened, privileges were withdrawn and ordinary prisoners were introduced to the wings where political prisoners were held. Most prisoners still refused to sign, and while large-scale releases began regardless from August, these were not happening quickly enough to defuse the rising anger among men in the prisons and internment camps at the fact that they were still detained after the courts had agreed with Frank Aiken that the war was over.[29]

In October a mass hunger strike began in Mountjoy Prison, with 424 men participating. Ten of them, including Ernie O'Malley, were now TDs; but, as O'Malley realised, 'it would have been better to have selected a number of really determined men, who might have been more fitted for such an ordeal than the heterogeneous complement of the four wings.'[30] As we have seen (chapter 7), more than fifty women prisoners joined the hunger strike but, as with the men, large numbers could not stay the course after the original enthusiasm faded. The prospect of release for those willing to come off the strike also removed the *raison d'être* of the protest.

On 20 November 1923 Denis Barry died in Newbridge camp, and two days later Andrew Sullivan died in Mountjoy after fasting for forty days. The strike was called off, and by the end of the year there were 1,852 prisoners left, compared with 11,840 in July. By May 1924 there were only 618, and these included men who had been sentenced to death and others who were under investigation by the Garda Síochána for offences not linked to the Civil War.[31]

———

Jim Larkin was the stormy petrel of the Irish labour movement. He was known as the 'Impossibilist', even by many of his supporters, because 'it was impossible to do anything with him and impossible to do anything without him.' He had built the Irish Transport and General Workers' Union almost single-handedly in its formative period and dragged the old craft-based trade union movement, with its guild mentality, into the twentieth century. He had survived the employers' offensive in the great Dublin Lockout of 1913, only to depart on a fund-raising tour of America in October 1914 and disappear from the Irish scene as suddenly as he had burst upon it seven years earlier.

His career was equally tempestuous in America, and in May 1920 he was sentenced to five to ten years' imprisonment for 'criminal anarchy'. Emmet Larkin described his speech in his own defence as 'an eclectic stew of Christianity, socialism, syndicalism, communism and Irish nationalism.'[32] A celebrity in America, he was transferred to Clinton Prison in Dannemora, New York, a remote prison near the Canadian border, but the move rebounded on his captors, who had to transfer him back to Sing Sing Prison in New York to stem public outrage. John Devoy and Harry Boland were among those who campaigned for his release, as did Charlie Chaplin, who sent presents to Larkin's estranged wife, Elizabeth, and children in Dublin.

A member of the newly formed Communist International, Larkin was elected in February 1922 to the Moscow Soviet by a union composed mostly of tailors who had returned to Russia from America after the revolution. He declined an invitation to be nominated for the Labour Party in North Co. Dublin in the 1922 election, intended to publicise his continued incarceration. Nevertheless the international campaign for his release finally succeeded in January 1923 when he was pardoned by the Governor of New York State, Al Smith. The British government had lobbied Smith to prevent Larkin's release, fearing he would throw his support behind the anti-Treaty forces when he returned to Ireland. While still in prison Larkin had issued a statement condemning the Treaty as a 'plan for the nation's destruction,' and some of his speeches on his release continued in this vein,[33] but his attitude had certainly changed by the time he arrived in Dún Laoghaire at 5 p.m. on 30 April, the day the IRA called an end to offensive operations. This may well have been the result of his discussions *en route* with leading members of the Communist Party of Great Britain in London. He was searched as he disembarked and characteristically growled, 'I haven't got a gun—yet, anyhow.' Outside Liberty Hall that evening he enjoined a crowd of four thousand to remember that 'unity is strength,' only to immediately condemn the 'lack of faith and limitation of vision' of some of those he had left behind to build the labour movement.

But neither the British nor the Free State government need have worried about which side Larkin would take in the Civil War. 'The time has arrived when peace should be their motto, and peace should be their work,' he said. He concluded with a warning that 'any section that continued the strife would be remembered as traitors to the nation and renegades to their God.'[34]

Some attacks continued, despite Aiken's order to cease offensive operations. Dundrum Barracks was fired upon the following weekend, as well as the home of Senator Martin Fitzgerald. The attackers in the senator's case were described as three women, who escaped in a car.[35] On 6 May the ITGWU celebrated 'Labour Day', with music, a hurling match and other games at Croydon Park, its recreational centre in Fairview. Larkin told the audience: 'It was easy to preach hate and destruction … Two armies were contending for power in the nation but he was speaking to the greatest army of all of them, and it was the working classes who were going to bring peace.' He continued in the same vein at the Connolly Commemoration in the Theatre Royal that evening.

> Everybody was sitting down like cowards afraid to speak. People thought it was courageous to take a gun or a mine and use it, but it required more courage to speak the truth … They had assassination by word and by deed but the worst form of it was moral assassination. They would have to get rid of this curse which was bringing their country into contempt of the world.

He then asked all those in the audience 'who desired peace' to rise. All rose. When they sat down Larkin asked 'all who believe in a continuance of this fratricidal strife to rise.' No-one stirred; but a voice from the dress circle cried, 'We are for peace with honour,' to loud cheers. 'There can never be dishonour in peace,' Larkin responded.[36]

He continued his crusade as he toured the ITGWU branches, expanding on the theme of 'no dishonour in peace' by arguing that if Connolly and Pearse and Clarke and the others who formed the galaxy of Irish heroes of 1916 were big enough to give up their arms for a time and give them up in the face of certain death, I say to you ... that there can be no dishonour in giving up arms.[37]

Yet within a few weeks he would have ignited his own war to regain control of the union he had founded. He had difficulty adjusting to a situation where the union, which had barely clung to its predominantly Dublin base in the aftermath of the 1913 Lockout, was now established throughout the country, with a membership and staff that did not know him. It would have been difficult for anyone, let alone a man within whom the 'impossibilist' element was almost eternally uppermost.

At first things went well. The ITGWU was now the largest civil society organisation in many towns, and many of his visits had not alone union members but trades councils, mayors, councillors and the general public flock to greet the returning hero. But Larkin discovered that his closest ally in the union, P. T. Daly, had been marginalised by William O'Brien, a loyal if not uncritical ally in the Dublin Lockout of 1913. The young O'Brien had not even been in the ITGWU but represented tailors on the Dublin Trades Council. Now he was general treasurer of the ITGWU, a member of the third Dáil and a Dublin city alderman. He had been brought in by the president of the union, Tom Foran, to help reorganise it in the chaos that followed the 1916 Rising, and the duo had virtually rebuilt it. The membership of between 3,500 and 5,000 in 1916 had reached a peak of 120,000 in 1921 and was still 100,000-strong in 1923. Despite the recession, the union comprised half the membership of the ILP&TUC, of which O'Brien was also treasurer.[38] They were understandably proud of their achievements and instinctively feared the erratic, adventurist streak in their returned general secretary.

It was clear from Larkin's cables concerning union business before his return that he intended resuming his autocratic style of leadership. In particular he had demanded £5,000 with which to purchase a ship that he would bring back from America with him, because he had a 'monopoly contract' with a 'certain Eastern Government' to fulfil, and it would be useful for other, ill-defined purposes. The government concerned was that of the Soviet Union, which had lost much of its romantic revolutionary allure for Irish labour, and the demand gave the new leadership a perfect pretext for calling a special delegate conference and changing the union rules so that, in Foran's words, 'one man could not be a law to himself.'

The conference was held in Dublin, with almost indecent haste, on 24 and 25 April 1923. The change in the rules was certainly needed if they were to control Larkin, who had never surrendered his position as general secretary. O'Brien told the seventy-five delegates that they 'had not sufficient time to study the draft new Rules in detail,' but he explained the general thrust of them, which was that in future the delegate conference would be the supreme governing body of the union. There would be a seven-member Executive Council, together with the general officers, to run the union's affairs between conferences. Larkin's powers were restricted and, crucially, all important decisions would have to be taken collectively.

The new rules were adopted almost unanimously, demonstrating the power of the O'Brien-Foran axis. Delegates were asked to consult their branches, and the conference was reconvened for 14 May.[39] It proved to be an anti-climax: anticipated rows about the ship, the purchase of Liberty Hall, the treatment of Daly and the new constitution did not occur. When Larkin suggested that a proposal in the new rules to appoint a political secretary be redrafted to ensure that the person was subordinate to the Executive Council, O'Brien agreed immediately that it could be referred back to a future delegate conference. Larkin concluded his address by telling delegates:

> Don't submit your minds to any one man. Think these problems out yourselves. A leader who can lead you out of the wilderness can lead you back again. If there is a thinking, intelligent movement, no leader can mislead you.[40]

He was about to put his own union to the test.

Larkin continued his triumphal tour of the branches, breathing new inspiration into the members who flocked to hear him. On Sunday 3 June it was the turn of Dublin No. 1 Branch, which, in Foran's words, was the 'cradle of the Union' and 'the heart of the Union,' whose branch committee had served as the ITGWU executive in its early days.

Larkin used the occasion to turn on O'Brien. Emmet Larkin[41] concludes that his tour of the branches had convinced Larkin that the real purpose of the change of rules was not to increase democracy within the union but to consolidate the power and influence of O'Brien, at his expense. He told members of the branch that he had discovered that many of the delegates at the special conference had not been elected by members, and he asked them if they had elected their own delegates, to which there were cries of 'No.' When he asked one of the delegates who elected him, the delegate replied, 'The branch committee.' Larkin declared: 'Tammany Hall never had a machine like this. All down to one man.' He singled out O'Brien as the machiavellian figure behind this takeover of the union, but Foran warned him that they might have 'come to a parting of the ways.'[42]

Larkin summoned a meeting of the Executive Council to inform it that the new rules were invalid and should not be registered, because they had not been introduced in accordance with the old constitution. The executive held its nerve and insisted it would hold by them. The only concession it was willing to consider was putting the questions raised by Larkin to the general membership. Instead Larkin decided to revert to the old rules and the old way of doing things by appealing to the rank and file, particularly in Dublin, where many members remembered the glory days of the union. He now used these meetings to tell members that he had uncovered documents proving the misuse of funds and secured the suspension of O'Brien, Foran and their allies while they 'looked on helplessly, no match for the demagogue in full flight.'[43]

On 11 June, Larkin seized Liberty Hall and the new ITGWU offices in Parnell Square. The executive responded by resorting to the courts and secured an interim injunction against him. He surrendered both premises; but the breach was now irreparable. Not only was the country's largest union split but the fissures inevitably spread throughout the whole movement. Anyone who took the side of the ITGWU executive incurred Larkin's wrath, including Thomas Johnson, secretary of the ILP&TUC and leader of the Labour Party in the Dáil.

Having revived the *Irish Worker,* Larkin denounced Johnson as 'the King of the Labour Party' and an 'English anti-Irishman,' although the two men had in fact been born within a few streets of each other in Liverpool. The *Voice of Labour* would eventually respond with cartoons ridiculing Larkin and his Liverpool accent. Reminding readers of Larkin's beginnings as a British union organiser, a cartoon history depicted 'Captain Larkin' saying, 'Ere I am Captain of a real h-Irish ship at last. It's much more comfortable than working as Third Mate on a h-English ship.'[44]

Denied access to union premises, Larkin unsuccessfully sought an injunction on the eve of the ILP&TUC conference in August to prevent the executive from using union funds to attend. His supporters held a mass picket outside the Mansion House, where it was taking place. The *Irish Times* reported that 'a series of the most discreditable scenes' occurred from 11 a.m. when a picket blocked the entrances.

> Newspaper representatives and camera men were treated with indignity and violence. One of the latter had his camera injured by a kick and was thankful that he escaped personal injury. A woman attempted to stab a reporter with a hat pin as he ascended the steps leading to the hall door and he was opportunely saved from mob violence by the Lord Mayor's lady secretary. Any man who, even unsuspectingly, attempted to approach the garden door was immediately surrounded by a mob of infuriated women, young and old, who pelted and scratched like tigresses and screamed like lunatics.

One girl 'no more than eighteen' broke her umbrella over the head of a delegate but 'found consolation in the fact that she could buy a new umbrella but "he could not buy a new head".'[45]

It was more than two hours before business could begin. Welcoming the delegates, the president of the ILP&TUC, Luke Duffy of the Irish Union of Distributive Workers and Clerks, said that Larkin had declared there would be no conference and had 'attempted to use the machinery of the law to prevent

Congress being held, and having failed in that he now invoked the aid of the rabble.' Nevertheless Larkin allowed his name to go forward as chairman; Duffy defeated him overwhelmingly, by 147 votes to 27.[46]

Meanwhile the divisions within the labour movement had already begun to exact a price from workers and from the city in general. The employers' offensive to cut pay and conditions, begun in 1921 with the engineering trades, had continued unabated, and in July 1923 dockers were told they would have to accept another cut of 2s a day. Larkin immediately took charge of the situation. The dockers had been the foundation on which he had built the ITGWU, and the union now found itself financing a dispute that Larkin was running. With an election looming, the Free State government did not want a confrontation with the legendary union leader. Cosgrave set up an inquiry, which asked the employers to defer the cuts and seek no more than 1s a day reduction. But the employers scented blood, and demands for pay cuts spread to other areas. Soon 'more than 8,000 men and 90 women were on strike for "Death or Liberty," but the docks, ships, factories and shops were still working.'[47] Even employers who wanted a settlement found the split in the ITGWU a problem. As one senior manager confided to the board of the GSWR,

> one of the difficulties is that there is no strike leader to rely upon or negotiate with owing to Foran and Larkin being at loggerheads. The Shipowners realise that they are fighting an economical battle for every employer in the Free State including the Railways, and they ask the Railways not to do anything that would assist outsiders or retard them in securing what they are out for.[48]

The employers eventually agreed to accept the government's compromise proposal of a reduction of 1s a week. On 26 October the ITGWU executive declared the dispute over and stopped strike pay. Sixty per cent of the dockers voted to stay out, but resistance collapsed once strike pay ended. Other groups, including carters, coal-heavers and seamen, accepted the cuts as well. Larkin castigated his opponents for selling out the strikers, but he had no alternative strategy to offer. Once again workers found that militancy could not defy economic gravity indefinitely, and pay cuts in the Free State simply replicated those already imposed in Britain.

The price of militancy could be high. Far from capitulating supinely, as Larkin alleged, the ITGWU had financed disputes around the country, but to no avail. As we have seen (chapter 7), in 1923, for the first time, ITGWU funds paid out in strike pay exceeded income from all sources. While income came to £84,122, dispute benefit cost £128,724. With each defeat, membership fell and unemployment rose. Membership of the ITGWU would almost halve, to 51,000, by 1925 and fall to 14,600 by 1930.[49]

In the meantime the civil war in the ITGWU had been won by the Executive Council. On 12 February 1924 Larkin's case came before the Master of the Rolls.

Not for the first time, he represented himself and was 'vituperative, petty and unfair to witnesses,' even to Tom Foran, who had helped him found the union and whom he now accused of ill-treating his family while he was in America. In fact the ITGWU had paid Elizabeth Larkin more than £2,000 towards her upkeep and that of her sons.

On 20 February 1924 the court found against Larkin, and on 14 March he was expelled from the union he had founded. He would go on in 1925 to lead the Workers' Union of Ireland and take two-thirds of the Dublin membership with him but only twenty of the three hundred provincial branches.[50] The ITGWU and WUI would in time become the country's largest and second-largest unions, respectively, and in 1990 they would reunite as SIPTU. But there is no denying that the split seriously weakened the trade union movement in Dublin for more than two generations.

Yet the split was inevitable. The precocious child that was the Dublin labour movement had been robbed of any chance of developing maturely with the advent of the First World War and all that flowed from it. O'Brien was essentially a bureaucrat with conservative instincts who, for all his left-wing rhetoric, saw the movement's future development in close alignment with such figures as Collins and McGrath, then later with de Valera and Lemass, while Larkin never lost his youthful vision of unions as a weapon for the revolutionary transformation of society. Both men were also haunted by the legacy of James Connolly. Larkin resented the fact that his place in the pantheon of Irish radicalism would always be overshadowed by his martyred subordinate, and yet he never made any attempt to lay out his own ideas in an ordered way that might have provided a comparable intellectual legacy. Instead he left a personal legacy of incorruptible outrage at social injustice and economic exploitation.

O'Brien had a very different relationship to Connolly. He was in practice his literary executor. It was almost as if he sought to compensate for the constant compromises with the dominant conservative forces in Irish society that marked his own career by promoting the ideas of the lost revolutionary leader as the next-best thing to implementing them. Larkin once described O'Brien, cruelly but not inaccurately, as living 'in the ghostly mantle of a man who is now dead in the flesh.'[51]

Even if Irish workers had been united, a reckoning after the halcyon years from 1917 to 1920 was inevitable. The arbitration system that the British government introduced during the war had meant *de facto* union recognition for many groups of workers, such as women and agricultural labourers. It gave the trade unions a strength and their members a confidence they never felt before. This carried them through the early stages of the recession in 1920 and 1921. But the lack of a strong political movement to offset the power of the employers, and the underdeveloped nature of the economy, meant that when British state controls were withdrawn that confidence proved misplaced.

Workers themselves had unrealistic expectations of what was achievable. For instance, in 1920 Port and Docks Board labourers were earning £3 10s a week for a 47-hour basic week, plus a residual 'war bonus' of 31s a week, a total of £5 1s, compared with 18s a week in January 1914.[52] Despite the militant image of the ITGWU, it was a major engineering strike in 1917 that secured the greatest pay increases for the work force in the war years; and the first significant indicator that the good times were over came with the protracted engineering strike that ended in October 1921. Craft workers had to accept a cut in pay of 6s a week, which had already been accepted by their colleagues in England six months earlier. Labourers' rates followed suit. By 1922 labourers had also lost their 'war bonus' and had taken a further reduction of 4s in basic pay. By 1924 the rate was down to £2 16s 3d. Meanwhile inflation, having soared by as much as 240 per cent in the war years, was back to 1913 levels, so Port and Docks labourers remained, in relative terms, in possession of significant pay rises and reductions over the decade.[53]

The price of militancy could also prove excessive. Employees of Dublin Port and Docks Board were protected by the fact that it was a statutory body; and some private firms, such as those in the building industry, were also protected from international competition to some extent. But this was not the case for all workers. The Dublin Dockyard Company, which had been established in 1901 and had given good employment to engineering workers for a generation—many of them members of the Irish Citizen Army and Irish Volunteers—had secured industrial peace by agreeing to pay 'Clydeside' rates. Using the huge Scottish shipyards as a comparator was no problem while wages were rising in the war years, but shipbuilding was particularly hard hit when the war ended. Pay cuts in line with the fall in Clydeside rates were accepted in 1921, but when the company proposed phasing out the war bonus, worth 26s 6d, in two instalments in 1922 there was a strike.

A conference was organised at the Ministry of Labour. The company said it could not afford to pay so much over the rates of its competitors in Britain, or Belfast for that matter, while the unions argued that their rates were being reduced far more than comparable rates in the Port and Docks Board, Dublin Corporation and the building trades. The men resumed work when the pay cuts were withdrawn pending further negotiations, but some incidents of industrial sabotage threatened further trouble ahead.

By now market conditions were changing so rapidly that the yard saw its core business of maintaining and repairing vessels going elsewhere. The owners sought a subsidy from the government, arguing the strategic importance of the industry to an island economy; but the Civil War was raging and the Cabinet had other priorities. Having failed to obtain state aid, the company proposed reintroducing the pay cuts but phased in over three stages instead of two. The strike resumed in August 1922. Joe McGrath tried to secure a wage subsidy from the Ministry of Finance, without success, and the company went into voluntary liquidation in 1923. The yard was bought by the British engineering giant Vickers for £63,000, which was the price it put on the scrap metal value of the facility alone. There was a 4,000-ton vessel almost completed, and the yard was considered more useful than some of the large British yards for coping with the post-war demand for smaller vessels. The directors and shareholders were delighted at the price of £3 for every £1 share.

The unions continued to black the yard when it reopened. The new company secretary, Frank Strickland, said that, 'in consequence, only blacklegs or non-union men could be employed, but there was agreement with black squads, namely platers, caulkers, riveters etc.' Even employing these men on lower rates failed to revive its fortunes. 'Under these adverse conditions we struggled along from 1925 to 1938, only to prove the old company correct—that there was no future [in the yard].' Nevertheless it carried out an 'extensive amount of repair work,' built '55 vessels including several barges,' and 'fabricated 3,000 to 4,000 tons of structural steelwork a year.' Strickland conceded that Vickers had paid far too much for the facility; the former owners had 'sold out when the going was good.'[54]

'THE NCOS BELIEVED THAT THE OFFICERS WERE AFRAID THEY WOULD LOSE THEIR WELL-PAID POSITIONS IN THE EVENT OF FAILURE'

The creation of the Irish Free State and the restoration of Dublin to its traditional role as a capital city should have heralded a new beginning for the city council. Instead 'the oldest political structure in Ireland', created by a charter of King John in 1192, was abolished.[1]

The government inquiry into the South Dublin Union inevitably reflected badly on the city council, as most of the Board of Guardians were members, former members or associates of members. The government now sought to portray the Corporation as the South Dublin Union writ large. Corruption and inefficiency had always been a problem in City Hall and, while the new administration dominated by Sinn Féin and Republican Labour had begun well, old practices continued. Alderman William O'Brien, for instance, leader of the Republican Labour group, who had previously worked as a tailor in the North Dublin Union, would issue pension cheques to himself as a member of the Estates and Finance Committee.[2] Many appointments and promotions were still decided by councillors. Far more employees were in prison than during the War of Independence, including senior anti-Treaty officers at the national level, such as Rory O'Connor, employed as an engineer, and senior commanders in the city, such as Joseph O'Connor and Harry Colley, both rate-collectors, and Noel Lemass, a company commander who worked as a fitter in the Stanley Street workshop.

Many of these men continued to be paid while on the run; indeed those most conscientious in carrying out their duties were most at risk of being apprehended, as Joseph O'Connor found when he was arrested while signing the attendance book in the City Rates Office at the end of October 1922. He had just authorised the attack on Oriel House that led to the first official executions of the Civil War. These were followed by the death of Rory O'Connor and his comrades in an 'administrative reprisal' a month later. Harry Colley was also arrested but survived internment and hunger strike in the Civil War to become a Fianna Fáil TD and senator. Noel Lemass escaped from custody and fled to England; he returned after the Civil War only for his body to be discovered in the Dublin Mountains, so badly mutilated that he had to be identified by his clothing. O'Connor's targets, the CID men in Oriel House, were the main suspects in Lemass's death.

By 1923 more than a hundred Corporation employees were imprisoned, and the Lord Mayor, Laurence O'Neill, facilitated the families of internees in addressing the city council. So did his deputy, another independent TD, Alfie Byrne.

Prisoners continued to be a major issue. On 24 September 1923 a motion was passed by the council calling for the release of all political prisoners; it condemned Mulcahy's refusal to allow visits, 'a right accorded to them during the Black and Tan regime.' On 5 November anti-Treaty councillors moved 'the release of Mr de Valera and all imprisoned or interned Republican deputies as the first step to national unity, peace and prosperity.'[3] When this too was rejected by the government the council sought the right of appeal to the Dáil, as it had been able to appeal Dublin Castle decisions to the House of Lords before independence; but this was not provided for in the Constitution of the Irish Free State.

The Corporation was finding that more national freedom could mean less domestic liberty. Meanwhile its criticism of the treatment of men and women in custody embarrassed the government and provided the anti-Treaty IRA and Sinn Féin with a valuable political asset when their own hunted activists could do little.

Another problem for a cash-strapped government was the soaring cost of running the city. As we have seen (chapter 6), the payroll alone had increased by 62 per cent since 1919 and by 1923 stood at £287,117, or a quarter of the budget. A combination of strong unions, a large Labour Party representation on the city council and several sympathetic Sinn Féin members, as well as populist independents such as O'Neill and Byrne, had defeated all efforts to cut pay rates while those of workers in other employments, such as the docks, transport and engineering, were falling rapidly.

Another means of ushering in change would have been to call local elections, but the government was becoming increasingly distrustful of the electorate. The constantly deferred local elections meant that the city council had been in office continuously since 1920. During that time several members had died and others, particularly government supporters, such as Seán McGarry, Michael Staines and Jennie Wyse Power, were increasingly involved in other duties. Pressure for suspending the council was mounting from quarters as varied as the Local

Government Board, the Greater Dublin Movement and senior Corporation managers, just as the Board of Guardians had been dissolved earlier.[4]

The clash over prisoners was especially unfortunate in its timing and played into the hands of the abolitionists' lobby, as Dublin urgently needed central government support if it was to overcome the many obstacles to transforming it into a modern capital city. The biggest problem it faced was the lack of adequate housing. In 1914 it was estimated that the city would need 14,000 new dwellings to clear the worst slums; by 1916, with the closure of many tenement houses as unfit and the destruction wrought by the 1916 Rising, the figure had risen to 16,500, and by 1920 it stood at 20,000. Progress had been hampered by lack of finance, wartime shortages of building materials and industrial and political unrest. What funds had flowed into the city from Britain after the Rising were gobbled up by William Martin Murphy and his business allies as compensation for their own premises destroyed in the fighting. By 1921 a mere 769 rooms had been provided in houses and flats, mostly consisting of one-room or two-room dwellings.[5]

The vision of the future on display in the new suburban 'cottage estate' pioneered by the Irish Sailors' and Soldiers' Land Trust in Killester provided a tantalisingly unattainable vision that had been held out ever since the proposals put forward by Lord Aberdeen's town planning competition in 1914.[6] When Alfie Byrne put his Dáil question to the Minister for Local Government, Ernest Blythe, in May 1923 about the urgent need for slum clearance (see chapter 8) it was a challenge but also a reminder of the incorrigible failure of local government in the city and the need to do something about it. Even with sufficient funds, the city's narrow limits made possible nothing but high-density flats to replace the tenement houses.

The extension of the city northwards into the county to acquire more land and southwards into the Pembroke and Rathmines townships to acquire more ratepayers was essential; but could the city fathers be trusted? Blythe was an abolitionist, and so was his successor, James Burke, when the former moved on to the Department of Finance, and to infamy as the man who cut the old-age pension. Of course the city council condemned the cut in the pensions as part of its continuing campaign of defiance against the government.[7]

If anything, Burke was an even more enthusiastic abolitionist than Blythe. The only Tipperary TD to vote for the Treaty, he had helped Cosgrave and O'Higgins make the Dáil Éireann government's alternative Ministry of Local Government a reality.[8] Over the next four years he would replace nineteen local authorities with full-time managers or 'commissioners'; but Dublin was his biggest trophy.

It was an indication of how different the view was from inside Government Buildings that the three men most involved in using local authorities to create a dual-power structure between 1919 and 1921 now dismantled so much of it. It was also a sign of how far local government had slipped down the agenda that

Burke was not a member of the Executive Council (cabinet). He was also given responsibility for public health, which suggests that it too was not a political priority in the wake of the Civil War.

It was a portent of what was to come when the government sent no representative or condolences to the funeral of Laurence O'Neill's wife on 18 January 1924 in Portmarnock. Messages of condolence poured in from others, including Cardinal Logue, Count Plunkett and P. J. Ruttledge, who was acting President of the Irish Republic while de Valera was in prison, trade union leaders such as William O'Brien and even former representatives of the British government, such as Andy Cope, and the former British army commanders Bryan Mahon and Neville Macready.[9] William O'Brien's letter encapsulated the common experience of those who encountered O'Neill in times of adversity when he wrote that the ITGWU

> has always felt itself under a deep obligation to your Lordship since the days when it had very, very few friends outside its own ranks for the stand which you then took when the employers, with the help of the Government of the day, sought to crush the union and outlaw its members.[10]

W. T. Cosgrave, a former city councillor, Kevin O'Higgins and Richard Mulcahy had all availed of O'Neill's hospitality in hosting Dáil courts, facilitating meetings of Sinn Féin and Dáil Éireann and providing shelter for those on the run. Now O'Neill was part of the problem rather than the solution.

––––

On 20 February 1924 Burke wrote to the Town Clerk informing him that an inquiry into 'serious complaints' over the administration of the Corporation was to be undertaken under section 12 of the Local Government (Temporary Provisions) Act (1923). It did not specify the nature of the complaints or identify the complainants. The Evening Herald welcomed the news, alleging that 'jobbery and corruption' were 'rampant in City Hall.' Dublin citizens had 'been disgusted at the action of this gang in refusing to accept the Government's grant of £10,000 for the benefit mainly of ex-soldiers of the National Army.' In fact the grant would only have temporarily inflated the number of employees before the council either laid them off or increased the burden on the ratepayer. But the city fathers were now routinely depicted in the press as 'corrupt and unscrupulous brutes [which] is the only description we can apply to a large proportion of members of the Corporation.'[11] O'Neill defended the record of the Corporation vigorously at a Council meeting on the same day that Burke's fatal letter arrived, pointedly reminding the government of the time when the men and women of this Council faced prison, and even assassination, and when they loyally stood behind President Cosgrave, then a member of the Corporation and Minister of Local Government. It is my belief that if this Corporation faltered then, and did not take up a stand in giving a lead to the country, it is questionable whether you would have a Free State Government in power today.[12]

The plight of all veterans of the recent conflicts, and the unemployed generally, was aired at a meeting of the Dublin Trades Council at the very time that O'Neill was defending the council's record in the Mansion House. The president of the Trades Council, Edward Tucker, declared that 'all the unemployed were in the same boat, and there should be no distinction between ex-Army men and civilians.' Six hundred men were signing on at the local labour exchange who had paid insurance contributions but had not been paid in weeks. 'What they really want is work, and not charity,' James Larkin told the Trades Council, and, in one of his more constructive moods, he suggested that the unions set up their own unemployment fund and seek a matching moiety from the government.

Cosgrave had other ideas for solving both the housing and the unemployment problem. At a meeting of the Rotary Club in Clery's newly opened restaurant in O'Connell Street he reminded the audience that he had always been interested in slum clearance and housing policy as a means of urban renewal for the city. But he went on to demonstrate that he remained Ireland's most conservative revolutionary. He acknowledged that 'people required better houses and more space than their fathers were content with. But the difficulty in … supplying the need was the high cost of building and the high rate of interest, and the unwillingness of many tenants to pay suitable rates.' He dismissed previous experiments at providing local authority housing as 'impracticable'; instead he suggested that the way forward was encouraging private house-building. Everyone had a role to play,

the Government and municipalities by way of grants, architects by economic design and construction, and by the use of suggestive plans; builders by limiting profits on sale and in construction, workers by increased output, and tenants by payment of suitable rents.

But he made it clear that 'it was not intended that local authorities should undertake building.' In a nod to the Labour Party and the 'sympathetic hearing' it had given the government's Housing Bill in the Dáil he said that a 'final opportunity' might be afforded to local authorities to build houses 'where no private individuals … undertake the business,' but the 'Government had come definitely to the conclusion that there was only one real method of making this service a success and that was by giving private enterprise full and complete freedom.' The government would therefore contribute £100 towards the cost of a standard £500 house.[13]

Ironically, the controversy over the tenant-purchase scheme at Fairbrother's Fields, off the South Circular Road, now provided ammunition for the government in establishing an inquiry into the Corporation's general affairs. Yet so determined was it to promote home ownership that it remained committed to tenant purchase as the solution to the city's housing problem. Schemes begun after 1924 in Fairview and Inchicore were for tenant purchase. Even when flat complexes were being built, such as Ormond Market, Boyne Street and Keogh Square, the majority were on the tenant-purchase model.[14] It was only when de Valera's new party, Fianna Fáil, came to power in 1932 that the unavoidable necessity of housing the working poor was finally addressed; but Cosgrave had laid down a template for the future of state housing policy that would endure well into the next century.

———

The inquiry began on 12 March and was chaired by Nicholas O'Dwyer, chief engineer with the Local Government Board. He had already been one of the officials charged with supervising the South Dublin Union, now that the Board of Guardians had been dissolved. The opening proceedings were overshadowed by the army mutiny that erupted in the same week as well as by two by-elections in the Dublin region. The first by-election was in the county, where an unknown Republican candidate, Seán Lemass, secured 42 per cent of the first-preference vote, giving the successful Cumann na nGaedheal candidate, the bacon factory owner James O'Mara, a close run for the seat. Many people attributed Lemass's success to a sympathy vote after the discovery of the mutilated body of his brother, Noel, and the disturbing evidence presented at the inquest the previous autumn.[15] There was no Labour Party candidate. A former Unionist, John O'Neill, ran as a 'Business' candidate; his transfers helped O'Mara secure the seat.

The second by-election was in Dublin City South, where Archie Heron, a son-in-law of James Connolly, stood for the Labour Party. Batt O'Connor, a Collins loyalist, was the Cumann na nGaedheal candidate, and he easily saw off the challenge of the Sinn Féin veteran Seán MacEntee, while Dr Michael Good, another former Unionist running as a 'Business' candidate, transferred heavily to O'Connor.

Heron finished last. His case was not helped by Larkin disrupting the Labour Party election rallies by travelling around on a lorry from which he could easily drown out the voices of Heron and his supporters by denouncing the party's policies.[16]

By the time the government inquiry into the Corporation began to receive any public attention, the main witnesses for the prosecution, the Citizens' Association and the Town Tenants' Association, had already given their evidence. Despite their names, both were primarily lobbying groups for commercial ratepayers, the latter representing smaller businesses and shopkeepers who rented their premises. Both concentrated their fire on the soaring numbers employed by Dublin Corporation, the generous pensions that could amount to two-thirds of pay, increases that brought the wages of the same employees significantly above those in comparable private-sector employments, and the built-in inefficiencies in running some departments, such as the Stanley Street workshops and the city's power station.

All these complaints had been well aired in the council chamber and newspapers for several years, and it was very much a case of publicly counting the chickens as they came home to roost rather than exposing any new scandals. The byzantine arrangement of the Corporation's accounts also made it possible to point the finger of suspicion at almost any area of municipal activity, whether corruption existed there or not. The findings of the investigation into the South Dublin Union, along with those into other Poor Law unions that had been dismantled around the country, were published during the inquiry to further undermine public confidence in the municipality.

Special attention was given to some of the activities of relieving officers, such as supplying cheques to recipients of outdoor relief who had no means of cashing them and failing to return the unclaimed funds to the South Dublin Union, the payment of cash to recipients whose income was far above the level specified in the means test, and continuing to draw money for people who no longer applied for relief or were even dead. The *Irish Independent* gave particular emphasis to the finding that 101 out of the 230 cases investigated had been struck out as fraudulent or highly irregular.[17]

The city council was finally abolished on 20 May 1924, on the strength of the inquiry's findings, though these were never published. It did not help the credibility of the exercise when it later emerged that Laurence O'Neill had been offered a job as one of the three commissioners who now ran the city. The three subsequently appointed were all full-time civil servants: Séamas Ó Murchadha, Dr W. O'Dwyer and P. J. Hernon. The latter two were already supervising the South Dublin Union.

In a final act of defiance the city council struck a rate of 19s 11d in the pound at a special meeting on 19 May 1924. The vote was unanimous.[18]

The decision to suspend the city council was generally welcomed. The *Irish Times* editorial said that

the people of Dublin cannot but welcome this decision. The fact that their Corporation for many years has been inefficient and extravagant is humiliating but indubitably true ... The ratepayers merely existed for the purpose of footing the annual bill and criticism of any kind was resented bitterly. The rake's progress of the Dublin Corporation could not be allowed to continue.[19]

The *Irish Independent* was more measured. It acknowledged that

> some members of the Council strove to serve the citizens with fidelity and
> efficiency, but unfortunately they were outnumbered. As the Minister for
> Local Government observes, their efforts to secure efficient and economic
> management of the business of the city were unavailing in the absence of
> support from the majority of the Council ... Pending a scheme of reform,
> which we hope will be thorough ... the Commissioners appointed by the
> Minister for Local Government will act as managers in Dublin.[20]

As with the prisoners issue, the Labour Party was the most vigorous champion of
the Corporation in the Dáil. Thomas Johnson described its suspension as 'a very
extraordinary and unprecedented action' and warned that 'we are rapidly going
towards oligarchy and dictatorship.' Alfie Byrne listed the 'very many resolutions'
passed by the council 'asking for the release of prisoners ... examination of the jails,
inspections by our medical officer' as among the real reasons for the suspension of
the Corporation, 'and not the inspector's report.'[21]

With the exception of the Municipal Reform Association, the majority of
members fought the threatened dissolution as best they could, led by the Lord
Mayor. The day after the order O'Neill told the *Irish Times* that he would be staying
in the Mansion House. 'Are the citizens to be deprived of a civic head?' he asked. He

> would remain until he was able to return the chain of office to those who had
> elected him, after a new municipal election. I want to maintain for the citizens
> the position of Lord Mayor ... The office dates back for hundreds of years,
> and I think it is not fair to the citizens that any Government with the scratch
> of a pen should destroy that office. I could understand if a man occupying the
> position of Lord Mayor committed any offence.[22]

He called a meeting of councillors on Monday 26 May in the Mansion House,
where he proposed that members 'get the Government by the throat and demand
an election, so as to give the Council an opportunity of rendering an account
of their stewardship to the citizens. It is for the citizens and the citizens only to
decide.' P. T. Daly proposed a motion instructing the Lord Mayor to call a meeting
of the burgesses to campaign for an election. It was passed, but nothing happened.
There were no funds for a campaign and apparently little appetite for one.

The meeting proved to be the swan song of local democracy. Tom Farren, a
veteran of the trade union movement and the struggle for independence, summed
up the feeling of many of his colleagues when he said that 'the Corporation was
the first citadel of the ascendancy in Ireland that was captured for the people,' and
now it had been 'lost'.[23]

The government remained unmoved. The first meeting of the commissioners took place on 29 May, and they would administer the city for the next six years. O'Neill continued to reside at the Mansion House for over a year and continued to serve on various bodies as Lord Mayor, including the Port and Docks Board and the National University. His decision not to accept appointment as one of the city's commissioners cost him dear, as his biographer Tom Morrissey has pointed out. He had been occupied virtually full-time as the city's chief magistrate since 1917 and had neglected his own business interests over the years. He eventually returned to Portmarnock to live out his retirement. Many former business associates had traded on his generosity and had not repaid debts. On 15 May 1928 he was forced to write to his old colleague—and still a friend despite their differences—W. T. Cosgrave, to seek help.

> I am dreadfully pressed at the moment. I had hoped [for] an account due me for £900 ... but again disappointed, and, you would hardly believe it, I have received a writ for my Corporation rates. Consequently, for old times' sake, I will be frank with you, you are the only one in this world I would approach, as the bank has turned me down. If you ... give me a sum between £250 and £500 to tide me over present difficulties I shall make every effort possible to have it paid back as soon as I can collect what is due to me. I know I am asking a great deal, but I think you know me sufficiently well in the past to know only it is a case of absolute necessity I would not trespass on you otherwise.

A week later he met Cosgrave, who authorised a loan of £250 from the Dáil Special Fund, followed by another £250 on 25 June.[24] Cosgrave also supported O'Neill's successful bid for a Senate seat in a by-election following the resignation of the Marquis of Lansdowne. He would be elected an alderman for the city when the council was reinstated. He held his Senate seat until its abolition under de Valera's Constitution in 1938. Although he was an outspoken critic of the Fianna Fáil government, de Valera appointed him to a vacancy in the new Seanad in 1940. It was an indication of the affection he inspired in those who met him, from revolutionaries and trade union leaders to civil servants and British generals, that personal bitterness never entered his dealings with allies or opponents in those turbulent years. He died peacefully in the summer-house in his garden shortly after his nomination to the Seanad.[25]

———

By March 1924 the Civil War was not quite a memory—occasional shootings and bank robberies still occurred—but the main items of public interest in Dublin were the pending by-elections in the south city and north county, the spring sales, and a proposal from Siemens for a hydro-electric scheme on the Shannon that could supply all the Free State's electricity needs. The author of the proposal was a young Dublin engineer, Dr T. A. McLaughlin, a graduate of the National University whose contemporaries included John A. Costello, Kevin O'Higgins, Patrick McGilligan, Michael Tierney and others who would play prominent roles in the new Free State.

McLaughlin was working as a trainee on hydro-electric schemes for Siemens in Germany when he persuaded his superiors that a Shannon scheme was feasible. Until then proposals for hydro-electric schemes had concentrated on the Liffey, because of its proximity to Dublin, and were part of the piecemeal growth of the electricity supply business, which had resulted in 160 undertakings by the early 1920s, many of them serving one or two businesses and a handful of domestic customers. Only Dublin and Cork and the local authorities in Kingstown, Rathmines, Terenure and Pembroke had more than a thousand customers each. Even in Dublin only a third of households had electricity. The new scheme would not only supply all existing needs for urban dwellers and agriculture but would provide an energy grid for the development of an industrial base.[26]

McLaughlin's efforts bore fruit rapidly with a proposal from Siemens to the Executive Council in February. The government responded with a white paper on energy on 7 March 1924. However, its attention was gripped next day by a sudden political challenge from within its own armed forces.

On 9 March the *Sunday Independent's* front page was dominated by a headline proclaiming 'Amazing army development.' It reported that the arrest of two senior officers, Major-General Liam Tobin and Colonel Charlie Dalton, had been ordered and that searches were under way for them and their accomplices. By Monday more details were available, including the information that rifles, machine guns, ammunition and other equipment had been taken from barracks at Gormanston, Clonmel, Cashel and Templemore and the Air Corps base at Baldonnel. The Minister for Defence and former commander in chief, Richard Mulcahy, issued a statement that the two officers on the run had 'attempted to involve the Army in a challenge to the authority of the Government.'[27] This was followed on the 11th by the President of the Executive Council, W. T. Cosgrave, reading out a letter in the Dáil that he had received the previous Thursday from the missing officers. It had informed him that

the IRA only accepted the Treaty as a means of achieving its objects—namely, to secure and maintain a Republican form of Government in this Country. After many months of discussions with your Government, it is our considered opinion that your Government has not these objects in view.

The writers then expressed their own core beliefs.

Our interpretation of the Treaty was that expressed by the late Commander-in-Chief, General Michael Collins, when he stated 'I have taken an oath of allegiance to the Irish Republic and that oath I will keep, Treaty or no Treaty.' We claim Michael Collins as our leader ... Both in oath and honour bound, it is our duty to continue his policy and therefore present this ultimatum, to which we require a reply by 12 noon, March 10th, 1924.

In the ultimatum the writers demanded

a conference with representatives of your Government to discuss our interpretation of the Treaty on the following conditions:
The removal of the Army Council
The immediate suspension of army demobilisation and reorganisation
In the event of your Government rejecting these proposals we will take such action that will make clear to the Irish People that we are not renegades or traitors to the ideals that induced them to accept the Treaty.

Cosgrave was characteristically taciturn in his report to the Dáil. He said he was confident that deputies,

having heard the text of the document ... will have no difficulty in agreeing that it constitutes a challenge which no Government could ignore without violating the trust conferred on it.

I do not propose to discuss any political point connected with the document. I consider that in the circumstances, such a discussion would be indefensible, and I may say that this Government has never discussed questions of politics with Army Officers.

He assured deputies that 'the necessary administrative and disciplinary steps' would be taken 'to deal with this conspiracy.' Orders had been issued for the arrest of the signatories, and 'the Headquarters Staff has been strengthened by the appointment of General Eoin O'Duffy to be General Officer Commanding the Defence Forces.'

If the decision to bring back the newly appointed Commissioner of the Civic Guard was a surprise, it was nothing compared with the announcement by Joe McGrath, Minister for Industry and Commerce. He rose to announce that he had resigned from the Executive Council the previous Friday night, when it was decided to arrest Tobin and Dalton. He wanted it understood that he was not in agreement with the mutineers but he believed the present situation had been 'brought about by absolute muddling, mishandling and incompetence on the part of a Department of the State.' He would clarify his position the next day.

As usual, the Labour Party leader, Thomas Johnson, gave a reasoned and over-reasonable response from the bewildered opposition benches. In trying to provide some information in response, Mulcahy only added to the confusion. He confirmed press reports that incidents had taken place at a number of barracks and that

certain officers have absconded, taking with them small quantities of stores ... A small number of resignations have taken place throughout the country, particularly here in Dublin—approximately, about 20. There is a certain atmosphere of threat that a large number of officers throughout the Army are preparing to resign if the threat contained in the letter to the Government is not carried out; that they are prepared to set themselves up in arms in defiance against the Government is another threat.

He wanted to assure deputies that

there have been no incidents of irregularity, and I am absolutely certain of our control of the forces over the whole country with the possibility—and it is only a possibility ... that there may be some defections, whether from the point of view of resignations or from the point of view of seizing some military posts that are in the Cork area.[28]

It was a strange way of reassuring the Dáil. But Mulcahy was in a difficult situation, as were McGrath and Cosgrave, for the mutineers had been in protracted contact with them since the previous summer. Cosgrave had been involved in at least one direct meeting with them in June 1924 and had in effect lied to the Dáil.[29] There were also far more mutineers than Mulcahy cared to admit, and they included quite a number of senior officers.

———

The movement owed its origin, as the letter suggests, to Michael Collins, or rather to the death of Collins. The core group were Dubliners, working-class and lower middle-class IRA members who had undertaken much of the dirty work in the city during the War of Independence. One of the signatories to the letter was Collins's former deputy director of intelligence, Liam Tobin; another conspirator was Tom Cullen, the man who told Collins after the Treaty was signed that most of the Dublin IRA activists would accept it on the grounds 'that what was good enough for him was good enough for them.'[30] They had undertaken the same sort of dirty work in the Civil War and, while 'street-smart', were politically naïve. They had trusted Collins to see them right and took his 'stepping-stone' strategy at face value. When he died they were left in midstream, divided by a river of blood from their former comrades in the anti-Treaty forces and loathed, as well as distrusted, by some members of the Free State government, notably Kevin O'Higgins and Ernest Blythe. By the end of the Civil War in 1923 it was clear to even the most optimistic of these officers that the Executive Council was embarked on a course of consolidation and survival rather than renewing the march towards the Republic.

The mutineers had first met on 29 January that year. Among those attending were Major-Generals Liam Tobin, Tom Cullen, Emmet Dalton and Tom Ennis; colonels present included Kit O'Malley, Pat McCrea, Dalton's younger brother Charlie, Jim Slattery, Frank Thornton, Seán O'Connell and Joe O'Reilly. All of them were former Collins apparatchiks. On 2 February they met again, agreed objectives, and appointed Tobin and Cullen to organise them into a group.

> The policy decided on was to get in touch with all IRA men serving in the National Army and if they believed in our ideals to link them together in an *Organisation* which when strong enough would demand a strong voice in army policy with a view to securing *complete independence* when a suitable occasion arises. It was also decided that members of the new Organisation would make every effort to get control of the vital sections of the Army and oust those *undesirable persons* out who *were* and *are* holding these posts. (Emphasis in the original.)[31]

The IRA Organisation, as it came to be called, was based on 'clubs' within army battalions, which were to meet at least fortnightly. They would elect a delegate to liaise with other clubs and represent them at general meetings. Members were warned to be cautious in selecting recruits. 'Their past and present outlook from a National point of view should be the ... deciding factor,' and 'all those approached should be warned as to the seriousness of indiscriminate discussion of the organisation.'

The group met again in April. Major-General Paddy O'Daly attended on this occasion, while some senior officers, including Major-General Seán Mac Eoin and Colonel Dan Bryan, sent their apologies. There was agreement that the organisation was making good progress and it was decided to contact GHQ and seek formal recognition. O'Daly, who had not attended the earlier meetings, disagreed with this approach and left, saying that they 'could rely on him to stand by us whatever action we decided to take.'

On 22 June a delegation consisting of Tobin, O'Malley, Dalton and Thornton met Mulcahy and Cosgrave, to whom they presented a document outlining their position.[32] Mulcahy had previously met the officers informally, but little progress had been made. The central disagreement was over policy and army appointments. Mulcahy appeared willing to tolerate the organisation as a debating society that could air the views of some disgruntled officers, but nothing more.

When Cosgrave met them in June he appeared to be much more conciliatory. This may have been because there was an election looming and he saw no advantage in gratuitously antagonising the army constituency; but he may also have welcomed the opportunity of hearing what they had to say. Since the death of Collins the government had been almost entirely dependent on Mulcahy for its dealings with the army, something the latter's colleagues were not always happy to do. However, if Cosgrave thought that Mulcahy's briefings about the IRA Organisation might have been unduly critical or misleading, he was about to be disabused. The 'Document' they submitted demanded to know,

> Does the C in C [commander in chief] understand the temper of the old IRA who are now in the National Army? He does not: Your Army is not a National Army. It is composed of 40 per cent old IRA, 50 per cent ex-Britishers and 10 per cent ex-civilians. The majority of civilians were and are hostile to the National Ideals.

It even asserted that some 'ex-Britishers' were active intelligence agents for their former political masters. The organisation asked for a committee of inquiry to be set up 'to investigate the advisability of retaining or dispensing with the services of any Officer gazetted or otherwise.' It sought equal representation on this committee for the IRA Organisation and a 'full and frank discussion' on other issues. These included the composition of the Dublin Command, the appointment of an 'ex-Britisher', Major-General W. R. E. Murphy, as Commissioner of the DMP, the status of 'peace overtures to the irregulars,' and the establishment of a Secret Service Department. The document warned the government that 'unless satisfactory arrangements are come to between us, Our Organisation will take whatever steps they consider necessary to bring about an honest, cleaner and more genuine effort to secure the republic.'

In an effort to appear reasonable, the delegation said it did not want to cause 'any rupture which would give satisfaction to the enemies of Ireland' and appealed to Mulcahy 'to meet our efforts in the same spirit [with] which he would have regarded them in 1920 and 1921'. Mulcahy responded by walking out of the room. Cosgrave remained, but no record appears to have survived of the subsequent conversation.

Mulcahy was persuaded to meet the organisation again with Joe McGrath at an unspecified date in June or July 1923, possibly while the two men were discussing plans to find employment for soldiers facing demobilisation. Nothing came of the meeting, but Mulcahy appeared in a more conciliatory mood when he met another delegation on 23 July. This group included regional representatives from Cos. Cork and Limerick. Mulcahy agreed to meet the organisation again as occasion demanded 'for consideration of any representations they wished to make on matters considered vital to the progress of the Army on National lines with a view to the *Complete Independence of Ireland.*' (Emphasis in original.) He accepted the 'absolute honesty and ideals' of the representatives and would 'leave nothing undone' to prevent misunderstandings with the 'men who had made the present position of the country possible.'[33]

This happy state of affairs did not last. Mulcahy's biographer, Maryann Gialanella Valiulis, has tended to dismiss the IRA Organisation as 'men who once enjoyed the adventure and mystique of being "gunmen" ... now being asked either to return to civilian life or to assume less prestigious positions within the army.'[34] She sees the political aspirations cited in their ultimatums as 'dressing up their demands in the rhetoric of republican nationalism.'[35] But their concerns were no more or no less legitimate than those of the men in the anti-Treaty forces or in the new Free State political elite. Whatever about Mulcahy, men such as O'Higgins and O'Duffy also excelled at dressing their personal agendas in political rhetoric, and each had a sense of entitlement that would brook few equals. Colonel M. J. Costello, who was heavily involved in the National Army intelligence operation against the IRA Organisation and knew many of the mutineers well, did not question their bona fides.[36]

What is striking about the leadership of the IRA Organisation is how deeply embedded their thinking and aspirations were in the pre-Truce milieu, as illustrated by their persistence in referring to Mulcahy as the commander in chief or chief of staff long after he had become Minister for Defence and Seán MacMahon had succeeded him as head of the National Army. Nor were their fears completely groundless. Emmet Dalton had been succeeded in Cork by David Reynolds, and Paddy O'Daly had been superseded in Co. Kerry by W. R. E. Murphy, both former British army officers. But the group's resentment often extended to any professional soldier, such as John Prout, who was a Great War veteran of the United States army and served with the pre-Truce IRA in Co. Tipperary. The main complaints against him, when he was put in command of National Army forces in the South-East over the heads of more senior IRA veterans, were that he did not execute enough irregulars and failed to impose discipline in his own ranks.[37]

About the only senior officers with British service who did not excite resentment were such figures as Emmet Dalton and Jack MacSweeney, who were part of the Collins cabal, and Charles Russell, who brought a special expertise to the vital if unspectacular battle to save the railways. If, as the IRA Organisation claimed, there were more former British officers in the National Army than pre-Truce IRA officers it was a cause for understandable concern; and no-one appears to have disputed their figures. Of course such a high ex-British element in the officer corps merely reflected the situation in the rank and file, where half the men were also 'ex-Britishers'. The IRA Organisation does not seem to have appreciated the advantage this gave them in the Civil War, especially in the opening, conventional stages, when organising and deploying men in large numbers was clearly beyond their opponents' capacity. Instead it left many of the Collins old guard feeling deeply insecure, because they lacked the type of organisational skill and the temperament needed to manage complex military organisations.

Some were shunted sideways. Liam Tobin, one of the organisers of the IRA Organisation, was despatched as aide-de-camp to the new Governor-General of the Irish Free State, T. M. Healy. Tom Ennis was put in charge of the Army Inspectorate but given no executive authority. Charlie Dalton was transferred to the post of adjutant of the Air Corps. Professor James Hogan, a protégé of Eoin O'Duffy, who replaced Tobin as director of intelligence for the National Army in 1923, described some of these veterans of the IRA Organisation as men 'float[ing] about the country unattached ... Their duties not clearly defined.'[38]

In a regime fighting for survival there was little understanding of or sympathy for these men within the new army, least of all from the beneficiaries of their earlier sacrifices who were now sitting at the cabinet table. The one who should have had some insight into their situation was Mulcahy, but his ascetic nature and natural aloofness did not lend themselves to such things. Joe McGrath, who did understand the men, had only come lately into the military structures, and his primary responsibilities lay elsewhere. In the event, both men would soon become collateral casualties of the mutineers' activities.

––––

What brought matters to a head was not disagreements over how to re-establish the Republic but the question of demobilisation. Far from wishing to expand the National Army further to resume the onward march to the Republic, the Free State government wished to shrink it now that the Civil War was won.

At the beginning of 1923 the National Army was accounting for a third of all current expenditure by the state.[39] As we have seen, recruitment in the months before the Civil War had been desperately haphazard. At Beggarsbush Barracks, the birthplace of the National Army, 'periods of Enlistment were indefinite and attestation was nominal.' There were no records before July 1922, except for a list of three thousand men who passed through the Curragh. Pay varied from 3s 6d a day for some men, with an allowance of 4s for dependants, to flat rates of £3 10s, £4 or £4 10s a week, inclusive of dependants' allowances, for others.

Some enthusiasts were not paid anything at all, and did not ask for payment.[40] Martin Conlon, a member of the Supreme Council of the IRB, who played a significant role in 1916 and subsequently in intelligence work, never held any rank except private in the pre-Truce IRA, although he was the substitute delegate for Michael Collins on the Executive of the Irish Volunteers. In early 1922 he served as a lieutenant in the National Army but was never attested, or paid. Ironically, his main task was assisting in the organisation of the new force. He served on the GHQ staff until late September or early October 1922, when he returned, at his own request, to his job as a sanitary inspector with Dublin Corporation.[41]

In these chaotic early months, junior officers or even sergeants made promotions as the need arose. When general fighting broke out in early July 1922 and pre-Truce Volunteers, such as the men of the 2nd Battalion of the Dublin Brigade, were recruited *en masse*, they were supposed to sign on for six months, but many signed on for anything from eighteen months to five years, or even longer. No doubt an excess of patriotism was reinforced by fear of unemployment. When the six-month term for which most men enlisted ran out in January 1923 the government appealed for more recruits, only to find that a mere 420 existing soldiers had opted to leave.

The total strength of the army rose to 3,000 officers and 52,000 other ranks by May 1923, when overt hostilities were coming to a close.[42] Most of the handful who left early were men such as Conlon or railway workers who had a job to return to. Some of these men had taken severe cuts in pay, or no pay at all, to serve in the National Army. Their patriotism was certainly not of the mercenary variety. Of course by the same token members of the anti-Treaty IRA also suffered economically, relying on erratic levies on local authorities and businesses or on straightforward 'expropriations' to survive. What is more, many anti-Treaty Volunteers had no prospect of being re-employed when hostilities ended, or when they were released from internment.[43]

Mulcahy and his colleagues on the Army Council kept the process of demobilisation very much to themselves at first,[44] although they had to liaise with the government's own Council of Defence, a subcommittee that served as a watchdog on the generals. Mulcahy served on both bodies. In June 1923 he contacted Joe McGrath's Department of Industry and Commerce to seek assistance in approaching firms that soldiers had left to join the National Army, as well as other employers, to see if they would 'give preference to ex-Army men when filling vacancies.' Mulcahy proposed

that all vacancies for temporary clerks, porters, messengers, park keepers, under government departments should be offered to ex-Army men;

That special provision should be made in respect of ex-Army men in all civil service examinations

That public bodies should be approached by Government Departments … with a view to their giving vacancies to ex-Army men until such time as the percentage of their employees shall be 10 per cent of ex-Army men

That Government Departments should approach Public Bodies with a view to their employing ex-Army men to the extent of at least 50 per cent on schemes of road re-construction

That the Minister for Agriculture should ascertain what preference could be arranged for ex-Army men in the provision of land [and] what facilities could be provided in the way of loans.

McGrath agreed that 'every department must help in every way to shoulder the burden of demobilisation.' By then 28,000 soldiers had filled out civil employment forms, including those for disabled men. Major-General Éamonn Price was transferred to a special section of the Department of Industry and Commerce to liaise on demobilisation with McGrath. Meanwhile Mulcahy succeeded in securing special privileges for soldiers applying for civil service jobs (see chapter 6) and extending the age limits for army candidates entering the DMP, the Civic Guard and the Customs Service. He even discussed with Joe McGrath putting ex-servicemen on the dole, proposing that the Department of Defence could foot the unemployment insurance bill, but this was not found to be practicable.

Mulcahy did manage to secure approval for a redundancy package that provided for a small lump sum, up to £5 in the case of officers, and two months' pay, followed by two months on half pay for all ranks. Extra discretionary payments were made to some pre-Truce officers. While better than nothing—which was the fate of most other workers losing their jobs—this was a much poorer demobilisation package than the British government had provided for ex-servicemen and female members of the Voluntary Aid Detachments in 1919.[45] As John P. Duggan has pointed out, 'the raising, equipping, training and maintaining of an army ... under active service conditions had been a stupendous feat,' but the price in poor discipline, poor morale and ill-health had been enormous.

By October 1923 some 12,858 men had been weeded out of the army, with ill-health accounting for 3,941 and unsuitability accounting for many others, who were described as 'the dregs of British post-war demobilisation.' Not that health problems were confined to the medically unfit: in 1923 there were 51,138 cases of lice infestation, 2,038 of scabies and 1,888 of other preventable diseases, including 638 of sexually transmitted infections.[46]

Officers proved more difficult to shift than other ranks, although it was estimated that there were already nearly a thousand surplus to requirements when reorganisation began. The first batch of 284 left in October 1923 when drastically reduced terms of pay and conditions were introduced. These reductions followed discussions with all nine regional commanders, who agreed to take a reduction in rank from major-general to colonel, resulting in pay cuts of almost 30 per cent, from 35s a day to 25s, plus related reductions in allowances. Part of the trade-off was that they retained much of their regional autonomy. Demotions were imposed on all their subordinates, with complementary pay cuts and straightforward reductions in pay and allowances for NCOs and privates. The aim was not just to reduce pay but to make military service so unrewarding that many soldiers would not re-enlist. Warnings from the IRA Organisation that this would lead to trouble were dismissed by Mulcahy as 'the bluff of children,'[47] despite his assurances to them in July that he would 'leave nothing undone' to avoid future misunderstandings. Besides, the cuts hit privates hardest: not only was pay reduced from 3s 6d to 2s 6d a day but new recruits would be paid only 2s until they successfully completed their training, and unmarried men would be losing all allowances for dependants. This meant cuts in real pay of between 7s and 28s a week. It particularly hit families in which a soldier was the sole breadwinner or on whom ageing parents or younger siblings were dependent.[48]

The Secretary of the Department of Defence accepted that 'the reductions were drastic. In other walks of life they would surely cause strikes.'[49] If there was no strike among the other ranks, the mutiny can be seen as an officers' strike of sorts. The first signs of resistance occurred in the Curragh, where the large concentration of troops provided a hotbed for dissent. On 9 November 1923 seven candidate officers refused to accept demobilisation papers and were placed under arrest. They said they had joined the IRA Organisation and, adopting the language of the 'Document', declared that they had taken an oath not to lay down their arms until Ireland was an independent republic. They were charged with insubordination, and some of them went on the run.[50] So did up to sixty officers who also refused to accept their demobilisation papers.

Despite his efficiency in handling the organisational challenges of first creating and then disbanding a large military force, Mulcahy's impersonal style and poor political antennae meant he had no close allies in the government. As Maryann Gialanella Valiulis puts it, he 'had a way of becoming totally absorbed in the tasks which were before him' that 'sometimes blinded him to what was happening around him.'[51] On this occasion his failure to engage with the IRA Organisation meant that they began lobbying various Cumann na nGaedheal TDs, particularly Joe McGrath.

On 26 November 1923 the government formed a new subcommittee to deal with demobilisation issues, which included the Minister for Education, Eoin MacNeill, the Minister for Finance, Ernest Blythe, and McGrath. It was empowered to investigate complaints by pre-Truce officers about their dismissals, to evaluate the validity of their concerns over preferential treatment being given to former British officers and to look into the cases of the candidate officers at the Curragh. It proved a futile exercise. None of the complainants was reinstated, but government fissures deepened, with McGrath resigning on 5 December 1923 when he discovered that some officers whose cases he was investigating had already been demobilised. He reconsidered only after Cosgrave assured him that the recommendations of the committee would be binding on the Army Council.

Unfortunately, there was no sign that Mulcahy had acquired any greater appreciation of the need to consult his colleagues more fully. Not only McGrath but

O'Higgins had developed a passionate interest in defence matters, albeit for very different reasons. O'Higgins seems to have fallen under the influence of Colonel Jephson O'Connell, a suspended priest and former British army chaplain who had been made director of inspection after the first director, Major-General Tom Ennis, took sickness leave.[52] It was widely, and mistakenly, believed that Mulcahy was president of the IRB, and O'Connell fed O'Higgins's increasing paranoia about that organisation, although O'Higgins himself had been a member in his younger days, when such things were an asset for young revolutionary careerists. O'Connell's claims were made all the more credible by the fact that the Army Council was widely suspected of doubling as the IRB's Supreme Council and by Mulcahy's decision to add O'Connell to those earmarked for demobilisation.[53]

The fact that the Army Council accepted that it had to meet the government's budgetary target of reducing the Defence Forces (as they were now called) to 1,300 officers and 30,000 other ranks by January 1924 cut little ice with any of its critics, as it was not only a question of how many but who. A subsequent government inquiry criticised the 'secret' nature of the Army Council's discussions and the fact that decisions were 'largely verbal'. Ironically, far from posing a threat to democracy, Mulcahy and MacMahon, the chief of staff, owed their predicament in large part to their taking a stronger line against the IRA Organisation than their political masters. MacMahon feared that the organisation would turn the army 'into an armed mob,' instead of being 'forced into a military machine that will be the right arm of any Government the people wish to place in power.'[54] The inquiry in effect scapegoated Mulcahy for provoking a situation that resulted from the government's own instruction to impose draconian cuts in pay and conditions.

Fortunately, the idea of tapping into such unrest was largely at odds with the outlook of the IRA Organisation, and that of the anti-Treaty IRA, who, in their different ways, shared a low opinion of the army's rank and file. That opinion was widely shared by deputies in the third Dáil. Reports of offences, including assault, robbery, arson and 'alleged criminal conduct' towards women were common (although there was always a reluctance to pursue prosecutions where anything of a remotely sexual nature was concerned).[55] The Biggs case (see chapter 3) would remain a solitary example of a woman (and in this case also her husband) openly accusing the offenders, and its outcome hardly encouraged others to come forward. Nor was such casual brutality restricted to combatants, or even civilians. In August 1922 the British government protested at a serious assault on one of its officers outside the Four Courts Hotel by 'Provisional Government' soldiers. He was 'hit in the face and over the head several times, even by an "officer" of the guard. Most abusive language ... was also used, and further ill treatment was only stopped by the arrival of the senior Provisional Government officer of the post.'[56]

The activities of the CID at Oriel House and Military Intelligence at Wellington Barracks were well known by now and documented, thanks to Dublin Corporation and such champions of civil liberties as Hanna Sheehy Skeffington. Officers often took the lead in the ill-treatment of prisoners for interrogation purposes. Such encounters could assume a degree of personal vindictiveness that was only possible because the interrogator and the interrogated knew each other. In Wellington Barracks it was the sergeant of the guard who did what he could to protect prisoners, not former 'comrades in arms'.

Even senior officers were implicated in such behaviour, most notably Major-General Paddy O'Daly, former commander of the Squad. As officer commanding in Co. Kerry he not only tolerated but encouraged 'routine and uncontrolled excesses,' including the unofficial execution of prisoners. In the most infamous incidents, at Ballyseedy, Killarney (Countess Bridge) and Cahersiveen, seventeen prisoners were killed in controversial circumstances in retaliation for the deaths of five National Army soldiers in a booby-trap explosion at Knocknagashel.[57] A court of inquiry was established but, as it was presided over by O'Daly, its findings, exonerating the alleged culprits, were predictable. Nor was O'Daly a respecter of property, persons or propriety when dealing with non-combatants, commandeering premises and assets as required, including a Buick touring car, from local pillars of the establishment.

The worst incident, in June 1923, involved O'Daly and two of his officers who had previously been accused of killing captured irregulars. All three men were now accused of assaulting the daughters of a local doctor in Kenmare, Dr Randal McCarthy. The two women claimed they had been flogged and had grease poured over their hair. O'Daly dismissed the incident by blaming the victims; he said they had associated with British officers before the Truce, and one of them had 'jilted' a National Army officer.

O'Higgins, who was receiving reports on irregularities from the new Civic Guard, was outraged and demanded action at the request of the Judge Advocate General, Cahir Davitt. It took Mulcahy's intervention to save O'Daly's career. It may have been old loyalties, or Mulcahy's desire to keep O'Daly from becoming more heavily engaged in the IRA Organisation, but the inevitable outcome was a further souring of Mulcahy's relationship with his government colleagues.

What was particularly damaging for Mulcahy and the Collins cabal was the fact that the Kenmare incident was far more resented than allegations about killing prisoners. It was 'an assault on the social order, and worse still a sexual assault on the middle class'—even, as John Regan points out, an attack on O'Higgins's own caste by undesirable social elements that had infiltrated the new order.[58]

The Biggs case in Co. Tipperary was, of course, much worse, but it had occurred during the Truce, and the perpetrators were anti-Treaty Volunteers. O'Daly was a very different proposition. He was not only a former commander of the Squad but probably the most effective of the Collins old guard, after Emmet Dalton. He seems to have had an animus against the Free State's middle-class supporters to a pronounced degree. He certainly resented former British officers in National Army ranks, such as Major-General W. R. E. Murphy, whom he replaced in Co. Kerry after the latter's conventional sweeps through the countryside yielded few results. Murphy's distinguished record in the First World War, where he had been decorated for bravery and temporarily commanded a brigade, did not impress O'Daly, whose gruesome counter-insurgency methods certainly yielded more results, or at least a higher body count.

Another former British officer with a good war record, Major Tom Ryan, who had also temporarily commanded a brigade, had been appointed commandant in command of the garrison at Ballymullen Barracks, Tralee, and he sought a court of inquiry into his own treatment by O'Daly.[59]

———

Labour Party members of the Dáil, who had been particularly assiduous in drawing attention to cases of misconduct by the National Army against trade unionists, now joined the public outcry against the IRA Organisation. In describing the ill-treatment of one of his own ITGWU members in custody, Cathal O'Shannon made the more general point that

> the military spirit is as deep in one section of the Army as it is in another, and the reason is that both came with prestige out of the guerrilla warfare against England, and they have got such swelled heads that the only authority they have is the authority of the gun.[60]

Yet the Labour Party's reaction to Cosgrave's reading of the IRA Organisation's ultimatum into the record of the Dáil was surprisingly mild. Cumann na nGaedheal, on the other hand, whose deputies included several army officers besides McGrath, held a six-hour meeting to discuss the crisis. At the meeting McGrath opposed the government's approach to the mutineers. While not agreeing with the IRA Organisation's document he criticised the way in which the Department of Defence and the Army Council had handled the problem. He then characterised the mutiny as a row between the IRA Organisation and the IRB about how the army should be reorganised.

Mulcahy said little, partly for fear of revealing too much about his earlier discussions with the organisation but also, Valiulis believes, because he felt he could still resolve the differences with the mutineers. Indeed while the Cumann na nGaedheal meeting was taking place Mulcahy was offering the IRA Organisation an interview with Seán MacMahon, the chief of staff. Liam Tobin agreed to meet MacMahon, provided he came 'as head of the Army, with full powers to discuss all Army affairs.'[61] Such a response showed the continued failure of the IRA

Organisation to appreciate the nature of political realities within the new state. Valiulis believes the offer was made by Mulcahy because MacMahon was president of the IRB but that the IRA Organisation, apparently unaware of this, missed the significance of the gesture. Even if they had known this, or that another member of the Army Council and Quartermaster-General, Seán Ó Murthuile, was secretary of the Supreme Council, it is hard to see what could have been achieved, apart from some *modus vivendi* between two secret organisations. Short of a coup, neither of them could avert the mass demobilisation which would end the IRA organisation's hopes of achieving the 'complete Independence of Ireland.' The pro-Treaty faction of the once all-powerful IRB was still committed to re-establishing the Republic as a long-term objective, but its immediate preoccupation was to prevent the anti-Treaty faction in the IRA from acquiring possession of the IRB by default.[62]

Meanwhile McGrath's tactic of portraying the mutiny as a spat between two secret societies worked in the short term. The meeting of government TDs authorised him to meet the mutineers, resolve any misunderstandings and make them withdraw their ultimatum. McGrath understood this to mean there would be no victimisation of the men, but some government members only saw it as an offer of leniency to enable the IRA Organisation 'to retreat gracefully from the rebellious position of the ultimatum.'[63] As the party meeting had no legal standing within the formal state structure, it bequeathed McGrath a mandate that could not be enforced if his government colleagues decided otherwise.

According to the mutineers, when they met McGrath on 12 March he

came from the President [of the Executive Council], and, with the concurrence of the Committee of Cumann na nGaedheal, offered us the following terms to which we agreed:—

(*a*) The setting up of a Committee of Enquiry into Army administration. In the event of this Committee finding for the removal of the Army Council, they [were] to be replaced by neutral officers who were not connected with either side.

(*b*) The personnel of the Army to be reviewed with the object of making it an IRA Army. All men with active service records, even though demobilised, to be placed, so long as the Army estimates did not exceed £4 million.

(*c*) Suitable arrangement to be arrived at whereby all our officers and men would return to their posts with any arms removed from same, it being distinctly understood that there would be no victimisation.

There were to be no further raids or arrests and both sides were to co-operate in preserving order.[64]

The 'arrangement' began to unravel even while it was being agreed. Lieutenant George Ashton, one of the principal officers on the run, was fired upon in Wicklow

Street. He escaped, only to be taken prisoner in the Phoenix Park the following Sunday.[65] Ashton had been involved in taking equipment from Gormanston Camp in Co. Meath on 8 March, the day the ultimatum had been delivered to Cosgrave. He then used a Crossley tender to remove twenty-seven rifles, four Lewis machine guns and forty-six Lewis magazines from the Air Corps base at Baldonnel, with the assistance of its commander, Major-General Jack MacSweeney, and the adjutant, Charlie Dalton.[66]

MacSweeney was one of the many waifs and strays Collins had picked up along his revolutionary way. Of a Manchester-Irish family, he had joined the IRA in the War of Independence and struck up a friendship with two other Great War veterans who had joined the IRA, Emmet Dalton and Charles Russell. MacSweeney was made general officer commanding the Air Corps on the strength of two years in the Royal Flying Corps and Royal Air Force. With Russell, who had also served in the RFC, he purchased a Martynside biplane for £2,600 in 1921 to whisk Collins back from London if the Treaty talks broke down. The Martynside became the first plane in the Air Corps fleet and was inevitably renamed *The Big Fella* after Collins's death.[67]

Valiulis, by no means sympathetic to the mutineers, accepts that subsequent events support the interpretation that McGrath and the mutineers put on the agreement reached with the Executive Council and the Cumann na nGaedheal deputies.[68] Despite the Ashton incident, general raiding for fugitives did indeed cease, and the Executive Council ordered a full inquiry into the administration of the army. McGrath was to be consulted on how it should be conducted. Lulled into a false sense of security, Liam Tobin and Charlie Dalton, who was acting as secretary to the IRA Organisation, now sent a letter to Cosgrave explaining that

> we were forced to present the document [ultimatum] to bring to your notice and that of the Dáil the seriousness of the situation. We ... fully recognise that the Army just as the police must be subject to the absolute control of the civil authority, and further that the Army should not have within its ranks any sections or organisations tending to sap the allegiance from the only and proper constitutional authority, viz. the Government of the people, which we fully recognise.
>
> We are satisfied that we have brought the matter sufficiently before the people, and will consider our object achieved if, as a result of our action, the Army situation is righted.[69]

This second letter was fatal to the prospects of the IRA Organisation. As Valiulis points out, 'the mutineers had publicly repented. They now professed their loyalty ... acknowledging the supremacy of civil authority over the military and deploring the detrimental effects of secret societies within the army.'[70] By no longer challenging the legitimacy of the state or reiterating its own demands, the IRA Organisation ceased to pose a threat to the government.

The implementation of the terms now fell a long way short of what the organisation thought had been agreed. While all officers who absconded with arms were afforded the opportunity of returning them, they were arrested and released on parole while the Minister for Defence reviewed each case, the final decisions to rest with the Executive Council.

The hunt now began in earnest for the mutineers, fuelled by intelligence reports that they had been in touch with some NCOs to gauge the mood of the troops, and also with the Irregulars. Joe McGrath's home was among those searched for fugitives, as well as those of some anti-Treaty IRA members.

Things quickly came to a head on 18 March 1924. M. J. Costello, who had succeeded Hogan as colonel in charge of Military Intelligence, had been tapping the phone of a colleague, Commandant Frank Saurin, who he knew was in the IRA Organisation. Through this it was possible to identify and listen in on several other conspirators through the Crown Alley telephone exchange. On hearing that leading members of the IRA Organisation, including Tobin, were meeting in Devlin's Hotel in Parnell Street, one of Collins's old haunts, Costello alerted GHQ. Troops were positioned around the hotel and waited for Tobin to arrive. When he stepped off the tram and saw two lorryloads of soldiers and an armoured car he decided to go elsewhere.

Eventually Colonel Hugo MacNeill, who was in charge of the operation, was ordered by the Adjutant-General, Gearóid Ó Súileabháin, to go ahead at 1 a.m. on 19 March and force an entry if necessary. MacNeill met no resistance except for a barricade on the stairs. The mutineers retreated to the rooftop, where they seemed determined to fight it out. It was a cold night, and after a while Costello, who had joined MacNeill, said their 'martial ardour' gradually cooled. Tobin contacted McGrath, who arrived at the hotel apparently 'under the influence of drink' just after the surrender. His main contribution to the proceedings was to insist on buying the mutineers a round at the bar before they were driven off. The only further incident that night was an unsuccessful attempt at escape by Colonel Jim Slattery, another old Squad member.[71]

The raid turned out to be a far greater setback for army commanders than for the mutineers. Although Eoin O'Duffy had been brought back from the Civic Guard to take charge of the army, his appointment had been fully regularised only on 18 March, the day of the raid. He had not been informed of the decision to carry it out. In other circumstances the urgency of the situation might have been a justifiable defence of the Army Council's handling of the affair, but the government scented blood and demanded the resignation of the council's members. Mulcahy resigned in solidarity with them. At one stroke the old Collins cabal in the IRA Organisation and the IRB faction in charge of the National Army were gone. Ever the democrat, Mulcahy said he was sure 'that General O'Duffy will get the absolute and scrupulous service of every officer in the Army, not touched by mutiny.'[72]

The mutineers, by contrast, while required to resign their positions—a significant economic penalty given the dire unemployment situation—were not otherwise disciplined. The other main casualty of the affair was Joe McGrath, and arguably his departure from the government was the greatest loss. One of life's born fixers, he had shown sympathy for the underdog, whether postal clerks, railway workers or army officers, that was curiously absent from most of the new Cumann na nGaedheal establishment.

The great survivor was, of course, Cosgrave, who fell ill during the crisis, as he had done on several critical occasions during the War of Independence. John Regan, who has written one of the most authoritative accounts of the period, suggests that 'on the evidence available it would seem that Cosgrave was confined to his bed by O'Higgins, not by his doctor: and there he stayed until the danger ... passed.'[73]

The clear victor was Kevin O'Higgins. His main targets were not the mutineers but Mulcahy, the military elite, and McGrath. A stern defender of the parliamentary process as the best defence of his own class in an unstable world, O'Higgins had little sympathy for losers or underdogs of any description. He became increasingly enamoured of the British imperial connection. A social climber, he conducted a secret adulterous affair with Lady Hazel Lavery yet sought to personify the public virtues of a deeply conservative Catholic state. When he was eventually killed by gunmen in 1927 it was thought at first that the perpetrators might be old IRA Organisation members, but it eventually emerged that it was an opportunist attack by four IRA volunteers. The irony was that practically all the protagonists in the mutiny, including O'Higgins and O'Duffy, were IRB members. Far from showing how all-powerful that body was it demonstrated its impotence. Unable to influence policy, let alone direct it, it was no longer relevant to the realities of political life in the Free State, as opposed to the aspirational Republic of 1919–21.

By the end of the year both the pro-Treaty and anti-Treaty IRB factions had decided to wind up their affairs. The treasurer, Eoin O'Duffy, disbursed the funds, £2,500 of which was to go to the writing and publishing of a history of the 'Organisation'.[74] It never appeared.

The IRA Organisation was not quite spent. Its call of 'Back to the spirit of 1916-1921 and the Completion of the work' evoked an immediate response in Cork, the stronghold about which Mulcahy had expressed most concern during the crisis. On 21 March a British Navy launch full of servicemen on leave from the base at Spike Island was fired on in Cóbh. Seventeen men were wounded and one, eighteen-year-old Herbert Aspinall, was killed. The attackers, wearing National Army officers' uniforms, used sub-machine guns and escaped in a motor car. If it was intended to provoke British retaliation it failed. No-one was ever charged in relation to the attack.

Nearly 130 officers resigned from the National Army following the mutiny. All resignations were post-dated to 7 March 1924, the day before the IRA Organisation's ultimatum was sent to Cosgrave, to avoid the need for courts-martial. The officers who resigned included five major-generals: Liam Tobin, Tom Ennis, Paddy O'Daly, Jack MacSweeney and Tom Cullen; eight colonels, including Charlie Dalton, Pat McCrea, Jim Slattery, Frank Thornton, Chris O'Malley and Joe Leonard, all former close associates of Collins; thirty-six commandants, including Squad members such as Vinnie Byrne and Joe Dolan, the man who ordered soldiers to fire on the prisoners in Mountjoy in July 1922; fifty-seven captains, including Frank Bolster, who had acquired such a ferocious reputation as an interrogator at Wellington Barracks and O'Daly's alleged accomplice in the Kenmare assaults; twenty-three lieutenants, including George Ashton, who took the weapons from Gormanston and Baldonnel; and ten second lieutenants. There were no NCOs or private soldiers involved, at least overtly.[75]

Arms seized during the mutiny[76]

Place and name of custody officer	Type of munitions	Quantity	By whom taken	Still missing, 12 April 1924
Dublin Command				
Baldonnel, Maj.-Gen. MacSweeney, 8/3/1924	Rifles	27	Lt George W. Ashton, 8/3/1924	0
	Lewis guns	4	J. Foy, Reserve, 8/3/1924	0
	LG magazines	46	J. Foy, Reserve, 8/3/1924	0
Gormanston, Lt G. W. Ashton, 8/3/1924	Bayonets	21	Cmdt Donnelly, Air Services, 8/3/1924	0
	Web equipment	2		0
	.303 ammunition	7,500		0
Athlone			Captain F. Madden (date?)	
	Bayonets	24		21
	Rifles	48		14
	Scabbards	13		9
	.303 ammunition	3,370		1,012
	Bombs	40		20
	Grenade cups	2		2

Waterford (Templemore, Cashel, Clonmel)			Captain M. Small (Templemore), Lt J. Morris (Cashel). Col. J. T. Prout (Clonmel), 10/3/1924	
	Rifles	142		65
	Lewis guns	8		0
	Bombs	80		0
	.303 ammunition	35,000		4,902
	LG magazines	71		0
	LG handles	34		0
	LG magazine carriers	5		0
	LG spare parts	2 bags		0
	Officers' kits and revolvers	19		19
	Men's uniforms	45		45
Roscommon	Rifles	48		14
	Bayonets	24		21
	Scabbards	13		9
	.303 ammunition	3,370		1,012
	Bombs	40		20
	Grenade cups	2		2
All returned through Joe McGrath, individual officers, or unnamed civilians				

Demobilisation of National Army personnel, December 1922 to March 1924[77]

	Officers	Men
December 1922	0	2
January 1923	0	420
February 1923	0	572
March 1923	0	1,356
April 1923	0	1,044
May 1923	0	1,043
June 1923	0	914
July 1923	0	2,351

August 1923	0	2,677
September 1923	0	2,479
October 1923	284	3,235
November 1923	294	3,804
December 1923	196	3,722
January 1924	154	3,517
February 1924	79	4,325
March 1924	940	6,820

There were still quite a few weapons missing from National Army stocks at the end of the mutiny, including twelve rifles, nineteen revolvers, more than a thousand rounds of ammunition and twenty hand grenades, not to mention personal weapons that many members of the IRA Organisation retained.

The government had reason to be concerned. There had been a sympathetic response at first to the mutineers' approaches from some former IRA comrades in Dublin, although Liam Lynch's successor as IRA chief of staff, Frank Aiken, quickly issued an order that no

> demobilised or resigned [National Army] officer is to be taken into the ranks of the IRA unless there is good reason to show such are acting on principle and not from some motive of self-interest. Any such will be looked on as recruits and appointments will depend on reliability and energy in the cause.[78]

Nor had the IRA Organisation disappeared from National Army ranks. Some NCOs were approached to ascertain

> what backing the officers would have in the event of a coup d'etat. The coup was to have taken place on three different occasions but for some unknown reasons it never materialised ... but the NCOs believed that the officers were afraid they would lose their well paid positions in the event of failure.[79]

If the veterans of the IRA Organisation no longer constituted a military threat, it was by no means clear that they did not pose a political one. They remained in touch with Joe McGrath and disgruntled elements in Cumann na nGaedheal, and bided their time.

Chapter 11 ∾

'A BARBARISM OF WHICH THE MOST PITILESS SAVAGE WOULD BE ASHAMED'

The Dublin Metropolitan Police was to have a far cleaner and more honourable end than the Collins cabal in the National Army. On Saturday 5 May 1923 a guard of honour of the DMP paraded in the Upper Castle Yard to be inspected by the Minister for Home Affairs, Kevin O'Higgins, and their new Commissioner, General W. R. E. Murphy, still wearing his National Army uniform. Murphy's predecessor, Lieutenant-Colonel Sir Walter Edgeworth Johnstone, had retired in April 1923, the last British army officer to serve as Commissioner of the force.

The DMP had weathered the storm of recent years remarkably well, given its involvement in the Dublin Lockout of 1913, when its name had become a byword for brutality and defence of the status quo.[1] Subsequently many DMP men had shown considerable sympathy towards the trade union and independence movements. After the 1916 Rising about half the force joined the Ancient Order of Hibernians in an unsuccessful attempt to overcome the ban on trade unions. In 1918 a group of DMP members let the Dublin Trades Council know they wanted to be regarded purely as law enforcement officers and not an arm of the state; and in October 1920 an agreement was reached with Michael Collins that they would not carry arms or assist the military, in return for an undertaking by the IRA not to regard the DMP as legitimate targets. Members of G Division (the detective branch) were excluded from this agreement, although some individuals ended up working for Collins, most notably Éamonn Broy and David Neligan.

The reality was that the survival strategy for most DMP members was a combination of retreat from the streets and co-operation with the IRA, to the extent that many of its surviving records from 1920–21 ended up in the hands of the IRA's Dublin Brigade.[2] Between the Truce and the Civil War, members underwent further significant rehabilitation with Dubliners while working with the Republican Police to maintain public order.

Nevertheless it was members of the newly formed Civic Guard who took over policing duties at Dublin Castle in August 1922, not the DMP, despite a shaky start for the new force, including a mutiny at its training base in the Curragh in May 1922. This may partly have been because the DMP had difficulty adjusting to the demands of the new regime, which saw the National Army as its first line of defence.

The DMP had failed dismally from the Provisional Government's point of view in the postal strike, when constables showed a marked reluctance to break up the picket lines.[3] Ten months later, with the city returning to something resembling normality, there was room for optimism about the future. The men on parade on 5 May were a combination of veterans of the past turbulent decade, such as Superintendent George Willoughby, who had saved his fellow-parishioner Seán O'Casey from a beating on Bloody Sunday in 1913, and recruits drawn from the DMP training depot at Kevin Street Barracks.

Kevin O'Higgins was in his element, able to contrast the DMP, almost ninety years old, with that troublesome infant, the National Army. The DMP 'was not young or raw, or hot blooded,' he said. 'There was no danger of your pot boiling over.' Nor should the assembled constables regard themselves 'in any sense as the stepchildren of the new regime.' On the contrary, he assured them of 'a cordial welcome to their new status as servants of the democratic state that had been founded.' With a native government established, 'observance of the law in Ireland is now for Irish citizens the highest form of self-respect, and their highest civic interest.'

Nevertheless, Murphy's appointment showed that some National Army commanders were to be trusted; in fact it was the former chief of staff and new Commissioner of the Civic Guard, Eoin O'Duffy, who had insisted on Murphy's appointment. Introducing their new commander, O'Higgins assured the men, and the wider public, that 'the greatest care was taken' in Murphy's selection. Referring to his distinguished war record in the British army, O'Higgins said he had joined 'at a time when the then representatives of the Irish people advocated such a course. No responsible spokesman of Sinn Féin ever suggested that, because there was a political landslide three years later, those who went to that war, believing that to be the best way of serving their country, should be stigmatised.'[4] Ironically, the man who had replaced Murphy in Co. Kerry, the War of Independence veteran Paddy O'Daly, inspired anything but confidence in his superiors, although he was the son of a DMP constable.

Murphy would do much to restore the morale of the force, re-establishing the international reputation of its legendary tug-of-war team and establishing a boxing club that would soon evolve into the Garda Síochána Boxing Club and win more than seventy amateur boxing titles before Murphy's retirement as Deputy Commissioner of the latter force in 1955.

Unfortunately it would require more than sports trophies to save the DMP. Less than two years later it would be merged with the Civic Guard, by then reconstituted as the Garda Síochána. The government had wanted to merge the two forces in 1923 but deferred a decision for fear that it would trigger mass resignations from the older force at a time when the new one was still finding its feet.

The fears were well founded. Article 10 of the Anglo-Irish Treaty provided for the transfer to the United Kingdom or retirement of all public servants, on relatively generous terms. In the case of the DMP, members could avail of ten to twelve additional years added to their pension entitlement before seeking alternative employment.

While the economic outlook was uncertain, so was the political one. Altogether 574 men availed of the early retirement offer, out of 1,126 officers and men. As the DMP was already forty-five under strength, this posed a serious challenge that the government hoped to meet with a recruitment drive. Not surprisingly, it decided to restrict recruitment to National Army men, ensuring the political reliability of new members and facilitating demobilisation at the same time. It also deferred retirement for some older constables until the new recruits were trained. Altogether 719 men were recruited, and 37 DMP members who had taken the early retirement option under the Treaty successfully reapplied to join the force. These were a decided bargain, as not only did they come ready trained but they only had to be paid the balance between their pension and the new salary scales.[5]

As it happened, very few demobilised National Army men from Dublin eventually qualified for the DMP, suggesting that they did not meet the physical or the educational requirements. The force did not change its essential social profile as a career path for farmers' younger sons. By June 1924 it was back up to a strength of 40 officers, 200 sergeants and 1,000 men. The biggest difference was that its personnel were much younger. Sergeants now had an average of seven years' service before promotion, compared with the traditional fourteen years. Not only that but the composition of the force, with its mixture of pre-Truce IRA and National Army veterans, resembled more closely the composition of the Civic Guard.

Besides, the cessation of hostilities saw a rapid drop in the incidence of serious crime in the city. The number of murders fell from 23 in 1922 to 2 by 1924, attempted murders from 53 to 15, malicious wounding from 112 to 3, armed robbery from 479 to 142, arson from 30 to nil, and malicious damage to property from 917 to 607. The logic of having a separate force in Dublin was rapidly disappearing, especially after the dissolution of Dublin Corporation. If an institution that was seven hundred years old could disappear, why not a sprightly 89-year-old?[6]

———

The dramatic fall in reported crime in Dublin that would follow the ending of the Civil War was by no means obvious in 1922 or 1923, when some Free State ministers took a dystopian view of their fellow-citizens and the world at large. Typically it was Kevin O'Higgins who set the ball rolling. He demanded an urgent conference on 'the maintenance of law and order' in the wake of the Nora Connolly O'Brien *habeas corpus* decision. (See chapter 9.) But the government also had to deal with some law and order problems of its own making, of which Joe McGrath had been the main author. Before his resignation from the government he had proposed some specific measures, as he envisaged an upsurge in crime, especially armed robbery, 'owing to the demobilising of a large number from the Army and the releasing of prisoners ... who have been used, for so long, to conditions which have torn moral standards to shreds.' McGrath's views probably reflected his own experiences during the War of Independence, when one of his main functions for Collins was to oversee IRA armed robberies in the city. If there is a certain brutal clarity in the visions of O'Higgins and McGrath, it also reveals their own lack of confidence in the moral fibre of their fellow human beings and what O'Higgins described as 'the moral disintegration' of the country by the 'Irregulars'.[7]

Their agendas, if complementary in some respects, conflicted in others, for both men had a vested interest in determining the future of the justice system in the Free State. Although McGrath was Minister for Industry and Commerce, his empire extended to Oriel House and Military Intelligence. In a memorandum to the government before O'Higgins's conference, McGrath's department concluded that

> in the light of experience gained in the late Civil struggle it seems that the maintenance of a strong and efficient armed detective force will be an absolute necessity for some time to come. It is understood that the Minister for Home Affairs is arranging for the amalgamation of the best elements of the C.I.D. and the 'G' Division, DMP into a permanent detective force with jurisdiction over the whole Free State.

But, the memorandum insisted, there was still a need to maintain the 'Protective Corps' which provided security for government ministers, and it suggested that yet another 'Auxiliary Corps of temporary Detective Officers' be set up 'from demobilised Army Officers and CID Officers.' It accepted that the detection of ordinary crime would be coped with by the ordinary permanent police forces but it would seem as if the Crimes Branch of the Civic Guard should be strengthened by the picking out of special men in each Police Area to be employed only on detective work. This special force would be the body which would ask for and obtain where necessary the assistance of the Armed detective force. In a few words the new armed force should be utilised by the supreme police authority to perform only those duties which could not be performed by ordinary police officers without undue risk.'[8]

It would have been an extraordinary submission from Industry and Commerce if the Minister had been anyone other than McGrath, and it showed the difficult and fractured legacy the Civil War had left, compounded by the death of Collins. By now even McGrath realised that the existence of Oriel House was an embarrassing reminder of the Free State's murkier origins. Its methods were no longer necessary, or acceptable, and were becoming increasingly damaging on the political front. For instance, the reopening of the Mallow Viaduct on 15 October 1923, restoring the main railway link between Cork and Dublin, which should have been a cause for celebration, was immediately overshadowed by the start of the mass hunger strike in Mountjoy Prison and by the inquest into the death of Noel Lemass.

Lemass was a veteran of the War of Independence who had taken the anti-Treaty side in the Civil War. He seems to have been one of those individuals, like Darrell Figgis and Erskine Childers, who generated a particular animosity in some of his enemies. The British authorities had reputedly issued an order that he could be shot on sight; on one occasion his younger brother, Seán, had been arrested mistakenly by British Military Intelligence and then released. In the Civil War he appears to have been one of that numerous band of Dublin Corporation employees who were paid their wages while engaged in various revolutionary activities.

Having escaped from Free State custody twice, and being blamed for various deaths, ranging from Sergeant Paddy Lowe to General Seán Hales on the Free State side, Lemass fled to the Isle of Man, only returning in the summer of 1923. He sought out the superintendent of the Corporation's Cleansing Department, J. J. Devine, for the purpose of getting his old job back. They met for lunch in the Wicklow Hotel on 3 July and left together. A short distance along Exchequer Street they were stopped and searched by two armed men in plain clothes, who took them to within sight of Oriel House. Devine was released once he satisfied his captors that he was who he said he was. He was told to keep quiet about the incident. Noel Lemass was never seen alive again.

His body was found on Glendoo Mountain, near Glencree, on Friday 12 October 1923. It was badly decomposed but had clearly been mutilated. The South County Dublin Coroner, Dr J. P. Brennan, told the jury that from the reports he had received 'it would appear that the teeth were torn from the jaw and that, in conjunction with the fact that hairs were found beside the body, suggested a barbarism of which the most pitiless savage would be ashamed.'

The dead man's father, John Lemass, identified the body from the clothing and a rimless lens, part of a pair of rimless spectacles of the type worn by his son. Other items that confirmed his identity included spats, black silk socks and tan shoes. He had been the well-turned-out son of a long-established family of milliners and hatters in the city, who had been meeting his former supervisor to pick up the pieces of his life when he met his abductors. The case was adjourned to allow for a full post-mortem examination of the body.

That afternoon Dublin Corporation adjourned after passing a motion of sympathy with the Lemass family. It was proposed by Laurence Raul, who had once supported the dead man's application for half pay while interned, and seconded by another Sinn Féin councillor, Joe Clarke, who had himself experienced the hospitality of Military Intelligence a few months earlier. The council 'condemned the death of Noel Lemass, an esteemed and worthy officer of this Council whose body had been discovered, foully and diabolically murdered.' It instructed the Lord Mayor and the Law Agent to attend the inquest, and it further condemned 'the system that organises and sustains these murder gangs.' Alderman J. J. Murphy declared, without any sense of irony, that it was 'men of the type of Noel Lemass that had won this country the position in which it stood today.'[9]

The next day the Sinn Féin ard-fheis adjourned to allow members to attend the funeral of the dead man. Until then it had been largely the funerals of the Free State's martyred dead that had attracted the crowds, but Republicans now had a rare opportunity to rally support in what became a massive demonstration of strength. The body was brought from Rathmines Town Hall, where the inquest had been adjourned, through the main thoroughfares to the Pro-Cathedral, with Cumann na mBan providing a guard of honour, led by Constance Markievicz. The coffin was draped in the Tricolour as it lay in state in Marlborough Street.

The following day thousands thronged the city centre as the hearse began its long journey not so much through the city as around it. Leaving the Pro-Cathedral, it crossed O'Connell Street, proceeded past the Lemass shop in Capel Street, then across the river for a circuit past City Hall and Trinity College before returning over the Liffey to continue up O'Connell Street and on to Glasnevin cemetery via Whitworth Road, the nearest it was allowed to Mountjoy Prison. The Lord Mayor, city councillors, delegates to the Sinn Féin ard-fheis, including Count Plunkett and Mary MacSwiney, released prisoners and another contingent of Cumann na mBan, augmented by women members of the Irish Citizen Army, joined the procession. It took more than two hours to reach its destination.

Earlier, at the Sinn Féin ard-fheis, Mary MacSwiney urged the young men of Ireland to adopt a policy of passive resistance to the Free State, as now was not the time for armed force.[10]

The government still had to endure the findings of the inquest when it resumed. The main focus of interest was the intimidation of witnesses, who were all young friends or acquaintances of Lemass. A copy of a threatening letter sent to each of the witnesses was read out. It was headed *Headquarters Defence Unit, Old IRA* and informed each recipient that

Owing to your lying statement one of our members has been placed under arrest. This order is served on you in order that you may know the position.

Take notice that:

(*a*) You have been sentenced to death for making statements likely to cause disaffection to our forces;

(*b*) You will attend forthwith at Military Headquarters, Dublin, and deny absolutely that Captain J. Murry ever stated to you that he shot the late lamented Mr. Lemass.

(*c*) If you or any person states that the officer mentioned had anything to do with the execution of Lemass they will be dealt with as at (*a*).

The death sentence would be commuted if they carried out the instructions in the letter.

Lemass is gone and the earlier he is forgotten the better. Take care you do not meet the same fate. Signed Fifty Members of the Old IRA.

There was no Captain J. Murry, but there was a Captain Henry Murray, who had questioned one of the young witnesses about Lemass's disappearance. Murray was a veteran of the 1916 Rising, who had served in the IRA before the Truce, had then joined the National Army and taken part in the attack on the Four Courts. After serving for a brief time in Military Intelligence as an assistant to Joe McGrath he had transferred to the CID in Oriel House and had been involved in establishing the Protection Corps to provide bodyguards to government ministers.[11] 'Old IRA' was a name sometimes used to refer to the IRA Organisation, but the amateurish attempts at intimidation hardly looked like the work of men such as Murray, and the only other officer allegedly involved, named Sears, did not exist. Nevertheless the whole affair was deeply embarrassing for the government, with Eoin O'Duffy being called to give evidence and pleading privilege about the identity of some of those investigating Lemass's death.

The jury returned a verdict that the dead man was 'brutally and wilfully murdered.' There was insufficient evidence to establish the identity of the perpetrators but, the jury said, 'we are convinced that armed forces of the State have been implicated in the removal and disappearance of Noel Lemass from the streets of Dublin.' It demanded a judicial inquiry. Kevin O'Higgins, as Minister for Home Affairs, pointed out that the inquest itself was a judicial inquiry, and he rejected the jury's opinion that the armed forces of the state were involved as 'entirely unsupported by the evidence.'[12]

Once Joe McGrath was gone from the government, the days of the CID were numbered. It was disbanded following the Lemass inquest, and in April the DMP would follow, its constables becoming members of the Civic Guard. They continued operating on the same beats they always had in what was now the Dublin Metropolitan Area of the Garda Síochána. None of them could be deployed outside Dublin without their own consent. Thus two more Dublin institutions disappeared, the DMP perhaps the more lamented of the two.[13]

———

Another casualty of Noel Lemass's brutal death and the recovery of Republican fortunes was Séamus Hughes, who lost a South Dublin by-election to Seán Lemass in November 1924. Cumann na nGaedheal had faced a series of setbacks that year, culminating in the resignation of Joe McGrath and eight other deputies, who formed a 'National Group' in October 1924. Faced with the prospect of another pro-Treaty party and a raft of by-elections in the new year, the Cumann na nGaedheal executive set up a new organising committee that sidelined Hughes. It was chaired by J. J. Walsh, the Postmaster-General who had clashed with McGrath over the handling of the postal strike, with an executive secretary, Liam Burke, appointed on a higher salary than Hughes.

It was a repeat of events in the ITGWU.[14] On this occasion, however, Hughes's luck changed. He left Cumann na nGaedheal to become the first announcer on the Free State's new radio station, 2RN, which opened on 1 January 1926. Based first at studios in Little Denmark Street, it soon moved to the GPO. The station was grossly understaffed, but it was the sort of pioneering activity at which Hughes excelled. His carefully modulated tones made him an ideal announcer, and he also produced a traditional music programme, greeted guests, and served as general factotum. He was appointed acting assistant director to the station in 1929.

When Fianna Fáil came to power in 1932 the station was reorganised and Hughes, as someone strongly associated with the former regime, once more found his wings clipped. Then, in 1940, cut-backs occasioned by war in Europe brought his secondment from the station to the postal censorship section of the Department of Defence.

Throughout this time his religious convictions took precedence over his previous commitment to politics. From 1924 he wrote a column in the *Catholic Herald*, joined the newly established Catholic social movement An Ríoghacht in 1926, and in 1930 joined the Knights of Columbanus. He would later be a founding member of the

Irish Christian Front, which sent aid to General Franco during the Spanish Civil War—an unexpected destination for a former follower of Larkin and Connolly.[15]

Joe McGrath underwent a similar transformation. His National Group never mounted a challenge to Cumann na nGaedheal and quickly disappeared, leaving the IRA Organisation without any potential political vehicle or direction. It staggered on for some eighteen months after the mutiny and was kept under investigation by Military Intelligence. There were several dismissals of Organisation activists from the National Army in early 1925 when it attempted to extend its influence there and it resumed contacts with anti-Treaty IRA personnel, especially in Dublin. Some IRA units indicated a willingness to take Organisation men into membership. There were also contacts with some Sinn Féin TDs, as well as Dan Breen, who had been elected for his native Tipperary and took his seat in Leinster House as an independent. Attempts to infiltrate the Association of Ex-Officers and Men of the National Army, set up to lobby the government for members' welfare, came to nothing, for it was in no better shape than the IRA Organisation.

By October 1925 Military Intelligence reported that no meetings of the IRA Organisation had been held for two months, 'and many who were ardent supporters of Tobin ... have fallen away in disgust at the lack of policy and general ineptitude of the whole group.' The ultimate humiliation was for it to be bracketed with other marginal groups, such as the communists, part of an exercise in intelligence bookkeeping rather than signifying anything in its own right.[16]

Meanwhile McGrath went to work for Siemens-Schuckert on the Shannon hydro-electric scheme that he had initiated in the Dáil when Minister for Industry and Commerce. He soon made a name for himself as a strike-breaker, bringing in ex-servicemen and seeing off a campaign for union recognition by his old comrades in the ITGWU and the Limerick Trades Council. But it was his involvement in the Irish Hospitals Sweepstake with the bookmaker Dick Duggan that transformed his fortunes. He was able to use his old revolutionary contacts to create an international network of agents, particularly in North America. The former finance officer of the ITGWU went on to become one of the richest men in Ireland and its most successful racehorse owner. His attitude to unions was totally opportunist, recognising them in some companies that he acquired, such as Waterford Glass and the Irish Glass Bottle Company, while keeping them at arm's length in those where he could, such as the Hospitals Sweepstake. His main interests outside business were religion and gambling. Despite his strong associations with Oriel House and Free State atrocities in the Civil War, he was reconciled with Seán Lemass in the 1930s, and they belonged to the same poker school.

Some of McGrath's old associates did not fare so well. Emmet Dalton, Thomas Ennis and Paddy O'Daly, the trio of Dubliners who secured the capital for the Free State in the crucial week of fighting that began with the attack on the Four Courts, found it hard to adjust to civilian life. Dalton resigned his commission on 9 December 1922 in the aftermath of the reprisal executions. Although he sanctioned summary executions in his own command area in the early stages of the Civil War, his attitude changed subsequently, and in November he made it clear to Mulcahy that he wished to resign.[17] Dalton personified the hybrid patriot who came from a strong Home Rule family background. He served in the British army, the IRA and the National Army in an almost instinctive way, responding to the national mood rather than because of any underlying political ideology. Other senior officers from similar backgrounds, such as Charles Russell and W. R. E. Murphy, do not seem to have engaged with the IRA Organisation, and Dalton himself probably acted on the strength of close personal relationships he had formed with the Collins military cabal during the War of Independence. Once confronted with the logic of the choices posed by the IRA Organisation's policy he quickly found the potential consequences unacceptable. He seems to have acted often on honourable impulses without considering their long-term consequences. On this occasion he was offered the £1,000-a-year clerkship of the Seanad by W. T. Cosgrave; but an equally impulsive decision to become guarantor for bank loans taken out by relatives proved fatal to his public-service career and he once more resigned. His initial business ventures ranged from selling encyclopaedias to working as a private detective. He enjoyed little financial success and developed a serious drinking problem that he overcame only in the 1930s. Eventually he moved to England, where he became a successful sales agent for Paramount Studios and then a film producer. His most lasting material legacy was Ardmore Studios in Bray, which was part-financed by the Industrial Development Authority. Seán Lemass played a central role in promoting the project as Minister for Industry and Commerce. The studios survived receivership in 1963 to provide a base for the Irish film industry. Dalton's younger brother, Charlie, who had been forced out of the National Army by the mutiny, became a manufacturers' agent until Joe McGrath gave him a job on the board of the Hospitals Sweepstake. However, he developed paranoid schizophrenia, probably triggered by his experiences in the War of Independence and Civil War. Again Lemass assisted Dalton's destitute wife, Theresa, in securing a disability allowance and supporting her four young children while her husband was in St Patrick's Psychiatric Hospital.

Paddy O'Daly was less fortunate. He saw the writing on the wall with the army mutiny debacle and resigned his commission in March 1924 to become a building contractor, giving work to National Army veterans. But by the 1930s he was working as an overseer in the Board of Works (later the Office of Public Works). He re-enlisted during the years of the Second World War, serving as a company commander in the Construction Corps, before returning to the building trade. He also became a member of the Third Order of St Francis.

Tom Ennis, who worked for a time as a private detective with Emmet Dalton, was appointed bailiff of the Phoenix Park, with a relatively comfortable salary of

£300 a year. He also had a wound pension of £120 a year for an injury sustained during the attack on the Custom House in the War of Independence. Personal tragedy affected his family too when his daughter was killed by her fiancé, who then shot himself.

Without Collins, most of these men had no political compass to guide them through the rapidly changing 1920s and 30s. Perhaps the 'mutineer' who made the most successful adjustment was Liam Tobin, Collins's deputy director of intelligence during the War of Independence. As Patrick Long points out, 'Tobin sought a political "third way", anticipating the constitutional republicanism of Fianna Fáil, while running the Gresham Motor Hire Service.' He organised a short-lived political party, Clann na nGaedheal, and, like some of his old comrades, worked for McGrath's Irish Hospitals Trust in the United States. Unusually, he then re-entered the public service, becoming superintendent of the Oireachtas in Leinster House from November 1940 until his retirement in December 1959. The appointment was a tribute to the respect in which he was held by former friends and foes. Like so many of his contemporaries, his religious beliefs deepened, and he regularly organised retreats to the Jesuit Centre at Milltown. One of those who shared his enthusiasm for these retreats was Richard Mulcahy. There was a collegiality of beliefs among these men that embraced more than the standard war veterans' camaraderie. Most of them continued to live in the city and the state they had helped to create, and some, like many veterans, would come to resent the public's indifference. Like so many of his former comrades, Tobin was accorded military honours when he was buried in 1944 in Glasnevin Cemetery.[18]

————

On Saturday 9 August 1924 there was a garden party at Beech Park, Templeogue, Co. Dublin, to coincide with the Dublin Horse Show. The *Irish Times* reported:

> It was the first 'At Home' given by President Cosgrave in his newly reconstructed house, and it brought to a very happy close the round of social engagements associated with Dublin's first gala week.
>
> The large and fashionable gathering present was representative of all interests in the Free State, and included several distinguished guests from home and foreign parts. Delightful weather favoured the event. The rendering of a very select programme of music by Colonel Fritz Brase, contributed much to the general enjoyment.[19]

It was almost exactly three years since the same newspaper enthused over the prospect of the Treaty negotiations coming to a swift and happy conclusion. Much had changed, and much remained the same. An Irish army band conducted by a German officer with seventeen years' foreign service was one of the newer and pleasanter aspects of the change. Figures such as the Earl and Countess of Fingall had been attending such events since the previous century, and it was a sense of continuity that predominated, confirmed by the presence of veteran constitutional nationalists such as T. M. Healy, the Governor-General, William Field, former Parnellite MP for Dublin, and Major Bryan Cooper, former Unionist MP for South County Dublin. The current crop of Free State ministers and military men were all neatly packaged on the lawn that afternoon in their frock coats and uniforms, there was a strong contingent of clergy, and even the arts were represented by such well-established pre-war figures as W. B. Yeats, Sir John and Lady Lavery, G. K. Chesterton and John McCormack. The weekend was also marked by the Tailteann Games, which had been planned to celebrate the false peace of 1921 but deferred. They proved a qualified success.

A more substantial contribution to marking a new beginning for the Free State came four months later when the government decided to draw a line under the past. On 7 November 1924 an amnesty was declared, dropping all prosecutions for criminal offences between the signing of the Treaty on 6 December 1922 and 12 May 1923 where these arose 'out of the 1922–23 armed campaign against the State.' All convicted prisoners still in custody would be released. Criminal acts committed by Free State forces in the suppression of these 'disturbances' were also covered. Cosgrave said that the government's decision was induced by a 'belief that the highest interests of the state and the protection of law and order would best be served by the generous course it is now taking.' The fact that two by-election campaigns were under way no doubt reinforced this desire to be 'generous'. Besides, fewer than two hundred political prisoners were left in custody.

The amnesty also dealt with the constitutional anomaly first brought to public attention by Cormac Breathnach, the INTO delegate at the ILP&TUC conference in August 1922, when he asked which was the legal government: 'Is it the Provisional Government or the Dáil Government?' As the terms of the Anglo-Irish Treaty did not come into force until 6 December 1922, it could be argued that every act performed by the authorities before then was illegal; not only that but the executions, the army mutiny and the litany of atrocities on both sides could have far-reaching consequences for all concerned if a line was not drawn under them. To that extent, 7 November 1924 might be taken as marking the end not alone of the Civil War but of the 'Troubles' of the previous decade.[20]

––––

Dublin had played a unique role in those events, beginning with the Lockout of 1913, which shone a spotlight on the city's sweatshops and slums. It was in an effort to address at least some of these problems that the Viceroy, Lord Aberdeen, had offered a prize of £500 for the best plan for the urban renewal of the capital in the summer of 1914, only for any potentially benign future scenarios to be obliterated by the 'desolating cloudburst of war.' Instead the 1916 Rising established Dublin's revolutionary credentials and asserted the primacy of the physical-force tradition; but the fighting was neither long enough nor ferocious enough to level the slums. Keen to rebuild and restore normality, the British government made the fatal mistake of decoupling grants for reconstruction from compliance with new plans to rejuvenate the centre city. Commercial property-owners, led by William Martin Murphy, doggedly rebuilt what was there before, in spirit as well as body.

On the other hand, the revolutionary agitation that had been fomenting since the Lockout took a new direction. The syndicalist tradition of class war gave way to militant nationalism. Workers' militancy was inadvertently facilitated by the more benign negotiating structures introduced by the British government to secure industrial peace during its life-and-death struggle with imperial Germany. *De facto* trade union recognition saw wages rise and workers' confidence with them. It also channelled that militancy into the work-place rather than onto the street.

Women worked outside the home in far greater numbers than ever before, and separation payments to the wives of British soldiers and sailors saw the greatest transfer of wealth into the Dublin tenements in their history. The concession of the vote to women over the age of thirty in 1918 was a major advance for the feminist cause that enabled beneficiaries of third-level education, such as Hanna Sheehy Skeffington, Kathleen Lynn and Louie Bennett, to play a more effective role in society; but in general the demands of the struggle for independence saw female activists inducted into Cumann na mBan and reduced to the role of handmaidens to the Volunteers, just as the Irish Labour Party and Trade Union Congress became an auxiliary of Sinn Féin. In Dublin 'Republican Labour', led by William O'Brien and the ITGWU, underpinned the supremacy of militant separatism in the city's governance; even Southern unionists, such as the banker Andrew Jameson, facilitated this process as they saw dominion status becoming inevitable.

———

The main institutional beneficiary of independence was the Catholic Church. Its impact on education, social welfare, cultural mores and all that this implied for the daily life of its citizens was far more significant than the disputes over whether the 26 Counties should be a Free State or a Republic. It had been the leading civil society group to stand unequivocally behind the new state, and 'there was now a perfect fit between the outlook of the hierarchy and its political counterparts.'[21]

Partition was the other factor that changed the outlook and prospects of the mass of the population with the creation of two sectarian states in Ireland. The polarisation of the population on religious lines was part of a longer process that predated 1914, and David Fitzpatrick has argued convincingly that the years from 1920 to 1923 accelerated rather than started the Protestant exodus from the South.[22] If it was particularly marked in Dublin city and county, this reflects the high proportion of Protestants in the British administration and armed forces. These groups accounted for about a quarter of the total outflow of 106,456 in the Free State between 1911 and 1926, and the figure was disproportionately higher for the capital, making the indigenous outflow relatively meagre. The dispersed nature of Dublin's Protestant population, the city's strong British cultural heritage and the relative anonymity of suburbia probably made it a less alienating environment than many parts of the new Free State.[23]

On the other hand, despite the Belfast pogroms there was little to attract Northern Catholics to the South; indeed Southern nationalists, afraid of competition for scarce jobs and housing in Dublin and other centres, urged refugees to go home and 'fight their corner.'

The outcome of the Boundary Commission's deliberations in 1925, which finally secured the future of Northern Ireland, was a blessing in disguise, for, as Bill Kissane has pointed out, acceptance of the border gave the Free State a definable geographical structure with which citizens could identify, and reunification became an increasingly marginal irredentist project.[24]

In Dublin, as elsewhere in the South, the sharpest impact of the Troubles was on the working poor. For them the new Free State was a harsher place than its more secular, interventionist British predecessor. After the post-war boom there was no dole except for a minority of unionised workers with insurance schemes. Even these faced destitution if they were unemployed for any length of time. Working-class juveniles leaving school without skills, and their older counterparts who were too elderly or too weak to work, were dependent on Catholic charity. Men such as Frank Duff and Matt Talbot—and it was largely men—symbolised the new order. Their values were adopted in the private lives of nationalist crusaders such as Richard Mulcahy and Liam Tobin and even such unlikely candidates as Paddy O'Daly and Joe McGrath. Colourful, larger-than-life characters such as Jim Larkin, Ernie O'Malley, Liam O'Flaherty and Seán O'Casey provided an entertaining contrast to the drab new conformity, but they did not challenge it. All four spent significant parts of their lives abroad or on the margins. O'Casey would become a permanent exile. Like any highly conformist society, the Free State was not only a boring place to live in but a hostile one for minorities or dissidents of any type. It would be fifty years before significant cracks appeared in the edifice.

———

From the Truce until the Civil War fizzled out, militarism in all its variants reached its apogee. Acts of violence have a unique capacity to freeze a moment in time, whether it is a man bearing a woman around a table or two armed groups colliding. Normality is suspended until they are over and often transformed in the process. In Dublin, where its excesses were curbed, ironically, by the presence of a large British garrison, militarism still impinged on the lives of citizens to a degree out of all proportion to the number of activists involved. Militarist values and the belief that men, and women, who had dedicated their lives to the profession of violence were entitled to impose themselves on civil society were shared across the political divide. It was so ingrained that not only the vast majority of members of this self-electing elite believed it was natural to think of themselves in such terms but so did a much larger number of fellow-travellers and celebrants of that tradition. Fortunately there was no unified ideology to give coherence to this movement, as there was in parts of Continental Europe. In October 1922, at the height of the Civil War, Mussolini seized power in Italy, and paramilitary groups had a long and significant impact in states such as Spain, post-war Germany and the Baltic republics.[25] By contrast, the antipathy of the anti-Treaty IRA leadership to 'politics' and its inability to agree an effective military strategy for defending the Republic ensured that its opposition to the Free State would be a very localised affair.

The reinstitution of the parish pump as the fount of political power after the 'four glorious years' of national revolution began with the Truce and culminated in the attack on the railway network in the Civil War. It was a process personified in the death of Michael Collins in August 1922, probably the only individual whose survival might have changed the political nature of the Free State. If a highly conservative form of parliamentary democracy eventually triumphed, among the casualties was local democracy, not least in Dublin. None of this was obvious to the people most involved in the revolution when the prison gates opened in 1922 and again in 1924, least of all many of the prisoners.

Far from reflecting on the lessons of the past, even in the immediate aftermath of the Civil War, many of the survivors doggedly set to work rebuilding the IRA. In Dublin there was even a plan to disrupt the Tailteann Games, although nothing came of it.[26] In the wider world, business and employment levels remained subdued. Most people tried to put the Civil War behind them. The split in the IRA was discussed only once by the executive of the Irish Engineering and Industrial Union, itself a creation of the IRB, when it was agreed that members who joined the army (it did not specify which army) would have to pay only 9d a week in contributions instead of 1s 6d until their return to civilian employment.[27] But that was not much help to members released from prison, or demobilised, who had no job to return to. Many activists in the labour, republican and loyalist movements found emigration the only alternative to destitution at home.

The career of Thomas Leahy encapsulates the experience of many ordinary activists. He was a young Dublin boilermaker who owed his political education as an apprentice to rallies and meetings addressed by such figures as James Connolly, Jim Larkin and P. T. Daly. As was common for his generation of engineering craft workers, he had to emigrate to England after serving his time and ended up in a shipyard at Barrow-in-Furness making submarines for the Royal Navy. While there he became involved in local Irish clubs, including a company of the Irish Volunteers. Remarkably, and possibly reflecting the strong local left-radicalism of the yards, the Volunteer company not only supported the Provisional Executive when it broke with Redmond but decided to break all links with the Irish Party. Leahy returned home in November 1914 and found work in that hotbed of radicalism, the Dublin Dockyard. Having fought in the 1916 Rising, he made the unusual decision afterwards to transfer to the Irish Citizen Army, but he continued to be active in Sinn Féin rather than the Labour Party. He became a founder-member and trustee of the Irish Engineering and Industrial Union.

Having taken the anti-Treaty side in the Civil War and evaded capture in the July fighting, Leahy was arrested in October while trying to combine union work with that of intelligence officer for the Citizen Army. He was taken to Mountjoy Prison and subsequently interned at the Curragh. Released on 6 August 1923, he returned home,

> quite unexpected by my family. I found that Jim Larkin had just been there with some help for them which, I could see, was badly needed. After a week or so, I found I could not get employment at the Dockyard as a riveter ... on the grounds that my place had been filled, and if anything turned up I would be sent a message. I never received it.

Leahy was forced to look for work once more in Britain, where he discovered that his membership card for the new Irish union he had helped found was not recognised and he had to renew his membership of the Boilermakers' and Iron Shipbuilders' Society. Finally he secured steady employment in Scotland, working on the 'Clydeside rate' that he and his fellow-workers had spurned in Dublin. He brought his family to live with him in Glasgow, and during the Second World War he rose to be a senior shop steward in the shipyards, representing workers in national negotiations with the British government. He secured far better pay and conditions than he ever dreamed possible in his Dublin days, but he never forgot the

> men or events in those stirring and glorious years, and [I] trust that God in his mercy and own time will spare all those who fought the good fight for the Republic to meet again with all our people, north, south, east and west, under the flag of a United and Gaelic Free Ireland.[28]

For men like Leahy the revolutionary experience gave them a memory of life lived beyond the drabness and predictability of the everyday. Figures such as Joe McGrath, Kevin O'Higgins and Frank Duff may have been the temporal heirs of the revolutionary decade that shaped the lives of Dublin's citizens for generations to come, but the legacy of the Thomas Leahys proved equally enduring, offering a glorious if sometimes incoherent vision of the future as well as the past. In this he was a true disciple of Big Jim Larkin, the man who started it all in 1913 with his feet on the ground and his eyes set on the stars.

NOTES

Chapter 1

1. *Irish Times,* 14 July 1921.
2. *Irish Times,* 14 and 15 July 1921.
3. *Irish Independent,* 14 July 1921.
4. *Irish Times,* 15 July 1921.
5. Bureau of Military History, Liaison and Evacuation Papers.
6. *Irish Times,* 14, 21 and 27 July and 8 August 1921. For a legal analysis of the case see Enright, *The Trial of Civilians by Military Courts,* especially chap. 16.
7. *Irish Independent* and *Freeman's Journal,* 14 July 1921; Parkinson, *Belfast's Unholy War,* chap. 10.
8. *Freeman's Journal,* 16 July 1921.
9. *Irish Times,* 14 July 1921.
10. *Irish Times,* 8 and 11 August 1921.
11. Morrissey, *Laurence O'Neill,* p. 201–2.
12. Labour Party and ITUC Report, 1921. The report of the Standing Orders Committee states (p. 75) that membership is 300,000. However, the paid-up membership of affiliates in the financial report is only 196,000. See Nevin, *Trade Union Century,* p. 443–5.
13. Minutes of ILP&TUC, 2 August 1921, p. 89–93.
14. ILP&TUC Report for 1920–21, p. 3–21. One Labour Party and ITGWU member, Richard Corish, Mayor of Wexford, stood and was elected to what became the second Dáil on the Sinn Féin ticket (ILP&TUC Report for 1920–21, p. 111). See O'Connor, *Syndicalism in Ireland,* p. 44–6 and 51–3, for the spread of soviets in the pre-Truce period; Fitzpatrick, 'Strikes in Ireland,' for analysis of strike patterns and comparisons with Britain.
15. Minutes of Executive Committee, IES&FTU, 27 November 1920.
16. ILP&TUC Report for 1920–21, p. 34–39.
17. *Irish Times,* 3 January and 18 February 1921. Apprentices do not appear to have won any increase. The IES&FTU had sought 3d an hour for them.
18. Minutes of Resident Executive Committee, IES&FTU, 29 July 1921 (TEEU). *Irish Times,* 29 and 30 July 1921.
19. *Irish Times,* 2 August 1921.
20. Minutes of Resident Executive Committee, IEIU, 10 August 1921 (TEEU).

21. Minutes of Resident Executive Committee, IEIU, 24 August 1921 (TEEU), set no. 1. Minutes of Resident Executive Committee, IEIU, 30 September 1921 (TEEU).

22. Minutes of Resident Executive Committee, IEIU, 24 August 1921 (TEEU).

23. Minutes of Resident Executive Committee, IEIU, 24 August 1921 (TEEU), set no. 2. For the background to the DTC-DWC split see Cody et al., *The Parliament of Labour,* p. 126–135; *Irish Times,* 4 and 19 January 1920.

24. Minutes of Resident Executive Committee, IEIU, 2 September 1921 (TEEU).

25. Minutes of Resident Executive Committee, IEIU, 24 August and 2 September 1921 (TEEU).

26. *Irish Times,* 5 October 1921; Minutes of Resident Executive Committee, IEIU, 7 October 1921 (TEEU).

27. *Freeman's Journal,* 1 October 1921; Minutes of Resident Executive Committee, IEIU, 7 October 1921 (TEEU).

28. Minutes of Resident Executive Committee, IEIU, 15 September 1921 (TEEU).

29. Minutes of Resident Executive Committee, IEIU, 19 September 1921 (TEEU).

30. Minutes of Resident Executive Committee, IEIU, 21 September 1921; Minutes of National Executive Council, IEIU, 24–6 September 1921 (TEEU).

31. Bureau of Military History, Christy Farrelly (WMSP34REF20605), Martin Conlon (W24P10720), Joe Toomey (WMPS34REF21715), Luke Kennedy (WMPS34REF21389).

32. Minutes of Resident Executive Committee, IEIU, 16 September 1921 (TEEU).

33. Minutes of Resident Executive Committee, IEIU, 10 September 1921 (TEEU).

34. *Freeman's Journal,* 24 October 1921.

35. Minutes of Resident Executive Committee, IEIU, 24 October, 4, 9 and 28 November and 7 and 12 December 1921 and 10 January, 2 February and 6 March 1922 (TEEU). The motor trade employers settled for 3s a week but forced through a second cut of 3s from January 1922. Dublin Corporation eventually froze wages and salaries for six months, except where they were regulated by outside agreements. This condition disproportionately affected IEIU members.

36. Minutes of Resident Executive Committee, IEIU, 16 September 1921 (TEEU).

37. *Irish Times,* 4 and 11 October 1921; Minutes of Resident Executive Committee, IEIU, 7 October 1921 (TEEU).

38. Minutes of Resident Executive Committee, IEIU, 28 October 1921 (TEEU). He subsequently established a successful business making metal bed frames (Seán Redmond family memoir, 2007).

39. Minutes of Resident Executive Committee, IEIU, 14, 15, 22 and 25 November 1921 (TEEU); Robbins, *Under the Starry Plough,* p. 211; Minutes of Resident Executive Committee, IEIU, 3 January, 26 November and 10 and 12 December 1921 and 3 and 10 January 1922 (TEEU).

40. Minutes of Resident Executive Committee, IEIU, 26 November and 10 and 12 December 1921; also 3 and 10 January 1922; Robbins, *Under the Starry Plough*, p. 211.

41. Department of Agriculture and Technical Instruction, *Journal*, XVIII, p. 308–20; *Labour Gazette*, May 1921.

42. Ó Broin, *No Man's Man*, p. 3–10.

43. Ó Broin, *No Man's Man*, p. 75.

44. Ó Broin, *No Man's Man*, p. 75.

45. Ó Broin, *No Man's Man*, p. 90–96. It may of course be true that the Brennan family business benefited from the demise of a Protestant business rival, but no evidence was produced to show their complicity in such activities.

46. Pakenham, *Peace by Ordeal*, p. 227; Ó Broin, *No Man's Man*, p. 99–109; Maguire, *The Civil Service and the Revolution in Ireland*, p. 128.

47. Bureau of Military History, Truce Reports (LE/4).

48. Lady Alice Howard's Diary, 14 December 1921 and 27 January 1922 (NLI, ms. 3625).

49. Bureau of Military History, Military Archives, CD 6/48/1.

50. National Archives (London), CO 762.

51. National Archives (London), CO 762.

52. National Archives (London), CO 762.

53. Dublin Corporation Minutes, 6 March 1922; *Irish Times*, 7 March 1922.

54. Dublin Corporation Minutes, 7 June 1920, 6 December 1921.

55. Kennedy, *Frank Duff*, p. 46 and chap. 6.

56. Morrissey, *Edward J. Byrne*.

57. Murray, *Oracles of God*, app. 2

Chapter 2

1. MacMahon had attended Blackrock College, which also gave him a useful link with the President of Dáil Éireann, Éamon de Valera (Witness Statements, WS0465); Patrick Maume, 'James MacMahon,' in *Dictionary of Irish Biography*; Morrissey, *Laurence O'Neill*, p. 199, 205.

2. Morrissey, *Laurence O'Neill*, p. 206; Laurence O'Neill Papers, ms. 35,294/13.

3. Townshend, *The Republic*, p. 273–5.

4. Kissane, *The Politics of the Irish Civil War*, p. 67.

5. *Irish Times*, 2 and 3 January 1922. Paddy Belton boasted that he had recruited Collins to the IRB when they were both young emigrants in London. Brugha was a director of Lalor Ltd, candle-makers, for which he worked as a travelling salesman. He declined to draw a salary as Dáil Minister for Defence, living on his commercial income.

6. The censors chosen came from across the political spectrum. They were A. J. Murray, Joseph Cleary and Liam R. McGuirk (Irish Vigilance Association), Alderman Kathleen Clarke TD (anti-Treaty Sinn Féin), Alderman T. P. O'Reilly (Republican Labour), Alderman Thomas Lawlor (Trades Council Labour), Councillor Jennie Wyse Power and Councillor Elizabeth Ashton (pro-Treaty Sinn Féin), John Russell Stritch JP (Municipal Reform Association), P. T. Daly (Trades Council Labour), Mrs S. Russell Stritch and Mrs McKean (Poor Law Guardians).

7. *Irish Times* and *Irish Independent*, 3 January 1922.

8. The bill for Deedes, Templer and Company was later reduced to £45,000 by the commissioners appointed to examine claims, as the company could not seek compensation for the cost of reopening the premises when it did not intend to do so. Against this must be set the cost to Balbriggan of the loss of its largest employer (Fitzpatrick, *Terror in Ireland*, chap. 6). Cork faced an even bigger bill of £2 million because the 'guardians of law and order' had burnt down the city centre in retaliation for an ambush at Dillon's Cross.

9. Malicious damages and injuries awards presented to date for the period leading up to the Truce in Dublin City (Dublin Corporation Minutes, 2 January 1921, and Corporation Reports, vol. 2, 1921, item no. 208).

10. Rumpf and Hepburn, *Nationalism and Socialism in Twentieth-Century Ireland*, p. 34–6; Costello, *The Irish Revolution and Its Aftermath*, p. 300–301; *Irish Times*, 4 January 1922.

11. Robinson, *Memories*, p. 325–6.

12. Macardle, *The Irish Republic*, p. 649–51.

13. Witness Statements, Laurence Nugent (WS0907).

14. Quoted by Hopkinson in *Green Against Green*, p. 58–9.

15. Frank Aiken, commander of the 4th Northern Division, quoted by Hopkinson in *Green Against Green*, p. 41.

16. *Irish Times* and *Irish Independent*, 2 May 1922. Several bank branches refused to disclose the amounts taken.

17. *Irish Times* and *Irish Independent*, 5 March and 3 August 1922, 31 July 1923; *Weekly Irish Times*, 4 August 1923; Yeates, *A City in Wartime*, p. 204–9; Irish Prison Records, 1790–1924, Mountjoy Prison (http://findmypast.ie/record?id=ire%2fp risr%2frs00018281%2f4492735%2f00296&parentid=ire%2fprisr%2frs00018281 %2f4492735%2f00296%2f018).

18. Witness Statements, Oscar Traynor (WS0340); Duggan, *A History of the Irish Army*.

19. Pinkman, *In the Legion of the Vanguard*, p. 86–9. Once arrived in Kilkenny, A Company mutinied over the lack of uniforms, boots and decent food.

20. Witness Statements, Laurence Nugent (WS0907).

21. Townshend, The Republic, p. 356–7.
22. Witness Statements, Laurence Nugent (WS0907). Members of the Dublin ASU were offered positions in the Dublin Guard or told to return to their Volunteer companies.
23. Oscar Traynor Papers (Military Archives).
24. Andrews, *Dublin Made Me*, p. 103, 214–5.
25. Witness Statements, Laurence Nugent (WS0907), Oscar Traynor (WS0340); File CD 6/49/1 (Military Archives). For the occupational composition of Dáil members see Rumpf and Hepburn, *Nationalism and Socialism in Twentieth-Century Ireland*, p. 35. They do not give the occupations of sixteen deputies, twelve of whom voted for the Treaty and four against.
26. Townshend, *The Republic*, p. 432 for O'Duffy quotation and p. 440 for Lynch.
27. Dublin Corporation Minutes, 5 March 1923, item 182: Report 308, 1923.
28. Dublin Corporation Minutes, 28 December 1921 and 6 June 1922, 5 March 1923; *Irish Times*, 29 December 1921 and 7 June 1922.
29. Dublin Corporation Minutes, 5 December 1921 and 25 January 1922, item 75; *Irish Times*, 6 December 1921; Yeates, *A City in Turmoil*, p. 218–21.
30. Dublin Corporation Minutes, 30 January 1922, item 77; Witness Statements, Oscar Traynor (WS0340). One possible reason for the high rate of unemployment is that a significant number of Dublin Volunteers interned in 1921 may well have forfeited their jobs.
31. *Irish Times*, 31 May 1923.
32. Report of the Committee on the Complaints of British Ex-Servicemen, para. 34 (National Archives, Department of the Taoiseach, S5560).
33. O'Sullivan, 'Houses for Heroes'. The Legion Hall in Killester was subjected to an arson attack in April 1928, and shots were fired at it the following October.
34. Phelan was sentenced to death in England in 1923 for IRA activities, but the sentence was commuted to life imprisonment. He wrote his first best-seller, *Lifer*, after fourteen years in Dartmoor Prison.
35. Fallon et al., *Come Here to Me!* p. 167–170; *Irish Times* and *Irish Independent*, 19, 21 and 23 January 1922; and Séamus Phelan for information on his father's part in the occupation.
36. ILP&TUC, Report of National Executive to 28th Annual Congress, 1922.
37. *Irish Times*, 19 January.
38. *Irish Times*, 3 January 1922.
39. The three hospitals are now incorporated in Beaumont Hospital, Dublin. The health service seems to have been the one area where significant increases continued to be secured for IEIU members: see, for instance, the settlement at Stewart's Hospital in Minutes of Resident Executive Committee, IEIU, 2 March 1922 (TEEU).

40. Nevin, *Trade Union Century*, p. 433.

41. Minutes of Dublin Trades Council, 25 March 1922; Minutes of National Executive Council, IEIU, 16 November 1921 (TEEU).

42. See Minutes of Resident Executive Committee, 10 January 1922, for application of the principle at the Pigeon House power station. The IEIU also lobbied the Department of Labour and Department of Trade and Commerce over companies and 'Catholic Institutions' giving contracts to Belfast firms: see, for instance, Minutes of Resident Executive Committee, IEIU, 23 March 1922 (TEEU).

43. Minutes of National Executive Council, IEIU, 30 November 1921 (TEEU).

44. Minutes of Resident Executive Committee, IEIU, 21 December 1921 and 23 March 1922; Minutes of National Executive Committee, IEIU, 31 December 1921 (TEEU).

45. Minutes of Mass Meeting, Abbey Theatre, Dublin, 1 January 1922.

46. Minutes of National Executive Council, IEIU, 31 December 1921 (TEEU).

47. Minutes of Resident Executive Committee, 17 January 1922.

48. Minutes of Resident Executive Committee, IEIU, 13 February 1922. Even the bingo sessions were showing a healthy profit after initial losses: Minutes of Resident Executive Committee, IEIU, 15 and 27 March 1922 (TEEU). The purchase of the linoleum sparked a strong reaction from one member of the committee, J. Maguire, who described it as a 'ridiculous' decision.

49. Minutes of Resident Executive Committee, IEIU, 13 and 20 February 1922 (TEEU).

50. Minutes of Provisional Committee, IES&FTU, 16 and 25 September 1920; Minutes of Resident Executive Committee, IEIU, 10 April 1922 (TEEU). At the time of writing the Electrical National Joint Industrial Council's registered employment agreement is facing a legal challenge from a number of employers.

51. Ministerial positions were somewhat flexible in the early days of the Free State. Blythe would also act as Minister for Local Government before becoming Minister for Finance in 1923. Minutes of Resident Executive Committee, IEIU, 25 January 1922 (TEEU). See Smellie, *Ship Building and Repairing in Dublin*, for a discussion of the problems in implementing the 'Clydeside' rate in the Dublin shipbuilding and repair industry.

52. Minutes of Resident Executive Committee, IEIU, 19 January 1922 (TEEU).

53. The Irish Trades Union Congress and Labour Party was established in 1914 as a result of a resolution of the Irish Trades Union Congress in 1912. In November 1918 the name was changed to Irish Labour Party and Trade Union Congress.

54. Witness Statements, T. Leahy (WS0660).

55. See, for instance, Witness Statements, Martin Conlon (W24SP10720), Luke Kennedy (W24B860) and Joseph Toomey (WMSP 34 REF 2175) on Michael Collins

and his 'secret intelligence unit'. It is not clear what the status of this unit was and whether it operated under the auspices of the IRB, the IRA or Dáil Éireann's Department of Finance; what is clear is that it was controlled by Collins.

56. ILP&TUC, Report of 28th Annual Meeting, held in the Mansion House, Dublin, August 1922, and of the Special Congress on Election Policy held in the Abbey Theatre, Dublin, 21 February 1922.

57. McCarthy, 'Labour and the 1922 General Election.' All other quotations are from the ILP&TUC Reports for 1922 (ICTU Archive).

58. A 1913 veteran, McPartlin would die the following year.

59. It is unlikely that all 245 accredited delegates attended the conference; nor are any abstentions recorded.

60. A strong Labour Party supporter all his life, Frank Robbins makes no reference to his role at the ILP&TUC conference in his memoir, *Under the Starry Plough.*

61. Minutes of National Executive, IEIU, 21 April 1922 (TEEU).

62. *Irish Times,* 22 February 1922; ILP&TUC Minutes for Special Delegate Conference on Election Policy, 21 February 1922; Minutes of Resident Executive Committee, IEIU, 20 February 1922 (TEEU); *Freeman's Journal,* 23 February 1922; *Irish Independent,* 22 February 1922; Mitchell, *Labour in Irish Politics,* p. 154.

63. *Irish Times,* 28 March 1922 and 2 February 1924.

64. *Irish Times,* 15 April 1922; Kostick, *Revolution in Ireland,* p. 202–6; *Irish Independent* and *Irish Times,* 19 May 1922, and *Irish Times,* 8 June 1922.

65. *Irish Times,* 23 May 1922.

66. *Irish Times,* 25 May 1922.

Chapter 3

1. *Irish Independent,* 25 April 1922.

2. ILP&TUC Report, 1922, p. 27.

3. Hanley, 'The Irish Citizen Army after 1916'; Fox, *The History of the Irish Citizen Army,* chap. 17; Robbins, *Under the Starry Plough,* p. 232–3.

4. *Irish Times,* 28 June 1922. For the role of the Carpenter family in Dublin's radical politics see http://1913committee.ie/blog/?p=542.

5. *Irish Times,* 26 April 1922.

6. Claim by E. M. and H. K. Biggs, National Archives (London), CO 762.

7. Clark, *Everyday Violence in the Irish Civil War,* p. 187.

8. *Irish Times* and *Irish Independent,* 26 May 1922.

9. *Irish Times,* 26 April 1922.

10. *Evening Telegraph,* 1 April 1922.

11. *Irish Times*, 4 April 1922.

12. Witness Statements, Maud Gonne MacBride (ws317).

13. *Irish Independent*, 11 April 1922.

14. Joseph O'Connor says that the anti-Treaty forces took over the Freemasons' Hall only after it had been occupied by refugees to ensure that it was not damaged: Witness Statements, Joseph O'Connor (ws544).

15. Masonic Grand Lodge of Free and Accepted Masons, Ireland, Annual Report, 1922; Witness Statements, Joseph O'Connor (ws544).

16. *Irish Independent*, 23 March 1922.

17. Robbins, *Under the Starry Plough*, p. 230–32.

18. *Freeman's Journal*, 2–9 May 1922.

19. Steam Coal Chartering of Steamers re Belfast Boycott, Irish Railway Record Society Archives, Dublin (3288B).

20. Dublin Corporation Minutes, 10 May 1922; *Irish Times* and *Irish Independent*, 10 May 1922.

21. William Murphy, 'Darrell Figgis,' in *Dictionary of Irish Biography*; *Irish Times* and *Irish Independent*, 18–21 June 1922.

22. Macready, *Annals of an Active Life*, Vol. 2, p. 654. The instructions two months earlier related to the deaths of three British officers in Co. Cork in controversial circumstances, when Macready was told not to aggravate the situation by taking action, although it was a breach of the Truce.

23. O'Malley, *The Singing Flame*, p. 89–90.

24. The British government may have despatched an artillery unit to Dublin from Northern Ireland to assist. An unpublished memoir by Lance-Bombardier Percy Creek of the Royal Field Artillery, found by the historian William Sheehan, states that Creek's unit, stationed in Co. Fermanagh, had been despatched to Dublin and fired two rounds at the Four Courts before being ordered to stop. There are problems with this account, especially over the timing and siting of the battery when it was engaged, but if it is accurate it means the threat of major British military intervention was even more immediate than previously thought. *Irish Times*, 5 November 2012; Hennessy, 'Four Courts still in headlines.'

25. Macready, *Annals of an Active Life*, Vol. 2, p. 655.

26. Deasy, *Brother Against Brother*, p. 49.

27. Deasy, *Brother Against Brother*, p. 113.

28. Gillis, *The Fall of Dublin*, p. 53.

29. O'Malley, *The Singing Flame*, p. 103.

30. Macready, *Annals of an Active Life*, Vol. 2, p. 656.

31. Fox, *The History of the Irish Citizen Army*, p. 221.

32. Claims submitted to Dublin Corporation. The bill for war materials supplied by the British government to the National Army would not come until the Statement

of the Financial Position and the Estimates of the Value of Transferred Property were agreed between the two governments in July 1923.

33. Witness Statements, Seán Prendergast (WS802).
34. Pinkman, *Legion of the Vanguard*, p. 119–20.
35. Dorney, 'Casualties of the Irish Civil War in Dublin.'
36. Letter by Father Albert, 12 August 1923 (Irish Capuchin Provincial Archives).
37. Andrews, *Dublin Made Me*, p. 234.
38. Witness Statements, Seán Prendergast (WS802).
39. Pinkman, *Legion of the Vanguard*, p. 128–9.
40. Ó Duigneáin, *Linda Kearns*, p. 69; *Irish Times* and *Irish Independent*, 10 and 11 July 1922.
41. Witness Statements, Annie Farrington (WS749).
42. Reilly, *Joe Stanley*.
43. Canning, *British Policy towards Ireland*, chap. 3; Hopkinson, *Green Against Green*, p. 83–6.

Chapter 4

1. Walsh, Oonagh, *Anglican Women in Dublin*, p. 35–6. She makes the point that the exploits of 'diehards' such as 'Ernie O'Malley, Liam Mellows or Liam Lynch do not arouse the same irritated hostility' as women opposed to the Treaty.
2. Morrissey, *Edward J. Byrne*, p. 88–9.
3. *Irish Independent*, 13 July 1922.
4. The *Irish Independent*, 12 July 1922, has a photograph of members of the 2nd Battalion joining the National Army before the public 'Call for Arms' was published. For the role of the IRB at this point in the crisis see Regan, *Myth and the Irish State*, p. 14–30.
5. Dublin Corporation Minutes, item 439, 18 July 1922.
6. Morrissey, *Edward J. Byrne*, p. 90–91.
7. *Irish Independent* and *Irish Times*, 13–20 July and 31 July 1922.
8. Boyne, *Emmet Dalton*, p. 176–7; Yeates, *A City in Turmoil*, p. 49–50, 218–19.
9. Cottrell, *The Irish Civil War*, p. 45; Hopkinson, *Green Against Green*, p. 145; Witness Statements, Laurence Nugent (WS0907). John Dorney (www.theirishstory. com/2012/06/19/casualties-of-the-irish-civil-war-in-dublin) puts the number of men arrested in the attempt to destroy the bridges at about 150.
10. *Irish Times*, 23 August 1922.
11. Irish Grants Commission, Sir Henry Robinson File, National Archives (London), CO 762.
12. Robinson, *Memories*, p. 330.
13. Irish Grants Commission, Sir Henry Robinson File, National Archives (London), CO 762.

14. Irish Grants Commission, James Crofton Dodwell Murray File, National Archives (London), CO 762.

15. West, *Horace Plunkett,* chap. 11 and 12. Besides having access to Plunkett's papers, West interviewed George Gilmore.

16. West, *Horace Plunkett,* p. 208–12, 217–19.

17. The demand for beds would fall to 28,823 by 1928 and the demand for meals to 60,237, but this was still far higher than anything seen in the Lockout or since the end of the post-war boom.

18. Annual Reports, Society of St Vincent de Paul, for Back Lane Shelter, 1912–25 (Dr Byrne's Laity Papers, AB7/Lay Organisations 476, Box 1).

19. *Dictionary of Irish Biography.*

20. *Dictionary of Irish Biography.*

21. *Dictionary of Irish Biography.* On 7 June 1925 (Trinity Sunday) he collapsed and died from a heart attack while hurrying to Mass at St Saviour's Church outside my grandmother's front door in Granby Lane, off Parnell Square. She had moved there after the Civil War incident mentioned in chapter 3.

22. Raftery and O'Sullivan, *Suffer the Little Children,* p. 19, 70.

23. My father was sent to Little Denmark Street Industrial School for mitching. Established by Dr Walsh in 1912, it was the only non-residential industrial school in the country, a half-way house to Artane and other institutions. Nevertheless, the discipline was ferocious and physical punishment a daily occurrence.

24. DMP Prisoners Books, 1907–9, 1911–13, 1916–18. Raftery and O'Sullivan, *Suffer the Little Children,* p. 26, 62.

25. *Irish Ecclesiastical Record,* vol. 18–20.

26. Dublin Diocesan Archives (Archbishop Byrne Laity File, AB7/Lay Orgs, 476, Box 1).

27. Dublin Diocesan Archives (Archbishop Byrne Laity File, ab/Lay Orgs, 476, Box 1). The Irish figures cover Northern Ireland as well as the Free State. The records suggest that at least some of the married women did not want husbands or immediate family to know of their pregnancy.

28. Eighth Annual Report of the Catholic Protection and Rescue Society (Dublin Diocesan Archives, Archbishop Byrne Laity File, AB7/Lay Orgs, 476, Box 1).

29. Rotunda Girls' Aid Society, Annual Reports, 1922–31 (Dublin Diocesan Archives, Archbishop Byrne Laity File, AB7/Lay Orgs, 476, Box 2).

30. Annual Reports for Catholic Girls' Club and Hostel (Dublin Diocesan Archives, Archbishop Byrne Laity File, AB7/Lay Orgs, 476).

31. 'Unions' were groups of parishes that combined to operate a poorhouse or workhouse, an obligation on parishes under the Poor Law.

32. Annual Report, Society of St Vincent de Paul, 1922.

33. Diarmaid Ferriter and Finola Kennedy, 'Frank Duff,' in *Dictionary of Irish Biography.*

34. Ó Broin, *Frank Duff,* p. 2–5. See also Kennedy, *Frank Duff,* chap. 3–4.

35. ILP&TUC, Conference Report, 1922, p. 237–8.

36. British soldiers who suffered from disabilities as a result of their service received pensions, but these were quite modest, as were payments to war widows. The basic widow's pay was 13s 9d, with 5s for a first child and diminishing amounts down to 3s for a tenth child.

37. National Library of Ireland (Ir 1792).

38. ISPCC, 36th Annual Report (National Library of Ireland, Ir 1792).

39. Commission to Inquire into Child Abuse, Report, Vol. 5, p. 5.

40. Yeates, *A City in Turmoil,* p. 32–7.

41. *Irish Independent,* 6 December 1921.

Chapter 5

1. *Irish Times,* 11 August 1922.

2. Maguire, *The Civil Service and the Revolution in Ireland,* p. 137.

3. The only exceptions were the four Unionist members for the University of Dublin (Trinity College) constituency, who refused to take their seats until the Dáil reconvened for one day as the 'House of Commons of Southern Ireland,' and Richard Corish, the Wexford trade union leader, who was elected with Sinn Féin approval. This did not prevent him incurring the disapproval of senior figures in the ILP&TUC.

4. There had been at least two unsuccessful attempts in Dublin.

5. *Irish Times* and *Irish Independent,* 14 August 1922.

6. *Irish Times,* 24 August 1922.

7. Boyne, *Emmet Dalton,* p. 229–35, 241.

8. *Irish Independent,* 8 August 1922.

9. ILP&TUC Conference Minutes, p. 155, 9 August 1922.

10. Dublin Corporation Minutes, 9 January 1922, item 59; *Irish Times,* 10 January 1922.

11. *Irish Independent,* 2 March 1922.

12. Maguire, *The Civil Service and the Revolution in Ireland,* p. 146.

13. Maguire, *The Civil Service and the Revolution in Ireland,* p. 147.

14. Brennan, 'The postal strike of 1922,' at www.theirishstory.com/2012/06/08/the-postal-strike-of-1922.

15. Memo from W. O'Brien, Department of Finance, on Cost of Living Report for Cabinet, 9 August 1922 (National Archives, TAOIS/S1802).

16. Quoted by Brennan in 'The postal strike of 1922,' at www.theirishstory.com/2012/06/08/the-postal-strike-of-1922.

17. *Irish Independent* and *Irish Times,* 12 September 1922.

18. National Archives, TAOIS/S1802.

19. Brennan, 'The postal strike of 1922,' at www.theirishstory.com/2012/06/08/the-postal-strike-of-1922.

20. The other mimeographed issue was on 9 July 1922, when a raid disrupted production for three days.

21. Irish Capuchin Provincial Archives. Brian Kirby, archivist of the order, points out that it has a fairly complete set of *Poblacht na hÉireann,* including multiple copies of some issues, suggesting that someone was using its premises in Church Street as a distribution centre.

22. *Poblacht na hÉireann,* issues 1–3, June 1922 (Irish Capuchin Provincial Archives).

23. Irish Capuchin Provincial Archives (CA/IR/1/7/3/1 to CA/IR/1/7/3/43).

24. A rhyme my mother taught me.

25. *Irish Times,* 11 October 1922.

26. *Irish Times* and *Irish Independent,* 21 September 1922.

27. *Irish Times,* 7 October 1922.

28. *Irish Times,* 5 October 1922.

29. Minutes, Dublin City Council, 9 October 1922; *Irish Times* and *Irish Independent,* 9 October 1922.

30. *Irish Times,* 24 October 1922; Minutes, Dublin Corporation, 23 October 1922; Morrissey, *Laurence O'Neill,* p. 218.

31. Details are taken from reports in the *Irish Independent* and *Irish Times* between 10 October and 16 November 1922. Emmet Dalton was married in Cork on 9 October, the day the inquest began in Dublin.

32. Pauric Travers, 'Michael Comyn,' in *Dictionary of Irish Biography.*

33. This would appear to have been the youngest but the tallest and oldest-looking youth, Joseph Rogers. If he was carrying them in his trench coat it may have been because, unlike the others, he was a new recruit and unknown to Dalton.

34. The fourth man arrested had given a false name and address and proved untraceable.

35. He subsequently served as Attorney-General to Cosgrave's government, advising on the ill-fated Boundary Commission. Appointed to the High Court in 11 January 1926, he ordered the release of General Eoin O'Duffy by the Fianna Fáil government at the height of the Blueshirt controversy. Nevertheless, in 1940 he was appointed to the Supreme Court and in July 1947 delivered his most celebrated judgement in the Sinn Féin funds case. Gerard Hogan, 'John O'Byrne,' in *Dictionary of Irish Biography.*

36. The British Prime Minister, Andrew Bonar Law, was reluctant to accept the nomination: he complained that Healy talked and drank too much. Frank Callanan, 'T. M. Healy,' in *Dictionary of Irish Biography.*

37. National Archives, TAOIS/S3331; Owen McGee, 'Henry Harrison,' in *Dictionary of Irish Biography*.

38. Witness Statements, Ernest Blythe (WS0939). Thomas Gay, an IRB member and long-standing intelligence operative working for Collins from the Black and Tan War, who was a librarian in Capel Street Library, may also have played a role in the formation of this unit.

39. Witness Statements, Patrick Michael Moynihan (W34SP15720), Ernest Blythe (WS0939), David Neligan (WS0380). Moynihan eventually paid a price for the unsavoury nature of his work when he was turned down for a veteran's pension. Fortunately, he already had one from the Post Office.

40. O'Halpin, *Defending Ireland*, p. 11–13.

41. Witness Statements, J. O'Connor (WS544); *Irish Independent*, 1 November 1922.

42. Witness Statements, J. O'Connor (WS544).

43. The *Irish Times* and *Irish Independent* of 9 November 1922 report that one National Army soldier was killed and seventeen others, as well as two civilians, wounded. They also state that the firing lasted fifteen minutes. The initial report for Military Intelligence by W. Fayne, brigade intelligence officer, states that one soldier was killed, fourteen soldiers wounded, and two attackers killed. A subsequent operational report dated the same day by Lieutenant Saurin gives a figure of twenty-two for National Army wounded and adds one civilian fatality to the total. Both reports state that the firing lasted only five minutes and 'that only slight [enemy] sniping was indulged in' after that. The second report says that fourteen prisoners were taken in the pursuit but makes no mention of any prisoners being shot.

44. *Irish Times*, 9 November 1922; Witness Statements, Cahir Davitt (WS1751). There was a similar attack the following night that disrupted a card game in the Judge Advocate's office. Two officers, who were lawyers on secondment to the National Army (and were losing heavily), grabbed their guns and ran out to help repel the attack, while the others continued playing. There were no casualties except for one of the lawyers, who ran into a barbed-wire barrier in the dark (www.theirishstory.com/2010/06/09/wellington-barracks-dublin-1922-a-microcosm-of-the-irish-civil-war/).

45. Witness Statements, J. O'Connor (WS544).

46. www.theirishstory.com/2010/06/09/wellington-barracks-dublin-1922-a-microcosm-of-the-irish-civil-war/.

47. National Army witnesses at these inquests were not usually named (*Irish Times*, 10 November 1922; *Poblacht na hÉireann*, 18 November 1922). A soldier called Christy Clarke was the implied assassin according to *Poblacht na hÉireann* (http://comeheretome.com/2013/02/04/james-spain-of-geraldine-square/).

48. Divisional Intelligence Department, Portobello Barracks, 3 November 1922; *Irish Times*, 4 and 23 November 1922.

49. *Irish Times*, 5 November 1922; Geraghty and Whitehead, *The Dublin Fire Brigade*, p. 174–5.

50. Share, *In Time of Civil War*, p. 74–5; *Weekly Irish Times*, 11 November 1922.

51. Irish Railway Record Society. There is no letter on file from Cosgrave, and the newspapers managed to call Glynn 'Tierney' in their reports. I am indebted to Peter Rigney for this information.

52. Debate on Emergency Powers Resolution, *Dáil Debates*, 27 September 1922.

53. National Archives, Department of the Taoiseach, S1369, 1 January 1923. The senior British civil servant who dealt with the request for help in finding a convenient offshore detention centre for Republican prisoners was Mark Sturgis, who was Assistant Under-Secretary for Irish Services after serving in Dublin Castle in the closing stages of the War of Independence and the Truce.

54. National Archives, Department of the Taoiseach, S1369, 1 January 1923.

55. *Irish Times* and *Irish Independent*, 28 September 1922.

56. *Dáil Debates*, 28 September 1922.

57. Murray, *Oracles of God*, p. 75–6.

58. *Irish Times* and *Irish Independent*, 18 November 1922; Witness Statements, Cahir Davitt (WS1751).

59. Cox, *Damned Englishman*, p. 271.

60. Davitt was a former judge of Dáil Éireann Circuit Court and a son of Michael Davitt, founder of the Land League.

61. Witness Statements, Cahir Davitt (WS1751).

62. Witness Statements, Ernest Blythe (WS0939).

63. Witness Statements, Ernest Blythe (WS0939).

Chapter 6

1. See, for instance, Republican leaflet issued after a raid on the home of Patrick Pearse's mother at St Enda's, Rathfarnham (National Archives, CA/IR/1/7/3/4).

2. O'Malley, *The Singing Flame*, p. 179–87.

3. Irwin, *Betrayal in Ireland*, p. 123.

4. *Irish Times*, 12 November 1922.

5. Bonar Law did indeed win the election and did honour the Treaty's terms.

6. A complicating factor in making direct comparisons between the Free State and Britain was the variation in weights and measures.

7. *Irish Times*, 9 September 1922; ILP&TUC Report for 1920–21, p. 34–9 (1922); Cabinet Minutes, 22 March 1922 (unnumbered), PG 23, 24 May 1922. See also letter from Ministry of Economic Affairs to Secretary of Post Office, 16 June 1922,

and Report to Minister of Economic Affairs, 9 August 1922 (National Archives, TAOIS/S1211).

8.   See *Irish Times,* 24 October 1922.

9.   Memo, 3 October 1922, National Archives, TAOIS/S1211; *Irish Times* and *Freeman's Journal,* 21 October 1922. Sir James Craig was no relation of the Northern Ireland Premier. He was an academic and physician whose primary political interest was in public health.

10. Local commissions were established for Co. Cork and Co. Waterford in February 1923.

11. Report of Commission on Prices, 3 November 1922 (National Archives, TAOIS/S1802).

12. *Irish Times* and *Irish Independent,* 11 November and 6 and 23 December 1922.

13. Report of Commission on Prices, 3 November 1922 (National Archives, TAOIS/S1802).

14. Darrell Figgis, Note to the Report of the Commission on Prices (National Archives, TAOIS/S1802).

15. Very little information is provided on prices in other towns.

16. Report of Commission on Prices, 25 July 1923, p. 14 (National Archives, TAOIS/S1802).

17. The president of the INUVGATA in 1920 was Patrick Moran, who was subsequently hanged in Mountjoy Prison for his involvement as an IRA officer on Bloody Sunday.

18. Yeates, *A City in Wartime,* p. 178–80, 308.

19. Report of Commission on Prices, 3 November 1922, p. 14 (National Archives, TAOIS/S1802).

20. National Archives, TAOIS/S1802, Correspondence, 15 August 1922 (1211), 19 August 1922 (E662) and undated (E706).

21. Report to Minister of Economic Affairs, 9 August 1922 (National Archives, TAOIS/S1211).

22. Report of Commission on Prices, 3 November 1922, p. 16 (National Archives, TAOIS/S1802).

23. William Murphy, 'Darrell Figgis,' in *Dictionary of Irish Biography.*

24. Six of the men who joined the British army had been among those locked out but had been taken back. One man was a strike-breaker; he was one of the two men who joined the Royal Navy.

25. Dublin Port and Docks Board, Namebook, 1895–1925 (Dublin Port Company Archive).

26. Pension file, Thomas James Ennis (w24sp7, 328).

27. Dublin Port and Docks Board, Namebook, 1895–1925 (Dublin Port Company Archive).

28. Report of the Committee on Claims of British Ex-Servicemen, General Observations, para. 7 (National Archives, Taoiseach S5560A).

29. Re-Employment of Disabled Soldiers and Sailors, List of GSWR employees who resumed employment after army service (Irish Railway Record Society Archives, IRRS 2877).

30. Rigney, 'Military service and GS&WR staff.'

31. Arthur Guinness, Son and Company Ltd, 'Roll of Employees who Served in His Majesty's Naval, Military and Air Forces, 1914–1918.'

32. European War, Allowances of Half Wages to Employees, 11 November 1919 (Guinness Archive, GDB/PE03.01/0661).

33. Two widows married before the war ended, saving the company any further payments to them (Memorandum, 23 December 1918, Guinness Archive, GDB/C004.06/0040.06).

34. Memorandum 3135, 13 November 1918 (Guinness Archive, GDB/C004.06).

35. Guinness Archive, GDB/C004.06/0040.07.

36. Report, Medical Department, 7 May 1921 (Guinness Archive, GDB/PE03.01/0661).

37. Report, Registry Department, 29 March 1923 (Guinness Archive, GDB/PE03.01/0661).

38. National Archives (AGO/92/2/1449, CSO G4034-21, FIN/1/48); Report of the Committee on British Ex-Servicemen's Claims, General Observations, para. 14 (National Archives, Taoiseach S5560A).

39. The other members of the committee were Cecil Lavery KC, who was briefly a Fine Gael TD and became a Supreme Court judge (chairman), J. F. Baxter, St Aidan's, Cavan, a large farmer and government supporter, and M. J. Beary, Department of Finance (secretary).

40. Report of the Committee on Claims of British Ex-Servicemen, General Observations, para. 18–28 (National Archives, Taoiseach S5560A).

41. Report of the Committee on Claims of British Ex-Servicemen, General Observations, para. 91 (National Archives, Taoiseach S5560A).

42. National Archives (AGO/92/2/1449, CSO G4034-21).

43. National Archives (AGO/92/2/1449, CSO G4034-21, appendix A).

44. Memorandum, 18 August 1921 (National Archives, AGO/92/2/1449 CSO G4034-21). Boyne, *Emmet Dalton*, p. 48.

45. *Irish Times*, 2 September 1921 and 31 May 1923.

46. *Irish Times*, 26 March 1921. One of them, Denis Lenehan, was a former sergeant-major in the Leinster Regiment, 'shot and left for dead' on his way home from Islandbridge Barracks. Kavanagh fails to mention that the only fatality in the attack was a twelve-year-old girl, Hanna Keegan. Another civilian was seriously injured.

47. Civil servants were entitled to full pay and the war bonus of 130 per cent on top of their army pay if they joined up.

48. Maguire, *The Civil Service and the Revolution in Ireland*, chap. 1. Nor was the Free State the only culprit: E. M. Tuite of Harcourt Street was seeking compensation from the Ex-Servicemen's Committee for the loss of his job with the Sailors' and Soldiers' Trust.

49. National Archives (TAOIS 3/495, Boxes 25–9, F/25 and F/49).

50. Nine hundred marks were needed to qualify for a job, with an additional 10 per cent for answering in Irish. National Army members who achieved this figure were then allocated another 150 marks, which improved their position on the panel and their level of entry to the civil service.

51. The NPGCA strongly contested the Department of Finance figure, claiming that far more ex-servicemen were employed as temporary clerks in 1922.

52. Report of the Committee on Claims of British Ex-Servicemen, para. 120–23.

53. Report of the Committee on Claims of British Ex-Servicemen, para. 131–32.

54. Report of the Committee on Claims of British Ex-Servicemen, para. 133.

55. Report of the Committee on Claims of British Ex-Servicemen, para. 137. Twenty cases were outside the terms of reference of the committee.

56. This was equivalent to the amount spent on the Governor-General's office in its first year—a comparison that no-one drew at the time.

57. Report of the Committee on Complaints of British Ex-Servicemen, para. 89. Society of St Vincent de Paul, Annual Reports, 1918–24: spending was £38,414 in 1918, £38,647 in 1919, £49,639 in 1920, £61,943 in 1921, £64,117 in 1922, £58,412 in 1923 and £65,996 in 1924.

58. Report of the Committee on Claims of British Ex-Servicemen, para. 89.

59. Report of the Committee on Claims of British Ex-Servicemen, para. 139.

60. Report of the Committee on Claims of British Ex-Servicemen, para. 103.

61. See, for instance, *Irish Times*, 10 February 1928, and *Irish Independent*, 11 November 1929.

62. *Irish Independent*, 30 May 1927.

63. Dolan, *Commemorating the Irish Civil War*, p. 40.

64. The *Irish Independent* was far more inclined to publicise the grievances of ex-servicemen than the *Irish Times*; the latter dwelt more on formal commemorations, fund-raising activities for ex-servicemen, and attacks on British Legion and related premises: see, for instance, *Irish Times*, 23 and 30 October and 30 December 1928; *Irish Independent*, 16 November 1927, 24 January, 10 February and 6 September 1928, and 25 October and 11 November 1929.

Chapter 7

1. Maguire, *The Civil Service and the Revolution in Ireland*, p. 137.
2. Maguire, *The Civil Service and the Revolution in Ireland*, p. 137–8. Maguire also points out that Murphy was the first person to be awarded a PhD by the Royal University. He used to lecture in philosophy.
3. Morrissey, *A Man Called Hughes*, p. 12.
4. Paul Rouse, 'James Joseph (Seamus) Hughes,' in *Dictionary of Irish Biography*.
5. Liberty Hall had been so badly damaged by British artillery in 1916 and again by Auxiliaries in 1920 that it was used only as a branch office.
6. Morrissey, *A Man Called Hughes*, p. 137–8.
7. Devine, *Organising History*, p. 93, 112; Nevin, *Trade Union Century*, p. 433.
8. Morrissey, *A Man Called Hughes*, p. 144–56.
9. Morrissey, *A Man Called Hughes*, p. 158–9.
10. Morrissey, *A Man Called Hughes*, p. 163.
11. *Irish Independent*, 14 October 1922.
12. *Irish Times*, 14 October 1922.
13. *Irish Independent* and *Irish Times*, 14 October 1922.
14. Morrissey, *A Man Called Hughes*, p. 142.
15. Minutes, Dublin Corporation, 11 December 1922, items 666 and 683.
16. Minutes, Dublin Corporation, 20 November 1922.
17. *Poblacht na hÉireann*, 11 November 1922 (Irish Capuchin Provincial Archives).
18. Dublin Corporation Minutes, Public Health Committee Report no. 88, 20 November 1922.
19. *Irish Times*, 5 December 1922.
20. Dublin Corporation Minutes, items 645 and 646, 4 December 1922.
21. There were four pay increases in 1915, eight in 1916, ten in 1917, twelve in 1918, eighteen in 1919, seventeen in 1920 and one in 1921—seventy in total. The war bonus system introduced in 1917 tracked these increases.
22. Dublin Corporation Minutes, 9 January 1922, item 59; *Irish Times*, 10 January 1922.
23. *Irish Times* and *Irish Independent*, 5 December 1922.
24. *Irish Times*, 15 December 1922.
25. McDunphy had been dismissed from the British civil service for refusing to take the oath of allegiance and had been a member of the 2nd Battalion of the Dublin Brigade in the War of Independence, when he worked as a travelling salesman.
26. *Irish Times*, 20 December 1922.
27. See Michael McKenna's excellent blog and subsequent exchanges at 'The Irish Story' (www.theirishstory.com/2013/09/02/who-was-seamus-dwyer).
28. Cited by Michael McKenna in Seán O'Mahony Papers (National Library of Ireland, ms. 44,055/10).

29. *Irish Times* and *Irish Independent*, 21 December 1922.

30. Witness Statements, Katherine Barry Moloney (WS0731).

31. *Irish Times* and *Irish Independent*, 27 December 1922. There has been speculation that the attack on Dwyer, like those on McGarry, Walsh, McDunphy, Mulcahy and other prominent Treaty supporters, was because they had been in the IRB, and certainly there was great antipathy towards this oath-bound society within the anti-Treaty ranks, from Éamon de Valera down; but there were IRB members on the anti-Treaty side as well. The primary reason for the attacks was the prominence of the victims within the new regime.

32. Witness Statements (WS1054).

33. *Poblacht na hÉireann*, 11 December 1922 (Irish Capuchin Provincial Archives). For Jameson's role in the War of Independence see Yeates, *A City in Turmoil*, p. 119–20, 150, 253–4 and 282–3.

34. Morrissey, *A Man Called Hughes*, p. 166

35. Dublin Fire Brigade, 60th Annual Report, 1922 (Dublin City Archives).

36. A new church was built on the site and the opportunity taken to extend Gloucester Street to O'Connell Street. The new thoroughfare was named Cathal Brugha Street, after the anti-Treaty leader who had died nearby; Gloucester Street was renamed Seán MacDermott Street, in honour of the 1916 leader Seán Mac Diarmada.

37. Dublin Fire Brigade at this time had four stations, designated in the order of their opening. The first was A, the central station in Tara Street; the second, B, was in Dorset Street; the third, C, was in Buckingham Street; and the fourth and newest, D, was in Thomas Street. Rathmines, Pembroke and Kingstown (Dún Laoghaire) had their own brigades.

38. Dublin Fire Brigade, 60th Annual Report, 1922 (Dublin City Archives); Geraghty and Whitehead, *The Dublin Fire Brigade*, p. 171–5; Fallon, *Dublin Fire Brigade and the Irish Revolution*, p. 39, 85–7.

39. Dublin Corporation Minutes, 27 November 1922.

Chapter 8

1. *Irish Times*, 27 December 1922; *Irish Independent*, 4–8 January 1923.

2. O'Connor, *Syndicalism in Ireland*, p. 162–3; Kostick, *Revolution in Ireland*, p. 205–7.

3. Transfer and Demobilisation Return for Period ended 24 July 1923 (Military Archives, BIC/RC/Lot 39, Department of Reports and Statistics, RPRMC).

4. *Irish Times*, 7 June 1923.

5. Incidents no. 218 and no. 249, GSWR and GNR Incident Log (Military Archives, IE/MA/RPRMAC/15 Lot 59).

6. Letter from E. A. Neale, general manager, GSWR, to Ministry of Economic Affairs, Transport Department, 17 July 1922 (Military Archives, IE/MA/RPRMAC/15 Lot 59).

7. Letter from George Gibson, manager, Dublin and Blessington Steam Railway Company, to Ministry of Economic Affairs, 14 July 1922 (Military Archives, IE/MA/RPRMAC/15 Lot 59).

8. *Irish Times,* 4 January 1923.

9. Insurability of Certain Members of the RMRPC, 5 September 1923 (Military Archives, RPRMC/A/06).

10. Share, *In Time of Civil War,* p. 61–2. Share does not appear to be aware of McGrath's meetings with the unions and attributes the initiative to the employers.

11. Dates of meetings and minutes were not kept. The RMRPC eventually reached a strength of 3,095 by June 1923 before its members were reallocated within the National Army.

12. Hopkinson, *Green Against Green,* p. 199.

13. ILP&TUC Annual Report, 1922–3, p. 18–9; *Irish Times,* 17 October 1922 and 4 January 1923; *Irish Independent,* 1, 4 and 13 November 1922; Share, *In Time of Civil War,* p. 71–8.

14. *Irish Independent,* 9 August 1922.

15. Share, *In Time of Civil War,* p. 15–16.

16. Deasy, *Brother Against Brother,* p. 118–20.

17. Irwin, *Betrayal in Ireland,* p. 127–8.

18. *Irish Independent,* 23 December 1922; *Weekly Irish Times,* 23 December 1922; *Irish Times,* 4 January 1923; Macready, *Annals of an Active Life,* Vol. 2, p. 673–4.

19. *Weekly Irish Times,* 23 December 1922.

20. *Irish Independent,* 14 November 1922.

21. *Irish Times* and *Irish Independent,* 20–24 November 1922.

22. Lawrence William White, 'Thomas MacDonagh,' in *Dictionary of Irish Biography;* Yeates, 'Craft workers during the Irish Revolution'; *Irish Times,* 27 December 1922.

23. Dublin Corporation Minutes, 19 February 1923, items 146 and 147.

24. Dublin Corporation Minutes, 19 February 1923, item 150.

25. O'Flanagan, 'Dublin City in an Age of War and Revolution,' p. 115.

26. McManus, *Dublin,* p. 76–7.

27. Extract from Cabinet Minutes, 30 October 1922 (National Archives, TAOIS/S1369 1-22).

28. Memorandum for Conference on Law and Order, 26 September 1923 (National Archives, TAOIS/S3306).

29. Response to Memorandum from Eoin MacNeill (National Archives, TAOIS/S3306).

30. The last incident noted was an attempt to derail a Midland Great Western train at Ashtown, Co. Dublin, on 14 December 1922 (Military Archives, RPRMC/A/08).

31. Bolster's rank varies according to the witness, from lieutenant to captain and commandant. His rank when he left the National Army on 7 March 1924 was commandant (Military Archives).

32. Signed Statement by Thomas McCarthy (National Archives, TAOIS/S1369 1-22).

33. Signed Statement by Christopher Ferguson (National Archives, TAOIS/S1369 14-22).

34. Signed Statement by James Kelly (National Archives, TAOIS/S1369 1-22).

35. Sworn Statement by Austin McDonald (National Archives, TAOIS/S1369 1-22).

36. The *Irish Independent,* 11 September 1922, states that there were 702 people on board but quotes no source; the figure may include crew and soldiers.

37. Signed Statement by Commandant C. Mackey (National Archives, TAOIS/S1369 1-22).

38. Extract from a summary of conditions in various places of detention (National Archives, TAOIS/S1369 1-22).

39. *Irish Times,* 9 September 1922; *Freeman's Journal,* 4 September 1922; *Irish Independent,* 11 September 1922.

40. Letter dated 11 September 1922 to Town Clerk of Dublin (National Archives, TAOIS/S1369 1-22).

41. O'Malley, and Dolan, *No Surrender Here!* p. xxxviii.

42. O'Donnell, *The Gates Flew Open,* p. 9–10.

43. O'Donnell, *The Gates Flew Open,* p. 9–10.

44. *Irish Independent* and *Irish Times,* 15 July 1922; Carey, *Mountjoy,* p. 198.

45. Peadar O'Donnell claimed that a full uniform was smuggled into the prison, but only a cap was uncovered in a search after the attempted escape described later in the chapter.

46. Greaves, *Liam Mellows and the Irish Revolution,* p. 363.

47. *Irish Independent,* 22 September 1922.

48. O'Malley, and Dolan, *No Surrender Here!* p. 129.

49. Greaves, *Liam Mellows and the Irish Revolution,* p. 358.

50. Mellows, *Notes from Mountjoy Jail.*

51. Mellows, *Notes from Mountjoy Jail.*

52. O'Malley, and Dolan, *No Surrender Here!* p. 152.

53. ILP&TUC National Executive Report, 1922, p. 39.

54. O'Malley and Dolan, *No Surrender Here!* p. 152, 155, 191.

55. Mellows, *Notes from Mountjoy Jail.*

56. Details of times vary slightly between accounts, but the main sequence of events is not contested. This narrative is based mainly on the findings of the inquiry by Commandant-General Dermot O'Hegarty and Commandant-General Seán Ó Murthuile, supplemented by statements submitted to them by prisoners and

government witnesses (National Archives, TAOIS/S1369 1-22); *Irish Times* and *Irish Independent*, 11 and 12 October 1922; MacEvilly, *A Splendid Resistance*, p. 99–106; O'Donnell, *The Gates Flew Open*, p. 30–34.

57. In the report and in all government statements to the press regarding the incident the military policemen were referred to as police rather than soldiers.

58. Ethel Voynich, born in Cork, was the daughter of the mathematician and social reformer George Boole.

59. *Poblacht na hÉireann*, 4 December 1922.

60. English, *Radicals and the Republic*, p. 57.

61. O'Donnell, *The Gates Flew Open*, p. 36–40; Greaves, *Liam Mellows and the Irish Revolution*, p. 388–90.

62. Conlon, *Cumann na mBan and the Women of Ireland*, p. 267–8. To add confusion to the situation, the Cork District Council of Cumann na mBan also supported the Treaty but refused to drop the name Cumann na mBan (Matthews, *Dissidents*, p. 14).

63. Matthews, *Dissidents*, p. 63.

64. Matthews, *Dissidents*, p. 45–6.

65. Matthews, *Dissidents*, p. 52.

66. Matthews, *Dissidents*, p. 56.

67. Buckley, *The Jangle of the Keys*, p. 31, quoted by Matthews in *Dissidents*, p. 59.

68. Hannah Moynihan, preface to her Prison Diary, p. 17–18 (Matthews, *Dissidents*, p. 67).

69. Hannah Moynihan, preface to her Prison Diary, p. 17–18 (Matthews, *Dissidents*, p. 67).

70. National Archives, TAOIS/3/1369.

71. National Archives, TAOIS/3/1369.

72. There remained 323 women in the other two prisons.

73. Matthews, *Dissidents*, p. 117.

74. Campbell, *Emergency Law in Ireland*, p. 241.

75. See *Poblacht na hÉireann*, 30 November and 1 December 1922 for Mary MacSwiney, also 12 and 28 December 1922 and 5 March 1923 on the treatment of women prisoners.

76. Carey, *Mountjoy*, p. 204.

77. DMP Arrest Book, 1916–18.

78. DMP Annual Report and Statistical Returns, 1912–19. See also Yeates, *A City in Wartime*, p. 308–9.

79. Annual Reports, Catholic Male Discharged Prisoners' Aid Committee, 1922 and 1925 (Dr Edward Byrne's Laity Files).

Chapter 9

1. South Dublin Union, Reports and Minutes, 1922–4 (National Archives).
2. South Dublin Union, Reports and Minutes, 1922 (National Archives). The audited accounts for the six months ending 31 March 1920 were only submitted in February 1922.
3. There were 205,000 Irish old-age pensioners, out of 942,000 throughout the United Kingdom.
4. South Dublin Union, Reports and Minutes, 1922, p. 129–132, 280 (National Archives).
5. Yeates, *A City in Wartime*, p. 247–8. The investigation found that no regulations had been broken, but neither had best practice been followed. It was another bout of bad publicity for the institution.
6. Letter from Office of National Education to Board of Guardians, 29 June 1920, South Dublin Union, Reports and Minutes, p. 460, 461 (National Archives).
7. South Dublin Union, Reports and Minutes, 1922, p. 278–82 (National Archives).
8. O'Flanagan, 'Dublin City in an Age of War and Revolution,' p. 107–8.
9. Until 1918 there were two workhouses, those of the North Dublin Union and the South Dublin Union. Ratepayers on the north of the Liffey paid a higher rate of 3s 6¾d in 1914, before their amalgamation, because the poor composed a larger proportion of the population.
10. Irish Labour Party and Trade Union Congress, 29th Annual Report, p. 16. Postal and railway workers' unions were large enough to set up their own societies in Ireland.
11. South Dublin Union, Reports and Minutes, 1923, p. 401–2 (National Archives).
12. Extracts from the Report of the Local Government Board taken from the copy in South Dublin Union, Reports and Minutes, 1923, p. 405–515 (National Archives).
13. *Freeman's Journal*, 13 February 1922. He resumed his medical practice in Dublin in 1924.
14. Campbell, *Emergency Law in Ireland*, p. 167.
15. Campbell, *Emergency Law in Ireland*, app. 2.
16. Curran, *The Birth of the Irish Free State*, p. 272–3.
17. Campbell, *Emergency Law in Ireland*, app. 2; *Irish Times*, 22 February 1923.
18. Durney, *The Civil War in Kildare*, p. 104–5; *Irish Times* and *Irish Independent*, 2 December 1922.
19. Ephemera Collection, Dublin City Archives (BOR F22–24).
20. Ephemera Collection, Dublin City Archives (BOR F09–01). The irony of the fact that half the National Army was composed of British ex-servicemen seemed lost on McGrath.
21. *Weekly Irish Times*, 5 May 1923.

22. Letter to Robinson, 9 October 1922, cited by Murray in *Sean O'Casey*, p. 140.

23. Murray, *Sean O'Casey*, p. 146–8, 171–2, 176–7; *Irish Independent*, 23 February 1926.

24. Morrissey, *A Man Called Hughes*, p. 171.

25. *Weekly Irish Times*, 5 May 1923.

26. Curran, *The Birth of the Irish Free State*, p. 273.

27. O'Malley, *The Singing Flame*, p. 229–30.

28. Mitchell, *Labour in Irish Politics*, p. 189–216.

29. *Irish Times* and *Irish Independent*, 31 July and 2 August 1923; Campbell, *Emergency Law in Ireland*, p. 232–41.

30. O'Malley, *The Singing Flame*, p. 251.

31. Macardle, *The Irish Republic*, p. 867; Campbell, *Emergency Law in Ireland*, p. 240–43.

32. O'Connor, *James Larkin*, p. 64.

33. www.thejournal.ie/james-larkin-deportation-1923-710632-Dec2012/.

34. Larkin, *James Larkin*, p. 254.

35. *Irish Times*, 7 May 1923.

36. Larkin, *James Larkin*, p. 258–9.

37. Larkin, *James Larkin*, p. 260.

38. Annual Reports of the ILP&TUC, 1916–23.

39. O'Connor, *James Larkin*, p. 68–72; Larkin, *James Larkin*, p. 264–6.

40. Larkin, *James Larkin*, p. 266.

41. No relation, but the author of the first serious and generally sympathetic biography of the trade union leader.

42. Larkin, *James Larkin*, p. 267.

43. O'Connor, *James Larkin*, p. 74.

44. Devine, *Organising History*, illustrations from *Voice of Labour* between p. 304 and 305.

45. *Irish Times*, 7 August 1923.

46. ILP&TUC Conference Report, 1923.

47. Devine, *Organising History*, illustrations from *Voice of Labour* between p. 304 and 305.

48. GSWR Secretary, Steam Coal Supplies (Irish Railway Record Society Archives, IRRS 3288).

49. Devine, *Organising History*, membership table, p. 183, and dispute pay table, p. 188.

50. O'Connor, *James Larkin*, 76–9.

51. Morrissey, *William O'Brien*, p. 294.

52. Board rates were used as comparators for other employments in the area.

53. Yeates, 'An injury to one is the concern of all.'

54. Smellie, *Ship Building and Repairing in Dublin*, p. 172–7; Sweeney, *Liffey Ships and Shipbuilding*, p. 157–64.

Chapter 10

1. O'Flanagan, 'Dublin City in an Age of War and Revolution,' p. 155.

2. *Irish Times*, 3 July 1923.

3. Morrissey, *Laurence O'Neill*, p. 220.

4. O'Flanagan, 'Dublin City in an Age of War and Revolution,' p. 153–5.

5. McManus, *Dublin*, p. 165.

6. O'Flanagan, 'Dublin City in an Age of War and Revolution,' p. 115.

7. Morrissey, *Laurence O'Neill*, p. 220.

8. Pauric J. Dempsey, 'James A. Burke,' in *Dictionary of Irish Biography*.

9. Morrissey, *Laurence O'Neill*, p. 225.

10. Laurence O'Neill Papers (National Library of Ireland, ms. 35,294/15).

11. *Evening Herald*, 21 February 1922.

12. Morrissey, *Laurence O'Neill*, p. 226.

13. *Irish Times*, 26 February 1924.

14. McManus, *Dublin*, p. 148.

15. *Irish Independent* and *Irish Times*, 12 and 14 March 1924.

16. *Irish Times*, 25 February 1924.

17. *Irish Independent* and *Irish Times*, 12, 14 and 20 March 1924.

18. Dublin Corporation Minutes, item 319, 19 May 1924.

19. *Irish Times*, 21 May 1924,

20. *Irish Independent*, 21 May 1924,

21. McManus, *Dublin*, p. 81,

22. Morrissey, *Laurence O'Neill*, p. 229–31.

23. *Irish Times* and *Irish Independent*, 27 May 1924; Morrissey, *Laurence O'Neill*, p. 229–31.

24. National Archives, TAOIS/S7474.

25. Morrissey, *Laurence O'Neill*, p. 237–60.

26. Manning and McDowell, *Electricity Supply in Ireland*, p. 15–23.

27. *Sunday Independent*, 9 March 1924; *Irish Times*, 10 March 1924.

28. All quotations from *Dáil Debates*, 12 March 1924.

29. The verdict of the historian of the army mutiny, Maryann Gialanella Valiulis (*Almost a Rebellion*, p. 54), on Cosgrave's speech is that 'at best the President's statement [to the Dáil] was misleading; at worst, a deliberate falsehood.'

30. Pauric J. Dempsey, 'Thomas (Tom) Cullen,' in *Dictionary of Irish Biography*.

31. At this point Emmet Dalton had resigned his commission and was clerk of the Free State Senate. Army Mutiny Files, Military Archives, J 26 D21,50.

32. Tobin, *The Truth about the Army Crisis*, p. 10. This contains a copy of a letter from Cosgrave's secretary dated Wednesday 20 June 1923 confirming that he will meet them on the following Friday.

33. History of Events, Cork, 12 September 1923 (Military Archives, Army Mutiny Files, J 26 D21,50).

34. Valiulis, *Almost a Rebellion*, p. 31. Regan, *The Irish Counter-Revolution*, provides what is still by far the best account set in a political context to the mutiny.

35. Valiulis, *Almost a Rebellion*, p. 51.

36. National Archives, TAOIS/S3678D.

37. Ex-Commandant Tony Lawlor, Intelligence Report, 7 May 1924 (Military Archives, Army Mutiny Files, I 26 D21,50). Nor was Lawlor alone in his criticism of Prout, who was regularly reprimanded by GHQ and poorly rated by his opponents.

38. Military Archives, Army Mutiny Files, A/Intelligence: No. 3 8/12/25-26. Tom Ennis's career is particularly problematic, because of the chaotic nature of National Army personnel files in the early months of the Civil War. The briefing document for the Inspection Branch was adopted by the chief of staff's office only in April 1924, a month after Ennis had resigned. See also Valiulis, *Almost a Rebellion*, p. 34.

39. *Irish Times*, 2 June 1923.

40. Mulcahy Papers, P7/C/1.

41. Military Archives, Pension File WS4SP10720; Witness Statements, Martin Conlon (WS0798).

42. Mulcahy Papers , P7/C/1.

43. Irish Railway Record Society Archives, GSWR File 3923.

44. The other members were the chief of staff, Seán MacMahon, the adjutant-general, Gearóid Ó Súileabháin, and the quartermaster-general, Seán Ó Murthuile.

45. Mulcahy Papers , P7/C/1.

46. Duggan, *A History of the Irish Army*, p. 138, 145.

47. Valiulis, *Almost a Rebellion*, p. 42.

48. Defence Order No. 30; *Irish Times*, 24 March and 12 October 1923.

49. Mulcahy Papers , P7/C/1.

50. Valiulis, *Almost a Rebellion*, p. 45.

51. Valiulis, *Portrait of a Revolutionary*, p. 48-9.

52. Ennis had been seriously wounded in an ambush in Gardiner Place, Dublin, on 18 March 1923.

53. Regan, *The Irish Counter-Revolution*, p. 176.

54. Mulcahy Papers, P7/C/1; Regan, *The Irish Counter-Revolution*, p. 175-6; Valiulis, *Almost a Rebellion*, p. 45.

55. National Archives, TAOIS/S3678B.

56. National Archives (London), CAB/24/138.

57. Tom Keogh, a friend of O'Daly and former member of the squad, had been killed by one of the first booby traps at Carrigaphooca, outside Macroom, on 16 September 1922.

58. Regan, *The Irish Counter-Revolution*, p. 173–5; Lawrence William White, 'Paddy O'Daly,' in *Dictionary of Irish Biography*.

59. *Irish Times*, 1 May 1923; Mulcahy Papers, P7/C/1-42.

60. *Dáil Debates*, 27 September 1922.

61. Tobin, *The Truth about the Army Crisis*.

62. O'Beirne-Ranelagh, 'The IRB from the Treaty to 1924.'

63. Valiulis, *Almost a Rebellion*, p. 58–9.

64. Tobin, *The Truth about the Army Crisis*.

65. *Irish Independent*, 13 and 17 March 1924.

66. Military Archives, A/Intelligence, No. 3, 8.

67. Witness Statements, Emmet Dalton (WS0641). Dalton identified Leopardstown racecourse as a suitable landing site, showing his lifelong interest in horseracing.

68. Valiulis, *Almost a Rebellion*, p. 60.

69. Tobin, *The Truth about the Army Crisis*.

70. Valiulis, *Almost a Rebellion*, p. 61.

71. National Archives, TAOIS/3678D.

72. Valiulis, *Almost a Rebellion*, p. 76. Mulcahy even privately counselled his brother Patrick, another serving officer, to make sure there was no disloyalty to O'Duffy.

73. Regan, *The Irish Counter Revolution*, p. 196.

74. O'Beirne-Ranelagh, 'The IRB from the Treaty to 1924'; Ó Broin, *Revolutionary Underground*, p. 210.

75. Army Mutiny Files, Military Archives, J 26 D26.

76. Military Archives, Army Mutiny Files, Sub-Files (10) F. The totals, some of them handwritten, do not always tally.

77. Mulcahy Papers, P7/C/1-42.

78. National Archives, TAOIS/S388/5, Sub-Files (10) F; Copy of Aiken order of 8 April 1924 (Military Archives, Army Mutiny Files).

79. Handwritten note dated 20 May 1924 (Military Archives, Army Mutiny Files, J 26 D21,50).

Chapter 11

1. Yeates, *Lockout*.

2. Yeates, *A City in Wartime*, p. 309; Yeates, *A City in Turmoil* p. 161, n. 38; Brady, *Guardians of the Peace*, p. 123–4.

3. Cody et al., *The Parliament of Labour*, p. 131; Yeates, *A City in Wartime*, p. 140–41; Yeates, *City in Turmoil*, p. 161.

4. McGarry, *Eoin O'Duffy*, p. 118; *Irish Times*, 5 May 1923.

5. However, new pension entitlements accrued to these constables for their final retirement.

6. *Irish Times*, 17 February 1955; Herlihy, *The Dublin Metropolitan Police*, p. 182–90; McNiffe, *A History of the Garda Síochána*, p. 64.

7. Kissane, *The Politics of the Irish Civil War*, p. 160.

8. Memorandum for Conference on Law and Order, 26 September 1923 (National Archives, TAOIS/S3306).

9. Anne Dolan, 'Noel Lemass,' in *Dictionary of Irish Biography*; Pinkman, *In the Legion of the Vanguard*, p. 115–7; *Irish Times* and *Irish Independent*, 16 October 1923.

10. *Irish Times* and *Irish Independent*, 17 October 1923.

11. Henry S. Murray (Military Archives, W24SP3522).

12. *Irish Times* and *Irish Independent*, 24 October and 13 December 1924.

13. *Irish Times* and *Irish Independent*, 23 and 24 October 1923; O'Halpin, *Defending Ireland*, p. 12–15; Herlihy, *The Dublin Metropolitan Police*, p. 182–8.

14. Mel Farrell, 'Renewing the party: Cumann na nGaedheal's Executive Organizing Committee, 1924–25,' *New Hibernia Review*, vol. 18, no. 3 (autumn 2014), p. 63–5; Morrissey, *A Man Called Hughes*, chap. 10.

15. Paul Rouse, 'James Joseph (Seamus) Hughes,' in *Dictionary of Irish Biography*; Morrissey, *A Man Called Hughes*, chap. 11–12.

16. Military Intelligence Briefings, January–October 1925 (Army Mutiny Files, Military Archives).

17. Boyne, *Emmet Dalton*, p. 250–52, 262–3.

18. Patrick Long, 'Liam Tobin,' in *Dictionary of Irish Biography*.

19. *Irish Times*, 11 August 1924.

20. *Irish Independent*, 8 November 1924; ILP&TUC Report, 1922, p. 155–6.

21. Kissane, *The Politics of the Civil War*, p. 161.

22. David Fitzpatrick, 'Protestant depopulation and the Irish Revolution,' *Irish Historical Studies*, 38, no. 152 (November 2013).

23. Delaney, *Demography, State and Society*, p. 71–2.

24. Kissane, *The Politics of the Civil War*, p. 166.

25. Gerwarth and Horne, *War in Peace*.

26. Military Intelligence, Fortnightly Report No. 7, 21 July 1924 (Military Archives, Army Mutiny Files).

27. Minutes of Resident Executive Committee, IEIU, 3 March 1922 (TEEU).

28. Witness Statements, T. Leahy (WS0660); also Thomas Leahy (WMSP34REF321). Ironically, it was Oscar Traynor who supported his pension application, which was disputed by some members of the Irish Citizen Army.

SELECT BIBLIOGRAPHY

The bibliography includes only sources cited in the text or the notes.

Primary sources
American Commission on Conditions in Ireland (National Library of Ireland)
Bank of Ireland Archive
British Labour Commission to Ireland (National Library of Ireland)
Cameron Papers (Royal College of Surgeons in Ireland)
Church of Ireland, Stained Glass in the Church of Ireland (www.gloine.ie)
Colonial Office Files (National Archives, London)
Dáil Éireann, *Minutes of Proceedings,* Dublin: Stationery Office, 1919–21
Dáil Éireann Reports, 1919–21 (National Archives, Dublin)
Department of Agriculture Files (National Archives, Dublin)
Department of Justice Files (National Archives, Dublin)
Department of the Taoiseach Files (National Archives, Dublin)
Dr Edward Byrne, Laity Papers, Dublin Diocesan Archives
Dr William Walsh, Laity Papers, Dublin Diocesan Archives
Dublin Corporation Minutes and Reports, 1911–24 (Dublin City Archives)
Dublin Metropolitan Police, Bi-Weekly Precis of Reports of Important Occurrences in DMP Area, 1921 (Military Archives, Dublin)
Dublin Metropolitan Police, Prisoners Books, 1907–9, 1911–13, 1916–18
Dublin Port and Docks Board Archive
Ephemera Collection, Dublin City Archives
Find My Past (http://search.findmypast.ie)
Guinness Archive, Dublin
Intelligence Notes, 1922–3 (Military Archives, Dublin)
IRA GHQ and Dublin Second Battalion Papers (National Library of Ireland)
Irish Capuchin Provincial Archives, Dublin
Irish Engineering, Shipbuilding and Foundry Workers' Trade Union Archive (Technical, Engineering and Electrical Union, Dublin)
Irish Grants Committee, Colonial Office Files, CO762 (National Archives, London)
Irish Labour Party and Trade Union Congress Archives, 1901–25 (Irish Congress of Trade Unions, Dublin)
Irish Railway Record Society Archives, Dublin
Lady Alice Howard's Diary (National Library of Ireland)
Laurence O'Neill Papers (National Library of Ireland)
Liaison and Evacuation Papers, Bureau of Military History (Military Archives, Dublin)
Masonic Grand Lodge of Free and Accepted Masons, Ireland

Military Service Pensions Collection (Military Archives, Dublin)

Mulcahy Papers (UCD Archive)

National Society for the Prevention of Cruelty to Children, Annual Reports, 1911–24 (National Library of Ireland)

Report of the Committee on Claims of British Ex-Servicemen, 1928 (National Archives, Dublin)

Society of St Vincent de Paul Archives, Dublin

South Dublin Union Reports and Minutes, 1912–24 (National Archives, Dublin)

Witness Statements, Bureau of Military History (Military Archives, Dublin)

Newspapers and periodicals

Cuala News

Evening Telegraph

Freeman's Journal

Irish Bulletin

Irish Ecclesiastical Record

Irish Independent

Irish Times

Poblacht na hÉireann: War News

Weekly Irish Times

Articles in periodicals, articles on web sites, and papers delivered at seminars and conferences

'1923 docs reveal Britain's fears over James Larkin's return to Ireland,' *The Journal*, 16 December 2012 (www.thejournal.ie/james-larkin-deportation-1923-710632-Dec2012).

Benton, Sarah, 'Women disarmed: The militarization of politics in Ireland, 1913–23,' *Feminist Review*, no. 50 (summer 1995), p. 148–72.

Bielenberg, Andy, 'Exodus: The emigration of Southern Irish Protestants during the Irish War of Independence and the Civil War,' *Past and Present*, vol. 218, issue 1 (2013), p. 199–233.

Brennan, Cathal, 'The postal strike of 1922,' The Irish Story (www.theirishstory.com/2012/06/08/the-postal-strike-of-1922).

Dorney, John, 'Casualties of the Irish Civil War in Dublin: Towards a figure for Civil War casualties in Dublin and environs, January 1922 to November 1924,' 19 June 2012 (updated August 2014) (www.theirishstory.com/2012/06/19/casualties-of-the-irish-civil-war-in-dublin).

Farrell, Mel, 'Renewing the party: Cumann na nGaedheal Executive Organising Committee, 1924–5,' *New Hibernia Review*, vol. 18, no. 3 (autumn 2014), p. 58–76.

Fitzpatrick, David, 'Protestant depopulation and the Irish Revolution,' *Irish Historical Studies*, vol. 38, no. 152 (November 2013).

Fitzpatrick, David, 'Strikes in Ireland, 1914–1921,' *Saothar*, 6 (1980), p. 26–39.

Hanley, Brian, 'The Irish Citizen Army after 1916,' *Saothar*, 28 (2003), p. 37–47.

Hennessy, Mark, 'Four Courts still in headlines, 90 years after attack,' *Irish Times*, 5 November 2012.

Hogan, John, 'Payback: The Dublin bricklayers' strike, 1920–21,' *Saothar*, 35 (2010), p. 23–33.

Howell, Philip, 'The politics of prostitution in the Irish Free State,' *Irish Historical Studies,* May 2003.

Howell, Philip, 'The politics of prostitution in the Irish Free State: A response to Susannah Riordan,' *Irish Historical Studies,* November 2007.

McCarthy, Charles, 'Labour and the 1922 general election' (document study), *Saothar,* 7 (1981), p. 115–21.

McGrath, Sam, 'James Spain of Geraldine Square,' Come Here to Me (http://comeheretome. com/2013/02/04/james-spain-of-geraldine-square).

McManus, Ruth, 'A beacon of light': Canon Hall and St Barnabas' PUS,' paper delivered at East Wall History Week, Dublin, 16 October 2011.

Moffitt, Miriam, 'The Protestant experience of revolution: The fate of the unionist community in rural Ireland, 1912–27,' paper given at Centre for Contemporary Irish History, Trinity College, Dublin, 20 October 2010.

O'Beirne-Ranelagh, John, 'The IRB from the Treaty to 1924,' *Irish Historical Studies,* vol. 20, no. 77 (March 1976), p. 26–39.

O'Flanagan, Niall, 'Dublin in an Age of War and Revolution, 1914–1924,' MA thesis, University College, Dublin, 1985.

O'Sullivan, Jan, 'Houses for heroes: Life in the Killester colony, 1919–1945,' *Dublin Historical Record,* vol. 65, nos. 1 and 2 (spring–autumn 2012).

Rigney, Peter, 'Military service and GS&WR staff, 1914–1923,' *Journal of the Irish Railway Record Society,* no. 161 (October 2006).

Riordan, Susannah, 'Venereal disease in the Irish Free State: The politics of public health,' *Irish Historical Studies,* 35 (May 2007), p. 345–64.

Ward, Margaret, 'Conflicting interests: The British and Irish suffrage movements,' *Feminist Review,* no. 50 (summer 1995), p. 127–47.

'Who was Seamus Dwyer?' The Irish Story (www.theirishstory.com/2013/09/02/who-was-seamus-dwyer).

Yeates, Pádraig, 'An injury to one is the concern of all: Dublin Port, the namebook, the 1913 Lockout and the sympathetic strike,' *Saothar,* 38 (2013).

Yeates, Pádraig, 'Craft workers during the Irish Revolution, 1919–22,' *Saothar,* 33 (2008), p. 37–56.

Books

Abbot, Richard, *Police Casualties in Ireland, 1919–1922,* Cork: Mercier Press, 2000.

Andrews, C. S., *Dublin Made Me: An Autobiography,* Dublin and Cork: Mercier Press, 1979.

Anonymous [Caroline Woodcock], *Experiences of an Officer's Wife in Ireland,* Edinburgh and London: Blackwood, 1921; reprinted London and Dublin: Parkgate Publications, 1994.

Bartlett, Thomas, and Jeffrey, Keith (eds.), *A Military History of Ireland,* Cambridge: Cambridge University Press, 1997.

Boyne, Sean, *Emmet Dalton: Somme Soldier, Irish General, Film Pioneer,* Naas: Merrion Press, 2014.

Brady, Edward M., *Ireland's Secret Service in England,* Dublin and Cork: Talbot Press [1928].

Buckland, Patrick, *Irish Unionism, One: The Anglo-Irish and the New Ireland, 1885–1922,* Dublin: Gill & Macmillan, 1972.

Buckley, Margaret, *The Jangle of the Keys*, Dublin: James Duffy, 1938.

Campbell, Colm, *Emergency Law in Ireland, 1918–1925*, Oxford: Clarendon Press, 1994.

Canning, Paul, *British Policy towards Ireland, 1921–1941*, Oxford: Clarendon Press, 1985.

Carden, Sheila, *The Alderman: Alderman Tom Kelly (1868–1942) and Dublin Corporation*, Dublin: Dublin City Council, 2007.

Carey, Tim, *Croke Park: A History*, Cork: Collins Press, 2004.

Carey, Tim, *Hanged for Ireland: The Forgotten Ten: Executed 1920–21: A Documentary History*, Dublin: Blackwater Press, 2001.

Carey, Tim, *Mountjoy: The Story of a Prison*, Cork: Collins Press, 2000.

Clark, Gemma, *Everyday Violence in the Irish Civil War*, Cambridge: Cambridge University Press, 2014.

Clark, Mary, and Doran, Gráinne, *Serving the City: The Dublin City Managers and Town Clerks, 1230–2006*, Dublin: Dublin Public Libraries, 2006.

Clarkson, J. Dunsmore, *Labour and Nationalism in Ireland*, New York: Columbia University Press, 1925; reprinted 1978.

Cody, Seamus; O'Dowd, John; Rigney, Peter, *The Parliament of Labour: 100 Years of the Dublin Council of Trade Unions*, Dublin: Dublin Council of Trade Union, 1986.

Comerford, Máire, *The First Dáil*, Dublin: Joe Clarke, 1969.

Commission to Inquire into Child Abuse: Report, Dublin: Stationery Office, 2009.

Conlon, Lil, *Cumann na mBan and the Women of Ireland, 1913–25*, Kilkenny, 1969.

Connell, Joseph E. A., *Where's Where in Dublin: A Directory of Historic Locations*, Dublin: Dublin City Council, 2006.

Costello, Francis J., *Enduring the Most: The Life and Death of Terence MacSwiney*, Dingle: Brandon Press, 1995.

Costello, Francis J., *The Irish Revolution and Its Aftermath, 1916–1923: Years of Revolt*, Dublin: Irish Academic Press, 2003.

Cottrell, Peter, *The Irish Civil War, 1922–23*, London: Osprey Publishing, 2008.

Cox, Thomas J., *Damned Englishman: A Study of Erskine Childers (1870–1922)*, Hicksville (NY): Exposition Press, 1975.

Craig, Maurice, *Dublin, 1660–1860*, Dublin: Allen Figgis, 1969.

Crozier, Frank P., *The Men I Killed*, London: Michael Joseph [1937]; reprinted Belfast: Athol Books, 2002.

Cruise O'Brien, Conor (ed.), *The Shaping of Modern Ireland*, London: Routledge and Kegan Paul, 1960.

Curran, Joseph M., *The Birth of the Irish Free State, 1921–1923*, Tuscaloosa (Ala.): University of Alabama Press [1980].

Dalton, Charles, *With the Dublin Brigade (1917–1921)*, London: Peter Davies, 1929.

Deasy, Liam, *Brother Against Brother*, Cork and Dublin: Mercier Press, 1982.

de Búrca, Séamus, *The Soldier's Song: The Story of Peadar Ó Cearnaigh*, Dublin: P. J. Bourke, 1957.

Delaney, Enda, *Demography, State and Society: Irish Migration to Britain, 1921–1971*, Liverpool: Liverpool University Press, 2000.

Devine, Francis, *Organising History: A Centenary of SIPTU, 1909–2009*, Dublin: Gill & Macmillan, 2009.

Doherty, Eddie, *Matt Talbot*, Milwaukee: Bruce Publishing Company, 1953.

Dolan, Anne, *Commemorating the Irish Civil War: History and Memory, 1923–2000*, Cambridge: Cambridge University Press, 2003.

Dublin's Fighting Story, 1916–21, Told by the Men Who Made It, Tralee: Kerryman [1950].

Duggan, J. P., *A History of the Irish Army*, Dublin: Gill & Macmillan, 1991.

Durney, James, *The Civil War in Kildare*, Cork: Mercier Press, 2011.

Dwyer, T. Ryle, *The Squad and the Intelligence Operations of Michael Collins*, Cork: Mercier Press, 2005.

Eagar, J. F., *The Inception and Early History of the Irish Bank Officials' Association*, Dublin: Robert T. White, 1920.

Ellmann, Richard, *James Joyce*, London: Oxford University Press, 1959.

English, Richard, *Radicals and the Republic: Socialist Republicanism in the Irish Free State, 1925–1937*, Oxford: Clarendon Press, 1994.

Enright, Seán, *The Trial of Civilians by Military Courts: Ireland, 1921*, Dublin: Irish Academic Press, 2012.

Fallon, Dónal; McGrath, Sam; Murray, Ciarán, *Come Here to Me! Dublin's Other History*, Dublin: New Island, 2012.

Fallon, Las, *Dublin Fire Brigade and the Irish Revolution*, Dublin: South Dublin Libraries, 2012.

Farrell, Brian, *The Founding of Dáil Éireann: Parliament and Nation Building*, Dublin: Gill & Macmillan, 1971.

Farrell, Michael, *Northern Ireland: The Orange State*, London: Pluto Press, 1970.

Ferriter, Diarmaid, *The Transformation of Ireland, 1900–2000*, London: Profile Books, 2004.

Fingall, Elizabeth Mary Bourke Plunkett, Countess of, *Seventy Years Young: Memories of Elizabeth, Countess of Fingall (as told to Pamela Hinkson)*, London: Collins, 1937; reprinted Dublin: Lilliput Press, 1995.

Fitzpatrick, David, *Harry Boland's Irish Revolution*, Cork: Cork University Press, 2003.

Fitzpatrick, David (ed.), *Terror in Ireland, 1916–1923*, Dublin: Lilliput Press, 2012.

Fox, R. M., *The History of the Irish Citizen Army*, Dublin: James Duffy, 1944.

Foy, Michael T., *Michael Collins's Intelligence War: The Struggle between the British and the IRA, 1919–1921*, Stroud (Glos.): Sutton Publishing, 2006.

Gallagher, Frank, *Days of Fear: A Diary of a Hunger Strike*, Cork: Mercier Press, 1967.

Gaughan, J. Anthony, *Thomas Johnson, 1872–1963: First Leader of the Labour Party in Dáil Éireann*, Dublin: Kingdom Books, 1980.

Geraghty, Tom, and Whitehead, Trevor, *The Dublin Fire Brigade: A History of the Brigade, the Fires and the Emergencies*, Dublin: Four Courts Press, 2004.

Gerwarth, Robert, and Horne, John (eds.), *War in Peace: Paramilitary Violence in Europe after the Great War*, Oxford: Oxford University Press, 2012.

Gillis, Liz, *The Fall of Dublin: 28 June to 5 July 1922*, Cork: Mercier Press, 2011.

Gleeson, James, *Bloody Sunday*, London: Four Square Books, 1963.

Greaves, C. Desmond, *Liam Mellows and the Irish Revolution*, London: Lawrence and Wishart, 1971.

Griffith, Kenneth, and O'Grady, Timothy E., *Curious Journey: An Oral History of Ireland's Unfinished Revolution*, London: Hutchinson, 1982.

Hall, F. G., *The Bank of Ireland, 1783–1946*, Dublin: Hodges Figgis, and Oxford: Blackwell, 1948.

Henderson, Frank (Michael Hopkinson, ed.), *Frank Henderson's Easter Rising: Recollections of a Dublin Volunteer,* Cork: Cork University Press, 1998.

Herlihy, Jim, *The Dublin Metropolitan Police: A Short History and Genealogical Guide …* Dublin: Four Courts Press, 2001.

Hittle, J. B. E., *Michael Collins and the Anglo-Irish War: Britain's Counterinsurgency Failure,* Dulles (Va.): Potomac Books, 2011.

Hogan, David [Frank Gallagher], *The Four Glorious Years,* Dublin: Irish Press, 1954.

Hopkinson, Michael, *Green Against Green: The Irish Civil War,* Dublin: Gill & Macmillan, 1988.

Hopkinson, Michael, *The Irish War of Independence,* Dublin: Gill & Macmillan, 2002.

Irwin, Wilmot, *Betrayal in Ireland: An Eye-Witness Record of the Tragic and Terrible Years of Revolution and Civil War in Ireland, 1916–24,* Belfast: Northern Whig, [1966].

Kearns, Kevin C., *Dublin Tenement Life: An Oral History,* Dublin: Gill & Macmillan, 1994.

Kee, Robert, *The Green Flag: A History of Irish Nationalism,* London: Weidenfeld and Nicolson, 1972.

Kenneally, Ian, *The Paper Wall: Newspapers and Propaganda in Ireland, 1919–1921,* Cork: Collins Press, 2008.

Kennedy, Finola, *Frank Duff: A Life Story,* London: Burns and Oates, 2011.

Kissane, Bill, *The Politics of the Irish Civil War,* Oxford: Oxford University Press, 2005.

Kostick, Conor, *Revolution in Ireland: Popular Militancy, 1917–1923,* London: Pluto Press, 1996.

Laffan, Michael, *The Resurrection of Ireland: The Sinn Féin Party, 1916–1923,* Cambridge: Cambridge University Press, 1999.

Larkin, Emmet, *James Larkin: Irish Labour Leader, 1876–1947,* London: Routledge and Kegan Paul, 1965.

Luddy, Maria, *Prostitution and Irish Society, 1800–1940,* Cambridge: Cambridge University Press, 2007.

Luddy, Maria, *Women and Philanthropy in Nineteenth-Century Ireland,* Cambridge: Cambridge University Press, 1995.

Lyons, F. S. L., *John Dillon: A Biography,* London: Routledge and Kegan Paul, 1968.

Macardle, Dorothy, *The Irish Republic: A Documented Chronicle of the Anglo-Irish Conflict and the Partitioning of Ireland, with a Detailed Account of the Period 1916–1923,* Dublin: Irish Press, 1951.

McBride, Lawrence W., *The Greening of Dublin Castle: The Transformation of Bureaucratic and Judicial Personnel in Ireland, 1882–1922,* Washington: Catholic University of America Press, 1991.

MacDonagh, Oliver, 'The Victorian bank,' in F. S. L. Lyons (ed.), *Bicentenary Essays: The Bank of Ireland, 1783–1983,* Dublin: Gill & Macmillan, 1983.

McDowell, R. B., *Crisis and Decline: The Fate of Southern Unionists,* Dublin: Lilliput Press, 1997.

MacEvilly, Michael, *A Splendid Resistance: The Life of IRA Chief of Staff, Dr Andy Cooney,* Dublin: Éamonn de Búrca, 2011.

McGarry, Fearghal, *Eoin O'Duffy: A Self-Made Hero,* Oxford: Oxford University Press, 2005.

McGuire, James, and Quinn, James (eds.), *Dictionary of Irish Biography: From the Earliest Times to the Year 2002,* Cambridge: Cambridge University Press, 2009–2014.

Mackay, James, *Michael Collins: A Life,* Edinburgh and London: Mainstream, 1996.

McManus, Ruth, *Dublin, 1910–1940: Shaping the City and Suburbs*, Dublin: Four Courts Press, 2002.

McNiffe, Liam, *A History of the Garda Síochána: A Social History of the Force, 1922–52, With an Overview of the Years 1952–97*, Dublin: Wolfhound Press, 1997.

Macready, Sir Nevil, *Annals of an Active Life, Volume II*, London: Hutchinson [1924].

Maguire, Martin, *The Civil Service and the Revolution in Ireland, 1912–1938: 'Shaking the blood stained hand of Mr Collins,'* Manchester: Manchester University Press, 2008.

Maguire, Martin, *Servants to the Public: A History of the Local Government and Public Services Union, 1901–1990*, Dublin: Institute of Public Administration, 1998.

Mandle, W. F., *The Gaelic Athletic Association and Irish Nationalist Politics, 1884–1924*, Dublin: Gill & Macmillan, 1987.

Manning, Maurice, and McDowell, Moore, *Electricity Supply in Ireland: The History of the ESB*, Dublin: Gill & Macmillan, 1984.

Marreco, Anne, *The Rebel Countess: The Life and Times of Constance Markievicz*, London: Corgi Books, 1967.

Matthews, Ann, *Dissidents: Irish Republican Women, 1923–1941*, Cork: Mercier Press, 2012.

Matthews, Ann, *Renegades: Irish Republican Women, 1900–1922*, Cork: Mercier Press, 2010.

Mellows, Liam, *Notes from Mountjoy Jail*, London: Irish Communist Group, 1965.

Midleton, William St John Fremantle Brodrick, Earl of, *Ireland: Dupe or Heroine*, London: William Heinemann, 1932.

Mitchell, Arthur, *Labour in Irish Politics, 1890–1930: The Irish Labour Movement in an Age of Revolution*, Dublin: Irish University Press, 1974.

Mitchell, Arthur, *Revolutionary Government in Ireland: Dáil Éireann, 1919–22*, Dublin: Gill & Macmillan, 1995.

Moran, May, *Executed for Ireland: The Patrick Moran Story*, Cork: Mercier Press, 2010.

Morrissey, Thomas J., *A Man Called Hughes: The Life and Times of Seamus Hughes, 1881–1943*, Dublin: Veritas, 1991.

Morrissey, Thomas J., *Edward J. Byrne, 1872–1941: The Forgotten Archbishop of Dublin*, Blackrock (Co. Dublin): Columba Press, 2011.

Morrissey, Thomas J., *Laurence O'Neill (1864–1943), Lord Mayor of Dublin (1917–1924): Patriot and Man of Peace*, Dublin: Dublin City Council, 2014.

Morrissey, Thomas J., *William J. Walsh, Archbishop of Dublin, 1841–1921: No Uncertain Voice*, Dublin: Four Courts Press, 2000.

Morrissey, Thomas J., *William Martin Murphy* (Life and Times Series, no. 9), Dundalk: Dundalgan Press, for the Historical Association of Ireland, 1997.

Morrissey, Thomas J., *William O'Brien, 1881–1968: Socialist, Republican, Dáil Deputy, Editor and Trade Union Leader*, Dublin: Four Courts Press, 2007.

Mulholland, Marie, *The Politics and Relationships of Kathleen Lynn*, Dublin: Woodfield Press, 2002.

Murphy, Brian P., *The Origins and Organisation of British Propaganda in Ireland, 1920*, Aubane (Co. Cork): Aubane Historical Society, 2006.

Murray, Christopher, *Sean O'Casey: Writer at Work: A Biography*, Dublin: Gill & Macmillan, 2004.

Murray, Patrick, *Oracles of God: The Roman Catholic Church and Irish Politics, 1922–37*, Dublin: UCD Press, 2000.

Neligan, David, *The Spy in the Castle*, London: MacGibbon and Kee, 1968.

Nevin, Donal (ed.), *Trade Union Century, 1894–1994* (Thomas Davis Lectures), Cork and Dublin: Mercier Press, for Raidió-Teilifís Éireann, 1994.

O'Brien, Joseph V., *Dear, Dirty Dublin: A City in Distress, 1899–1916*, Berkeley (Calif.): University of California Press [1982].

O'Brien, William, *Forth the Banners Go: Reminiscences of William O'Brien, as told to Edward MacLysaght*, Dublin: Three Candles, 1969.

Ó Broin, Leon, *Frank Duff*, Dublin: Gill & Macmillan, 1982.

Ó Broin, Leon, *Just Like Yesterday: An Autobiography*, Dublin: Gill & Macmillan [1986].

Ó Broin, Leon, *No Man's Man: A Biographical Memoir of Joseph Brennan, Civil Servant and First Governor of the Central Bank*, Dublin: Institute of Public Administration [1982].

Ó Broin, Leon, *Revolutionary Underground: The Story of the Irish Republican Brotherhood, 1858–1924*, Dublin: Gill & Macmillan, 1976.

Ó Broin, Leon, *W. E. Wylie and the Irish Revolution, 1916–1921*, Dublin: Gill & Macmillan, 1989.

O'Connor, Batt, *With Michael Collins in the Fight for Irish Independence*, London: Peter Davies, 1929; reprinted Aubane (Co. Cork): Aubane Historical Society, 2004.

O'Connor, Emmet, *James Larkin* (Radical Irish Lives), Cork: Cork University Press, 2002.

O'Connor, Emmet, *A Labour History of Ireland, 1824–2000*, Dublin: UCD Press, 2011.

O'Connor, Emmet, *Syndicalism in Ireland, 1917–1923*, Cork: Cork University Press, 1988.

O'Donnell, Peadar, *The Gates Flew Open*, Cork: Mercier Press, 1965.

O'Donoghue, Florence, *No Other Law: The Story of Liam Lynch and the Irish Republican Army, 1916–1923*, Dublin: Irish Press [1954].

O'Donovan, Donal, *No More Lonely Scaffolds: Kevin Barry and His Time*, Dublin: Glendale Press, 1989.

Ó Duigneáin, Proinnsíos, *Linda Kearns: A Revolutionary Irish Woman*, Manorhamilton: Drumlin Publications, 2002.

O'Halpin, Eunan, *Defending Ireland: The Irish State and Its Enemies since 1922*, Oxford: Oxford University Press, 1999.

Ó hÓgartaigh, Margaret, *Kathleen Lynn: Irishwoman, Patriot, Doctor*, Dublin: Irish Academic Press, 2006.

O'Malley, Cormac K. H., and Dolan, Anne (eds.), *No Surrender Here!: The Civil War Papers of Ernie O'Malley, 1922–1924*, Dublin: Lilliput Press, 2007.

O'Malley, Ernie, *On Another Man's Wound*, London: Four Square Books, 1961.

O'Malley, Ernie, *The Singing Flame*, Dublin: Anvil Books, 1978.

Pakenham, Frank, *Peace by Ordeal: An Account from First-Hand Sources of the Negotiation and Signature of the Anglo-Irish Treaty, 1921*, London: Geoffrey Chapman, 1962.

Parkinson, Alan F., *Belfast's Unholy War: The Troubles of the 1920s*, Dublin: Four Courts Press, 2004.

Perkins, Anne, *A Very British Strike: The General Strike, 1926*, London: Pan Books, 2006.

Pinkman, John A. (Francis E. Maguire, ed.), *In the Legion of the Vanguard*, Cork and Dublin: Mercier Press, 1998.

Raftery, Mary, and O'Sullivan, Eoin, *Suffer the Little Children: The Inside Story of Ireland's Industrial Schools*, Dublin: New Island, 1999.

Regan, John M., *Myth and the Irish State: Historical Problems and Other Essays*, Dublin: Irish Academic Press, 2013.

Reilly, Tom, *Joe Stanley: Printer to the Rising*, Dingle: Brandon Books, 2005.

Rigney, Peter, *Trains, Coal and Turf: Transport in Emergency Ireland*, Dublin: Irish Academic Press, 2010.

Robbins, Frank, *Under the Starry Plough: Recollections of the Irish Citizen Army*, Dublin: Academy Press, 1977.

Robinson, Sir Henry, *Memories, Wise and Otherwise*, London: Cassell, 1923.

Rumpf, E., and Hepburn, A. C. (eds.), *Nationalism and Socialism in Twentieth-Century Ireland*, Liverpool: Liverpool University Press, 1977.

Ryan, Desmond, *Sean Treacy and the 3rd Tipperary Brigade*, Tralee: Anvil Books [1945].

Share, Bernard, *In Time of Civil War: The Conflict on the Railways, 1922–23*, Cork: Collins Press, 2006.

Sheehan, William, *Fighting for Dublin: The British Battle for Dublin, 1919–1921*, Cork: Collins Press, 2007.

Sheehan, William, *A Hard Local War: The British Army and the Guerilla War in Cork, 1919–1921*, Stroud (Glos.): Spellmount Press, 2011.

Smellie, John, *Ship Building and Repairing in Dublin: A Record of Work Carried Out by the Dublin Dockyard Co., 1901–1923*, Glasgow: McCorquodale [1935].

Sturgis, Mark (Michael Hopkinson, ed.), *The Last Days of Dublin Castle: The Mark Sturgis Diaries*, Dublin: Irish Academic Press, 1999.

Sweeney, Pat, *Liffey Ships and Shipbuilding*, Cork: Mercier Press, 2010.

Tobin, Liam, *The Truth about the Army Crisis: With a Foreword by Major-General Liam Tobin*, Dublin: Irish Republican Army Organization [1924].

Townshend, Charles, *The British Campaign in Ireland, 1919–1921: The Development of Political and Military Policies*, Oxford: Oxford University Press, 1975.

Townshend, Charles, *The Republic: The Fight for Irish Independence, 1918–1923*, London: Allen Lane, 2013.

Valiulis, Maryann Gialanella, *Almost a Rebellion: The Irish Army Mutiny of 1924*, Cork: Tower Books, 1985.

Valiulis, Maryann Gialanella, *Portrait of a Revolutionary: General Richard Mulcahy and the Founding of the Irish Free State*, Blackrock (Co. Dublin): Irish Academic Press, 1992.

Van Voris, Jacqueline, *Constance de Markievicz: In the Cause of Ireland*, Amherst (Mass.): University of Massachusetts Press, 1967.

Walsh, Oonagh, *Anglican Women in Dublin: Philanthropy, Politics and Education in the Early Twentieth Century*, Dublin: UCD Press, 2005.

West, Trevor, *Horace Plunkett: Co-Operation and Politics: An Irish Biography*, Washington: Catholic University of America Press, 1986.

Whelan, Yvonne, *Reinventing Dublin: Streetscapes, Iconography and the Politics of Identity*, Dublin: UCD Press, 2003.

Wolfe, Humbert, *Labor Supply and Regulation*, Oxford: Clarendon Press, 1923.

Yeates, Pádraig, *A City in Turmoil: Dublin, 1919–21*, Dublin: Gill & Macmillan, 2012.

Yeates, Pádraig, *A City in Wartime: Dublin, 1914–18*, Dublin: Gill & Macmillan, 2011.

Yeates, Pádraig, *Lockout: Dublin, 1913*, Dublin: Gill & Macmillan, 2000.

INDEX